IGHTING
Warsaw

FIGHTING WARSAW

The Story of the Polish Underground State
1939-1945

STEFAN KORBONSKI

† *With a new Introduction by* ZOFIA KORBONSKI
† *Translated from the original Polish by F. B.* CZARNOMSKI

HIPPOCRENE BOOKS, INC.
New York

All illustrations courtesy of Zofia Korbonski.

First Hippocrene Books paperback edition published in 2004.
Hardcover edition published by Macmillan, 1956.
First paperback edition published by Minerva Press, 1968.

For information, address:
Hippocrene Books, Inc.
171 Madison Avenue
New York, NY 10016

ISBN 0-7818-1035-3

Cataloging-in-Publication data available from the Library of Congress.

Printed in the United States of America.

INTRODUCTION

by Zofia Korbonski

"The difference between the Polish Underground Movement that exist-ed during the Second World War and at the beginning of the anti-Soviet resistance, and similar movements in other countries, consists not so much in its having been the largest and the most active but, primarily, in its having achieved the form of a real underground state."

—Stefan Korbonski in his preface to the
1968 Minerva Press edition of *Fighting Warsaw*
(the first edition was published by Macmillan in 1956).

This statement is still valid in 2003. I recall those wartime years with great emotion and have come to the same conclusion: the Polish Underground State was the most glorious page in the modern history of Poland and one of the most important movements in the worldwide struggle against Hitler's Germany. It was in keeping with the best tra-ditions of the Polish struggle for independence and a continuation of the Polish Second Republic (1918-1939). It was a unique historic phenom-enon. Stefan Korbonski, one of the creators of the Polish Underground State, captured in *Fighting Warsaw* the nation's attitude, its will to fight in defense of independence and national identity—the imperatives of that period. The underground struggle was a universal and spontaneous reaction of the entire nation. (This fact cannot be altered by pseudo-his-torians now peddling their own versions of history.) The so-called civil resistance was the nation's soul. The heroes of this book came from all walks of life; from newspaper vendors to aristocrats, they were authen-tic, vibrant, full of imagination, defiant of death, and they served others without fanfare or patriotic cant. One might say they were "just ordi-nary heroes."

A significant part of the book is devoted to the secret radio stations, KWC ("Kierownictwo Walki Cywilnej" or "Directorate of Civil Resistance") and DAWN (SWIT), which gave London daily updates of what was happening to the Poles and the Jews in occupied Poland. This is one of the least-known aspects of wartime history. I commend this book with great pride and feeling to American readers who would like to meet true Polish heroes and learn of Poland's contribution to history.

I am deeply grateful to Hippocrene Books for reissuing this book on the 60th anniversary of the 1944 Warsaw Uprising.

Washington, D.C.
November, 2003

STEFAN KORBONSKI (1901-1989)
Polish Statesman, Lawyer & Writer

STEFAN KORBONSKI was one of the founders of the Polish Underground State during World War II. Throughout the war he was a member of the High Command of the Underground Home Army, the Chief of Civil Resistance and the last delegate in Poland (Deputy Prime Minister) of the Polish Government in Exile in London.

As a teenager, Stefan Korbonski fought in the defense of Lvov in December of 1918; then in 1920 he was a volunteer in the fight against the invading Soviet Army, and finally in 1921 he took part in the Third Silesian Uprising against the Germans.

He finished law school at the University of Poznan, and after three years of service in the Prosecutor's Office he moved to Warsaw, where he established a law practice with his cousin. On July 10, 1938, he married Zofia Ristau. Along with his professional activities, he undertook political activities in the ranks of the Polish Populist Party—he was the legal advisor of this party in Poznan. At the outbreak of the war in 1939 he was the President of the party in the Bialystok region, and a member of the National Directorate of the Party.

During the campaign of September 1939, he was a reserve officer and was taken prisoner by the invading Soviets. He escaped from a prisoners' transport into Russia, and returned to Warsaw, where he was instrumental in the founding of the Polish Underground State. As Chief of Civil Resistance, he directed all sorts of acts of sabotage and civil disobedience. He organized Polish Underground courts that tried, sentenced, and executed about two hundred collaborators and Gestapo agents. He established a network of clandestine radio stations that informed the West, and especially the Polish Government in Exile, of the events in Poland. His closest collaborator was his wife Zofia, who organized and led the cryptologic service of the radio stations.

After the war, upon the imposition of the Soviet occupation, after the arrest by the NKVD of the sixteen leaders of the Polish Underground Government, Korbonski became the de facto head of the Government in Poland, until his arrest, along with his wife, on June 28, 1945 in Cracow. He was released after the formation of the so-called

Temporary Government of the National Unity, became the President of the Polish Populist Party for Warsaw, and was elected to parliament from that city. At that time he became a member of the Executive Committee of the Populist Party.

Because of his anti-Communist activities, with his parliamentary immunity in jeopardy and threatened with arrest, he escaped in November of 1947 to Sweden, then went through England to the United States. Here he began intensive political and publication activities. He became the head of the Polish Political Council, then of the Polish Council of Unity in the United States, and also the President of the Assembly of Captive European Nations.

He wrote extensively in the American press, having many articles and letters published. He also was a member of the Polish Institute of Arts and Sciences in the United States, and of the International Pen Club in Exile. In addition, he authored ten historical books in Polish, of which seven also appeared in English and one in Spanish. His last book, titled *The Jews and Poles in World War II*, appeared in English only just before his death in 1989. His best-known titles include the trilogy *Fighting Warsaw, Warsaw in Chains*, and *Warsaw in Exile*. In 1973 he received the literary award of the Alfred Jurzykowski Foundation.

Stefan Korbonski received many decorations, including the Virtuti Militari Cross, Medal for the War of 1920, Cross for the Third Silesian Uprising, Golden Cross of Merit with Swords, Cross of the Home Army, Metal for the War of 1939-45, and others. In 1980, the Yad Vashem Institute of Jerusalem conferred on him the Medal of Righteous Among Nations for his work in saving Jews during the war. Polish President Lech Walesa granted him posthumously the Order of the White Eagle, Poland's highest decoration.

CONTENTS

CHAPTER I

The Birth of the
Polish Underground State

Warsaw, October, 1939

By the middle of October I had already been back in Warsaw for some days. I had been captured by the Russians near Vladimir Volynski, but I escaped from the transport, and having found my wife in Kovel, by walking part of the way and by getting lifts in a horse-drawn cart, we succeeded in reaching our home. I was still completely off my balance, I was still unable to live down the frightful experiences of the past few weeks, but I already felt safer, because I was back among my own people, in my old home. I walked about Warsaw and viewed the familiar landmarks, but felt that both the city and I myself lived in a different world. At first sight everything looked as it had before, but it was somehow different, submerged in the strange atmosphere of a city in mourning. Through the dense veil of dust its lovely features were hardly visible. No trace of its former elegance and gaiety remained. Everything was shabby and drab now; the crippled houses, with empty and blackened window-frames stood like rows of blind people. Everywhere lay masses of broken glass, that first victim of war. It screeched underfoot and got on one's nerves. The sidewalk slabs of concrete bore symmetrical patterns left by the explosions. The people too were somehow different, but I was not surprised, for I had seen that already on the other, the Soviet side. That appearance might be called protective, for it was assumed as a protection against the prying enemy. The ideal colour scheme was that of the houses and the pavements, on the principle that by no detail of one's clothes or movements and gestures should one attract attention. But what gave Warsaw its new look was the noisy shapes in grey-green uniforms, barking their every word and roaming the streets and open spaces of the City.

A Meeting with Mr. Speaker, Matthew Rataj

I went about visiting friends and acquaintances, and I received news of the early casualties of the war. I went to Buxom Street 14, the residence of the former Speaker of the House, Matthew Rataj, chairman of the Polish Peasant Party during the period when Vincent Witos lived in exile abroad. I wanted to know what had happened to him and to his family.

I found Mr. Speaker Rataj at his home, a modest four-roomed apartment on the first floor, with a few pieces of old furniture, well stocked book-cases and one or two pictures on the walls, including a large and fine portrait of Rataj's late wife. The place was run by Rataj's only daughter, Hanka, who opened the door to me, welcomed me with genuine pleasure, and showed me into her father's room. Rataj looked rather gaunt; his hair had turned a shade whiter during the few weeks since I had last seen him and he had grown a beard. I had a good look at his fine, prematurely aged face and I noticed that his head was shaking slightly. Having seated me in an easy chair he told me his adventures. After the outbreak of war, accompanied by his daughter Hanka, he had left Warsaw and made for the East. His son-in-law, Hanka's husband, Stankiewicz, had joined the Army and they had just received news that he had somehow succeeded in avoiding capture as a prisoner-of-war, and was living for the time being in Rataj's native village. Rataj himself was very happy to be back in Warsaw, but he had not yet recovered from the shock of the country's terrible defeat. For hours Rataj unburdened himself eagerly of the accumulated sorrows of the past, present and future. Sorrow and pain permeated his every word when he talked about the past, about the internal policy of the pre-war regime, about Beck's foreign policy, about the unpreparedness of the country for war, about Marshal Rydz-Smigly and so forth. He then reminisced about the more distant past, about the coup d'état of May 1926 and his conversation with Marshal Pilsudski at military headquarters in Saxon Square, during which he had reproached the Marshal for his high-handed action and had found him undecided and uncertain about the next move. Before I left, Rataj asked me to call on him as often as possible. 'Stefan, do come to see me whenever you are free. We must consider the future. Let's hope more of our people will come back; we shall have to stick together.'

A few days later I again visited Rataj, as I had something definite to put to him. The prospect of passively waiting for the end of the war did not appeal to me, even though I knew I would have to do something to earn my living. I had already had a foretaste of what was in store; I had to stay at home because of the curfew, and the house was crammed with all sorts of junk brought from destroyed buildings, and crowded with people who got in each other's way and were worrying over every trifle they lost. I could not possibly live like that till the end of the war. I was, of course, like thousands of others at that time, thinking about some kind of underground activity against the Germans.

The news that a new Polish Government was in the process of being set up in the West had already reached us. We knew that a new army was being formed in France, and that all those who were free to do so in the wide world were already preparing to continue the struggle. We expected all radio receivers to be confiscated any day, but for the time being we were listening in eagerly, and we knew what was happening. I was reflecting on the possibility of making my way through Hungary into France, as it seemed to me natural that I should try to rejoin the Army. Like the many thousand men in a similar situation, I felt that I had scarcely tasted war, and I had an irresistible urge to go back into the fray. Such desires, doubts and anxieties preyed on me and I decided to ask Rataj for his advice.

Rataj listened calmly while I unbosomed myself; he regarded me with much warmth, smiled wanly now and then, but became grave as soon as I mentioned conspiracy as an absolute necessity, to which political considerations and all our national characteristics were impelling us. When I had finished, Rataj placed one hand on my shoulder—he had exceptionally fine hands with long, alert and sensitive fingers—and shaking my hand firmly with the other, he said :

'I am glad you came to me before making a decision. From now on everything that passes between us will be strictly secret.'

For the next two hours, gripped to my very marrow, I listened to Rataj, who from time to time rose from his chair and paced the room, while he initiated me into the details of the conspiracy which was being hatched. He was already in close contact with Niedzialkowski, the leader of the Polish Socialist Party, and they were planning the organisation of underground action covering the whole country. The military disaster which has overtaken Poland meant the bankruptcy of the pre-war regime as well. The proposed underground activities would be directed by the opposition Parties, which had proved their loyalty to democratic ideals. The defeat should act as a cleansing fire; the Parties would have to get rid of all that had hindered their collaboration in the past.

'I shall not be privy to any factional bickerings or games,' Rataj said. 'The underground movement, like the Government in exile, must be based on democratic ideals.'

He gave me to understand that he himself, together with Niedzialkowski, would be in charge of all underground activities. Niedzialkowski never left Warsaw and during the siege he had been a member of the Citizens Committee for the Defence of the Capital. Among those already initiated he mentioned Stanislaw Dubois, a Socialist Member of Parliament.

'You will be glad to know,' he said, 'that we have included your friend Stan in our plans. You should keep in close contact with him.'

Continuing, Rataj told me that apart from myself he wanted to draw in only very few of the members of our Party, only those who in his opinion had the necessary qualifications for participating in a conspiracy. He therefore enjoined on me the necessity for not disclosing anything to our Party colleagues. My confidences had prompted him to speed up the

execution of the plans jointly decided upon with Niedzialkowski. In conclusion he expressed the hope that in the circumstances I would give up my intention of leaving the
country.

I agreed at once and I left him greatly reassured and contented. Now I had a clear aim before me. It made sense for me
to remain in my native country with the alluring prospect of
underground action. With that resolution all my worries and
anxieties were dispelled, and for the first time since the outbreak of war I felt plainly and simply gay. I was still young
enough to feel the attraction of an armed struggle, with its
sporting chances, its surprises, and its Great Adventure
written in capitals. My own generation, which grew up during the twenty years of Poland's independence, envied its
elders their conspiratorial past, which was enveloped in an
atmosphere of mystery and heroism. Conspiracy never ceased
during the century-long struggle for independence, and with
the restoration of that independence it occupied a place of
honour in the hearts of the Polish people. After such a conversation as I had just had, one should perhaps have been
shaken to the very depths of one's being, or one should have
become secretive—a quality which, as it turned out in hard
fact, was not at all synonymous with the rare ability to keep
a secret—or perhaps, having been placed in the very heart
of a conspiracy, one should have 'weighed within oneself
great schemes'. The truth is that at that moment I felt none
of these but, happy as a lark, I hurried back to my still legal
home.

As the conspiracy developed, the men of the underground
adopted an altogether sensible attitude. They realised the
gravity of their position, but they shunned pathos or national
mourning. We were of the opinion that mourning could not
go on for five years, and people were on the whole leading
normal lives; they conspired and . . . perished. Without
ostentation, without heroics, but heroes nevertheless. Officers
of the Regular Army moved about in bowler hats, wearing
galoshes and carrying umbrellas, while civilians sported
jackets of a military cut, peaked caps and military trousers.
Everyone tried to get rid of the garb he used to wear before

the war. The military men walked with a stoop, as if they had spent all their lives behind desks, while the civilians carried themselves as straight as if they had swallowed a stick. This degenerated at times into circumlocution and impenetrable secretiveness. Some characters flitted about in the manner of actors on the stage of a provincial theatre. They moved about silent, sombre, and hesitant if they had to speak, but their gait and their whole appearance seemed to be proclaiming to all and sundry, 'Look, I am a conspirator'. Such silly behaviour, however, did not prevent them risking death in their daily work, and when necessary dying like heroes. While on the subject of conspiratorial practice it may be said that during the winter 1939-40 Warsaw became the centre of some peculiar fashions. Young men of landowning families were sweeping the streets in fox-fur caps and bearskin furcoats reaching down to their ankles. Dressed in this way they visited cafes and bars in which society ladies were working as waitresses. These were mostly the wives, sisters or fiancées of military officers who worked to make their living. But some of the ladies worked there because it was fashionable to do so, and this fashion spread even behind the walls of the ghetto, where ladies of the leading Jewish families were working in a similar capacity.

Many women in Warsaw sported men's jackets with padded shoulders of all shades and colours and strutted about with masculine energy. Men had a special predilection for strong top-boots, but unfortunately the Germans soon suspected who had adopted this fashion and many a young man or boy risked arrest because of it. Nevertheless, the youngsters of the Underground Army paraded in such boots all day long disdaining the risks involved. One of my friends, who is now pining away in a prison in Poland, happened to be arrested by a German police agent in mufti while waiting at a bus stop. When he was taken to the police station in Basket Street, which now houses the Ministry of Public Security, he only got out by bribing the agent, who seemed to be a Volksdeutsche. When asked by my friend why he had arrested him the agent replied: 'Why the hell do you walk about in top-boots? Don't you know what sort of people wear such boots nowadays?'

During this period I kept in regular contact with Mr. Speaker Rataj and I was worried by what I observed in his apartment. Because of the throng of visitors the doors never seemed to close. His home became a meeting place for people of all parties and shades of opinion. Instinctively, men who seemed lost, who needed advice and guidance, flocked there. At first, I often took part in whatever conversation happened to be going on when I entered, but I soon avoided it in order not to draw attention to my close association with Rataj. The subjects of conversation were usually identical: the unexpectedly rapid defeat, the complete lack of preparedness for war, the Government in exile, General Sikorski, and the need to work for a different and better Poland in future. I noticed how great was Rataj's political and moral authority among the numerous visitors. We had no reliable news about the chairman of our Party, Witos, except that he was under arrest and could not be reached. Now, Rataj deputised for him, and his intelligence and high level of political thinking impressed all his visitors. He was full of enthusiasm, radiating an inner strength, and one could sense that he had a clear vision of the future, a definite plan, for the fulfillment of which he was keen to labour and to organise people. Before the war I knew Rataj well, though he occupied a much higher position in the Party hierarchy than I, but it was only now that I got to know him intimately, and my respect for him increased, together with a feeling of genuine affection.

During our many talks we discussed the structure of the conspiratorial Party organisation to be set up, and we agreed on the personalities who were to be invited to join in the numerous provincial centres. In his opinions on the suitability of individuals Rataj disregarded completely their respective importance in the Party hierarchy; the only criterion he applied was their suitability for underground activities.

I took it upon myself to draw Rataj's attention to the danger to which he was exposing himself by receiving so many visitors, but he said with a shrug:

'I realise it myself. But what can I do? I cannot keep the doors locked all day long. I might move to another place, but I won't do it, for I have got used to my home.'

Rataj's daughter, Hanka, warmly supported me, as she was well aware of what was going on and tried to limit the number of visitors by introducing some kind of selection, but it was of no avail.

To-day, while writing about it, I realise how careless and naive we were. Apart from military officers who had somehow succeeded in avoiding capture as prisoners of war, and the more prominent politicians who had been close to the Government and feared that the Germans might arrest them, and who therefore went into hiding, all others remained in their pre-war homes or returned to them from their war wanderings. They argued that if they behaved outwardly in accordance with the stipulations of international law and remained quiet, the Germans would have to respond in the same way. Everything concerning the position of an occupied country in international law was being studied, and people comforted themselves with the thought that the Germans could not do this or that. The conspiracy which was being organised was an altogether different matter, but the Germans knew nothing of it as yet and normal appearances were maintained. We had already received vague rumours about the mass murders committed in Posnania. There were grounds for fearing a persecution of the Jews, but in those early months of occupation no one envisioned such horrors as collective responsibility, arrests and imprisonments without any charges being preferred, or genocide. Manhunts, the horrors of the Pawiak Prison, of Auschwitz and the Ghetto were still to come. The first blow fell on November 9, 1939, when the Germans took hostages, and the second blow soon afterwards, when they carried out the terrible mass execution in Wawer.

Hostages

I was awakened at my home early in the morning by a violent banging at the door and a German voice shouting, 'Open the door'. Snatching whatever was handy to put on, I opened the door. A Gestapo man, accompanied by two gendarmes entered the room. He held a sheaf of papers in his hand and looking at a list he read out my name and occupation. When I admitted who I was, I received the order: 'Get dressed! You will come with us!' I started to dress very slowly, to gain time to overcome the shock. The gendarmes made a round of all the rooms. My hands were trembling slightly and all sorts of thoughts flashed through my mind. Was this the end of something that had hardly begun? How did they find out? Had Rataj been arrested? I could not tell.

The Gestapo man stood watching and urging me to hurry. My wife, pale but calm, handed me the various things I might need, a towel, a cake of soap, some underclothing. At last we left the house. A truck was waiting in front of the door and in it I noticed two crouching shapes. I thought their faces were familiar as those of people from the neighbourhood whom I used to pass in the street. The sobering thought occurred to me that this could not be connected with the conspiracy, and when, after a few minutes drive, the gendarmes led us into the great hall of the University in the Cracow Suburb Avenue, which was filled with several scores of people as frightened as we were ourselves, I had an inspiration. The surprise arrest could have nothing to do with the conspiracy and must have been connected with the Day of Independence, which was November 11. Presently, I was shaking hands with Henry Kolodziejski and Emil Breiter, who confirmed my supposition. After about half an hour, an officer of the Gendarmes informed us that as prominent citizens we had been taken as hostages responsible for public order in the city on November 11. Should any riots occur, we would be shot. Well, the conspiracy was not discovered. I regained my equanimity and fortified myself with a goodly portion of gruel and some tinned meat which the gendarmes brought to us, and lying on a mattress I chatted far into the night with Kolodziejski and Breiter, who occupied the mattresses next to me. They wondered why I was in such a good mood, but I could obviously offer no explanation; in the end however they too calmed down considerably. We carried on our talks for the next two days, until the afternoon of November 11, when the Germans were satisfied that the city was calm, and released us. My wife was waiting for me at the entrance to the University. We were happy to be going home, though we did not like the idea that the Germans had conferred this mark of distinction on me so soon.

The First Arrest of Mr. Speaker Rataj

A few days later, like a bolt from the blue, came the news that Rataj had been arrested. The Gestapo came in the early morning and took him away in such haste that they would not even let him put on an overcoat or take any personal effects with him. I was told all the details by Hanka, Rataj's daughter, whom I met in town with all the necessary precautions; she was calm though shaken. This was a blow at the very heart of the newly founded organisation. I was overwhelmed, but before anything else, I wanted to find out the reasons for the arrest. Within a few hours I knew that Niedzialkowski had not been arrested, but that a number of other people in the city had also been seized. I took counsel with Dubois and we agreed that the Germans must have acted without knowledge of our activities, and that they could not have any proofs of what we were doing. Dubois, with his well preserved pre-war portliness, and dressed in a wind-jacket and 'pumps', was roaming all over the working-class quarters of Warsaw, well liked by all and most welcome wherever he went. He also retained his good-natured jocularity and every time I met him I felt relaxed. We had many common memories to share, and we promised ourselves that when the war was over we would go climbing in the Tatra mountains with our friend Miet Thugutt, who was then out somewhere in the wide world and whom we greatly missed.

Hanka was doing her utmost to supply her father with clothing and a blanket, but she failed, and could not even get inside the building in Szucha Avenue, which was already acquiring its tragic notoriety. I determined to take a risk and visit the lion's den in my capacity as a barrister, retained by Rataj's family as defence counsel. To-day, the whole thing appears laughable to me, but at the time we did not know the Germans well enough. Hanka, carrying a parcel and accom-

panied by my wife, arrived in front of the Gestapo Headquarters at the same time as I arrived from the opposite direction, carefully groomed and with a document case under my
arm. We looked at the building, which used to house the
Ministry of Education, taking stock of the situation. A number of gendarmes guarded the modern, chromium-plated
entrance doors, barring them to the little groups of people
with anxiety and expectation in their faces, who were obviously members of the families of the men under arrest. A
number of suspicious characters were flitting here and there
who must have been either middlemen or agents of the
Gestapo. It was not long afterwards that the gruesome horror
which surrounded the building made everyone abandon the
Szucha Avenue, and the very name of that once quiet thoroughfare became a synonym for murder and crime. For the
time being, conditions were still tolerable and the gendarmes
gazed at the passers-by with perfect indifference. I went
boldly straight up to them, they clicked their heels and let me
pass. It was a good beginning. They took me for a German. I
wandered about the building for more than an hour without
being accosted by anyone. The corridors were clean and there
was a great deal of coming and going; officers and soldiers
of the Gestapo, in brown shirts and grey uniforms, were
rushing about with folders and papers in their hands. Here,
gendarmes were escorting a deathly pale man carrying a
pile of books, which he could only with difficulty manage.
In passing him I caught his scared, haggard and unseeing
gaze and I surmised that he must have been just arrested.
There, a group of civilians, with automatics in their hands,
was emerging from a room, laughing coarsely. I went on and
passed two Gestapo men escorting or rather dragging down
the stairs a groaning, bleeding woman with only the whites
of her eyes showing. No one paid the slightest attention to
me. Things were gradually getting on my nerves and I
knocked at a number of doors, enquiring in my rather poor
German where I could get any information concerning the
arrest of Matthew Rataj. Some replied politely, some rudely,
that it was not there. Finally, I was given a chit with the room
number. I accosted an elderly, shabbily dressed and rather

repulsive civilian to enquire which way I should go, and he replied in Polish:

'Who is it you are enquiring about?'

'The former Speaker of the Diet, Matthew Rataj.'

'What? Mr. Rataj has been arrested?'

I told him what happened and noticing that Rataj's name had made an impression on him, I solicited his help. But he only retorted:

'How did you get in here? Who are you, anyhow?'

He shook his head when I explained what I had come for and led me to a door marked 'Preventive Arrest', with the name 'Thiele' and the rank of an SS officer on it. He knocked at the door, and in response to a coarse invitation to 'Come in' bowed himself into the room. Presently, he reappeared at the open door and beckoned me in. I found myself in the presence of a Gestapo officer, who stood behind his desk, a giant of a man, looking at me sharply and unfriendly. He had a handsome face, with regular features that I can still remember vividly. I explained what I had come for, asked for permission to deliver a parcel to Rataj, and demanded to know the reason for his arrest. The huge man left the room and came back with an index-card. Looking at the card, he stated briefly that the 'author' Matthew Rataj was being held in prison in Division Street, where I could take the parcel and explain that he, Thiele, gave me permission to do so. He sat down and I understood that he had nothing more to say. However, that was not enough for me to tell Hanka, who was waiting in the street, so I screwed up enough courage to ask:

'Why was Mr. Rataj arrested and how long is he going to be kept in prison?'

Thiele's eyes flashed with anger, but before he could utter a word I was already in the corridor, pushed out of the room by the helpful civilian, who furiously shouted into my face:

'Are you crazy? A question like that is enough to get you behind bars!' I could still hear from behind the closed door the angry muttering of Thiele. I thanked the civilian, who showed me the way out with a final warning not to miss it, and in no time I was reporting to the two women. They had been walking up and down the street for hours, and had

already begun to pray for my safe return. Hanka went straight
to the prison in Division Street, but they would not accept
the parcel.

A Meeting with Niedzialkowski

Dubois arranged my meeting with Niedzialkowski for 8 a.m.
in the Café Napoleon, at the corner of New World Avenue
and Warecka Street. I protested against such an early hour,
but Stan cut me short by saying that 'Mek' was in the habit
of rising early, and that was that. Punctually at 8 a.m. the
following morning I was in the café, which had just opened
for the day and was deserted and as yet unheated. Two
elderly actresses, whom I knew by sight, were tidying up and
arranging the tables and chairs. I sat down in a corner, and
presently a man came in and sat down in another corner,
eyeing me discreetly. We were the only two customers in the
café. I repaid the man in the same coin until the arrival of
Niedzialkowski put an end to this mutual observation. Mek
gallantly kissed the two waitresses on the hand, bowed to the
unknown man, and sat down at my table. I knew him fairly
well, having met him frequently at the home of my kinsman,
Dr. Zygmunt Gralinski. Nevertheless, I had a good look at
him and found that he showed none of the marks of war. In
fact, he had not changed at all, with his old frameless pince-
nez, with the same unruly mop of upstanding hair, and the
same rather funny double chin. I looked at him with considerable curiosity, which was aroused by the part he had played
during the past few months. He had organised workers'
battalions during the siege of the Capital, he had been one
of the leading members of the Citizens Defence Committee,
he had collaborated closely with the Mayor of the City,
Starzynski; all this made me realise that here was a leader
who had already proved himself in action, to which he now
summoned other people. We exchanged a number of preliminary questions and I asked him who the man was whom he
had greeted on arrival. He answered mysteriously:
    'You will meet him presently.'
    In a whisper which penetrated to every corner of the

empty café, Niedzialkowski explained the position to me. I had to listen hard, because his speech was rather blurred and he mispronounced the letter S. He told me that Rataj had given him my name as one who would perform the same functions within the Polish Peasant Party as Dubois was performing within the Polish Socialist Party. Since Rataj was under arrest, I should assume his functions as a deputy and carry on the work in accordance with the agreed line. In his opinion Rataj's arrest had no connection with the growing conspiracy and he would surely be soon released. Enjoining me to observe the strictest secrecy, he told me that an executive political body to direct the conspiracy had already been formed and consisted of himself, Niedzialkowski, as chairman, representing the Polish Socialist Party, Rataj, representing the Polish Peasant Party, and the Dean of the Warsaw Bar, Leon Nowodworski, co-opted to represent the National Democratic Party. He also mentioned General Tokarzewski, as being in charge of the military side, and pointing to the man sitting at a table in the opposite corner, he added:

'The man over there has been sent by him. He will acquaint you with the methods of military action and put you in contact with whomsoever it will be useful for you to know.'

He introduced me to the man and left us. I had a close look at the new comrade. He had a ruddy complexion and black hair, but otherwise no 'distinguishing marks'. As soon as he spoke I knew that he was a native of Cracow. His name was Kortum, of the Supreme Command of the Service for Poland's Liberation, later transformed into the Union for Armed Struggle. We sat there, in that café, sipping a washy liquid, while I listened to a long exposition, in which Kortum defined the demands the military underground addressed to the political parties. He proceeded from the assumption that the past had been wiped out and would never be restored. Unity of purpose and unity in action was to be our slogan. I left him with the clear impression that we should have to meet these demands, and I informed my party colleagues accordingly.

By then I had already been joined in Warsaw by Jozef Grudzinski, a member of the Executive of the Peasant Party, who, until the arrival from Czechoslovakia of Casimir Baginski, acted as Secretary General of the Party, and Stanislaw Milkowski, Editor of 'Wici'. I saw no alternative but to initiate them into all the secrets rather than wait for Rataj to be released and do it himself. We discussed matters all day long and we agreed unanimously to proceed in accordance with the principles laid down by Rataj and with the information supplied by Niedzialkowski. We decided there and then that Grudzinski should make a tour of the provincial centres of our Party to establish contacts, to transmit indispensable information and to organise conspiratorial cells. Grudzinski, a smallish, ruddy and rather shy man, whom I ran into in the street by chance, was pleased that things were moving. He had intended to return to the countryside in the Lublin region and to lie low there, but now all his plans were altered. His only regret was that he had not met Rataj before the latter was arrested.

A Meeting with Rowecki

Very soon afterwards, through a contact from the Peasant Party, whom I knew well, I received an invitation to meet the Chief of Staff of the Military Organisation. I met the girl in the evening, somewhere near Basket Street. It was rather dark and I had difficulty in recognising the rather smallish woman standing in a doorway. She took me by the hand and led me up an unlighted staircase. She knocked at a door and whispered the pass-word. Presently I entered a dimly lit room, to be welcomed by a thick-set man in his forties, with fine features and dark hair which seemed to have been recently cropped close to the skin. We kept silent for a long while, looking at each other intently. I liked him. He impressed me as being energetic, he had a ready and pleasant smile, and his cold eyes looked straight into one's own. He had a masculine and melodious voice. I knew his real name, which meant nothing to me, just as my own name meant nothing to him. Our talk lasted for several hours, during which I was mostly a listener. We discussed the subject Kortum had already touched upon, namely the views and desires of the military organisation, which were now put in a more precise form. The underground political organisations would constitute the social basis for a purely military organisation subordinate to the Government. The young people active in the parties would gradually enter the ranks of the underground army. The definite organisation of the political body initiated by Niedzialkowski and Rataj was an absolute necessity. He emphasised his opinion that this body should begin to function as soon as possible. Moreover, the underground party organisations in the provinces should speedily make contact with the local military centres.

In this way, in a dark and cold room somewhere in Basket Street, I made the acquaintance of a man who was to bring many memorable experiences into my life. At that time I was not aware that I was sitting in front of a man who was to be one of the most heroic figures of the coming struggle. We chatted with considerable freedom and sincerity. We sat close to each other, face to face, and towards the end we touched upon all sorts of subjects, including personal and family affairs. I said goodbye to him with a most favourable impression, which in days to come never left me, though our future talks were by no means invariably friendly. Our views and opinions frequently clashed and tempers rose, and sometimes, as I remember, there was even some banging of fists on the table. Nevertheless, the favourable impression I received during my first meeting with Colonel Rowecki remained with me to the end.

Contact with General Tokarzewski

Ascending gradually the higher rungs of the military ladder, I met one evening General Tokarzewski, at that time Commander of the Union For Armed Struggle. I was given an exact address, with instructions on how to reach it. I had to commit it all to memory because the making of notes was forbidden. In the evening, I went along Rakowiecka Street repeating to myself the instructions, 'Entrance through the janitor's; if the latter should ask whom I had come to see, I was to tell him I had come to see the doctor; after passing the janitor's lodge, I was to pass the courtyard, turn right and take the third door; go up to the first floor, turn left, and give the pre-arranged knock on the door, two short, pause, one short. An elderly lady would open the door. Password: I have come from Praga. Reply: We are waiting with the dinner.' Such were the beginnings of a system the disregard of which could not only make a meeting impossible, but could result in the liquidation of the hide-out, alarms, etc. The person in charge of a hide-out might report:

'Someone I did not know came and said he was sure it was here that he was to meet another person, but he did not give the password. He looked suspect, was insistent, and it was necessary to abandon the place at once.' If something like that happened, the genuine conspirator might have lost not only the chance of a safe hide-out for the night but the contact as well, and he would be lucky if he were able to return empty-handed. So I kept muttering to myself . . . 'to the right, third door' . . . while turning over in my mind what I knew about General Tokarzewski. It was not much, but I remembered a pre-war Congress of the Peasant Party in Cracow. Rataj mounted the tribune with a bouquet of red roses in his hand, which he showed with a dramatic gesture to the crowded audience saying:

'The roses were sent to the Congress by a certain General.' Amidst the stormy applause with which these words were received, a shout went up in a corner of the hall: 'Long live General Tokarzewski!'

I shook my head with the rather melancholy thought that so much had changed in such a short time, but I had already reached Falat Street and was glad to find that my memory had served me well. I passed the janitor's lodge, the courtyard, another door, the staircase, reached the first floor, and stood in front of another door. I stopped, took a deep breath, and drummed off the signal. The door opened at once, and before I could open my mouth, an elderly lady pointed silently to a door leading to an inner room in the apartment.

My talk with General Tokarzewski lasted for some time, and he showed considerable knowledge of the problems and of the political set-up. What he was primarily interested in was the forming of the military organisation on a wide national front, and the calling into being of a supreme conspiratorial political body in accordance with the plan of Niedzialkowski and Rataj, with which he was familiar. The functioning of that body was being delayed owing to complications which had arisen within the National Democratic Party.

When the conversation was concluded, I already had behind me the first round of meetings with the higher commanders of the Union for Armed Struggle, and I had a pretty clear picture of the structure and the needs of the underground Polish Army.

Party organisation

Now that we had established initial contacts, we proceeded to plan the principles of co-operation between our underground party organisation and the military. It was not long before difficulties arose, due to the conflict between the tendency of the military to absorb everything and our desire to preserve the independence of our organisation. Our numbers increased, because at a conference with Grudzinski and Milkowski we decided to draw into the conspiracy certain additional members of the Peasant Party. We called the first enlarged meeting, and it took place in a small café in Raven Street. Everyone was extremely impressed with even the scanty information I was able to impart, and all declared their enthusiastic desire to join the underground movement. We all deplored the absence of Baginski, whose great experience as a conspirator would have stood us in good stead now. We had no news of him, except that during the critical September days he had left Warsaw and taken the road to the east, as so many thousand others had done. We fixed a special hide-out for members of the Peasant Party who would be coming to Warsaw from the countryside, in the old offices of the Party at 4, Princes Street, where a bookshop was set up to serve as a cover. Any of our people coming to Warsaw were always to call at the old office to enquire. The energetic Grudzinski undertook to visit all our more important centres and was going first to Cracow and then to Lublin. Milkowski took upon himself the province of Kielce, while I contacted the former deputy Wladislaw Praga, who before the war was secretary-general of the Executive of the Party in the province of Bialystok, of which I used to be chairman. Praga left for Bialystok soon afterwards, to take up the work of organisation, and it was not long before he gave his life in the service of his country.

The Arrest of Niedzialkowski

In the meantime I had several meetings with Niedzialkowski, to whom I related the results and my impressions of the conversations with the military people, and informed him of the progress of the work within the Party. I asked him when a joint meeting with the representatives of the National Democrats was to take place. Niedzialkowski, without entering into details, replied that owing to difficulties which had arisen in the internal councils of that Party, he would not, for the time being, call a meeting of the representatives of all three parties, but he hoped that it would be possible to arrange it soon. However, a meeting of this nature, with the participation of Niedzialkowski, a representative of the National Democratic Party and myself never took place. On another occasion Niedzialkowski told me that in the event of his being arrested, Dubois would take over; but I received the impression that he did not take such an eventuality seriously into account, because he continued to live in his pre-war apartment.

During the Christmas Holidays, however, the dreaded news broke that Niedzialkowski had indeed been arrested. It was brought by Dubois, who was shaken to his very core. Niedzialkowski had been taken for cross-examination to Gestapo Headquarters in Szucha Avenue at noon on December 23, the day before Christmas Eve. After a preliminary examination, he was ordered to report again on the following day, but he explained to the Gestapo that Christmas Eve was a solemn occasion in Poland, and asked that the examination should be concluded that day in the afternoon. The

Gestapo were courteous and understanding enough to agree and so, after a short adjournment for lunch, Niedzialkowski went back to the Gestapo headquarters, never to return.

We were thrust into utter despair. Both Rataj and Niedzialkowski were in prison. What could it mean? Could it be that contrary to our assumption the Germans knew the leaders of the underground movement already? We instituted a thorough inquiry, but obtained no definite proofs. It seemed that both Niedzialkowski and Rataj had been arrested simply because they were prominent politicians, and Niedzialkowski, moreover, was a Socialist.

Months passed without any reliable information as to the cause of the arrests. We only found out that Niedzialkowski was in Pawiak prison and that both physically and morally he was bearing himself magnificently. The information was gathered either from released prisoners—such things still happened at the time—or from Polish prison guards. However, during the second half of 1940 there were persistent rumours that, together with a large group of people, Niedzialkowski had been shot at Palmiry. We soon discovered the date of the execution: June 21, 1940.

Six years later I saw Niedzialkowski once again, in a coffin. His well-preserved body was exhumed from the mass grave at Palmiry, and a photograph of his wife, a cigarette case and visiting cards were still in the pocket of his jacket. I had to witness the falsehood and hypocrisy of a solemn 'State Funeral'. The comrades of his labours and struggles gazed wide-eyed from a distance at the tragic spectacle. By the coffin stood his widow, in deep mourning, and close to her the men whom Niedzialkowski hated most during his life, agents of the Secret Police, of the Security Police, in uniforms and in mufti, of the Soviet NKVD, detachments from the Public Security Police, some presenting, some concealing arms; and among them was Bierut and other dignitaries of the Communist regime, whose safety was well guarded amidst the mass of workers and peasants who had come to pay their last tribute to their dead leader. At the grave of Niedzialkowski stood those who had been the Germans' friends and collaborators at the time when they were torturing him to death, all with an assumed, hypocritical mask of mourning on their faces; and among them was the bald head and cynical face of the 'hog from Chicago', Cyrankiewicz. Bierut conferred on Niedzialkowski posthumously the highest decoration—the Cross of Grunwald. The decoration, thrown into the open grave, hit the coffin like a slap in the face.

The First Session of the Inter-party Political Committee

On February 7, 1940, I hurried stealthily and a little excitedly to the first meeting of the representatives of the three parties, the Polish Socialist Party, the National Democratic Party, and the Peasant Party, and the Commander of the Union for Armed Struggle, as the organisation of the Underground Army was to be called henceforth.

As I hurried along the streets of Warsaw, I discreetly cast glances around me to make sure I was not being shadowed. As the months and years went by, this habit sank into my very bones and became simply a mechanical function performed by the eyes, some cells in the brain and, most important of all, instinct. Constant practice sharpened my senses to such a degree that they automatically registered everything that was happening around me, and at the right moment presented the required picture. I was able, for example, to recognise an unknown person in the street whom I happened to run into twice in one day. If someone followed me for some time, I would sense it; there must be a sort of 'radar' concealed in the human body. In such cases I reacted by stopping in front of a shop window, by turning into a side street, by passing to the other side of the roadway, or by jumping on to a moving tram, to continue my observations. Everyone was keen to know all the buildings with a through passage, i.e. with exits into two streets. If a shadowing agent did not know it, he would wait in front of a house entered by his prey, and continue to wait for his emergence until doomsday.

It became standard practice, when going to an important meeting, to board a tram going in the opposite direction to one's destination, jumping on when it slowed down at a bend, for instance. Only when a conspirator was completely reassured that no one was following him did he change to a tram going the right way. And if there was the least doubt about the matter, the whole procedure would be repeated. One's feelings, too, were important; we all became very superstitious and sensitive to premonitions. If one day I suddenly felt I ought not to go along, say, Wilcza Street, I would go out of my way to avoid it. If I did not like a particular hide-out, I never tried to reason myself out of the feeling; I just stopped going there. The same applied to meeting new people; all my senses would automatically take in everything about them, and this would serve as a basis for determining the kind of relationship I should enter into with them. A well developed instinct of self-preservation saved many of us from arrest or death.

Having observed all the necessary precautions while on my way to the meeting, I finally reached the apartment in Independence Avenue that I was looking for. The door was opened by a young woman in a doctor's overall, who smiled at me meaningly. We exchanged the passwords, and a moment later I was seated in the waiting room of the surgery, in the company of General Tokarzewski, Colonel Rowecki, and a man who was introduced to me as 'the director', and who was none other than Kruk-Strzelecki, known later as Stefan, at that time chief of the Political and Propaganda Department of the Union for Armed Struggle. We chatted while waiting for the rest to arrive, and Tokarzewski told me that he had been informed that the Polish Socialist Party had delegated Puzak, and the National Democratic Party the former Member of Parliament, Alexander Debski. Presently, Puzak arrived, a tall man with a slight stoop, greying hair, and large spectacles with very thick lenses. His speech had a faint borderland accent. The last to arrive was Alexander Debski, a tall, gaunt man, also with a stoop and thick spectacles, but brisk and lively. The mood of the gathering was grave and attentive. We eyed each other closely, the military eyed the politicians and the latter eyed the former. It was indeed a strange coming together. Three representatives of the parties of the opposition and three former legionaries representing the Army, which had had so much say before the war. It seemed to me that all the men present were at that moment wondering if we should succeed in finding a common tongue and in agreeing on a common plan. The session was inaugurated by the host, General Tokarzewski, who proposed the agenda and suggested that the oldest among us, Casimir Puzak, should take the chair. After Puzak had taken the chair he called on Colonel Rowecki to speak, in accordance with the agenda. In this way the body, which for the next two years directed the nation-wide Polish conspiracy, began to function. All those present adopted pseudonyms, which were to be changed frequently in the days to come. Puzak changed into Basil, Debski into Stachurski, and I was henceforth to be called Nowak. Tokarzewski became a 'doctor' and 'Michael', Colonel Rowecki 'Engineer' and afterwards Rakon, Tur, John and Grot. The Polish Socialist Party became the 'Circle', the National Party the 'Square', the Peasant Party the 'Triangle', and the Union for Armed Struggle simply 'Z'.

The first session was devoted to considering the aims to be adopted and the organisation of the country under the occupation. The formulation of the aims produced short, impassioned and unanimous declarations of a life and death struggle against the Germans, to begin at once. No-one as much as suggested the possibility of passively awaiting the end of the war, of adapting ourselves to existing conditions, of adopting a policy of caution, or of seeking to come to terms with the Germans. Writing about it to-day, I am not at all sure we were right, because the problems deserved at least to be posed and considered. But they were not, because everyone had already digested the matter, both individually and in the organisations, while the irreconcilable attitude of the nation as a whole was common knowledge. We were of the opinion that the struggle had to be continued underground, and we wanted to make the struggle in our country a part of the general war against Hitler, a part which the Allies would be bound to recognise and to appreciate. We wanted to make our contribution to victory, and to become as big an item on the active side of the final balance sheet as possible. No prominent personality in the country, except Wladyslaw Studnicki, expressed a different opinion; our decision, moreover, har-monised with the policy of the Polish Government-in-exile. To-day, when through no fault of our own we find ourselves in the red, legitimate doubts may arise about whether the decision to carry on the struggle, taken so readily, was right, whether it was worth while to shed so much blood for such meagre results. But though such doubts may arise to-day, at the time and in the circumstances in which we made the deci-sion, no other was conceivable. Besides, the whole story has not yet been written, and it is difficult to draw final deduc-tions from history when the last chapter is still missing.

In that stand, the nation endured till the end and pro-duced no Quisling. It may be asked whether the Germans made any attempts to come to an understanding with the Poles during the occupation. The answer is that the Germans only tried to influence the Poles unilaterally and imperson-ally to supply labour for German factories, to deliver food supplies, to keep quiet and to give up all underground activi-ties. Many German declarations to that effect were put into circulation from Cracow, the seat of the Governor General, but they came up against a wall of hostility and hatred. As to the formation of a Government, the Germans considered such a possibility and took tentative soundings, echoes of which reached the underground authorities. The result of these attempts, which might have been undertaken on their own initiative by certain high officials of the Government General, must have been negative; they must have shown that the atti-tude of the Poles was more hostile than that of any other occupied country. The Polish people had their eyes fixed on the Government-in-exile; they gave their unstinted obedience to the underground authorities, of whose existence the Germans were well aware; and they would have rejected any suggestion of a compromise. The unsuccessful experiment with the Regency Council during the first world war may have had a sobering effect, as the Council was supposed to ensure the formation of a Polish army to fight on the side of Germany. On the other hand the Germans may have realised that any Government, even one called into being by them-selves and entirely subordinate to them, would still be a symbol of the Polish State and hence an obstacle to carrying out the policy of extermination and genocide. Moreover, as it turned out, the Germans granted governments only to those occupied countries which had already produced a potential Quisling before the war, no matter whether his name was Laval, Pavelic or Degrelle. The most likely Polish candidate, the irresponsible Piasecki—and it must be recorded to his credit—renounced from the first his brown cousins from the West and joined the ranks of the conspiracy. It should be added, however, that after Poland had been overrun by the Soviets, he collaborated closely with his red cousins from the East.

There was no attempt on the Polish side to form a Government under the German occupation, and, to repeat, Poland produced no Quisling.

During our first session, political and organisational problems formed the main subjects of discussion. We examined the suggestion that a Council of National Defence should be established, and it was then that I realised how much circumstances had altered, when 'Doctor' Tokarzewski emphasised that only the Parties which had been in Opposition before the war would be able to gain the support of the bitterly disappointed nation. However, the National Party regarded the formation of the Council as premature, so without abandoning the suggestion altogether, we decided for the time being to seek other forms of national representation.

We also discussed the question of establishing in the country a Plenipotentiary of the Government-in-exile. Some suggested that the Government should appoint as its Plenipotentiary somebody in Poland, nominated by the Parties, while others thought that the Government should send into the country one of its members.

During these deliberations I observed my colleagues. Basil was grave and tense; he argued dispassionately, with considerable power, punctuated occasionally by sarcastic remarks. He had had much experience in politics and conspiracy, gained during the struggle against Tsardom, which cost him eight years in the prison of Shlisselburg. The manner of those present towards him showed that he was the central figure in our little group. Debski, who spoke with great animation and intelligence, was against going too far and was rather restrained and circumspect in his approach. Tokarzewski had charming manners and spoke more like a politician than a military officer. It was evident that he was familiar with political problems, and advanced bold suggestions which we had to moderate. Rowecki, on the other hand, seemed rather uncertain in broaching political questions; he always impressed me as a man to whom politics did not appeal. The strongest impression I carried away from the meeting, however, was the desire of all to reach agreement and conciliation, and to ensure complete national unity for the duration of the war. It was the sound instinct of the nation, which prevailed in face of mortal danger.

When the session was adjourned, we left individually at intervals of several minutes. We agreed to meet in the same way in future, each arriving five minutes after the other, strictly in accordance with a time-table; for the simultaneous arrival of six people might have been too conspicuous even for a doctor's surgery.

In Pawiak Prison

On about February 20, 1940, at dawn, I was awakened by a banging on the door and German voices, which I had heard once before. We were still living at 10, Rose Avenue, where I was legally registered. Only half dressed, I opened the door. Several Gestapo men and gendarmes entered, asking for me by name. It was only a few minutes before I found myself in the street escorted by the Germans. I could see trucks and crowds of Gestapo and gendarmes everywhere and from every house men were emerging escorted by them. I noticed that in Basket and Mokotov Streets the same thing was happening, and I felt somewhat relieved that it had turned out to be a mass action and not the arrest of individuals. With the butt of his rifle a stout gendarme helped me into the truck, where a number of frightened men were sitting on wooden planks placed across it. They pushed into our truck Count Ronikier, President of the Central Welfare Council, who produced his identity card; but the gendarme would not listen to his explanations. From the direction in which the truck was being driven I knew that we were being taken to Pawiak Prison. On arrival there we were drawn up in the courtyard and all the arrested janitors were formed into a separate group.

With the curiosity characteristic of all convicts I looked around, taking in every detail. We were standing in the snow-covered yard, more than a hundred of us, and all around were high walls and iron-barred windows. It was mid-winter and I was chilled to the bone. In front of us stood several Gestapo officers and a civilian, whom someone recognised as a man of German origin who had been a lecturer in one of the Warsaw Colleges. The civilian advanced a few steps and announced in Polish that we would be detained for some time as hostages, and if any disorders ocurred in the City we would be shot. It was the second time I had listened to that kind of speech. The man then turned to the group of janitors saying:

'As for you, you may go home now and tell all and sundry what you have heard. Let everyone know that the fate of these hostages depends on the orderly behaviour of the inhabitants.'

The janitor of the house in which I lived, the small, shy Stanislav, ran up to me, pushed into my hand a bundle containing a loaf of bread, and whispered:

'Don't worry sir, everything will be all right.'

'Stanislav, will you go to my wife right now and tell her that they have only taken hostages.'

'I shall go at once and tell your lady.'

The janitors left reluctantly, looking back at us. Stanislav was one of those janitors of Warsaw whom I shall always remember with gratitude. They often risked their lives to hide me, though they only guessed that I might be working in the underground movement. When I moved into illegal domicile, I arranged with the janitors of my two official apartments that I should not check out. I expected that should the Gestapo search for me, they would go first to the apartment in which I was registered. My anticipation proved correct, and my apartment at 1, Amity Avenue, was in fact repeatedly visited by the Gestapo at night. Each time the janitor explained that I was living in the country now, that

I visited the apartment only occasionally, and that he did not know my address. The Gestapo threatened him with revolvers, arrest and execution if he would not tell them my address, but John—who was later murdered during the Warsaw Rising—would not be intimidated; he pretended to be a fool and kept on repeating, 'He didn't tell me'. Meantime, while the Gestapo were still in his lodge, his nine-year-old son would rush to the Prudential building, which was an emergency alarm point, and within half an hour I would know that the Gestapo had resumed their search for me. I should add that the German habit of being methodical served us in good stead; for whenever they resumed a search they always went first to the old official address.

We hostages were accommodated in two separate halls, equipped with iron bedsteads and mattresses, a table in the centre, and next to it an iron stove. The filth was unbearable, and the walls were dripping with water. The exit from the hall led straight to a lavatory. I found a place between the lavatory and a window that admitted some fresh air, and I was glad to find myself in a spot where the two air currents neutralised each other. I reclined on the bed and looked round the hall, filled with office clerks, merchants, shop-keepers, barristers, doctors—all of whom lived in the same part of the town. Little groups were already forming and engaging in conversations. A lean, sickly-looking man was complaining:

'I don't live in Warsaw at all, I live in the country. I came in early this morning to see a doctor in Chopin Street, and they took me away from his waiting room. They would not listen to my explanations that I was a stranger here.'

Count Ronikier, who had arrived from Cracow and was spending the night in Chopin Street had a similar experience. He was released after a few hours, but his brother, a taciturn, elderly man, remained with us to the end.

I was in turn amused and irritated by the position in which I found myself. Here I was, detained as a hostage, while my colleagues went on working hard. How long was this going to last? On the other hand, I was tickled to death by the thought that the Germans would have skinned me alive if they had known what was going on. But all in all, it was annoying, cold and hopeless.

Some days later the Polish prison guards brought us parcels from home; for in 1940 they were, luckily, still performing their duties in the Pawiak prison. I was munching a roll when I started to choke and felt something strange in my throat. It was a scrap of paper with a message from my wife, who informed me that the hostages had been taken because of the arrival in Warsaw of Governor Frank, who was in residence at the former Czechoslovak Legation in Chopin Street. The hostages had been taken from that neighbourhood. She also tried to console me with the thought that in a few weeks, after Frank had left, we would be released.

We were thus spending our time in a rather sullen mood, when one day the prison guard called me and my neighbour from Rose Avenue to fetch parcels which had arrived for the hostages. As we went along, escorted by the warder, I wondered why I should have been chosen for this task. We passed through inner doors and corridors to the clanking of keys and iron doors, till we emerged into a small yard, where prisoners were exercising by walking in a circle in single file. I recognised among them the well-known Chopin player, Professor Lewicki of the Conservatoire, and Count Branicki of Wilanow. We reached the guard-room next to the prison gate, which was slightly ajar. Through a chink I saw my wife's face, and dropping the basket I ran to the gate. The sentry on duty pushed me away with some violence. I pleaded with him, explaining that my wife was just outside. He proceeded to revile me, and losing my self-control I repaid him in the same coin.

At that moment, a man in a smart overcoat with the collar turned up approached, and raising his voice ordered the sentry in German to open the gate. The sentry hastened to obey. He opened the wicket gate and stood to attention. The German passed through and in that instant I saw my wife standing in a crowd of other women. She saw me and had time to wave to me before the wicket gate was closed with a bang.

We had been in the guard-room for some minutes, putting

the parcels into the basket, when we suddenly heard shouting and whistling, and saw two Gestapo men and a number of warders running towards the gate. 'He's escaped! He's escaped!' they shouted, and a row ensued. From the guardroom I could hear questions and curses in German, and through the window we could see that the sentry at the gate was helplessly waving his arms and explaining something away. Our warder, a Pole, winked at us:

'Quick, gentlemen, let's get out of here.'

Some hours afterwards, a warder told us all that had happened. It appeared that my wife convinced the warder with a quart of vodka that I was exceptionally well suited to carrying the parcels from the guard-room. He told us that two Gestapo men brought in by car a man who had been arrested for being in possession of firearms. They drove into the prison yard and took the arrested man into an office. There, they ordered a prison typist to take down personal details of the prisoner, while they themselves went into a cell to cross-examine another prisoner. The typist, being engaged on some other work, told the arrested man to wait in the next room. Presently, the prisoner went into the corridor and with the utmost composure ordered the sentry in German to open the iron door, which the sentry did, having seen him come in a few moments earlier with the two Gestapo men, and having taken him for a Gestapo man in mufti. I happened to witness the similar procedure at the main gate, and the ingenious and daring conspirator escaped. Much later, my wife told me that after emerging from the prison gate, the man sprinted as fast as his legs would carry him, to the utter amazement of the women who had been waiting for many days in front of the gate.

When I heard the warder's account I was glad that my row with the sentry at the gate had distracted his attention, but my neighbour sobered me with the observation that we might be involved in the matter. We enquired from the warder what had happened to the sentries in the corridor and at the gate.

'They were taken for cross-examination,' he said, 'but they let them go when they explained that they were not able to distinguish who is a prisoner and who a Gestapo man, because no one ever told them anything, and the Gestapo would arrive sometimes in uniform and sometimes in mufti.'

After a fortnight, dirty and unshaven, I returned home, and we at once carried out the decision I had made while in the Pawiak Prison, the decision to move. Within a day or two my wife and I were living unregistered in the Staszic Housing Estate.

The Organisation of the Inter-Party Political Committee

While I was pining away in Pawiak Prison, another meeting took place on February 26, 1940, between the representatives of the Parties and the Commander of the Union for Armed Struggle, at which 'Walenty'—Grudzinski—deputised for me. The records of that meeting included a minute, 'Nowak's absence justified'. Unanimous decisions were taken at the meeting and the aim was defined as 'the restoration of the independence of the country by means of an armed struggle against the two occupying Powers'. Means of action: the support of the work and plans of the UAS as the sole central military organisation called into being by the Government of the Republic, and the integration of all organisations and efforts for the purpose of carrying out the tasks and achieving the aims of 'Z', and also to produce the indispensable conditions and bases for creating a joint political organisation, the Council of National Defence.

The deliberating body, of which the Commander of 'Z' also became a member, was named the Political Consultative Committee, and it had been decided that members of the PCC should preside over its deliberations in rotation, each for one month. Finally, all those present took an oath, in the form of the 'Z' oath, which included the duty of absolute secrecy. After constituting itself, the Committee resolved that by March 25, 1940, all groups of a military type should report and be subordinated to 'Z'. It had also been decided that political and social organisations which were not represented on the Political Consultative Committee should be persuaded to subordinate to 'Z' their units of a military type.

I was able to attend the next meeting, called for March 4 in an apartment in Skorupka Street. I was given a warm reception, as the first 'prisoner from Pawiak' under the present occupation. Basil-Puzak regarded me with great affection and said jokingly:

'That's only a beginning, Nowak. You mustn't think it's all that's coming to you.' He was entitled to his little joke, having spent eight years in the dreaded Tsarist Schlisselburg fortress-prison.

As a rule, the meetings of the Political Consultative Committee were held weekly. I remained a member of this Committee for more than a year, until April, 1941. During that time the foundations of the Polish Underground State were laid and the mutual relationship between its institutions and the Government in London became clarified. The Government of General Sikorski recognised that the Political Consultative Committee spoke for the country, and furthermore, that it represented for the time being the exiled Government as its executive organ in Poland. This somewhat confused division of authority, caused by the conditions prevailing under the occupation of the country, continued until the Government Plenipotentiary was appointed.

The Political Consultative Committee dealt with all matters, with problems of a political, social, economic, and military nature, as well as with the ethical principles to be observed during the occupation. Everything that life under an enemy occupation brought with it came within the purview of the PCC, whose decisions were circulated throughout the country by means of the networks established by the Party organisations. Decisions concerning home affairs had to be unanimous, which, during the period in question, was not difficult to achieve. In the event of a conflict of opinion over what should be communicated to or requested from the Government, it was agreed that the attitude of each Party and of 'Z' should be explained to the Government in London. The contacts with that Government were not regular or frequent, and decisions concerning home affairs were mainly made by the PCC on their own responsibility.

The Political Consultative Committee maintained its

character as the supreme political institution throughout the whole period of its existence, with only one modification: as soon as the Government Plenipotentiary was appointed and joined the Political Consultative Committee, assuming its chairmanship, the Commander of 'Z' withdrew. Meanwhile, the relations between the politicians and the representatives of the military were shaping variously and not always well, as there were considerable differences in their approach to problems, arising from differing backgrounds and methods of thinking. Military men sometimes find it difficult to comprehend a political point of view; they are prone to take everything into their own hands and to direct everything, while at the same time keeping away from the limelight. On the other hand the politicians not only refused to be led, but rightly wanted to subordinate 'Z' to the political direction of the PCC, being suspicious and imagining military intelligence everywhere. There were therefore frequent quarrels and stormy discussions. The two contrary tendencies made themselves felt during the first period of the conspiracy; nevertheless, both sides were striving for a compromise, and consideration for Polish reasons of State usually prevailed; a consolidation was gradually achieved by a division of authority and delimitation of competence. The numerous sessions, each lasting for hours, led to a certain intimacy, to a drawing together of the various individuals, and, naturally enough, to some inevitable antipathies. In addition to formal discussions, confidences were exchanged and a happy harmony established.

General Tokarzewski's Departure

During one of our meetings General Tokarzewski informed us that he had received the order to take over the Command of the military organisation in the Soviet-occupied part of Poland, with his seat in Lwow, and that he would soon be leaving us. We were surprised by this unexpected decision, which we did not like, considering that General Tokarzewski had been a Commander of the Lwow Military District before the war, and was therefore well known there and would soon be caught. Moreover, we had got used to him and did not want an unnecessary change. The command of 'Z' was still unsettled, and we did not know whether the Government wanted to appoint two commanders, one for the German and one for the Russion zone of occupation, which would have meant a decentralised system of military work. We decided to inform the Government of our uncertainties, and we persuaded General Tokarzewski to postpone his departure until the receipt of a reply from the Government in London. We had difficulty in persuading him, and it was not for long. He had to carry out the order, and he left us. We were uneasy about his safety and the farewell was most cordial. We had already had reports from the Soviet-occupied zone, and we knew that the NKVD was a dangerous enemy. Tokarzewski was deeply touched by the warmth of our farewell; he shook each of us by the hand, and wished us success in our work; though we did not show it, we had grave doubts when he said: 'I hope we shall meet again'.

Not many weeks afterwards we received a report that he had been arrested by the Bolsheviks while crossing the frontier between the two zones.

First Emissaries of the Government

We lived through exciting days when the first emissaries of the Government-in-exile arrived in Warsaw. They were Wladislaw Gieysztor and Heller (pseudonym). We held many prolonged sessions with them. They gave us the Government's appraisal of the international situation, political reports, and detailed information. They were charged with the task of collecting all kinds of information about the country and about the underground movement, and with acquainting themselves with our wishes and needs. They had come without much difficulty through Hungary, and Heller, with whom I soon struck up a friendship, gave me privately a grim account of the conditions in Angers, the temporary seat of the Polish Government, to which he did not want to return, as in fact he did not. He described the strife, quarrels, intrigues, and manoeuvring for power and office among the emigrés, and I tried to discover what the essence of the problem was. It soon became clear to me that the impact of two worlds, the one which governed before the outbreak of war and bore responsibility for the crushing and rapid defeat, and the other, representing the Opposition, which had assumed power after years of political struggle against the Government, was an impact which could be likened to that of seething lava and water. In the Political Consultative Committee we had a similar phenomenon on a minor scale, but that was no consolation, especially since later news from the West did not indicate an amelioration of the sorry state of affairs.

Not long afterwards, another emissary, Karski, arrived and made a deep impression by the objectivity with which he presented all problems to the Political Consultative Committee, and by his extraordinary memory for even the minutest detail. He was followed by the 'diplomat' Borkowski (pseudonym), the technologist Moskal, of the Peasant Party (pseudonym Vojtek), and by George Lerski, who initiated the shuttle service of emissaries coming and going between Warsaw and Angers, and later Warsaw and London, which continued throughout the war.

The return and re-arrest of Rataj

After several weeks in prison, Rataj was released. The news at once spread through the whole of Warsaw; it was almost unbelievable how rapidly any news or even rumour of this kind reached everyone. I do not know if anyone has ever inquired into the laws and the mechanism governing this phenomenon, but it would be interesting to know what formula ensured the speed with which news spread under the German occupation. Every item of more important news, or even rumour, was the talk of Warsaw after a few hours. For instance, news monitored from the London radio, which was at that time communicated to relatively small groups in Warsaw, became the property of the whole city by the end of the very same day.

Everyone was delighted, especially the higher hierarchy of

the underground, for it also meant that the secret had been well preserved. We might even expect the release of Niedzialkowski. I set out for a meeting with Rataj in a mood of happy excitement. He had returned to his apartment in Buxom Street 14, and our meeting was to take place there. I found Rataj leaner and more aged than when I had last seen him, but happy to be home again. He gave me a full account of his detention in prison and of his cross-examinations.

'They were not able to convict me of anything and I soon realised that they had acted blindly. Nevertheless, they wore me out with their examinations for weeks on end. They wanted to know everything about me, my past, my views. . . .'

Rataj had nothing but praise for the Polish prison guards.

'I found there a little bit of Poland,' he said. 'They supplied me with underclothing, which they brought from their homes, they brought me food and everything I needed, including news from outside. I could feel their protecting hand everywhere, they tipped me off and instructed me how to behave.'

(Nearly all the guards from Pawiak prison were later deported to concentration camps, and a number of them were shot by the Gestapo on the spot.)

Rataj rejoiced in his freedom and the unexpected delights of experiencing it.

'You have no idea how it feels to touch the door handle and to see the miracle of the door opening. . . .'

I gave Rataj a detailed report of my conversations with Niedzialkowski, Tokarzewski and Rowecki; I described the establishment of the Political Consultative Committee; and I related the resolutions passed, the question of appointing a Government Plenipotentiary, the conditions in our own Party and in the other Parties, in short everything. Rataj was somewhat startled by my report, and when I had finished, he said, shaking his head:

'I can see that Niedzialkowski has advanced matters rather far, but I don't blame him, as the situation required it.' From what Rataj told me I gathered that Niedzialkowski had put into definite shape certain conceptions that had been only casually talked over with Rataj. After making my report, which took some hours, I informed Rataj that in view of his release I would regard my participation in the work of the Political Consultative Committee as terminated.

However, to my surprise, after further talk Rataj decided that I should continue to be a member of the Committee. He explained his point of view:

'You see, we don't know how the work of the Political Consultative Committee will develop. I have no desire to enter into old disputes and quarrels. If any misunderstandings should arise, either with the military or between the Parties, I would not like to be in the PCC. I gather from what you have told me that you have settled matters in principle only, that in the day-to-day work you are still seeking a common language, and co-operation has hardly begun. I prefer, therefore, not to commit myself. If the PCC comes through the testing time, which will not last long, I may eventually join it. Otherwise, I don't know if you would want to stay with them yourself. In any case, let us agree that you will discuss matters concerning the PCC with no one but me.'

I understood this to mean that I should not discuss the affairs of the PCC with the 'triumvirs' whom Mr. Speaker Rataj had appointed to direct the various operations of the underground organisation of the Peasant Party.

The unending stream of visitors to the apartment at 14, Buxom Street began again; their number ran to a dozen or more daily. Though I had more reason than the others to call frequently, I became a rare visitor. During this period I arranged that members of the Political Consultative Committee, Puzak and Debski, should meet Rataj. The majority of visitors, however, consisted of the same kind of people as before. Rataj's daughter Hanka, her husband, Tadeusz Stankiewicz, and I insisted that Rataj should cease to extend this dangerous hospitality to all and sundry, for it was bound to end badly. Rataj knew it himself, and when the most pressing matters had been settled, he agreed to leave secretly for Otwock, where he was to stay at the St. Joseph's Institute, run by the clergy. No-one except his daughter, his son-in-law and myself were to be told about it. I had certain connections with the Colgate-Palmolive people in Warsaw, an American firm, whose motor-car had not been requisitioned by the

Germans. One suitable day, in the morning, I drove this car to Rataj's apartment, and only two hours later he was in Otwock. He was put up in a timbered villa in the garden of the Institute. The snow covered everything with a mantle three foot thick, and there was peace and calm there, which made one forget the war and the whole world. Under the loving care of the clergy in charge of the Institute, Rataj slowly recovered. I visited him occasionally to report and to receive instructions.

Several weeks later Dr. W. Kiernik from Cracow arrived in Warsaw in order to see Rataj. When I informed the latter, he suggested that I should bring Kiernik to Otwock, observing the utmost secrecy. When I told Kiernik, the latter was visibly disgruntled:

'If I could come all the way from Cracow to see Rataj, he can easily come to Warsaw from Otwock.'

All persuasion remained unavailing and I left for Otwock in the company of Hanka. Rataj said resignedly:

'There you have the true Kiernik. To him this is primarily a matter of prestige. Well, it can't be helped. I shall go with you to Warsaw and come back here.'

Both Hanka and I tried vainly to dissuade him from going to the City; but Rataj was becoming bored by the peace and quiet at St. Joseph's and might have been glad to have a pretext for going. We entered the car, a half-truck, and shaken to the bone on the road—though covered by deep, fresh snow it was full of pot-holes—we finally reached Warsaw in the evening. There was no longer any question of Rataj's return to Otwock.

I arranged a meeting between Rataj and Rowecki. I had at my disposal a hide-out in the Prudential Building where I pretended to run a two-room office, complete with shelves full of files, a desk and a few chairs. At four o'clock in the afternoon I was to introduce the Commander of the UAS to Rataj. Rowecki came punctually at four, and we waited. After a few minutes there was a knock at the door in the pre-arranged pattern. I opened the door, but instead of Rataj I found a contact from the Party. As soon as I saw her pale and tired face my heart sank.

'Where is the Speaker?'

'He was arrested this morning. The Germans cordoned off Buxom Street between Raven Street and Three Crosses Square and took the Speaker away.'

Before questioning her further, I told Rowecki to leave the hide-out at once, as it was always possible that Rataj might have jotted down the address. I was completely crushed, and as I hurried home my mind worked feverishly. This time the arrest looked ominous, for it followed closely upon his release. They must have found a lead. Why did he ever leave Otwock? It was necessary to alert all concerned, for though Rataj would certainly not give anything away, they might find other clues.

I was haunted by the look in the contact-girl's eyes spelling disaster. The future had many such encounters in store for me, and they all seemed alike. The familiar face of the contact-girl would be changed, her eyes dilated with fear. Before she opened her mouth I would know I was to be told of a trap, an arrest, or a killing. The machinery of alarm would have to be set in motion, to freeze the hide-out, to change all addresses and pseudonyms, to warn those immediately threatened. The excitement of rapid action made one forget the heart-ache for a few hours, only to have it return afterwards with redoubled force. There would follow a brief period of relative quiet, and then the pale-faced contact-girl would be on the doorstep again.

Hanka was soon receiving scribbled notes from her father, smuggled out of the prison by the Polish warders, and judging by their contents the position looked serious. All our efforts to help Rataj failed, except for the means of communicating with him, which enabled us to organise something in the way of seeing him, though only from a distance.

At the pre-arranged time, Hanka, with my wife, and I, alone, walked along Division Street. Suddenly, at the window of the prison hospital, the emaciated face of Rataj appeared, his eyes glued on his daughter. Hanka stood at the kerb of the sidewalk, and smiling through tears, looked at her father. I passed close by, and with a nod Rataj signalled that he had noticed me. We remained on the sidewalk, gazing at the face behind the bars of the window. At last Rataj made a gesture for us to go away. We moved off, looking back at the pale face behind the window panes. Hanka was sobbing quietly. She had seen her father for the last time.

Then a message arrived foretelling disaster. Hanka, usually so self-possessed, came crying her heart out in utter despair and gave me a note to read, scribbled in Rataj's characteristic hand on a small leaf of paper torn from a notebook. I read it carefully with a feeling of helplessness. There could be no mistaking the message. Rataj knew that he was doomed and this was his final good-bye to Hanka and his son-in-law, to whom he sent his blessings. I did not even try to console them.

Months afterwards we received the information that Rataj had been shot on June 21, 1940, in a wood at Palmiry, together with Mieczyslaw Niedzialkowski, Pohoski, Kusocinski, Wojnar-Byczynski of the UAS and others.

The epilogue to the Rataj tragedy took place during the Warsaw Rising. One day, a contact-girl, covered with the dust of an explosion, rushed into my quarters shouting in despair, 'A bomb has buried Hanka, Tadeusz, the baby and the maid Bronia in the cellars at Buxom Street.' I ran like a madman to Raven Street by way of Jerusalem Avenue, while the air raid was still on and bombs were raining down. I turned into Buxom Street, which was no longer a thoroughfare, but a heap of rubble and craters filled with muddy and yellowish water. A cloud of smoke rose above the ruins of the house at No. 14; the people nearby were covered with powdered plaster from the blast. I leaped down the stairs into the basement. The passage was intact, but the entrance to the cellar was cut off by a wall of rubble, bricks and broken timber. I shouted, 'Hanka, Tadeusz, are you there?' But only a barking dog answered my cries from under the debris, and that dog was the sole survivor. The Stankiewicz family, together with a dozen other people, perished in the cellar.

The Question of a Civil Commissioner

The Government in Angers pressed the Political Consultative Committee to submit a candidate for the office of Plenipotentiary. This presented considerable difficulty, as it was not easy to find a personality who would command general support, as the PCC desired. Various alternatives were being considered.

One day I received an invitation from General Rowecki to meet him. The meeting was arranged to take place in his hide-out, which was carefully chosen and protected by an armed guard. Rowecki soon abolished the guard, because he thought it was too conspicuous and might produce the opposite result to that intended. On that particular occasion the guard was still there and a number of civilians moving about in the street kept me under thorough observation. Everything went smoothly, and following all the pre-arranged signals, I reached my destination. A smiling and serene Rowecki welcomed me. His dark hair was in full growth again, and he was dressed in a shabby lounge suit and a dark shirt, which became almost standard practice, as it could serve for pyjamas in casual night lodgings.

After a conventional exchange of civilities, I soon sensed that the talk would be of some importance. Rowecki opened by complaining about the delays in settling the question of appointing a Plenipotentiary, which had a harmful effect on military activities, and proceeded to explain what he had in mind:

'Listen, Nowak, why should you insist on appointing a Plenipotentiary, a new and untried office, when our laws provide for such an eventuality in a war emergency. All we need is simply the appointment in the country of a Civil Commissioner. I want to bring the matter up at the next meeting of the Political Consultative Committee, but before I do so I should like to have your opinion on it.'

I was rather startled by this proposal, but I wished to probe the matter to the bottom and asked:

'To whom, in your opinion, should the Civil Commissioner be responsible?'

'To the Commander-in-Chief.'

'Which one? To the one abroad, or to his corresponding number at home?'

'It would make no sense to make him responsible to the one

abroad. He would have to act under the Commander of the Home Forces.'

'That means under you, General?'

'Yes, under me.'

I objected to the suggestion most emphatically and said that the appointment of a Civil Commissioner subordinate to the Commander of 'Z' would mean the militarisation of the underground movement, to which the Party I represented on the Political Consultative Committee would never agree. Moreover, the office of Civil Commissioner had already been sufficiently compromised by the appointment of Kostek-Biernacki on the outbreak of war. Rowecki then brought his heaviest gun to bear on the target:

'I can understand why you should have such fears, but I hope they will be completely dispelled if I tell you that we shall offer the office of Civil Commissioner to a man of your Party.'

This bait notwithstanding, I still refused to agree to the proposal, arguing that the man would not alter the office, and that the acceptance of the proposal would mean that the Civil Commissioner, even if he were a member of the Peasant Party, would still be subject to the orders of the Commander of 'Z'. Rowecki was visibly disappointed, but in a lengthy discourse I tried to explain to him the grounds of my opposition, as a result of which it began to dawn on him that the matter was not as simple as he had imagined. We parted amicably, and before I left Rowecki told me that he would not put his proposal forward officially.

The September Manhunt

My wife and I continued to live on the Staszic Housing Estate, where we had two rooms rented in a false name. It was a little house with a garden, and it was quiet and peaceful there. So at least it appeared, but in fact the entire Housing Estate was honeycombed with secret hide-outs. Nevertheless, appearances were well maintained, and there was nothing to indicate that the district was of such importance to the underground movement in Warsaw. Next to it in order of import-

ance were, somewhat later, Mokotow and the City, then Zoliborz, and finally Praga. Manufacture of army supplies was
organised in the factory districts, while laboratories were hidden in the former colleges, of which the Polytechnic, with its
workshops and laboratories, was the most important.

This idyllic existence was interrupted one September morning in 1940 when the milkwoman told us that the entire
Staszic Housing Estate had been surrounded by the military
and gendarmes, and that a gendarme was posted in our very
street. I dressed in a panic. What bad luck! My wife, with the
assistance of a contact-girl, had been typing all night, copying
micro-films received from the Government-in-exile. The type-
writer must have been clattering away in the room while the
gendarme had paced up and down in front of the house since
dawn. We had the choice of either destroying the films and
all that had been copied or hiding them somewhere, since it
was possible that the German action had nothing to do with
us. We decided to hide everything in the loft, at least until
the position became clearer. It was not long before two gendarmes entered, and without asking my name took me with
them. The day was fine, the autumn sun shone brightly, and
there was a pleasant tang of coolness in the air. The entire
Housing Estate was bustling with activity. Heavy trucks
loaded with men were leaving and empty ones arriving. From
every house gendarmes were escorting little groups of men,
young and old, healthy and infirm. I helped one of the cripples
on crutches to mount the truck. Packed like sardines, we were
driven to the Light Horse Barracks beyond Lazienki. I again
felt a certain relief at the sight of a throng of over a thousand
men in the large barrack square. I continued to look after
the cripple, whom the gendarmes allowed to go out of turn.
Walking to the front of the crowd I passed a cross-section of
Warsaw: workmen, merchants, artisans, intellectuals; all were
standing there not knowing what to expect. By escorting the
cripple I committed a grave blunder, for I missed the first
selection, at which the Germans released all employees of
municipal power-stations, waterworks and other public utility
enterprises, and I happened to have on me just the necessary

documents to prove I was such an employee, though they were issued to me by the underground.

In the huge hall there were about thirty tables with type-writers on them. In front of each table there was a queue of men in the same predicament as myself. Officials took down personal details concerning each of us, and through the side entrance we were led in groups to the riding school of the Light Horse Regiment. There was strict discipline there. Hundreds of men were lying on the sawdust that covered the turf. No-one was allowed to stand up. In the wide gangway SS men marched up and down with whips in their hands, which they used unsparingly. On the side-galleries other SS men had machine-guns at the ready.

We lay there for two days, trying to guess why we had been brought there. The majority were convinced that we were to be deported to Germany as forced labour. There were about fifteen hundred of us. We were given some bread, but nothing to drink, not even cups with which to get water from the tap. Next to me lay a teacher suffering from hernia, and hoping that a medical commission would let him go, he asked me to enquire from an SS man when the examination was to take place. When an SS man escorted a group of us to the latrine, I fell behind and asked him:

'When is a doctor likely to come? We have sick people here.'

The SS man looked about him and answered, lowering his voice:

'There will be no medical inspection.'

'And where are we going to be sent?'

'You will be sent to a place where you will be sorry to have been born.'

An officer came up and the SS man roared:

'Schneller du! . . .'

In the evening of the second day, uniformed officials and a group of SS officers entered the riding-school, and at their head stalked a veritable giant of a man, in top boots and with a whip in his hand. Fifteen hundred men held their breath. The Germans called out names. The men whose names were called were ordered to stand aside. When I heard my own name I walked out of the crowd, while my casual comrades in misfortune sadly bade me farewell.

The men whose names were called out, to the number of about three hundred, were escorted by the SS men into the square, formed in two ranks, and ordered to take their hats off. A civilian whom I knew well by sight, having often come across him in the streets before the war, addressed us in Polish. He told us that we were being released because of the intervention of our employers. He expressed the hope that by hard work we would show our gratitude for the humane way in which the German authorities had treated us. He concluded:

'You are all men and you ought to be aware that it is necessary to know how to keep silence about certain matters, if one does not wish to go to a place from which there is no return. You must hold your tongues. Now you can go.'

Only a few minutes later I was telephoning from the corner of Basket Street to tell those who had to know that I had been released. I owed my release to a certain Polish institution, with the documents of which I had been supplied, and which did everything possible to get me out.

All those who remained, to the number of more than a thousand, were deported that same night to Auschwitz, where the majority met with a terrible death.

I met the giant SS officer once again in my life. As the head of Civil Resistance, I was called as a witness in the trial of the German Governor of Warsaw, Fischer, and others, held in Warsaw during 1946 under the Soviet occupation. When I entered the court-room I looked at the defendants in the dock. The face of one of them seemed familiar to me. During the adjournment a barrister showed me a photograph of the man in the uniform of an SS officer. I recognised him as the giant who had led the group of SS officers into the riding school at the cavalry barracks. Now, without uniform and badges, he looked less formidable as 'the defendant Meisinger'. Together with Fischer he was sentenced to death, and thus discovered that fortune was a fickle mistress.

I may add that I was not called to testify in that court. The names of witnesses were published in the Communist press, and immediately afterwards my name was struck off the list;

and I am sure someone got it in the neck for calling as a witness for the prosecution a 'notorious lackey of reaction'.

The Appointment of Plenipotentiary Ratajski

On Kwiecinski's[1] initiative and contrary to the wishes of the Polish Socialist Party and the Peasant Party, Cyril Ratajski was appointed to the office of Government Plenipotentiary. He was a former Mayor of the City of Poznan and a former Minister of the Interior. The objections to his appointment were of a political and, as it were, technical nature. His patriotism and former activities were highly regarded by all (he had been expelled from Poznan by the Germans before he came to Warsaw), but we were of the opinion that he was not a generally acceptable candidate, especially as he was too old to be a leader of the Underground and had no experience in conspiratorial work.

In these circumstances, the 'Triangle' and the 'Circle'—that is the Peasant Party and the Polish Socialist Party—resolved to draw Ratajski's attention to the fact that both Parties were opposed to his appointment, so as to enable him to appreciate the position before he made his decision to accept it. I was given the thankless task of informing Ratajski to this effect.

The first meeting of the Political Consultative Committee in which Ratajski participated was held in a building at the corner of Jerusalem Avenue and Lindley Street. We foregathered in an empty office with its windows giving onto the Avenue, and I was introduced to Ratajski, whom I remembered well from my student days in Poznan, when Ratajski had been Mayor of that city and had won general recognition as an able administrator.

It was my turn during that month to be chairman of the Political Consultative Committee, and after opening the meeting I informed the Committee of the appointment that had been received from the Government. Amidst dead silence I addressed Ratajski in my capacity as a representative of the 'Triangle', and appealed to him with great sincerity not to take what I was going to say personally, but solely politi-

[1] a leader of the Labour Party

cally. I told him of the critical attitude of the two Parties towards his appointment, and added that I was obliged to present these circumstances to him before he made a declaration of acceptance.

Ratajski, an elderly white-haired and rather big man, seemed to be greatly affected, but apparently prepared for the occasion, for he replied straight away:

'I have received my appointment at the hands of General Sikorski and his Government and the trust they have laid on me is of decisive importance to me. I accept the appointment and I request you to administer the oath.'

In view of this declaration on the part of Ratajski, which, by the way, the authorities of the two Parties had anticipated, there was nothing to be done but for me to carry out the duties of the chairman. I summoned all those present to rise to their feet and I administered the oath, which Ratajski pronounced in a voice trembling with emotion.

The Commander of the Union for Armed Struggle did not take part in the next meeting of the PCC, but sent a message to say that in view of the appointment of the Government Plenipotentiary and the delimitation of functions, he was withdrawing from membership of the Committee, and requested that, if needed, he should be summoned to meetings either in order to report or to give any information required.

In view of these developments we desired to strengthen the position of the Plenipotentiary by entrusting to him the permanent chairmanship of the Committee. He was very pleased with the decision, assumed the chairmanship, and he, and subsequently his successor, performed this function for as long as the PCC existed.

Plenipotentiary Ratajski

The anticipations of the 'Triangle' and the 'Circle' as to relations and collaboration with Plenipotentiary Ratajski turned out to be well founded. A man of the highest integrity and patriotism, and of a disarming enthusiasm, he was naïve and could not comprehend many phenomena inherent in conspiratorial work. He was not able to think and act constructively in those difficult and complicated circumstances. He was a man of advanced age who regarded everyone under forty as immature, and he was genuinely astonished that they should hold responsible positions in the conspiracy. When he assumed office, he wanted to pay official courtesy visits to each member of the PCC in the best tradition of more peaceful times. We tried to dissuade him without hurting his feelings. Personally, I was not surprised that he bore a grudge against me at first, because of the part I had had to play over his appointment. However, when he appointed me his plenipotentiary for Civil Resistance and we met more often, he soon got rid of it and told me so openly. He gave me extraordinary powers, including the authority to use my own code in the transmission of messages to London.

It took some time for Ratajski to assume all the powers of the office of Plenipotentiary and take over the political direction of the underground movement. The function of the Polish Consultative Committee was later limited to expressing the opinions and desires of the four major Parties, which represented the great majority of the Polish people. On his part, the Plenipotentiary solemnly undertook that in home affairs he would regard the opinions of the PCC as binding upon him, whereby he recognised a dual responsibility, both to the Government in London and to the PCC at home. This state of affairs continued throughout the existence of the PCC.

It is to the credit of Ratajski that under his rule various departments were created: of Justice, headed by the Dean of the Warsaw Bar, Leon Nowodworski; of Information and Propaganda, under Dolega, who survived in his office right to the end of the war; and also departments for Agriculture, Industry and Trade, Finance, Communications, etc. In addition, there came into being the Office of State Audit, run by the barrister Peszynski; the Plenipotentiary thus had an administrative organisation at his disposal, which survived until the end of the German occupation. Not least important in the Department of the Interior was the organisation of the cadres of the future civil service of the Polish Republic, which towards the end of the German occupation numbered many thousands of well-trained officers.

The Plenipotentiary maintained close contact with the Commander of 'Z', who was invited from time to time to attend meetings of the PCC at which military matters were to be discussed.

The time arrived when our doubts as to the suitability of Ratajski to lead the conspiracy were fully confirmed. He was unable to deal with the problems that arose, which in addition to normal administrative gifts required a capacity to act under conspiracy conditions, and also exceptional physical stamina. The underground groups throughout the country became increasingly restless and their dissatisfaction became known to the Polish Government abroad. After a year in office Ratajski was asked to resign, and as a mark of appreciation for his services and courage he was decorated with the Cross of Virtuti Militari. After his resignation he remained in Warsaw; but he was withering away and died soon afterwards. He was buried in the Powazki Cemetery in Warsaw under an assumed name.

Arrest of Debski

At about this time the Political Consultative Committee suffered its first casualty. Debski, the representative of the 'Square', fell into the clutches of the Gestapo. He had been warned in time that the Gestapo was searching for him. He therefore quitted his legal residence in Piekna Street, leaving the other members of his family behind, and used various hide-outs, including one in Nullo Street, where I visited him several times. But on one occasion Debski dropped in at Piekna Street for some underclothing and was immediately apprehended. It was obvious that the Gestapo had had the apartment under observation all the time, expecting that sooner or later he would want to see his family. Unfortunately their reasoning proved to be right.

The Situation in the Country

By the middle of 1940 round-ups and arrests had become the order of the day. Terrible stories were circulating throughout the country about the cruelties of Pawiak prison and the camps of Auschwitz and Oranienburg. Despondent families were receiving small boxes with the ashes of their dear ones, allegedly dead from some disease or other. This was a German perfidy which passed the comprehension of the Poles, and it began to be questioned whether the Hitlerites were human beings at all. Every inhabitant of Warsaw knew about Palmiry. Peasants from that region were giving reports of packed trucks rushing at night to the woods of Palmiry and of salvoes echoing in a forest clearing there. A pall of horror descended on the City, the streets of which were roamed by motorised squads of men with death's-head badges on their caps. The muzzles of automatic pistols were aimed at passers-by. Patrols of gendarmes in green uniforms were to be seen everywhere. Before the curfew hour throngs of people changed their abodes for the night. They hurried from Zoliborz to Mokotow, from Mokotow to Zoliborz in a veritable inter-migration of people. Everyone felt safer by spending the night at an address where he or she was not registered. After the curfew hour the deserted streets echoed the dull thuds of the heavy footsteps of the patrols. Behind the blacked-out windows, the city kept vigil. No-one knew where the searches and arrests were to take place that night. Was it to be here or elsewhere? Restlessness and anxiety made sleep impossible.

Men and women whom the war had jolted out of their normal routine had not yet entirely recovered; they were scarcely attempting to organise their lives, to work and to earn their living, and the year 1940 was one in which poverty, fear, terror and hunger held undisputed sway over the city.

But the underground, too, began to act and to strike. Here and there the first shots of retribution and vengeance were fired, and the first red posters with photographs of 'Polish bandits' were disfiguring the streets, and continued to do so until the end of the German occupation, ever more horrible, more dreadful in what they announced.

I leave the Political Consultative Committee

Debski's place was taken by a barrister, Trajdos, an elderly man and a representative specimen of the nationalist party of the old type. Being calm and phlegmatic, he was the anti-thesis of the excitable and lively Debski, of whom, for the time being, we had no news. Ratajski had been very fond of him, and it was evident that the two men had clicked.

My own activities underwent a change. The authorities of the 'Triangle' wanted to have their representative at the High Command of the Union for Armed Struggle and the choice fell on me, as I was well versed in military matters. In April 1941 I left the PCC, switching parts with Grudzinski, who took my place in the PCC, while I remained his deputy. In the latter capacity I attended a further meeting of that Committee, in August 1941, and, together with its other members and the Plenipotentiary, had a strange experience.

Grudzinski fell ill and as his deputy I attended a meeting to be held in an apartment in Marshall Street. As I entered, I noticed in the entrance hall a man who looked at me closely. It was too late to back out, so I mounted the stairs with the intention of warning those present. On the second floor I ran into another man, who also gave me a close look. I no longer had any doubt that the meeting was being watched, and I hurried on to alert everybody. Plenipotentiary Ratajski, the Director of the Political Department, Piotrowski (pseudonym), and Kwiecinski were already there. Before I had time to explain the position, the bell rang and the other members of the Committee arrived. They too had noticed that the place was under observation and came to warn the rest and decamp. We immediately adjourned the meeting, and the first one to go was making for the door when the door bell rang and the terrified lady of the house rushed in whispering, 'The Germans! This way out. . . .' and she pointed to the side door. I caught the door handle, but the door was locked. A second later we heard footsteps on the other side of the door, the key was turned, and two civilians with leather cases under their arms and with Nazi badges on their lapels entered the room. They gave us all a sharp look, ordered us to stay where we were, and asked in German for the owner of the apartment. In reply, Kwiecinski started on an involved explanation, obviously trying to gain time. I found myself behind the backs of the newcomers, so I tiptoed out of the room and through the next room into the corridor. I descended the staircase rapidly and again ran into the observer. He was visibly startled by my presence there, but did not budge when I passed him. Exactly the same thing happened with the second observer in the entrance hall. I emerged into Marshall Street, and hurrying along Wilcza I reached Ujazdow Avenue without being pursued.

When comparing notes with other members of the Committee afterwards, I learned that the Germans had gone to the telephone and informed some one that they had caught a number of Poles holding a meeting. During that telephone conversation all the others made their escape down the kitchen staircase, while Kwiecinski covered their retreat by engaging the Germans at the phone in desultory conversation. Finally, when the Germans proceeded to search the apartment, he, too, made his escape. All this took place in the apartment rented by Kwiecinski, who acted with great courage, like a captain on a sinking ship.

No one ever discovered what really happened and who the men were. Personally, I believe it was not a German raid or an accident, but an exploit of some underground gangsters known as 'Mousqueteers'.

Such was my last meeting with the members of the Political Consultative Committee, which in time was transformed into the National Political Representation, and finally became the Underground Council of National Unity.

All the members of the PCC with whom I worked while on the Committee met with a tragic fate. Rataj and Niedzialkowski were murdered at Palmiry. Debski was murdered by the Gestapo, and the same fate overcame his successor, Trajdos, who was captured by the Germans. A similar fate befell the successor of Trajdos, the former deputy Sacha, an experienced and cautious politician whom I met on several occasions.

The Editor Kwiecinski was arrested on January 19, 1942, and soon afterwards he was executed. His body was found only after the war, in a mass grave in the Kabacki Forest. The Gestapo seized him in a hospital where he was lying ill; they harassed and tortured him, but he gave no one and nothing away and died like a hero.

My successor on the Political Consultative Committee, Jozef Grudzinski, also perished, murdered by the Ukrainians in the Officers' Settlement during the Warsaw Rising.

General Rowecki perished much later, while Puzak died after the war in a Communist prison in Warsaw. But before that occurred I had many dealings with them, of which more in the following pages.

CHAPTER II

Radio Contacts
between London and Warsaw

Meeting Joey

I was walking briskly from Cracow Suburb Avenue in the direction of Kierbedz Bridge, inhaling the cool air coming from the Vistula. I was hurrying to a meeting with a man who was to help me make a dream come true, a secret radio contact with the Government in London, the lack of which was felt acutely in the underground movement.

I soon found myself on the fourth floor of a house in Downhill Road, No. 4. The door opened and a pale youngster, without saying a word, led me through a dark corridor into a room which at once impressed me greatly. It was dim; the windows were boarded with sheets of plywood, and over the tables were bright lamps with conic shades. The room was littered with cables, flexes, switches, instruments, tools, transformers, radio valves and a multiplicity of other strange implements. In short, it looked like a miniature electronic workshop full of prohibited objects. Noticing my curiosity, my host proceeded to give technical explanations, to which a cat playing on the table provided a distraction. I took the cat in my arms and stroked it, while Joey, for such was the name of my youthful new friend, told me how on one occasion the cat crawled on to a battery and received such a shock that sparks flew from its tail. However, he must have forgotten it by now, for he had been moving about boldly amidst all the paraphernalia of the workshop. The demonstration ended with a portable gramophone which had a radio receiver concealed within, and Joey suggested that in a few minutes we should listen in to London. I looked at him closely. He gave one the impression of being a grown-up, self-possessed and calm young man, and his replies were concise and to the point. He had clear, bright eyes, and his hands had the elongated fingers of an artist. I had no compunction in asking him how old he was. He answered, 'Seventeen,' and handed me the earphones. I heard London speaking in Polish. The reception was clear and the instrument functioned perfectly.

After these preliminaries we came to the point. Joey confirmed the information I had concerning him. All that was necessary to establish contact with London was a transmitter of less than 20 watts strength; the short-wave amateurs were familiar with all that. He would be able to construct a stronger transmitter, which would cost two or three thousand zlotys in all. I wanted to know more and asked him:

'Have you decided to operate the radio station and thereby join the underground movement?'

'I have already made up my mind,' Joey answered, 'and it goes without saying.'

We agreed that to camouflage it he would construct the transmitter in a pail with two bottoms; we settled details concerning cash, and we were about to part, pleased with each other. In pressing Joey's hand, I cautioned him:

'You cannot have all these things lying about like this. You must find a place to put them.'

'It shall be done,' Joey said smiling, and shut the door behind me.

He had to bear with my cautionary counsels for the next two years.

Emissary Wojtek

Joey worked on the transmitter day and night and made rapid progress. I frequently dropped in on him early in the morning and found him unwashed after a sleepless night, with dishevelled hair, but full of zest. He was practising Morse, for in addition to being a constructor, he also wanted to be a radio telegraphist. He had no skill at it, but while transmitting, he would be regulating the pace, while in order to receive messages, he intended to construct (the innocence of it!) a mechanical tape recorder, operated by a tiny electric motor. I visited him every few days and we had endless talks with each other. In technical matters he was the teacher and I the attentive pupil. In other matters, our parts were reversed. I learned to know him, and a friendship developed between us. He was truly a mature man and only his little practical jokes made one realise that he was only seventeen. I sensed that he had a great love for our mother country, but we never spoke about it. He was a genuine child of the Warsaw riverside by birth, upbringing and speech. I was amazed to discover that he had only had two years of elementary school education, but the spelling mistakes he made convinced me that it must have been so. He had gained all his immense technical knowledge by his own exertions, and whenever he had a few pence to spare, he spent them on scientific publications on radio technology. His lean appearance made me think that his people were of less than modest means and that his childhood must have been rather frugal.

At about this time, the first emissary, Wojtek,[1] was preparing to return to England. He had come from London by way of Gibraltar, Cairo, Cyprus and Constantinople, bringing with him codes for correspondence. I met him and told him of the efforts which were being made to establish radio communication. I gave him all the details, such as our basic wavelength, which was 7,174 kilocycles, suggestions for the wavelength of the Government transmitter in London, mutual call signs, and the date by which we should be ready to go on the air, namely April 1, 1941, at 19 hrs. our time. We would transmit for three consecutive days. In fixing the date we took into consideration the time necessary for Wojtek's return journey to London. Communications would be conducted in the code brought by him.

Wojtek listened to all this as to a fairy tale and, impressed by the boldness of the scheme, memorised all the details. When he reached London, his report created great enthusi-

---

[1] Engineer Moskal, at present in Canada

asm, because of the prospect of establishing direct radio communication, the lack of which was being felt acutely by the
Polish authorities in London.

In the meantime, I tried, through my trusted collaborator
Celine,[1] to check Joey's technical knowledge, and I gave her
the drawings and a description of the projected transmitter.

Soon afterwards Celine brought me the opinion of a Professor at the Technical High School; according to him the
power of the machine being constructed by Joey was quite
insufficient to communicate with England. This was a hard
blow and I was distressed by the thought that all our exertions would come to nought. In my quandary, I decided to
tell Joey frankly what the Professor said. Unshaken in his
absolute self-assurance, Joey sneered at the learned man.

'Don't you know that Professors know nothing about short-
wave transmissions? One of them tried to contact London by
means of a powerful transmitter, and failed because he forgot
to open a window.' He continued in this manner for some
time, and I must confess I never heard so many ingenious
epithets, spoken in the juicy language of the riverside.
Amused and reassured by Joey's certitude, I made up my
mind to wait and see.

The Transmitter completed

The day came at last when Joey told me that the transmitter
was ready. We met by the Cathedral of St. John and proceeded
to the Old City's Market Square. In a dark and empty shop
on the ground floor, after locking the door and switching on
the light, Joey proudly extracted from a brand new and shining pail a gadget in white metal, glittering with varnish and
multi-coloured flexes. It was the first time in my life I had
ever seen a transmitter, but I noticed that it was extraordinarily well, almost artistically, finished and I concluded that
Joey was a talented craftsman. He connected the apparatus
with the mains and the valves glowed. He mounted the quartz,
turned a knob, and the tiny control bulb burned brightly. He
smiled with self-satisfaction and finding that the quartz was

[1] Celine Holm-Broniewska, at present in U.S.A.

oscillating, he placed a wire ring with a tiny bulb in the centre close to the aerial hanging on the wall. When the bulb lit itself he announced that everything was in good order. I was startled, and all my earlier doubts were dispelled. I had never before seen a bulb light up by itself. I had not the slightest notion of the technical processes taking place before my eyes, but I felt that the deed was done. The flash of the little bulb persuaded me of it.

We were both pleasurably excited, and to honour the occasion, we proceeded to a little café, where Joey had coffee and a pile of pastries. It was really touching to see him munching one after another with the gusto of a 'teen-ager. We sat there, in the Zmijewski Café in the Cracow Suburb Avenue, and tried to anticipate the outcome of the real thing on April 1. All that remained for Joey to do was to complete the receiving set and the recorder for taking down the messages from London; but he regarded these as trifles compared with the feat of constructing a transmitter.

The First Attempt

At last the long awaited day arrived. We were accommodated in a hide-out as safe as a rock in distant Grochow, offered to us by Joey's chum. My wife Zosia and her helper Anna[1] who were let into the secret, transported the instruments, transformers and tools in the afternoon. Amidst general excitement Joey set up the station; he threw the aerial over the window sill, into the open, and fastened the further end to a tree. Outside, Joey's chum stood sentry, while Zosia and Anna circulated in the neighbourhood, observing the entire field. We were not afraid of a German raid, for we were in a deserted spot, but of being discovered by the enemy's mobile radio interceptors or listening posts, which we called 'gonia', and which covered by means of a network the entire territory of Poland under German occupation.

According to our incomplete information the country was divided into triangles. At the apex of each triangle were

[1] Mrs. Aniela Jachnik, at present in London.   Wife of Colonel Jachnik of the Polish General Staff.

listening posts, which for twenty-four hours a day watched every 5 - 10 metre band. Any station operating within a given band would be known to the enemy. If they heard any station of which they had not been notified in advance, they reported it immediately. If nothing was known about it, the ascertaining of its location would begin by means of directional aerials. The field of the aerial in which the reception was clearest would indicate the direction in which it should be sought. The point at which the lines drawn between two listening posts crossed indicated the region in which the station was to be found. Planes or mobile units equipped with measuring instruments would be dispatched into the region to locate the station with precision, and the Gestapo, the gendarmes, or the military would proceed with its liquidation. The only means of protection lay in a frequent alteration of all the operational elements, such as the call signs, wave-lengths and hours of transmission. Apart from these, a frequent change of premises was advisable, together with careful observation by look outs, which would enable a located station to close down in time and the crew to dismantle it, hide the equipment, and escape. Such were the conditions under which we worked . . . in theory. We were soon to discover what they were in actual practice.

Nineteen hours was approaching and our excitement grew. Joey was checking everything, and I could see that he was satisfied. We looked at our watches, which were regulated to radio time, and punctually at 19 hours, Joey pressed the key and for a minute or so tapped out our call sign; then, in international code, he announced that he was going over to reception. He adjusted the earphones and listened intently. I could see from the expression on his face that nothing was coming through. The wave-length agreed upon for London was silent. Joey repeated the call and mentioned the wave-length on which he expected a reply; after about half an hour a station replied. I immediately plugged in the tape recorder and observed the dots and dashes that appeared on it. Joey read off letter after letter, and when he had finished, to my horror I read in German: 'Sind sie eine militärische station?'—'Are you a military station?'

As quick as lightning we shut down, pulled in the aerial, packed everything into prepared bags, and hurried across the fields with Zosia and Anna towards the tram-car stop. It was getting dark, the curfew hour was approaching, and we had already passed the first patrol of gendarmes. We jumped on to the last tram, but seeing that we would not be able to get home in time, we got out near Kierbedz Bridge and dropped in for the night, together with our dangerous luggage, at the house of an acquaintance living nearby. Joey had only a few yards to his home in Downhill Road. We were all scared and downcast, having been located even before we were able to establish contact with London.

We repeated the attempt on April 2 and 3, when we were mostly listening and not calling so much, but with no result, except that the German station no longer interfered.

Succour

All my earlier doubts concerning the power of the transmitter were revived. I was furious with myself for having disregarded the opinion of the Professor at the Technical High School. Joey presented a picture of gloom, but insisted that the apparatus was in order. All the date-lines were past and no one listened in any more. In short, we were done for. Before a new emissary arrived, through whom we would be able to make new arrangements with London, much time would have been wasted.

I was considering all sorts of means to break the deadlock, and it occurred to me that I might consult the experts from the military organisation, i.e. the Union for Armed Struggle, whom I knew to be in radio communication with the Supreme Command in London, though it was kept a strict secret. My personal contacts in the underground movement enabled me to arrange a meeting with the chief of the military liaison, Zaremba,[1] a professional officer in the communications branch, to whom I explained the quandary in which we found ourselves. He was a young man still, of middle height, and sporting a small moustache. In his quiet way he explained

[1] Major Conrad Bogacki, at present in London.

that automatic recording of messages was useless for establishing contact, and that an experienced and skilled radio operator was indispensable, and finally that three attempts were not enough to establish the connection, and that constant daily monitoring would be required. He offered to test our apparatus and also to communicate, through his own channel, to the Government station in London details of the new communication link.

I was rather depressed by what he told me, and Joey was equally downcast when I passed on what I had just heard. Now, I could see clearly how silly we had been and what our blunders were, but at least I could see a way out.

To begin with, an attempt was arranged to obtain a connection with the Supreme Command station in London with our apparatus from Joey's home in Downhill Road. Zaremba arrived, accompanied by his contact, Halina, a young and good-looking girl, and his telegraphist, Wieslaw. As usual Joey proceeded to check the transmitter. I was talking with Zaremba, who told me the story of a raid which a German flying interceptor unit made on his radio station in Zoliborz, fortunately, without success. We discussed all the possible precautions against discovery, while Halina seated herself on the balcony and kept an eye on the street. Unfortunately, just opposite, in the building of the Schicht Soap Company, a German military hospital had been installed, and the convalescent patients, in their hospital pyjamas, were shouting to Halina across the road. The position was rather ticklish, for Halina could not leave her post, while the soldiers were encouraged by her presence to make vulgar jokes. They might have interpreted her continued presence on the balcony as an invitation to a visit. Fortunately, Halina's perfect composure made it unlikely. Despite all our anxiety we were rather amused by the grotesque situation, with a radio station just about to call London on one side of the road, and twenty yards away, on the other side, dozens of German soldiers watching the windows of our apartment.

Wieslaw went to work, and to our joy London replied at once that the transmission was audible, though faint. After about ten minutes the signal vanished, and that was the end of our first contact with the military station in London.

I thanked Zaremba effusively for testing our apparatus, and Joey was overwhelmed with joy when I congratulated him on the successful test. We had to make hay while the sun was shining, so I asked Zaremba to help us out until we got our own telegraphist by lending us Wieslaw, who was to transmit to the Government station in England our signals and other details through the military station in London, and also train our telegraphist. Zaremba agreed on condition that we supplied our own hide-outs and equipment and that, in addition to our own messages, Wieslaw would be allowed to transmit military messages. After the last German raid he was very short of safe hide-outs and wanted to use ours. In this way we came to know Wieslaw, a most likeable and courageous radio operator who simply loved his job.

The first successful contact

One fine summer day, we were again on our way to a new test. We all travelled by the same tram to Powazki, where I had secured a hide-out in a stone-mason's shed. Zosia transported the transmitter, while Wieslaw, Joey and I followed, each arriving separately. Our host, who was neither the owner nor the janitor of the place, overwhelmed us with all sorts of questions. For the time being, he concealed us in his own little room, as some of the workmen were still in the shed. There we waited, talking in low voices with his wife and playing with their child, who was very excited by the presence of so many strange people. We had brought some refreshments with us and now shared them with our hosts, who seemed to be rather down and out.

At last the workmen left, but our host informed us in a mysterious whisper that he had a secret radio receiver in the loft where we were supposed to work, and that two of his friends were in the habit of calling on him to listen in to London. It was necessary therefore to wait, as his friends were not supposed to know anything. We had to stay in a very uncomfortable, stuffy and warm room. After a long pause we heard the creaking of the gate and our host rushed outside and led the two newcomers to the shed. It was more than half an hour before the inopportune guests departed. We then picked up our packages and, one after the other, made for the shed. It was still daylight and we had a great deal of equipment to carry, because Wieslaw, to make sure, had brought his own transmitter as well. We were already in the dark shed when our host rushed in whispering, 'You must hide, they are coming back!' We hurried from the shed into a small yard full of grave stones, statues, blocks of marble and slabs of sandstone. I dropped to the ground next to a slab and gazed at the inscription, in which the next-of-kin was assuring the deceased of her 'loving memory'. Close by, someone was choking with suppressed laughter. I raised my head and could see Joey tickling Wieslaw, who lay stretched out next to him. I threatened them with my fist, while giving an admonitory glance at Zosia, to stop her throwing pebbles at them. By way of a change, she took up a position behind a mourning angel and assumed a similar posture. For some time we heard voices and the splash of water in the pond near the shed, until our host came and explained:

'Get up. They only came for a dip in the pond and are gone now.'

We clambered up a little ladder into the tiny loft, which was so low that it was impossible to stand erect. Joey and Wieslaw each assembled their transmitters, plagued by our host with endless questions. We fixed a long aerial so that it hung above the stone-cutting machinery, high up under a wooden roof. We judged that technical conditions were favourable, and the tuned-in transmitters were waiting for the pre-arranged hour. It was so hot in the loft that we had to take off not only our jackets but our shirts too. It was July, and the fourth month of our unrelenting efforts at establishing radio communication with London.

When everything was ready, Wieslaw called London on his transmitter, and presently he received confirmation that he was being heard with strength 1-2, which was 'faint' but made an exchange possible. It was a good beginning, anyhow. Wieslaw then signalled: 'I am going to test a new transmitter,' and when London signalled that they were ready to receive, he transferred the quartz from his transmitter to Joey's and repeated the call. The reply came immediately that he was being heard with strength 2-3, which was a degree higher. Wieslaw was amazed and admitted that our transmitter was much better. He then signalled that he had an urgent message for the Government station, and having received the reply 'ready', he tapped out the details of our working schedule. We all heaved a sigh of relief at the progress made. The long run of bad luck was over. Joey was pleased with himself, at seeing his transmitter function so well. There we were, in that loft, half naked, with perspiration running down our faces; but the transmitter worked, the control lamps blinked, and we were happy.

Our host, a little, thin man, was strangely fidgety. While the transmitter was being made ready, he calmly looked on at our doings, making pessimistic remarks about our ability to establish contact with London, but when he noticed that we were actually exchanging messages, he became very uneasy and kept on inquiring how long it was all going to last. We assured him that it would not be long; but this was our first hide-out for some time and Wieslaw had an accumulation of messages and had to go on for as long as possible. I went out into the open, where Zosia was sitting on a fence watching the approaches. The night was fine and calm and only occasionally did the hum of motor-cars driving down Powazki Highway disturb the nocturnal stillness. Owls were hooting in the cemetery. A cool, gentle breeze was blowing, and sitting at Zosia's side I inhaled the fresh air with delight. We remained at our post, closely observing the terrain, until dawn began to break.

I went back to the shed to find Wieslaw exchanging farewell courtesies with the telegraphist in London. Within ten minutes the dismantling and packing of the apparatus was completed, and everyone came out into the fresh air. Wieslaw wanted to have a wash, and as he leant over something dropped from his pocket and broke with the sound of glass. It was a porcelain statuette of the Virgin Mary which he always placed beside the transmitter when he was operating it. He was deeply affected, and we all tried to comfort him, though we felt it was a bad omen. A few months later, he fell into the clutches of the Gestapo while operating a secret military transmitter in Konstancin.

Our host became very excited and peremptorily demanded that we should leave at once, explaining that the workmen would be arriving presently. We knew this was not true, because it was not yet 5 a.m.—the curfew hour; but we had to leave. We had to wait for the first morning tram at the terminal stop in Powazki. Though we had had no sleep and were all tired, we enjoyed the bright, fresh morning in the green and sun-bathed countryside, pleased with our achievement. All we had to do now was to listen in to the Government station in London on the wave-lengths and at the times indicated by us.

At last the tram arrived and we got on it in two groups. However, we still had a surprise in store for us. Just before the tram started we heard German voices, and the car we were in was boarded by several German gendarmes who were obviously returning from a night patrol. The moment was tense, but the gendarmes were as tired and sleepy as we were ourselves; they gave us a casual glance and made themselves comfortable, taking off their steel helmets. Our two groups maintained perfect calm, neither chatting loudly nor whispering; we thus avoided drawing attention to ourselves by any unnatural behaviour. The apparatus, the transformers, and tools were concealed in the usual bags, of the kind carried by housewives out shopping, and they were covered over with various vegetables. At first there was no one in the car except ourselves and the gendarmes, but gradually other passengers got on. We breathed with relief when the gendarmes left on arriving in the centre of the city. Our task had been accomplished successfully in every respect.

At Last!

The eagerly awaited telegraphist, Johnny, arrived at last, recommended by the president of the Warsaw Union of Short-Wave Amateurs, Pokorski, who was later hanged by the

Germans. Joey, Johnny and myself met in the Zmijewski Café. Johnny impressed me as a smart, clever and cool boy who did not talk much, but observed everything. He knew what was expected of him and agreed to work with us, assuring me that he would be able to manage. To begin with, we discussed the question of a hide-out and salary, while people were playing billiards in the next room; then, after we had had a cup of the traditionally bad coffee and a few pastries, Joey took Johnny with him in order to initiate him and to find a hide-out for him.

A few days later we moved everything to Zielonka, a few miles out of Warsaw, where in the meantime a room had been rented for the station. Johnny moved in, pretending to his landlady, who was the wife of a gardener, that he was a student who could not afford the higher rents in Warsaw. Without a hitch, Zosia transported all the apparatus by train from Warsaw, which required some effort, considering the weight of the transmitter and transformers.

The station was assembled in a very small room, the V-shaped aerial being fixed to the ceiling. We tested the transmitter and found that everything was in perfect order, with the control bulb burning brightly and the quartz oscillating. Punctually at 19 hours, Johnny, with the earphones on, sat up in his chair saying: 'Here they are!' He took the earphones off and handed them over to Joey, whose face lit up with a blissful smile as he listened in, nodding to show that everything was functioning well; he then offered the earphones to me. I put them on and listened for a while to the regular rhythm of morse. Johnny, standing next to me, took one of the earphones and interpreted the signs, which made it clear that the Government station in London was calling us.

Our excitement rose when London signalled, 'Over to you,' and we knew that the hour of establishing contact with the Government in London had arrived at last, after nearly four months of effort. Pale with emotion and tense with concentration, Johnny put his fingers on the key and for the next two minutes proceeded to tap out the pre-arranged signals of our acknowledgement, finishing with 'Over to you'. The next second, Johnny leapt from his chair as if he had received an electric shock, adjusted the earphones, sat down again, snatched a pencil and began to take down the message. What a joy it was to know that they not only heard us, but heard perfectly! London could hardly believe it and requested a repeat. Amid general rejoicings the identification signals were mutually confirmed three times.

There could no longer be any doubt that we had established direct contact with the Government station in London. There followed an exchange of greetings and congratulations —radio operators are notorious for exchanging endless courtesies—with the letters OK, OK, OK appearing on Johnny's pad.

London signalled in code that an urgent message was to follow at once. Johnny started to take it down and in this way our work began; it was to go on for the next four years. The date was August 2, 1941.

We went through another trial of nerves waiting to hear whether the code in which the messages had been sent could be deciphered or not, but when in a few hours we received confirmation that it had been, all doubts were dispelled.

Our run of good luck held, for I met emissary Wlodek,[1] who, at a time when all the money I had for the construction of the transmitter was expended, gave me the dollars I needed to complete the work. Wlodek was overjoyed when he learned that we had achieved the longed-for liaison with London.

'I shall help you all I can,' he said.'Your work would be easier and quicker if you had your own individual code for communication with London. Here is my personal code, which I am letting you have on my own responsibility, though I shall get into trouble with the other people here.'

It was in this way that I was enabled to communicate with London in my own code, which was known only to Wlodek, Zosia and myself.

The First Stage

We were all going about transported with joy. We already had news from London that the radio station there was no less

[1] Engineer Czeslaw Raczkowski, at present in the United States.

overjoyed by the successful contact, and the Government regarded it as an event of considerable importance. All our troubles were forgotten and we concentrated now on the task of ensuring the efficiency, extension and safety of the station. Johnny received a pile of messages, with a detailed technical code, and we were at last able to do without the international code, which every German telegraphist at a listening post was able to understand perfectly, as it was a kind of Esperanto of the short-wave fans. The work in Zielonka proceeded smoothly, messages were being transmitted in large numbers, and Johnny struck up a friendship with his landlady and her family, whom he visited frequently. The only trouble was that his landlord had a pretty daughter, who attracted the attention of German soldiers billeted in Zielonka. They used to come in for a chat, which they carried on in broken German-Polish, insensitive to the carefully concealed hatred with which their visits were received. On one occasion we all went to Johnny's for a picnic. It was warm in the summer sunshine and we lounged on the lawn in the garden, enjoying hard-boiled eggs, radishes and other titbits prepared by Zosia. Joey, happy as a lark, teased Johnny, who repaid him in the same coin, and we all enjoyed ourselves greatly. However, I did not like the fact that the window of Johnny's little room on the ground floor was permanently closed and curtained, for his landlord might begin to suspect that something was going on.

As a workshop for Joey, I rented a separate apartment in Knights' Street in the Old City consisting of two small rooms and a kitchen in a pleasant old house, which he had to redecorate. In the meantime, at his home in Downhill Street, Joey had made a spacious hiding place under the floor, and was urgently constructing new sets. He had a helper, a youthful friend of his called Frank, a funny, broad-faced boy from the riverside who looked up to Joey as to a hero. Joey was very fond of him, but treated him rather condescendingly and was constantly telling him off. Work was proceeding apace and Joey was in a frenzy of buying up everything he could lay his hands on; he proclaimed proudly:

'With the stuff we've got put away under the floor, we can go on working for five years.'

One day he came to me beaming with delight and said: 'Guess where I've ordered first-class valves?' 'How would I know? Maybe from some short-wave fan in Cracow?' I replied. 'No . . . in Berlin!' Joey declared triumphantly, laughing like a lunatic.

Noticing my amazement, he explained that he had a friend, a Pole employed by a German firm, who was going to get them for him somehow. And, indeed, some days later Joey showed me a large cardboard box with German labels, bearing the name and address of the firm in Warsaw, filled with valves. We were greatly excited at the thought that we would be talking to London on equipment imported from Berlin. Joey was so amused by it that he mentioned it every five minutes.

New worries now began to beset us, owing to the flood of messages we had to send out. People seemed to be unaware of the limited capacity of our apparatus, not to mention the risks involved in extensive daily work. We only had two quartzes at our disposal and Johnny could therefore use only two wave-lengths, which greatly increased the dangers. The code in which messages were being transmitted required two figures to denote one letter, and thus took twice as long as an open message.

This was the beginning of a struggle I was to wage for four years for economy in messages sent by the Government Plenipotentiary and the political Parties, for avoiding repetitions, for abolishing adjectives, full stops, commas, in brief, for short, laconic texts. I asked all persons entitled to prepare texts to word them in the same way as they would if they had to pay a large sum of money out of their own pockets for every word. All my efforts were of little avail and I had many unpleasant encounters because of it. Jozef Niecko of the 'Triangle,' who died recently as a Communist member of the Council of State in Warsaw, and who promised to erect a monument in my honour if I succeeded in establishing permanent communications with London, did everything in his power to get control over the radio station, to introduce his own henchmen, and to appropriate the work himself. I fought back, and for a time we were left in peace.

Early Anxieties

Later in the month Johnny, breathless and greatly excited, arrived in Knights' Street and announced:

'They are searching in Zielonka. Mobile squads of gendarmes are searching every house there.'

From what he said it transpired that they had missed the little house in which the station was installed, that officially they were searching after an illicit still, but that the way they went about it indicated they were after our station. They examined all electrical installations carefully, testing even ordinary electric light bulbs. I ordered the immediate suspension of the work in Zielonka and transferred Johnny and the station to a rented room in Upper Silesia Street in Warsaw. This place had the serious disadvantage of being situated between the Parliament Building and the University Hostel, in both of which gendarmes were billeted. Joey thought it would be great fun for the station to produce ear-splitting noises in the radio receivers of the Germans. On the other hand, we thought that none of the gendarmes would suspect the effrontery of a secret station operating under their noses. To make sure, Johnny arranged with London that we would operate during the hours of the night, when no one would be listening to a radio. The drawback to this was that we would be unable to keep a look-out in the streets because of the curfew; but we had no choice, and Johnny started working in Upper Silesia Road. Occasionally Wieslaw would visit him there, as Zaremba was short of hide-outs, and they worked in turn through the night, one sending messages to the Government station in London, the other to the military station there.

The arrangement did not last very long; a tired and scared Johnny came running to us again:

'A stranger came to see my landlords and questioned them about me. So I moved the station and my things to Joey at once. I was lucky, because after I left the Gestapo arrived and took all the people away.'

I could not make out what it was all about, for Johnny had not been suspected up till then; the matter looked mysterious to me. Was the arrest of his landlords connected with the enquiry concerning himself? We never found out, but we were inclined to think that his landlords must have been engaged in some underground work of their own and slipped up. It could not have been due to a pursuing radio interceptor team, for if it had the Germans would have come during a transmission.

I was lucky enough to find a tiny one-roomed house in Lesna Podkowa; I rented it and Johnny moved in together with the transmitter. This house in Eagle Street had many technical advantages and the work went on smoothly, as Johnny was an exceptionally skilled radio telegraphist. He was able to send and receive messages at record speed and had a wonderful memory for figures. He also knew a great deal about the construction of apparatus, and whenever he fancied it he helped Joey in his work. The only obstacles were frequent power cuts at the generating station in Pruszkow; these always occurred at the wrong time. However, I was able to get in touch with the right people and Lesna Podkowa became a privileged locality as far as the supply of electric current was concerned. I had been warned, however, that fuses on the pylon close to our hide-out blew frequently, and this attracted the attention of the repairs squad.

At about the same time Anna obtained a job as a ticket seller in the box office of one of the little theatres in New World Avenue. As she had to sit in the box office all day long, I arranged a clearing post there, which made it unnecessary for me to meet Johnny in town. The arrangement functioned well, because in the afternoon there was a great deal of coming and going at the box office and no one paid any attention to the people who called there. Anna, in her best make-up, smart and brilliantly illumined, sat in the box office and welcomed all our agents with a smile, when under the pretence of buying tickets they delivered or collected messages.

Johnny used to come to Warsaw every day to call at the box office. By then I had come to know him rather well. He was on top of his job and was undoubtedly a patriotic Pole, but he was cold, calculating, and ambitious; he talked quite openly of wanting to make lots of money, run his own car, and possess other worldly goods. The modest salary of a radio operator was not enough for him, and as Joey told me, he was constantly speculating on the side. In our relations with him there was not much warmth of feeling, in contrast to our dealings with Joey, whom we all loved. Moreover, Johnny was too inquisitive, and was restless because he did not know what my real name was and what functions I had in the underground movement.

It sometimes happened that all of us met accidentally at Anna's box office, I, myself, Zosia, Joey and Johnny; and as each always had something to say to the other, I had to disperse them more than once.

The hide-out in Knights' Street was very cosy and inconspicuous amidst the innumerable houses of the Old City, so that we felt safe there. It is important in every conspiracy to have a nose for danger. A hide-out in which one does not feel comfortable should always be abandoned at once. I never expected a radio operator to work in a hide-out which he did not like, even if he could not say why. In the Knights' Street hide-out Joey altered the window-frame in such a way that it could be moved, and between the frame and the sheet-iron roof, which came down over the window at an acute angle, he fixed up a roomy store. He was supposed to put everything away there, but every time I arrived the table was littered with bulbs, valves, flexes, coils, batteries and the like.

The main stores were still kept under the floor in Downhill Road, and whatever Joey needed for current use he brought from there. He accumulated about thirty large boxes of radio equipment in his hide-out.

With Johnny's help the work was going on at full speed. We now had new transmitters, and to test the technical conditions of the Knights' Street hide-out, Johnny contacted London with them. The new transmitters were quite good, but as we had to observe the rule that the workshop hide-out must not be used for transmissions, we could not operate from Knights' Street.

The time was now ripe for trying out my new scheme of

constructing a sound broadcasting transmitter. I had planned from the very outset that after radio contact had been established with London, the next stage would require the construction of a radio transmitter on which we could broadcast from time to time programmes for home listeners, and maybe for listeners abroad as well. Joey was enthusiastic about the whole scheme and we discussed every little detail of it. We realised, of course, that there could be no question of broadcasting regular programmes. It would have been suicidal, for the Germans would have discovered it at once. Sound broadcasts could be detected much more easily than wireless telegraphy in morse, and all we intended was to venture on to the ether with a programme occasionally. Joey succeeded with the utmost difficulty in acquiring all the indispensable parts, above all powerful transmitting valves and a microphone. He told me, beaming with pride, that he would construct a radio transmitter of 300 watts power, which under favourable atmospheric conditions should be heard throughout Europe. He explained that during the last short-wave competition before the war, a programme sent out on a transmitter of less than 100 watts had been successfully picked up in England, and that our enterprise was practicable.

We went on conjuring up visions of our future exploits and the impression they would make on the Germans, with all the advantages it would bring to the underground work. Joey was sure the Germans would be raving mad, and with my final approval he started work on the transmitter.

Encounter with the Zarembas

A day or two later Zosia and I went to the Lowiczanka restaurant for dinner. The place was safe and most of the waitresses were members of the underground, so we went there frequently. From a corner someone nodded to us and I recognised that it was Zaremba and the contact Halina. We joined them at their table and found that they were both very worried. It was so obvious that I put the direct question to Zaremba:

'What's worrying you? Perhaps we can help you?'

'We slipped up,' he said, 'and the Gestapo raided our apartment. We are homeless and don't know where to turn for the night.'

Zosia looked at me, and noticing my approval said:

'We can put you up for a few days. We have an illegal place on the Staszic Housing Estate. It will give you time to find another hide-out.'

Zaremba and Halina, who, as it turned out, was his wife, came to live with us. From the point of view of security, in a conspiracy this was inadmissible, but we had no alternative. We had to help the Zarembas, although thereby the heads of military and civilian liaison came to live under one roof. I feel ashamed to admit that this 'crime'—according to all the rules of conspiracy—lasted for about a year. We happily shared two little rooms and in the evening, after dinner, we discussed our work. Sometimes, putting earphones on, we swirled round the room to dance music broadcast by the BBC in London, careful not to get entangled in the wires connecting the earphones with the receiver. The Zarembas were old hands at radio communication and survived several raids and slip-ups. The last one was rather serious as Zaremba lost a number of transmitters, but I was able to return the help he had given us some time before by offering him two transmitters of Joey's construction.

Johnny and Joey had to visit Zaremba's hide-out stations to teach the military how to operate our transmitters, and this led to an unexpected development, of which Joey came to warn me.

'They wanted to play you a dirty trick,' he said.

'What sort of a trick?' I asked.

'A chap, not Zaremba, who is a decent fellow, took me and Johnny aside and suggested that we should leave you. He promised us better pay, and as we would be working for the military, there would be promotions and decorations for us.'

'And what did you tell them?'

'Nothing. I only laughed, but Johnny seemed to be impressed and I have a feeling he will brood over it.'

Broadcast Programme

The transmitter for sound broadcasting was ready. I viewed it with respect, for compared with our earlier apparatus it looked like a Flying Fortress beside a fighter plane. We tested it successfully and I notified London that we had ready a sound broadcasting transmitter with a power of 300 watts, and that we proposed to broadcast a Christmas programme for the Polish army and people in exile, which the BBC could record on discs and re-broadcast for the world. Our proposals were received with some scepticism, but nevertheless accepted, and we fixed an hour in the evening of one of the weekdays before Christmas, and, in case of failure, an hour in the early morning of the following day.

In a series of journeys, Zosia transported most of the parts by the Suburban Electric Railway to Lesna Podkowa, while Joey and Johnny moved the remaining equipment. I prepared a talk, which included Christmas greetings from the people in Poland to the Poles in exile, all good wishes to the Polish Armed Forces in the West, and a call to continue the struggle against the Germans to the bitter end, assuring them that the nation would fight on until victory was won. A description of the situation in Poland under German occupation followed.

In the evening of the appointed day we all assembled in Lesna Podkowa. It was pitch dark when we groped our way to Eagle Road. The one-roomed apartment was carefully blacked-out. The interior was impressive even though we were familiar with radio work. The transmitter and six transformers occupied a large table. Multi-coloured bulbs glowed; we were especially captivated by the two mercury vapour rectifiers that burned with a violet light, and by the third, largest valve, which emitted a fantastic pinky-orange light. In this light Joey's face, bent over the apparatus, looked satanic. On this occasion he worked with solemn concentration and made no humorous asides. The sceptical smile on Johnny's face was absent and he, too, was rather solemnly grave, and for no obvious reason talked in a whisper, an example that was followed by all present. It did not prevent us from feeling hungry, however, and Johnny put on the kettle to make tea. We consumed our frugal meal in a hurry, watching the clock all the time.

The appointed hour was approaching. The transmitter had been tested, the quartz was oscillating and the meters indicated that everything was functioning well. We were all excited, but tried to appear calm. At last the hour struck and Johnny sent out the call signal. London replied at once that it was ready to receive the sound broadcast. The transmitter was adjusted from telegraphy to sound and Joey spoke into the microphone the weighty words:

'Can you hear me?'

'I am sorry, I cannot hear you at all,' London replied.

Our faces fell. Joey made another test with the same result. It became obvious that atmospheric conditions were unfavourable, especially as the interior aerial deprived the transmitter of much of its power. We informed London that we would resume the attempt in two hours, and with our spirits low we tried to snatch a little sleep. Zosia lay down on the bed, we men on the floor. After two hours rest we got to work again, with the same pitiable result. We had no alternative but to postpone the attempt until the alternative morning hour, hoping that conditions would improve in the meantime.

At dawn we got up again, still sleepy and worn out. Johnny was more depressed than usual, and Joey, unkempt and pale, tuned in the transmitter. The minutes were flying fast and finally, key in hand, Johnny again called London. This time London replied that though faint, they could hear us. The exhausting attempts continued for more than an hour, during which Joey tried to tune the transmitter to its maximum power, while the atmospheric conditions, too, were improving. We decided to take a great risk, and in broad daylight Johnny drew the aerial through the window into the garden, and fastened it to a shed on the opposite side. At last London signalled:

'OK. Proceed with the programme. We are ready.'

I got hold of the microphone and, profoundly moved, though suffering from the stage fright of a novice, I read the prepared address. Joey, ever vigilant and keyed-up watched the functioning of the apparatus and at the same time listened in on a tiny receiver. Everything seemed to be in order.

I finished my speech and Johnny went to the receiver, to find out how the programme had been recorded. As soon as he put the earphones on, his face changed. He beckoned to me and handed me the earphones; through them I could hear a monotonous, rising and falling roar. Johnny whispered into my ear:

'We are being jammed from a nearby German transmitting station. Let's run at once.'

Joey listened in for a second and confirmed Johnny's opinion. The transmitter, and therefore the Germans, must have been very near. There was no time to dismantle the station, so we just disconnected the apparatus, covered it up with a blanket, and in two groups decamped from Eagle Road in a hurry, each taking a different route to the railway station in Lesna Podkowa, where, without mishap, we boarded the Warsaw train and reached the city in safety. We at once proceeded to our Knights' Street hide-out, where at the regular hour for listening in, Johnny tuned in to London. Within minutes he received the following message:

'Immediately after you opened the programme, you were jammed by a powerful German station. Nevertheless, we could hear odd sentences. Thank you.'

An analysis of the events indicated that the Germans must have overheard our rehearsals for sound broadcasting, and guessing what we were after had no difficulty in preparing the jamming.

The following day we learnt that after our departure from Lesna Podkowa, the Germans had carried out searches all day long on the Electric Railway and in Podkowa itself, which showed that they must have located the station fairly accurately. In view of this development Johnny kept away from his hide-out for some days and returned to it only after we felt sure that it was safe.

I collected the whole team and asked them if they felt they could stand a repetition of the attempt at a sound broadcast before New Year's Eve, from a hide-out in Miedzylesie. I altered my talk so as to make it a New Year's message. I also made it plain that the decision rested with them, as everyone was somewhat exhausted, both physically and nervously. However, the entire team was determined and unanimously resolved to repeat the attempt. London, too, agreed to my proposal, whereupon Zosia and Frank transported the complete equipment by rail to Miedzylesie, carrying it in suitcases and parcels, having luckily evaded the gendarmes and the railway police. The preparations and the actual attempt were similar to those in Lesna Podkowa, except that the result was even worse. Each time we called London they replied, 'Sorry, we cannot hear you at all.' We gave up, and the entire equipment was transported back to Warsaw and the Knights' Street hide-out; we travelled recklessly, the whole team in one compartment, exhausted and disappointed.

By way of consolation, we heard in the evening of January 10, 1942, the BBC's broadcast of a speech by the then deputy Prime Minister in the Sikorski Government, Mikolajczyk, who, in an address to the people of Poland, thanked us for the first living word to reach England from Poland. As our enterprise had been kept strictly secret, Mikolajczyk's statement aroused keen curiosity in all underground circles. Colonel Rzepecki, chief of the Information and Propaganda Department of the Union for Armed Struggle, showed me a monitoring report of Mikolajczyk's speech and asked me if I knew anything about it. On the margin of the report I noticed a remark written in Rzepecki's own hand: 'This must be a hoax.'

The Dismissal of Johnny

I was taking a walk in the streets accompanied by Johnny, who was telling me a strange story:

'I spent the night in Warsaw,' he said, 'and returned to Podkowa in the morning to contact London at 8 a.m. When I arrived, the door was locked and everything seemed to be in order. On entering, I found everything upside down on the table. The light was on, although it was broad daylight, and the bed was all in a mess.'

'Had anything been taken away, or not? What about the ciphers and messages?'

'Nothing was missing. I had the ciphers and messages on me, but the station had been searched by someone, although nothing is missing. What do you think happened?'

'It must have been a common thief who, finding that he had come across some conspiratorial work, remembered that he was a Pole as well as a thief and did not pinch anything,' I explained to Johnny.

'I think so too,' said Johnny. 'But the trouble is the bum kept the light burning during the night without having blacked-out the window, and that might have attracted a patrol.'

'Have you noticed anything suspicious?'

'No.'

We discussed the incident at some length. In view of the fact that a third party knew our secret, we had to abandon the hide-out in Eagle Street, and had to work casually, wherever we could.

However, I did not like the way Johnny was carrying on. I already knew that he was jealous of Joey. As a constructor he had had better schooling, in fact he had matriculated when the war started, but now he had to subordinate himself to a boy who had hardly any education and yet was in charge of all the work. Johnny mentioned casually that he could do exactly the same work as Joey did, but I took no notice. Joey had told me some time before that Johnny was in touch with the UAS; now he began to arrive late or miss appointments altogether, and my observations led me to suspect that Johnny was trading in something. I had a frank talk with him and told him plainly that if he did not wish to work with us, he could go All I wanted was that he should tell me so, and I would find another telegraphist. I warned him that I would never allow him to make something on the side, because he might slip up in smuggling, and as it was he was getting quite enough and had no need to earn any extra.

'I warn you,' I added in conclusion, 'not to work for two parties, because you can't work well for both and the chances of a slip-up are considerably increased.'

Johnny assured me solemnly that he was not trading, that he was not working for anyone else, and that he would keep appointments punctually. We parted on friendly terms, but after a few days it became clear that nothing had changed, and that Johnny was absorbed by something besides his work at the radio station. I told Joey of my suspicions and he confirmed them, saying:

'I have noticed many things myself, and I shall try to find out exactly what the position is.'

It was not long afterwards that Joey told me Johnny had admitted to him that he was also working for the UAS, making purchases of equipment; that he was handling large sums of money and earning a lot, and had sneered at my credulity. I arranged with Joey that without telling Johnny anything we would look for another telegraphist. We were helped in our search by Pokorski, who put us in touch with Stanislaw, a man in his thirties, of middle height, with bulging eyes and a pug nose, a typical man of Warsaw. He was an experienced and highly skilled radio telegraphist. He enquired about the organisation of the work and was anxious to know what the security conditions were, which I appreciated very much, as it indicated that he was a sensible man. Keeping it secret from Johnny, Stanislaw contacted London, and when he had found his bearings, I had a final talk with Johnny. We parted on correct terms. Pressed, he admitted to having been working on the side, expressed his regret, and promised solemnly not to divulge our secrets. I could see that he was glad to be released, and when I later ran into him occasionally, we exchanged friendly nods.

Telegraphist Wladek

I had always felt that one telegraphist was not enough. Should he fall ill or slip up, liaison would be disrupted. As usual, I confided my anxiety to Joey, and we both kept a look out. It was not long afterwards that Joey introduced to me a shy and engaging young man, who was a skilled radio telegraphist. He had been through many hardships, for after the September defeat he escaped to France, re-joined the Polish army there, took part in the campaign of 1940, and was captured as a prisoner-of-war by the Germans. As he was not at all robust, he pretended to be gravely ill and was released from a Stalag. He felt it his duty to continue the struggle against the Germans, and he was glad to join us. We rented a little house in Jozefow, near Warsaw, for him; Zosia transported the equipment there, and Wladek—for such was his name—easily established contact with London. He was allotted his own hours, wave-lengths, call signs and a cipher, and in this way we had two independently run stations at our disposal. Should one of them slip up, the other would go on operating. The work proceeded smoothly, and I was again toying with the idea of sound broadcasting, which we planned to organise in Jozefow. Zosia again transported the equipment, Joey assembled the transmitter, and we were ready to make another attempt.

Wladek worked with the regularity of a clock, and most of our messages were being passed through him. On one occasion I told him how well satisfied I was with his work, to which he replied modestly: 'It's no credit to me, it's all in the transmitter. It's first class, and I'm sure it must have a power of at least 300 watts.'

'You must be mad. What do you mean, 300 watts? It's probably less than twenty at the outside.'

'That's impossible,' Wladek answered. 'I know something about transmitters.'

I felt uneasy.

'Which transmitter are you using?' I asked him.

'The one for sound broadcasting,' Wladek coolly replied.

I felt devastated. It transpired that on one occasion, when London could not hear him on the small transmitter, Wladek had brought the large one into action and had used it ever since, with excellent results.

'Don't you realise,' I stormed, 'that London is using a transmitter with a power of half a kilowatt, but that happens to be in England, while we here live under German occupation, and it is a miracle that you are still alive. You are a professional telegraphist and yet you did not realise that with such a powerful transmitter the risk of a slip-up is inordinately increased?'

I took immediate action, and not a minute too soon, for a few days later Wladek escaped from Jozefow in a fright just as he stood, reporting that German mobile squads were taking bearings there and the place was swarming with gendarmes. The hide-out was at once given up and all the work was transferred back to Stanislaw. For the time being we left the transmitters in Jozefow.

A Slip-up in Downhill Road

I knew that the Gestapo were searching for me all the time, as my pre-war apartment in Friend's Avenue was being visited by them regularly. I deliberately did not check out when moving. Each time the Gestapo came, the janitor, Stanislaw, a good patriot and a courageous man, sent me word through a chain of contacts. The Gestapo had raided the Prudential Building in Napoleon Square quite recently and searched the two rooms which I had used for a time. They seemed to be closing in on us, and for greater safety Zosia and I moved from the Staszic Housing Estate to friends on Saxon Isle.

One evening the telephone bell rang.

'Anna wants to see you at once and is waiting on Poniatowski Bridge, at the Praga end.'

I set out at once, and in a few minutes reached the bridge. From under the dark pillars emerged, not Anna, but Joey. He took me by the arm and leading me down the steps to the Miedzeszyn Dam, he whispered:

'A slip-up. Johnny has been arrested and the Gestapo are in Downhill Road.'

I was appalled and instinctively quickened my steps. Joey, clad in an outsize jacket, trembled as he continued:

'I went to Downhill Road to get urgently needed spare parts from the hidden store. I pulled the cardboard boxes from under the floor and was selecting the required parts from a list. All of a sudden I heard a knock at the door and the whistled signal I had agreed upon with Johnny. Naturally, I thought it was him, and without closing the store under the floor, I opened the door. Two Gestapo men burst in, shouting "Hands up!" followed by Johnny. I quailed, as I would sooner die than that. The Gestapo men pushed me with the butts of their revolvers into the corridor and from there, through the open door, into my parents' room. They had not yet been to the room on the right, where the hidden store and the open boxes were, but it was obvious that they would go into it now. They examined my parents' room and the kitchen and asked who else was in the apartment. I told them no one, as my parents were staying with relatives in the country. They put away the revolvers and proceeded with the search. I was standing by the door, and seeing that all was up, I leaped into the dark corridor and made for the staircase. The door was open; I banged it behind me and ran down. By the time they had got along the corridor and opened the door, I was already two flights below. They fired their automatics down the staircase, breaking a lot of plaster, but I got out of the house and into the street. There, a Gestapo man was sitting in a car, smoking a cigarette. He did not even look at me. I ran to the nearest contact point and they sent me to Anna. I escaped in my shirt-sleeves; Anna gave me this jacket and notified you. That's all.'

We both trembled with emotion. We had to think first of the safety of the people Johnny knew. Anna was already informed, but we had to warn the rest and the curfew hour was approaching. Unfortunately, Johnny knew our hide-out on Saxon Isle and we had to flee from it. I took Joey, who had already sent someone to warn his brother and his parents, who actually lived out of Warsaw, and we proceeded to our friends. Besides ourselves, they were also sheltering Casimir Baginski, who had only recently arrived from the Soviet-occupied part of Poland. With forced calm I announced:

'We have to run. All of us. Someone who knows this apartment has slipped up and is squealing.' I whispered to Zosia: 'It's Johnny,' and we all began to pack our things. We left at once, together with our hosts, and flitting along the dark and deserted streets of Saxon Isle—it was already after the curfew hour—we reached other acquaintances. They gave us shelter willingly, for it was a time of great solidarity among our people, who were ready to risk their own lives in order to save those who were in danger. We settled down for the night as best we could, but everyone was upset and no one had any sleep that night.

We reviewed the position from the beginning. What were the circumstances of Johnny's slip-up? Why did he squeal? Had they found the address on him, and had they found anything else? We came to the conclusion that it was most likely that Johnny, who occasionally dropped in on Joey for the night after leaving us—it was only now that Joey told me of it—was caught by the Gestapo and gave Joey's address as his domicile. We were all mad with Johnny, and we kept on repeating the most hated word in a conspiracy: 'He squealed.'

The following day Joey spent in the hide-out, while we circulated in the city warning all the people involved. Anna left the theatre at once and hid in the suburb of Czerniakow. On the third day I began to study the position carefully. The hide-outs that Johnny knew were undisturbed. In the afternoon Joey went out and came back deeply depressed. His parents, who had been warned, were safe; but his brother had disregarded the warning, remained in his room in the Old City, and the Gestapo had taken him. We knew, of course, that immediately after Joey's escape the Germans must have discovered the hidden store and realised what an important bird had given them the slip.

The Gestapo had laid a trap in Downhill Road and caught Frank, who went upstairs although warned by the janitor's wife that something suspicious was happening in the apartment. Another of Joey's friends, a man just released from Auschwitz, was also caught. When he realised he was trapped, he jumped from a fourth floor window into the courtyard. The Gestapo rushed downstairs and captured him alive, but with his legs broken. It was a terrible disaster. We had to evacuate the workshop in Knights' Street at once, as both Johnny and Frank knew it. We were worried about where to hide all the equipment.

Fortunately, none of them knew Stanislaw and his hide-out, thanks to which the work suffered no interruption and the exchange of messages with London continued. But Frank used to visit Wladek in Jozefow, and we had to remove everything from there, too. Wladek was in Warsaw and became visibly worried when I told him the position. However, he overcame his fear and went with Zosia to Jozefow. I accompanied Zosia to the tram stop, where I found a rosary, which I gave to her for luck. She has kept it to this day. In Jozefow everything was quiet, so they packed the entire equipment into two suitcases and carried them to the railway station. The burden was too heavy for Zosia and she had to stop frequently, while Wladek hurried on as if he were being pursued. The train was crowded with smugglers carrying bundles containing provisions. Two children sat on Zosia's suitcase munching sandwiches. On arriving in Warsaw, they made their way out of the station by following experienced smugglers and avoiding the points at which the gendarmes were on sentry duty. They dragged the suitcases along to Wilcza Street, near the Polytechnic, where Zosia and I were hiding in Cesia's apartment. First Zosia carried one suitcase to our new hide-out, while Wladek waited with the other in the doorway of a house in Wilcza Street, because we did not want him to know the address of our hide-out. When Zosia came back, just as Wladek was handing her the suitcase, it opened and all its dangerous contents spilled out on to the pavement. Wladek bolted, leaving Zosia all by herself. Fortunately, there were no Germans about and the passers-by pretended not to notice anything. With tears of anger, Zosia put everything back into the suitcase, fastened it with a length of flex and carried it to the Polytechnic.

The incident showed that Wladek was more profoundly shaken by the slip-up than I had thought. I was worried, because he was an excellent boy; it was just that his nerve had gone. As Joey said, he was scared. But he struggled to overcome his fears, and of his own free will continued to work with us. I respected him all the more for it. He found a hide-out in Lesna Podkowa East and operated from there.

For the time being Joey was hiding in distant Grochow. We used to meet in the fields there, away from the crowd. We used to spend hours lying in the grass making plans, while Joey played with a revolver which he always carried on him. He found a number of hide-outs for occasional work, and

Stanislaw was now operating in this neighbourhood. We went from one hide-out to another, intruding on our friends to secure a hide-out from which we could operate for even a single session.

Joey's Adventure in Brwinow

Despite all our troubles, we had not given up hope of sound broadcasting and we wanted to go on with the experiments in Wladek's hide-out in Lesna Podkowa East. We transferred the equipment in grand style, and both Zosia and I dressed especially well for the occasion. With two new suitcases and smart woollen rugs thrown over the left arm we drove in a cab to Novogrodzka Street Suburban Railway Station. We knew from experience that the Germans had a certain respect for well-dressed and prosperous-looking people. We boarded the train most nonchalantly and reached our destination safely. Wladek was living in a detached two-storey house surrounded by trees and shrubs. He lived in a large room, and had a kitchen in which to prepare his modest meals. His inventory included a few plates, tumblers, a kettle, and an electric heater, and his provisions consisted of bread, sugar and salt. A shabby bed, a table and three chairs completed his meagre household goods. Soon after our arrival Joey came in; he was temporarily sharing the hide-out with Wladek, and as the latter disliked solitude, he was glad to have Joey's company. However, he seemed to be disgruntled and complained that the work was not going well, and altogether things did not look right. When I pressed him to be more explicit he said:

'The landlords here are running an illicit still and a secret bakery. I am afraid I might get caught through them. They are also pinching the current; when they are at work the voltage drops and I cannot operate the transmitter. It's altogether too much, for an underground radio station, an illicit still, and a secret bakery to be housed under one roof.'

'What hours do they work?' I asked.

'All hours, but mostly during the night,' he answered.

'You must find out, and arrange with London for the hours during which the current is adequate.'

However, it was difficult to arrange such hours, and in the end Joey had to construct a special transformer on the spot to replace the loss of power. He also moved in a few of his personal effects; but he had little to do, and to while away the time he cycled around the neighbourhood.

It so happened that one day, while I was in Warsaw, I received an urgent summons through our secret channels to go immediately to an address indicated. I did not know why I was wanted, but I went at once, and on arriving I found Joey and Wladek having breakfast. On the table, apart from bread and butter, they had placed their revolvers and reserve clips of cartridges. They both looked fatigued, with traces of excitement in their eyes. Joey was in his socks, with no shoes on. I sat down beside them, and concealing my anxiety, I asked:

'I can see something has happened. Has the station been raided?'

'I don't think so,' Joey answered, 'but when you hear the story, you will be able to judge for yourself. You know we used to prepare our own meals; but they always consisted of the same old bread, sausage and tea. While cycling in Brwinow, I went into a restaurant to have a meal. I leaned the bicycle against the wall, sat down at a table, and ordered a cutlet. There were a number of customers present, including two blue policemen.[1] While eating my meal, I noticed that they were whispering something to each other and looking in my direction, so I was on my guard. When I had finished my meal and was paying the bill, one of the blues took up a position against the bar, with my cycle within his reach, while the other came up to me and demanded to see my identity card. There was no time to hesitate; I bolted through the open door and ran for my life. I soon noticed that they were hot on my heels, but at that moment I lost a shoe and couldn't run so fast. So I pulled the revolver out and let them have it. They ducked and paused so I got rid of my other shoe and sprinted in my socks. I threw them off and ran to Wladek, and we both hastily made for the Electric Railway. We were

[1] The Blue Police consisted of the pre-war Polish Police force; the Germans made them co-operate for the maintainance of public order.

lucky enough to board a train for Warsaw, and I took my socks off and travelled barefoot, as neither Wladek nor I had a spare pair of shoes. The conductor noticed my bare feet and pointed us out when the inspector came. It wasn't much, but to make sure we jumped from the moving train somewhere past Rakowiec. We reached Warsaw in the evening and made for the contact point. I shouldn't like to have such a silly adventure again.'

'It's too bad,' I said, 'but are you sure you gave the blues the slip?'

'Of that I am sure, and I think they gave up the pursuit when they discovered I had a revolver on me. But they will be on the look-out for me.'

'I take it they know nothing of Wladek?'

'No—nothing whatever,' Joey said.

'Nevertheless, we cannot take risks with Lesna Podkowa. Give me the keys, Wladek. Zosia will go there to-morrow and remove the lot.'

The following day, Zosia and Helena, a newly recruited look-out, a tall, good-looking girl, travelled to Lesna Podkowa and taking the utmost cautions approached the house Wladek used to live in. They sensed that everything was quiet, and Zosia called on the landlord, pretending to be Wladek's sister. As he had had to go away unexpectedly, she had come to fetch his belongings. At that moment she realised that she did not even know the name under which Wladek had checked in, and felt most uncomfortable. The landlord smiled at the word 'sister', but agreed that she could take the things away, as he had seen Zosia on previous occasions when she visited Wladek. But he wanted to know what she was taking away. Zosia pretended to be offended.

'What's on your mind?' she said. 'Don't you know me?'

Her audacity helped, and she and Helena removed everything. Loaded like two camels, they brought the suitcases safely to Cesia's, at the Polytechnic.

Thinking over all these events, I could not help feeling that fortune was unkind to us, but apparently it was to be our lot never to enjoy a moment's peace in our work.

New Men and Women

Helena had been drawn into the work by her friend Stanislaw, who occasionally operated from her modest apartment in Silver Street. Helena and her lodger girl friend became lookouts. The two-roomed, modestly furnished, but well-kept apartment was in the inner courtyard, and as the house was surrounded on all sides by blocks of buildings, we calculated that even if the radio interceptors pin-pointed us, they would find Helena's apartment only after a prolonged blockade and search. If this happened, Stanislaw would have enough time to dismantle and hide the transmitter. He liked working there and frequently went on all night. He also looked for other hide-outs, and found one in Milanowek, another in Muranowska Street, and a third in the cottage of Ralph, a workman living in Wola who later became a look-out at the station there.

Wladek had no hide-out, and I thus had to combine both stations and introduce him to Stanislaw, thereby giving up the idea of keeping the two stations isolated. However, pressure of work demanded it, as we were being flooded with messages which had to be sent out. Stanislaw took Wladek in hand, to the great advantage of our work.

On one occasion Wladek came to me and said:

'Would you like to engage an extra telegraphist? I have met a colleague, an excellent technician and a trustworthy man.'

I was glad to have him, and Wladek introduced me to a man of about forty, of middle height and with merry little eyes. He spoke with a noticeable borderland accent. He impressed me as being a sensible man, and so he proved; his solid work, his courtesy and willingness to oblige gained him the regard of all of us. I gave him the name Martin.

Dangerous attempts

The sound transmitter was still waiting, and it worried us. In addition to normal work, therefore, we made preparations for another attempt at sound broadcasting and informed

London accordingly, fixing a date for the beginning of August. We let Stanislaw into our secret; he, however, reacted to the scheme with a complete lack of enthusiasm. He looked at Joey and me with something near contempt, saying:

'I don't think it's worthwhile. The risk is enormous and the advantages trifling.'

I tried to explain to him the political and propaganda value of sound broadcasting from a country exposed to a frightful terror. He was sceptical and tried to dissuade me.

'Have this junk dismantled,' he persisted. 'Nothing good will come of it.'

'The matter is settled, Stanislaw,' I said. 'We need the help of a telegraphist, but if you have no heart for it, we shall have to look for someone else.'

'That has nothing to do with it. If you need a telegraphist, I shall take on the job,' he answered, thereby settling all his doubts.

We found a hide-out in Wesola, near Warsaw, and the team, consisting of Zosia, Joey, Stanislaw and myself, went there to have a look at it. The whole family occupying the modest little two-storey house received us with the utmost friendliness. It was July and the heat was unbearable. The people we met were living in a world apart, in a delightful quiet spot amidst green fields and gardens. Our hosts and their children, in swimming suits, were basking in the sun, unruffled and contented. They offered us tea, and when I let our host into our secrets, he was deeply impressed and said:

'The house is at your disposal at any time you may need it.'

On the appointed day I travelled to Wesola and inspected the station, which was assembled in the loft. Zosia and Helena had transported all the parts safely by rail a few days before. It was exceedingly hot under the roof and Joey and Stanislaw had to work there almost naked. The transmitter worked perfectly and Joey showed me the improvements he had made of his own invention. It was not an empty boast on his part, for he really had patented several little improvements in electro-technology before the war.

At exactly the pre-arranged hour Stanislaw called London and received the reply, 'We can hear you very well.' I glanced at Joey, and he looked at me, and we must have both been thinking that this time we would succeed. I had a script of my prepared address, and Stanislaw signalled:

'We are ready to begin the broadcast.' The telegraphist in London asked for fifteen minutes in which to decipher our message and to encipher his reply, and then signalled:

'I can't make out what you want.'

This was really more than we could stand. We checked all the messages in which we had fixed the day and the hour, and we found that there was no misunderstanding on our part. But London might have decoded our message wrongly. We repeated it; to receive the reply:

'I know nothing of a sound broadcast. I have several urgent messages. Are you ready?'

We were at the end of our tether and cursed London, its station, the BBC, and our own idea of attempting a sound broadcast. Stanislaw put the earphones on and resigned himself to receiving the messages London wished to unload on us; while I drafted a red-hot message of complaint, demanding to know why London had disregarded our efforts, undertaken at such great risk to our lives. Having transmitted the message, we had to wait patiently for an answer; in the meantime Stanislaw went on with his normal work.

Two days later I received an urgent summons to Wesola. I set out at once and found Joey and Stanislaw waiting for me in a state of nervous excitement. No sooner had I entered, when Stanislaw rapped out:

'A mobile interceptor is listening in within a radius of less than a kilometre. They are pin-pointing me from so close that the earphones are screeching like a rusty saw. They are also communicating with another station; I can hear their key hammering away. They must be within a stone's throw. We did not want to make a decision while you were away. What shall we do?'

'Dismantle, pack up, hide the apparatus, and leave at once.'

I could see that the disciplined Stanislaw approved of my decision and was glad to get out of the trap. Our host, an elderly man, carried the parts down from the loft and put them away safely outside the house. As I took my leave, I told him that in a few days the Germans would get tired and lose the trail, and that we should then fetch the transmitter.

We all returned to Warsaw, not knowing what we would do if, in reply to our message, London should inform us that they were ready. We could do nothing about it; until Joey managed to find a hide-out in the apartment of one of his chums, who lived in a Grochow side-street. Now we had only to transport the station from Wesola to be ready for any emergency.

The following day we received news from there that after we had left motorised German gendarmes had arrived and carried out mass searches, and arrested everyone who could not prove that he was registered as domiciled in Wesola. From this we deduced that the Germans already knew that our station was a kind of 'Flying Dutchman', and was not operated by the people of the locality. After the raid everything was calm again in Wesola, except that agents of the Gestapo kept the railway station under observation.

My problem was how to transport the station, packed in two suitcases and several bags, under the eyes of the Gestapo watch-dogs. I did not want to expose anyone in the team, especially as no one was keen enough to volunteer. All I said to Joey was that at about noon the next day the station would be delivered at the new hide-out.

In the morning of the following day Zosia and I set out on foot from the last tram stop in Grochow in the direction of Wesola. The road was pleasant and refreshing, as it led through shaded woodlands; however, we had to cover a distance of about five miles, and the heat was oppressive. When we arrived, our host was greatly relieved and brought the suitcases and the bags. We started back without delay, each of us carrying a suitcase and two bags. We had hardly begun, and had only walked a few hundred yards, before we were wet with perspiration and had to rest. That road became one long torture, and we slogged along, resting every few hundred yards, trying various ways of making the carrying of the burden easier, but without avail. In the end I took off my leather belt, strapped the two suitcases together, and lifted them on to my shoulder. I had scarcely moved more than a

few yards when the belt broke and one of the suitcases fell
to the ground, fortunately the one with the transformers.

Panting hard we struggled along until we reached the top
of a mound in the woods, and the sight that met our eyes
took our breath away. A company of German infantry, led
by an officer riding a horse, was marching in our direction.
They were not more than fifty or sixty yards away and we had
no time to turn or to hide, especially as the Germans had
already seen us. With a last effort we lifted the suitcases and
walked towards the marching column, grumbling to each
other about the heat. The soldiers passed a few yards away,
without paying any attention to us. They were obviously returning from some exercise and must have suspected us of
smuggling, but at that particular moment they did not seem
to consider it their concern, and they gazed at us with utter
indifference, assuming no doubt that we would be dealt with
by the gendarmes. Somewhat heartened by this lucky escape,
we moved on. I picked up a thick stick, put it through the
handles of the suitcases, and with each of us holding one end
of the stick, we reached the first cluster of houses in Goclawek.
I was utterly exhausted and Zosia was half dead. At last we
beheld the loop of the tram track and . . . a squad of gendarmes with their dogs, waiting at the tram stop. Fortunately
we were just in front of a little shop, so we hastily went in and,
ordering lemonade, we were able at last to take a little rest.

After about a quarter of an hour, the gendarmes departed
by the first tram, and we took the next one. When we reached
the hide-out, Joey was waiting for us; he made us comfortable
on a couch, served refreshments, and was altogether sympathetic. A message from London was also waiting for us, to
the effect that a final reply concerning the sound broadcast
would be sent within two days.

In the evening of the following day I went to Grochow
with the intention of remaining at the station all night. I
reached the hide-out in nice time, just before curfew, and in
the darkened room I found Joey and Stanislaw, who made
everything ready in case London should want to record the
sound programme at once. The telegraphic transmitter was
also ready. Joey switched on the large transmitter to test its

audibility, which took only a few seconds and involved no great risk. Stanislaw signalled the call and London replied that audibility was 3-4, or very good; then, without waiting to be told that we were ready to receive, the London operator proceeded to transmit messages. Stanislaw could do nothing but take them down. Messages flooded in as if the London telegraphist wanted to get rid of all arrears at once. Stanislaw had to repeat various signals intermittently, and we were all furious that London should have imposed this work on us in a hide-out reserved for sound broadcasting, instead of transmitting everything to Wladek and the new telegraphist, Martin.

The flood of messages came to an end at last, and we had to think what to do next. The regular listening hour was fixed for 7 a.m. and we decided to wait, hoping that London would perhaps be ready for the sound broadcast. We had to wait three hours, which we spent dozing in our chairs; then at 7 a.m. Stanislaw called up London to enquire about the sound programme. At that very moment the bell rang, and a few seconds later Zosia, whom we were expecting, rushed into the room. To our dismay, she announced:

'Three cars are converging on you. One is only a hundred yards away, while the other two are in the neighbouring streets.'

We looked at each other in consternation, and our first urge was to run for it. But we could not abandon the station. I had a sudden inspiration and called to Stanislaw:

'Send a message in international code that we shall resume the transmission in half an hour's time.'

Stanislaw understood, pressed the key, and repeated three times the signal familiar to every telegraphist in the world. I guessed that since the gendarmes, who were certainly waiting nearby, had not been let loose yet, we had not been pinpointed with sufficient precision. And if our pursuers heard that we intended to resume in half an hour's time, they would wait quietly until then, in order to complete their measurements prior to striking.

London confirmed reception of the signals and repeated them. Stanislaw tore the earphones off, rapidly dismantled the apparatus, and put his hat on; but I motioned him to wait and entered the lavatory giving on to the street. I looked through the little window and at no great distance I noticed in the sandy roadway a German saloon car. I withdrew at once and gave my decision:

'Zosia and Stanislaw will leave first. You will walk calmly like two people on their way to work.'

Stanislaw, glad to be going, left with Zosia, while I returned to the lavatory to observe their departure; from there I saw them walk along quietly, like two unconcerned passers-by, chatting all the while. I heaved a sigh of relief when they passed the car without being stopped. The transmitter was already packed up and Joey, together with his chum, carried the parts, the ciphers, and messages into the courtyard and then into the nearby ruins. I felt greatly relieved and experienced an upsurge of new energy. Joey must have felt the same, for he started joking, as was his way, and tempted me:

'Let's take the revolvers and pass close to them. We ought to see what they look like.'

I agreed, rather rashly, and after checking the revolvers, with our hands in our pockets, ready for anything, we emerged from the front door and advanced towards the stationary car in the roadway. As we passed it I glanced inside; in addition to the driver I could see two civilians sitting in the rear smoking cigars. One of them had earphones on his lap, a sure sign that our ruse had worked. They would be waiting, looking at their watches, for half an hour; until we were supposed to resume our work. We walked on for another twenty yards and turned into a side-street, where we passed another car, from which we were closely observed by its German occupants. We walked in the direction of Grochowska Street. Joey was laughing like mad.

'Aren't they idiots?' he exclaimed. 'How we've bamboozled them! They will sit there like fools without even suspecting that their quarry has vanished.'

As we approached Grochowska Street, we saw in the distance Stanislaw and Zosia looking in our direction. Suddenly Zosia pointed to something behind us, and then they both disappeared round the corner. We looked over our shoulders and saw the car we had just passed driving in our direction. Joey and I turned into a side-street, ran to the next corner, turned again, ran on, turned another corner, and rushed into a house, leaping up the stairs to the top floor, where we waited, holding revolvers at the ready. All ears, we panted with exhaustion and perspired from top to toe. The house was quiet, except for the distant hum of a motor-car. It passed the house and went on. Listening in dead silence, we heard the hum recede and then increase again; and now growl threateningly close. Joey whispered:

'It's cruising nearby, searching for us.'

When the car seemed to have finally departed, for good, I said to Joey:

'Now let's run for it before they alert the gendarmes.'

We emerged into the street, firmly grasping the revolvers in our pockets, each with the safety catch off. Making our way through side-streets, we headed for Praga and Kierbedz Bridge. On the roadway I noticed numerous tracks of motor-car tyres and pointed them out to Joey.

'They were cruising all night, getting our bearings, the scum. They wanted to come right up to our door, but missed it,' he said.

We passed Szembek Square at a reasonable distance, and in it we noticed the car that had chased us. Joey was again his old self.

'They can wait there till the crack of doom,' he said. 'Shall we have another look at them?'

I was furious with myself for having agreed to our act of bravado after having bolted from the station. Joey was entitled to such youthful recklessness, but I ought never to have agreed to anything so foolish.

I was also anxious about Zosia and Stanislaw, though Joey was sure they had escaped safely. As the drag-net had not been thrown out immediately, he was certain they would have reached home without trouble.

And so it turned out; when I reached home, Zosia was there waiting for me, with a message decoded a minute previously. It read:

'Are you ready with the sound broadcast? British Radio is overworked and it is only thanks to our intervention with the Minister of Information that we have been able to obtain half an hour. Let us know the time.'

The Broadcast from Skolimow

I called the whole team together, and after explaining the exertions we had been making, I read them the message from London. The effect was devastating; everyone cursed London. It was some time before tempers cooled and we were able to survey the new situation. I posed the straight question:

'Are you willing to try the sound broadcast once again?'

'Any time,' declared Joey.

Stanislaw took a little longer to make up his mind.

'I've really had enough of it,' he said, 'but we've put so much effort into it that it would be a pity to quit. But have you got a suitable hide-out?'

'If you are all willing to go on with it, I shall find a place. I have already got one in view.'

Several days later I went with Joey to Skolimow, to inspect the premises which an underground worker and his girl contact, Bura, were putting at our disposal. Joey thought the hide-out would do, and so the usual treadmill was put into operation. I assisted Zosia, Helena and Bura to get the heavy suitcases on to the Wilanow Railway at the Belvedere Street stop. There was a terrific crush of shouting and jostling people, with masses of luggage crowding the entrances to the carriages. Here and there uniformed Germans were leisurely making for the compartments marked 'Nur Für Deutsche.' Our girls managed to get in somehow and the train departed.

Together with Joey, I soon fixed the day and the hour for our sound broadcast, and we advised London accordingly. As it was already September, Joey came to the conclusion that the best results would be obtained in the morning hours, so we chose 7 a.m. for the first attempt.

All of us, except Stanislaw, met in Skolimow on the eve of the appointed day. The little timbered house stood in a wood, on the outskirts of the housing estate. We entered it by a shaky wooden staircase fixed to the outside wall, and found ourselves in a spacious, shabbily furnished room, with a verandah on one side and a loft under the eaves on the other. After a frugal dinner, we lay down on mattresses placed on the floor; at dawn we all got up. Joey assembled the transmitter and started tuning it in. All of a sudden the brilliant mercury vapour rectifiers went out and the apparatus was dead. Joey tried to discover what had happened, but could find no defects. It occurred to him to try the lamp suspended from the ceiling: there was no light. Though anxious, we thought that it was only a fuse; but when Joey went to find out, he came back with the sad news that the current had been cut off. We could do nothing about that.

Stanislaw, who never liked to do anything in a hurry, arrived at this juncture. When we told him what had happened, he waved his hand disparagingly and sat down without saying a word.

After a wait of about half an hour the lamp lit up, and we all jumped as if the electric current had passed through ourselves. As it was nearly 7 a.m., we had to hurry. Joey put the finishing touches to the preparations; Zosia and I muttered the texts we were to read. This time, in addition to my own speech, addressed to the armed forces and our fellow-countrymen abroad, Zosia was to make an appeal in English to the women of Britain and America, requesting help for struggling Poland. We were all old war horses by now, but on this occasion we were seized with excitement and full of hope. I sent Bura out as an observer, and although I did not expect a surprise, for the hide-out had not been used before, I placed four revolvers on the table. Punctually at 7 a.m. Stanislaw called up London and received the immediate reply:

'We can hear you four plus. We are ready to record the programme. Over to you and begin.'

Our excitement mounted. Stanislaw went on transmitting the signal preceding the programme and then stopped. Joey switched in the microphone and I began to read my address. Joey, with the earphones on, controlled my voice, and seizing my head with both hands placed it at the proper distance from the microphone. I could not wholly overcome my stage fright and my voice trembled with emotion, though I was trying to speak clearly and not too loudly. When I had finished, Zosia followed at once. Her voice sounded very clear. While she was speaking, Joey took me aside and whispered: 'During your speech the current suddenly weakened. Someone in the house must have switched on the kitchen stove.'

'Of course! It's breakfast time,' I answered, worried lest the failure of the current should spoil the transmission. When Zosia had finished, Stanislaw immediately tuned in to London, and looking over his shoulder I could see him scribbling down: 'OK', 'OK'. This was our reward, and we all rejoiced at the success of our first sound broadcast. Stanislaw went on taking down a coded message, Joey read the figures out as they were being pencilled, and I held the code in my hand, dictating to Zosia the decoded text. We were shaking with emotion as, word by word, the message came through:

'Congratulations. The major part of the programme successfully recorded. Full message to follow.'

We rejoiced like children, even at this partial success; but we had to remember that the greatest danger was only just beginning. The Germans had apparently been taken by surprise and had had no time to jam the transmission, but there could be no doubt that the listening posts had heard us and located our station. I anticipated that within half an hour Skolimow would be raided. I recalled Bura from her observation post, but found that she had not noticed anything suspicious. We dismantled the station, packed everything into suitcases, concealed them in the loft, and after another check of the immediate neighbourhood, I put the four revolvers under the floor-boards. Since the Germans had not caught us during the transmission, it was better for us to leave without carrying anything incriminating, for once we were a hundred yards away from the house we could pretend to be casual passers-by. Bura, too, advised us not to take anything with us, and when Joey was looking round for his new overcoat, she promised to bring it to Warsaw the next day. Joey however was determined to take the overcoat with him and he found it in the loft.

We left the house in pairs and returned to Warsaw, one

group taking the road through Grojec, the other through Konstancin. Neither in Skolimow, nor on the way back did we notice anything disturbing. We were as happy as larks; with this dangerous experience behind us, we hardly paid any attention to the gendarmes, who were on the train and at all the stations. The two groups joined up again in a café in Pulawska Street, where we celebrated the occasion with pastries and ice-creams, in which Joey beat all his previous records.

In the afternoon we received a message from London:

'Can you telegraph the unrecorded part of the speech? We shall then be able to reconstruct the whole and broadcast the programme through scores of Allied stations.'

Needless to say, I complied with the request.

The Transmitter disappears!

The following day, I went to meet Bura in Chalubinski Street, to make arrangements for the transportation of the transmitter back to Warsaw. I spotted her from a distance, hurrying in my direction. No sooner had she reached me, when she began:

'The station's lost. I saved myself by a miracle. During the night the Germans arrived in several motor-cars, surrounded the house, and banged at my door. I escaped down the pillar supporting the verandah and escaped in my night-dress. How could you do this to me? What shall I do now?'

She went on for some time, complaining bitterly, while I was so shaken by the news that I was hardly able to question her.

'Has anyone been caught? Have they taken the people living on the ground floor?'

'No, they left them alone, but I had to escape as I was. I've lost everything I had, and it's all your fault.'

'I am very sorry and you may count on our help. But are you sure they have removed the station? It was well hidden away.'

'I have already been back, and I found that the station and all my things had been removed. Except that I didn't know

where you had hidden the revolvers, so I couldn't check that.'
'I hid them under the floor-boards, to the right of the door.'
There was something about Bura's account and behaviour
that I did not like. I looked at her closely, and noticed that
she had on the same dress as she had worn on the day of the
broadcast; yet she was trying to tell me that she had escaped
in her night-dress and lost all her belongings. Moreover, she
was pretending she had been back to her home, when every
child in Warsaw knew that after discovering one of the underground's hide-outs the Germans kept it under close observation for days, and even weeks. The whole thing smelled
badly. I asked Bura for more details, which embarrassed her
visibly, and I soon found her contradicting herself. Then I
remembered the episode of Joey's overcoat; he had hung it
on a hook in the room and found it concealed in the loft. In a
flash I concluded that it was not the Germans, but Bura herself who had stolen the transmitter. Noticing my growing
suspicions, Bura waded on, with the utmost effrontery:
'You failed to take any precautionary measures, so that I
had to call up my own people to keep watch during the
transmission.'
'What people?'
'My friends.'
'Who gave you permission to do that? How dare you let
your friends into the secret without my knowledge? Who are
these people?'
At this moment Zosia and Stanislaw arrived, and I seized
the opportunity to ask Bura to repeat her story in full detail
in their presence. This she did and concluded:
'I can see you don't believe me. Perhaps you will be convinced when I tell you that they knew you, for as they were
coming up the stairs they talked about a tall, fair-haired man
and a freckled woman!'
It was true that Zosia had freckles, but it was obvious that
the remarks alleged to have been overheard were nonsensical.
Bura had lost her head and was talking nonsense. I asked
Stanislaw:
'What do you make of this story?'
Stanislaw was almost foaming at the mouth.

'It's a pack of lies,' he shouted. 'Does she think she can take us in with all these stupidities? We are too old hands for that! Out with the truth, woman, or you'll get it in the neck!'

Zosia, perhaps because of the freckles, could hardly contain herself:

'You're a common pickpocket! You thief!'

Bura became hysterical.

'You have no right to disbelieve me. I nearly got killed through you, and you dare to suspect me!'

By that time I realised that we were all shouting in a public thoroughfare, and that German soldiers passing by on the way to and from their nearby barracks were eyeing us; so I put an end to the scene.

'I shall investigate the matter and I shall see you afterwards,' I said.

We left Bura in tears, but noticed that she was joined by a young man.

'Look,' said Stanislaw, 'that's her accomplice. What a hag, what a rotten hag. She didn't think out her story well enough, and finding us too tough for her, got herself entangled in it. I am sure it was her, and her friends who were supposed to guard us, that have stolen the transmitter.'

I suddenly remembered that they had not found the revolvers, and that I had been rash enough to tell Bura where they were hidden. We were all very angry, till Stanislaw said:

'Perhaps it's as well that junk has been lost. I always had a feeling that sooner or later sound transmission would be our undoing.'

On the following day I sent two parachute commandos to Skolimow, to take stock of the situation there. They were both young men with their heads screwed on the right way; they had been parachuted into Poland some time before, with many adventures and German corpses to their credit. They soon cleared the matter up. It turned out that after the sound transmission had ended, Bura had remained in her apartment; she disappeared only after her row with me. They talked to the tenants on the ground floor, pretending to be police agents, and the tenants stated that during the night, after we had left, two motor-cars arrived; the men were very young, spoke Polish, and remained for several hours in Bura's apartment, drinking and shouting. Bura was with them all the time, and left with them when they raided a nearby villa in which some rich Jews were hiding, whom they robbed of everything. It was not the Germans, therefore, who liquidated the first underground broadcasting station, but a criminal gang.

I was determined to find Bura, as I could not let her get away with it. I informed her superior in the underground movement of her conduct, but he lost all contact with her, and our searches remained unsuccessful.

Years later, after the Warsaw Rising, I went to Komorow to meet the former Government emissary, Vogel. Turning into a fenced-off road I found myself unexpectedly face to face with Bura. She nearly collapsed at the sight of me and had to hold on to the fence to remain erect. I must have given her a fright, for she was trembling all over. I had a good look at her and went on without saying a word. I had no time for her. Judging from her appearance, she was going to become a mother within a few weeks.

The Raid in Czeska Street

We were now searching frantically for a new hide-out, for in addition to routine messages we had to communicate to London the missing parts of the broadcast speech. During this search I chanced on another piece of the Polish tragedy. One night, assisted by Zosia, I was fixing the aerial across the garden surrounding a villa in Zakopane Street, on the Saxon Island. Although the hour was late, by the light of the moon I noticed a woman approaching.

'How are you my dears? Don't be afraid, I can keep secrets,' she whispered.

On looking closer, we recognised her to be a woman we knew, Mrs. U. We also knew the dreadful tragedy that had befallen her entire family, and we had been worried lately because of the lack of any information about her. Mrs. U. had the misfortune to have an ancestor who was a Jew, which was sufficient reason for any German to murder her with impunity. She was in hiding in the villa we had been offered as a hide-out for our radio station. We chatted on a bench in the garden, while Stanislaw was at work. We talked about mutual friends, our conversation following the already established pattern: murdered, lost without trace, caught, executed. . . . I decided not to use the villa again, lest we might attract the Germans to it.

We succeeded in finding another hide-out on Saxon Island, in Czeska Street. Wladek operated the transmitter, and as conditions were favourable, he sent out one message after another with great speed. He worked well and London asked for no repetitions. Together with our host we watched the neighbourhood from the windows and from the terrace, but without noticing anything suspicious. A few minutes before curfew, I left with Zosia to continue as look-outs for the rest of the night from another hide-out in the next street; in case of emergency we were to warn Wladek by telephone. We crossed the garden, keeping a sharp look-out. We noticed that the traffic in the streets was quite normal, with a few passers-by hurrying to reach their homes before curfew.

When we reached the observation hide-out we took up our positions at the windows. Zosia kept an eye on the Miedzeszyn Dam, while I watched down Francuska Street. Some time later, a motor-car appeared on the Dam, pulled up, and switched off its headlights. At almost the same time other motor-cars drove into Czeska and Gallant Streets and switched off their headlights. There was not a moment to lose. Zosia rushed to the telephone and dialled the number. When our host answered, she said to him naggingly:

'You really must finish the rubber now. It's late and you will be tired out to-morrow morning.'

'We have just finished. Good-night,' the voice replied, and hung up the receiver.

We put out the lights, and by opening a window slightly, we could observe feverish activities on the part of the Germans, who were driving up and down Czeska and Gallant Streets. In the still night we could hear their guttural voices. It was obvious that they had located the station before curfew, and when the curfew hour struck they had come in their cars to complete the pin-pointing process undisturbed; for they knew that our look-outs in the streets would have been withdrawn, and no one would be watching what they were doing. If anyone left a house after curfew it could only be an escaping operator of an underground radio station.

With bated breath we observed the Germans' activity for nearly two hours. We had no means of finding out if they had discovered the hide-out. I risked another telephone call, but heard only the 'engaged' signal. What was the meaning of that? Were they talking to someone else on the telephone? If so, the Germans could not have raided the station, because if they had, we would have heard a stranger's voice speaking. But it could have been the Germans reporting their discovery of a radio station. Our anxiety grew when, after another hour, Zosia tried again and found that the telephone was still engaged. At last 'the motor-cars departed and everything was quiet once more, except that we could hear the sound of motor-cars crossing Poniatowski Bridge. We lay down fully dressed, waiting for what the morning would reveal. At about 7 a.m. Zosia 'phoned again and, greatly relieved, heard the voice of our host:

'I am feeling well and I shall be with you presently.'

Within a few minutes we were welcoming him as one who had had a miraculous escape. With a wave of his hand he bade us listen, and reported:

'Soon after you two left, I noticed from the terrace a number of converging motor-cars. Wladek dismantled the transmitter immediately and put it into a suitcase. The Germans cordoned off the exits from our street and proceeded to search one house after another, gradually getting nearer to us. I was scared to death and Wladek too. I told him to throw the transmitter out of the back window into a patch of potatoes in the garden. Though his teeth were chattering with fright, he refused; because it was the only apparatus in working order, after the other stations had failed us. He would not destroy the last available station. I must say he is a brave boy and did well not to listen to me. We concealed the suitcase with the transmitter in a container full of sand for extinguishing incendiary bombs—you will have the trouble of cleaning it up.

I also disconnected the telephone, because I was afraid you might 'phone again and attract the attention of the Germans, who were searching the house next door already. We sat there like two criminals about to die, waiting for the executioner's axe to fall. And would you believe it, the Germans ended their search in the very next house to ours, and departed. There are several entrances in our block, each with a separate number-plate. The number-plate of the house in which I live is very small, almost flush with that at the other entrance, and I think the Germans failed to notice it. Or it may be just luck. Perhaps fate has not decreed our end yet.'

About a year later, I was relating the incident to an underground worker whom we used to call Heimor, because when we first met him he suffered from an inflammation of the Heimor duct. He jumped up from his chair.

'Ah, it was you!' he exclaimed. 'Just imagine! That very evening I had visited friends in Czeska Street for a game of bridge, and was to spend the night with them. All of a sudden, there was a terrific banging at the door and a number of German gendarmes came in, followed by some Germans in mufti. They turned everything upside down, the beds, the wardrobes, divans; they looked into the pots in the kitchen and tapped all the walls, the ceiling and the floor. They were not specially interested in the people present. We could not make out what they were after; but now I know.'

The Transmission is killed

We succeeded at long last in transmitting to London the unrecorded portions of the broadcast, and we waited day after day to hear British stations re-broadcasting it. Instead, we received the following message:

'We have contacted the Government Plenipotentiary and the Commander-in-Chief of the Home Army to find out if they agree that your programme should be re-broadcast by a score of Allied stations. We are waiting for their replies.'

The message did not worry me, for the Government Plenipotentiary, Professor Jan Piekalkiewicz, who succeeded Ratajski, had seen my speech beforehand and had no objections; in fact he regarded the whole undertaking as very useful. At my next weekly meeting with the Plenipotentiary, I asked him if he had made a decision yet. The Plenipotentiary was pleased to tell me:

'I replied to General Sikorski that I not only approve of the re-broadcast but insist that it should take place. See to it that the message is sent right away.'

'I shall send it as an urgent message. And do you know what the Commander of the Home Army thinks about it?'

'I don't know, but what can he do? I shall ask him at the first opportunity, but I have no doubt that he has agreed.'

It came as a complete surprise, therefore, when I learned that General Grot-Rowecki intended to oppose the broadcast. In my anxiety, I asked him for an appointment, and when we met, I asked General Rowecki:

'Would you tell me, Commander, what decision you have made with regard to the re-broadcast of our programme?'

'How do you know that I have to make a decision in a matter which you have kept such a secret from me?'

'I kept it a secret because I did not know if it was going to succeed, and I am asking you because I have received a telegram stating that the broadcast depends on your approval, and that of the Government Plenipotentiary. Has he spoken to you about it?'

'He has not; but that is immaterial, as I have already sent a negative reply. My Chief of Radio Liaison categorically opposes the broadcast, which can only infuriate the Germans and provoke them into pursuing us with redoubled energy and thus destroy our stations.'

'General, I know something of your liaison. The Germans have already destroyed over a dozen of your stations; they know such stations operate and they already pursue them remorselessly. The broadcast cannot worsen the position, because on that sector the Germans are already acting to the very limits of their ability.'

The conversation went on for some time, and I put forward every possible argument to convince the General. I thought I had succeeded, for he said in conclusion:

'Perhaps you are right. But you must understand that I cannot go against the opinion of my Chief of Liaison in matters with which I am not familiar myself and, moreover, I cannot alter a decision I have made and already communicated to the Commander-in-Chief without any new circumstances having arisen and, as it were, solely on the basis of your own arguments. I am sorry it has happened this way, but now it is too late to do anything.'

And that is how the transmission was killed. The Germans were not able to prevent it; but envy on the part of our own countrymen killed it. I need not describe the reactions of our team, except to say that my vocabulary of invective during those stormy days became enriched by many new and ingenious expressions which I had not known before.

In the end, our broadcast was transmitted by a foreign station; but that was nearly a year after we had made it in Skolimow, and we did not know anything about it at the time. We only heard about it at the end of the war.

CHAPTER III

Underground Courts of Justice

A New Appointment

As a result of an understanding between General Rowecki and the 'Triangle' I joined the General Staff of the Union for Armed Struggle, which subsequently became known as the Home Army, to distinguish it from the Polish Armed Forces fighting in the West. I met General Rowecki to discuss my new functions with him. General Rowecki, looking extremely well and, as usual, smiling and friendly, came straight to the point:

'I should like to ask you to give me a straight and sincere answer to one question only. If for any reason you are unable to give it, I shall not mind at all. Well?'

'Put your question, General; I shall try to answer it in the way you wish.'

'The question is simple. I know your Party has delegated you to be its representative in the High Command so that you can be in a position to see what we are doing. Because of this I should like to know whether you wish to be in the Command as a kind of observer, or whether you would also like to have a definite function?'

Rowecki looked me straight in the eye, although he was slightly embarrassed. I always like to know where I stand, and as I had been thinking the matter over myself, I answered without a moment's hesitation:

'All I have to say, Commander, is that if you won't give me a definite function I shan't accept a purely titular or fictitious office; I would rather return to underground work in the Party. I want a definite function in the Command; I want work, I don't want to be a watchdog.'

Rowecki was greatly pleased and pressed my hand warmly. 'I am glad you put the matter like that. I shall talk to the Chief of Staff, and we'll find something that will suit you.'

Several weeks later, I was appointed the Commander-in-Chief's Plenipotentiary for matters of Civil Resistance, with which the Political Consultative Committee had dealt from its very inception. It included resistance to the German occupiers in every department of our national life, in all parts of the country, and by every available means. The resistance was to be passive (by undermining the decrees and rights of the occupying power) and active (by such deeds as the liquidation of Gestapo agents; in other words, armed resistance). Civil Resistance was to embrace not only the underground organisations but the whole Polish nation.

The Commission meets

The most immediately urgent matter that had to be dealt with was the drafting of the rules to be observed by every individual Pole living under the occupation. There were many unforseen questions, such as whether it was permissible to work in a factory whose management had been taken over by the Germans, or how to act when a German importuned a Pole with social invitations, or whether a Pole was free to enter a restaurant reserved for Germans, etc. The Commander-in-Chief had already appointed a team to draft the rules, and when I was appointed the Commander's Plenipotentiary, I assumed the chairmanship of this Commission and was invited to attend its meeting. On entering a smoke-filled room in Rakowiecka Street, I found ten people there waiting for me, which I did not like at all. Several slip-ups had already occurred because of meetings attended by too many people, and I well remembered a reception at Easter, 1940, given by a member of the Government Plenipotentiary's office for several dozen of his friends in the underground. On that occasion the large number of people was utterly unconspiratorial, and the subsequent arrest of one of them exposed all the others to the danger of being implicated.

I was introduced, by my pseudonym of course, by a functionary of the Office of Information and Propaganda and by one of the leaders of the Democratic Party, the technologist Makowiecki, known by the pseudonym of Malicki. I surveyed the company and discovered that apart from Malicki I only knew one other person. I addressed the meeting on the subject of the Commission's tasks, while the members, including one woman, sat around me in a circle. In conclusion I said rather acidly that in future we should not be meeting in such large numbers, as this was contrary to all the principles of conspiracy, and that the work in hand would be allotted to separate teams, each of three people. I could see that many of those present were pleased with this, though Malicki himself was somewhat embarrassed. As I took my leave and shook hands all round, an elderly gentleman, whom I knew, took me aside and whispered:

'I am glad you have put an end to these mass meetings.'

The old gentleman with thick spectacles, who later became the Government Plenipotentiary and deputy Prime Minister Jan Stanislaw Jankowski, was at that time an ordinary member of the underground; in 1945 he was one of the sixteen Polish leaders who were lured to Moscow, arrested, put on trial on trumped-up charges, and sentenced to eight years' imprisonment.

The Rules Governing Civil Resistance

The Commission drafted and issued rules for every section of the population, such as farmers, workers, industrialists, civil servants, clergymen, doctors, lawyers, judges, railwaymen, women, young people, etc. The basic instructions were to offer resistance to the occupying authorities always and everywhere, to remain intransigent, to sabotage all decrees and laws likely to harm the Polish nation or profit the Germans, a categorical prohibition against registering as 'Volksdeutsche', prohibition of all intercourse with the Germans and, finally, the duty of obedience to the underground authorities. In addition, the rules included definite instructions for particular professions, such as instructions to doctors, permitting them to issue false certificates if this would help a Pole to avoid forced labour for the Germans; to judges, that on principle they should not send cases from Polish to German Courts, etc. These rules were supplemented from time to time by appeals or instructions issued by Civil Resistance whenever it was necessary to deal with problems arising under the occupation.

Civil Resistance was particularly concerned with the protection of labour. During the second half of 1942, appeals to employers were issued demanding that they should seize every opportunity to raise the wages of their employees, and requesting them to find extra-legal means for increasing their earnings. The appeal demanded that every employer should look after the interests of his employees as if they were his own, and prohibited the basing of the profitability of undertakings on wage tariffs imposed by the German occupation authorities. It prohibited the use of German decrees that infringed the rights of the workers as one of the meanest methods of exploiting war conditions in order to get rich quickly. A separate prohibition was imposed on participation in the recruitment of workers for labour in Germany, and all employers were forbidden to select workers for deportation.

Further requests and instructions were issued concerning such matters as the boycotting of certain premises, boycotting the collecting of ski-boots, of the Polish-language newspapers published by the Germans (which, it should be stated, were the only legal source of information), of cinemas, and of lotteries run by the occupation authorities, etc. A special appeal was issued requesting the population to record all German crimes and to deposit the records with the underground authorities.

A separate series of decrees was issued concerning the sabotage of compulsory labour for the occupiers, such as the construction service (Baudienst), the departure of juvenile workers of both sexes for labour in Germany, etc. Finally, a warning was issued to functionaries of the Polish Blue Police and officials of the German Labour Board not to take part in mass round-ups for the deportation of people to Germany as forced labour.

Additional measures were enacted for sabotaging all kinds of compulsory deliveries, of grain, meat, dairy produce, etc., and for suppressing drunkeness, liquidating illicit stills, etc.

All such decrees were distributed by means of the underground press and through all underground organisations collaborating with Civil Resistance throughout the country; they told the Polish people what the underground authorities expected of them, and as the great majority were willing, the decrees were universally observed.

An exception to the applicability of the decrees was made in the western provinces, which had been incorporated into the Reich, because of the mass colonisation of these provinces by German settlers, and because of the extraordinary terror to which all Poles in that part of the country were subjected. The conditions prevailing in these provinces were so different that only certain of the principles of Civil Resistance, those concerning so-called 'petty sabotage', such as slowing down work in the factories and the wasteful use of raw materials, could be observed. It proved impossible to carry out in the western provinces all the underground activities conducted in the Government General.

Manifesto of the Government Plenipotentiary

In the meantime, the Government Plenipotentiary appointed me to be his own plenipotentiary for matters of Civil Resistance, which thereby became the joint responsibility of both the Government Plenipotentiary and the Union for Armed Struggle. When Civil Resistance became fully developed as an effective instrument in the struggle against the occupying Power, the scope and functions of the Directorate of Civil Resistance were officially defined. The Directorate consisted of the Chief of Civil Resistance and his staff. A special manifesto, signed by the Government Plenipotentiary, at that time Professor Jan Piekalkiewicz, informed the Polish people of the newly established underground authority, the Directorate of Civil Resistance (DCR); it defined its tasks, and concluded with the appeal: 'I summon the nation to observe unreservedly all the decrees, declarations and appeals of the Directorate of Civil Resistance.'

A Talk with Leon Nowodworski

As soon as the code of the Rights and Duties of Loyal Poles and Citizens had been distributed throughout the country, the Directorate of Civil Resistance proceeded to fortify it by an executive arm. Its purpose was not so much to ensure the observance of the instructions issued by the DCR, which in view of the unyielding attitude of the Polish people would have been unnecessary, as to prevent its infringement by unscrupulous individuals. For this purpose special Underground Courts of Justice were to be set up.

There was already a Department of Justice attached to the office of the Government Plenipotentiary, which by its nature was the proper authority to deal with this matter. The Department of Justice was headed by the Dean of the Warsaw Bar, Leon Nowodworski, whom I visited in order to discuss the matter. We met somewhere in Wspólna or Buxom Street, and when I arrived I found Nowodworski waiting for me in a study furnished with red velvet chairs and curtains, with tall tables bearing flower vases, and a couch with a curiously curved back, all of which to-day remains in my memory as something distant and exceedingly pleasant.

I had a good look at Nowodworski; for I had not seen him since 1938, when, following the election to the Bar of a number of new members from the Peasant and Socialist list, which included myself, he had made a demonstration of protest by leaving the Council. Our past relationship, therefore, was not one to promote an amicable atmosphere for our present conversation; but we were now under enemy occupation, which, if it did not wipe out past conflicts, suspended them for the duration of war.

I explained to Nowodworski the purpose of my visit and described to him the principles on which the functioning of the Underground Courts was to be based. Even while I was speaking I could see from the expression on Nowodworski's face that he did not like the idea, and we were soon involved in heated arguments. He agreed that it was necessary to punish traitors, but some of the suggestions offended the sense of legality of that distinguished jurist, and he was quite outspoken about it.

'I cannot conceive a situation,' he said, 'in which an individual should be sentenced to death without being heard, and yet you have just said that it is likely that the majority of sentences will be passed *in absentia*.'

'Mr. Dean,' I replied, 'we are in a state of war with Germany; in the face of the special emergency in which we find ourselves the natural objections of a lawyer must be overruled. Our proposals provide for the death penalty only in cases of high treason, in fact only in the case of those Polish citizens who become German agents; principally agents of the Gestapo. Do you think it possible to summon an agent of the Gestapo to attend a hearing of the Underground Court of Justice?'

'That would be nonsensical,' Nowodworski retorted. 'But in my opinion even the most extreme measures could be applied to them without recourse to Underground Courts of Justice.'

Here the Dean of the Warsaw Bar put his finger on the crux of the matter; but as it had been the subject of my prolonged conversations with the Government Plenipotentiary and the Commander of the UAS I was well prepared to advance a contrary argument.

'Don't you think,' I said, 'that many more "legal murders" would be committed if they were to be promulgated by administrative decrees without hearings, than if the death sentence were to be passed by an Underground Court of Justice, presided over by a trained Judge or professional lawyer, after an examination of the evidence in accordance with the usual Court procedure, and after hearing Counsel for the Defence, appointed *ex officio?*'

'Perhaps you are right,' Nowodworski answered, without conviction. 'If the Government Plenipotentiary should instruct me to organise such Courts, I shall obey the instruction. But I must say that it would be against my inclination.'

In my Department the work is being done with a view to the future, the organisation of the future judiciary in liberated Poland. If I may be allowed to make a suggestion, I would rather see the Directorate of Civil Resistance take the organisation of special courts of justice in hand, especially as it is obvious that you gentlemen are only interested in the present struggle and not in the future of the judiciary. However, I shall be glad to help in the drafting of regulations, instructions, etc.'

Further talks confirmed the impression that Nowodworski was dubious about the Underground Courts of Justice, whereupon the Government Plenipotentiary and the Commander of the Home Army entrusted the task to Civil Resistance, stipulating at the same time that the Home Army was to set up separate military Courts of Justice for members of the armed forces.

A Meeting with Bukowiecki

Notwithstanding the decision made by the Plenipotentiary and by the Commander-in-Chief, my talk with Nowodworski somewhat damped my enthusiasm for this particular task. However, after a few weeks I received unexpected support, which dispelled all my lingering doubts. In my search for a President for the first special Court of Justice, set up in Warsaw, I called on the President of the Procurator General's Office, Bukowiecki, who lived in Mokotow at the time. I had myself once worked in that office, and ever since I had had the highest regard and admiration for Bukowiecki. I am sure that everyone who ever met this extraordinary man, whose integrity was of the highest, shared my feelings. He was an eminent lawyer and exerted great moral authority, which was enhanced still further after he became blind.

He received me in a modestly furnished room equipped with two large bookcases, and not only remembered me but also enquired after my brother Stanislaw, for whom, as he said, he had high regard as an exceptionally able advocate. Turning his unseeing eyes on me, he told me that he had been warned that the subject of our talk and my name must remain secret, which condition he promised to observe, and with old-world courtesy asked me what he could do to help.

I explained my errand to him in great detail, without attempting to gloss over the dubious aspects of the problem, and ended by inviting him to accept the office of President of the Court in Warsaw. As I went on unfolding the matter, I noticed that Bukowiecki's face became slightly flushed, and that he was being overcome by some emotion. When I had finished, he thought it over aloud, analysing with the utmost gravity everything I had told him. He first expressed his deepest gratitude to the underground authorities for the honour of having offered him such a responsible office. I could see that he was genuinely grateful not to be regarded as a useless old man whose lot it was to linger on to the end of his days, but as a man still capable of taking part in the struggle, and of serving the country in an exposed position. However, he declined the offer.

'God in His mercy knows that I am not thinking of the miserable remnant of life that remains to me. I would gladly offer it to my country. But I am blind, and even under normal conditions I could not pass judgment on a man. How much more difficult would it be to do so where the judge has to bear much greater responsibilities. That cannot be undertaken by a man afflicted as I am, but only by one in the full vigour of his spiritual and physical strength. Besides, I cannot move about without a guide. A blind old man led by a guide to a meeting of the Underground Court of Justice might easily attract the attention of the Gestapo. However, if the underground authorities attach any importance to my opinions, I beg you to tell those concerned that, having considered the pros and cons of the matter, I am of opinion that the setting up of Underground Courts of Justice is right, because they are necessary. And to conclude; as I see it, almost the entire responsibility will rest on the Judges. You must therefore choose them with the utmost care. The kind of men you select will determine the kind of Courts you will have. May God guide and bless their labours!'

While speaking of the underground struggle, the disasters that had befallen the country, and its future liberation, he was carried away by his patriotic emotions and spoke like one inspired. I had never seen Bukowiecki in such a mood before. I was deeply moved by the other-worldly expression on the face of that imposing man, who, like Rataj in 1939, unfolded before me a vision of struggle and liberation. Though I parted from him empty-handed, I was convinced that he was right, that I should never have made such a proposal to him, but should have recognised myself that a blind man could not possibly preside over an Underground Court of Justice. Nevertheless, I carried away with me Bukowiecki's blessings on the idea.

Special Courts of Justice

Eventually, after several months of effort, special Underground Courts of Justice were set up in Poland, and towards the end of the German occupation there were about ten of them.

The original legal basis for the setting up of such Courts had been furnished long before by the following resolution of the Inter-Ministerial Committee for Home Affairs, passed in London on April 16, 1940:

'Special Courts are competent to pass sentences on oppressors, traitors, spies and *agents provocateurs. . . .*' The Courts were guided in their work by the Polish Penal Code and by the decrees of the competent underground authorities, especially of the Directorate of Civil Resistance. Most frequently applied were Articles 99-113 of the Penal Code of 1932, and special statutory laws concerning espionage.

As far as the procedure before special Courts was concerned, the principles applied were based on the Penal Code procedure, and defined by the Court itself. The bench consisted of three judges, of whom the presiding magistrate was as a rule a professional Judge, or a lawyer with the qualifications of a judge. The indictment was presented by a Public Prosecutor, and a Counsel for the Defence took part *ex officio*. The hearings could take place without the presence of the accused. Everything the Court regarded as material evidence was admitted. The evidence consisted of depositions of witnesses, reports of the underground authorities, photographs, documents, etc. There were three kinds of verdict: not guilty, remission of the case to the proper court after the war, and capital punishment. No appeal from the sentence of the Court was provided for, but each sentence had to be approved by the District Government Plenipotentiary. Should the Plenipotentiary refuse his endorsement, the case had to be reopened, or postponed until after the war.

However, in exceptionally urgent cases, in which no doubts arose and every delay—especially in the endorsement of the sentence—involved immediate and great danger, the District Director of Civil Resistance was empowered to order the execution of the person from whom the danger threatened, without waiting for the verdict. In such cases, after the execution had been carried out, the case went to a special Court, which dealt with it according to normal procedure. Should the Court arrive at a verdict of 'not guilty', the District Director of Civil Resistance could be prosecuted for abuse of authority. I remember only one case in which a special Court passed sentence of death after the accused had already been executed. The bailiff of a village was shot dead on his way to Gestapo headquarters with a list of members of the underground in his village. He had been threatening to do so for a long time, and he had finally blurted out when he was going two or three days beforehand. There was no time to apply to the Court. On his body was found a detailed list, which, together with the depositions of witnesses, was admitted as evidence of guilt in a subsequent hearing of the case.

As may be seen from this summary description, made from memory, of the procedure of the special Courts of Justice, everything depended on the unrestricted judgment of the Court, which, as President Bukowiecki and the Directorate of Civil Resistance anticipated, had to bear exceptional responsibility. To-day it may be said with complete certainty that not one of the judicial benches ever failed in its duty. They were composed of men with the very highest moral and professional qualifications. As proof of the circumspection with which sentences were passed, it may be said that about 90 per cent of the cases, all in which there was even the slightest doubt, were postponed until after the war; while the remaining 10 per cent—which involved about 200 executions in the whole country—were never questioned at the end of the war, when the cases and the personnel of the Directorate of Civil Resistance became publicly known. It was five years after my escape from Poland, which took place on November 5, 1947, that the Communist regime launched a campaign against the former Courts of Justice, of which more will be said in the following pages.

The Implementation of Sentences

When a sentence had been approved by the competent District Plenipotentiary, it was returned to the District Director of Civil Resistance, who then handed it over to the so-called Executive. The latter consisted of members of his own detachment, or men detailed by underground organisations collaborating with Civil Resistance. The Executive was divided into two teams, of which one had the task of making preparations for the execution of the sentence, and the other of carrying it out. The first, which included women, kept close watch over the condemned individual, and by ascertaining every detail of his daily life chose the most appropriate occasion for the execution of the sentence. Once this had been done, the matter was taken in hand by the execution team, which, however, was not bound by the opinion of the first team but was empowered to select, on the basis of the report submitted by the preparation team, a more suitable occasion.

The team carrying out the sentence consisted as a rule of three men. One did the shooting while the other two covered him, no matter whether the execution was carried out at home, where the cover had to terrorise the household, or in the street, where the Germans might have interfered. The execution team never bothered about the behaviour of passers-by. On the whole the latter, especially in Warsaw, realising that the underground was striking, hurried on, pretending not to have noticed anything. If circumstances permitted, the executioners read out to the condemned the sentence, which always began with the formula: 'In the name of the Polish Republic. . . .' This was usually possible when the execution was being carried out in a house, and even in the street the executioner was frequently able to pronounce the first words of that solemn formula.

The team carrying out the sentence was usually composed of young men. In such actions it was forbidden to employ boy scouts, as agreed between the Civil Resistance and the Command of the Grey Ranks, or women, or juveniles. On the other hand, the recommendation was issued that a man who had already taken part in carrying out three sentences should be relieved from duty in the second team. The Directorate of Civil Resistance considered that the killing of a man produced a great psychological shock in the executioner, a shock to which he ought not to be exposed too often; and, moreover, the Directorate desired to prevent the emergence of a professional group of killers.

The teams of the Warsaw executive sometimes undertook collective actions for special tasks. Their leader, Ambrosia, for example, organised a bold expedition against the John the Divine Hospital, to which the Germans sent sick prisoners from the Pawiak prison. The armed raid succeeded and the prisoners were liberated. However, Ambrosia could not provide any help for them after they had escaped, and they ran straight from their sick-beds into the street. He told me afterwards with admiring approval that the passers-by, guessing what was happening, offered their overcoats to the fleeing prisoners to hide their striped prison uniform. A similar armed raid on the same hospital was carried out later on by the Home Army.

During the Warsaw Rising the local Executive formed the backbone of the company defending Emilia Plater Street. One day, during the final stage of the Rising, the Warsaw Director of Civil Resistance came to me at my headquarters in Raven Street and on behalf of the Company commander invited me to dinner. I accepted the invitation gladly, as I wanted to meet the men whose work I knew so much about, but whom I had not met before, except for Ambrosia himself. The next day, the Director came to fetch me, and after a spurt across Marshall Avenue, which was already under enemy fire, we wound through a maze of underground passages. Masses of people were crouching in the cellars everywhere, trying to find shelter from the continuous bombardment from the air and from artillery and mortars, dubbed by our men 'the roaring cows' because of the characteristic sound they emitted on being fired. We made our way through the masses of poor, dirty and hungry people crowding the dark corridors of the vaults, which were lit only here and there by a candle or a paraffin lamp. The catacombs of the early Christians must have looked like this. Along the vaults and corridors, connected by openings made in the walls, one could pass from one end of the city, held by the insurgents, to the other. Bedding and blankets were everywhere, with an occasional bedstead in a corner occupied by several of the 'cave dwellers'. This was the name given to those who were psychologically incapable of venturing out into the open, which for them was full of great dangers; for weeks on end they never emerged from the underground vaults into daylight. They suffered many more fatal casualties in the cellars than those who studied the plan the Germans were adopting in their systematic bombardment of the city, and who had the strength and courage to move into another place when it became obvious that their building would be bombarded next.

We passed close to the stores in Buxom Street, where the miserable remaining stock of provisions was jealously guarded by the local command, and where an oil engine hummed uninterruptedly, operating a pump drawing water from an old well. To my astonishment, we emerged unexpectedly from the dark underground passage into a sunlit garden, full of shrubs and trees that were still green. Instinctively, I stopped at this enchanting sight. Green trees and patches of lawn presented an extraordinary picture to one accustomed to the rubble and dust of the inner city. Here the sounds of explosions were muted, or perhaps I refused to hear them amidst the charms of this retreat. However, time pressed and we descended again into the maze of meandering passages, to end our wanderings in the St. Joseph Hospital.

Here, in the middle of a barrack-like hubbub, was the smiling Ambrosia, neatly shaved and dressed up in an assortment of military garments.

Formal presentations followed, with clicking of heels and firm handshakes. I found around me young, weather-beaten and gaunt faces, looking at me with curiosity. We again descended into a vault and crossing an underground passage under Emilia Plater Street we reached a house on the opposite side. Here, another surprise awaited me. The windows were intact, the doors could be opened and closed, and the furniture was altogether comfortable.

'By what miracle has this house escaped destruction?' I asked Ambrosia.

'The miracle is simple,' Ambrosia answered. 'This is the only building in our hands on this side of Emilia Plater Street, which is the front line. The Germans are on three sides of us. They are here, behind this wall. That's why they don't bombard us, because with the least error they would hit their own people. This is the quietest place remaining in our hands.'

The dinner promised to be interesting. The presence of Germans behind a brick wall only 18 inches thick was something that impressed even our blunted nerves. But very soon I forgot all about our neighbours, absorbed in the consumption of a horse steak fried in onions, the flavour of which could not entirely overcome the rather high smell of the meat. I did not let that interfere with my appetite, but proceeded to devour a large number of talc-fried pancakes, supported by a cup of coffee. After a long spell of feeding on boiled wheat this was a real feast for my hungry stomach. To round it all off, there was also a bottle of illicit alcohol, whose blue colour made me rather suspicious, without cause as it turned out. During the dinner the atmosphere was as spirited as in any officers' mess. People were addressing each other as lieutenants or captains. The lowest rank was that of sergeant, the highest, a colonel. I was astonished to discover that this rank was held by the metropolitan Director of Civil Resistance, and though I felt a mere nobody in this company, I asked the Director in which formation he served.

'In the Corps of State Security,' he answered with the utmost gravity, as if it had been the General Staff and not a future police force.

The post-prandial talk lasted for several hours. I enquired what actions they had taken part in, what impressions they had received, and what opinions they had formed; while they wanted to know everything concerning politics, the Government in London, the fortunes of the Rising, and the future in store for us. It was a typical war-time talk with all its natural ingredients—death and heroism, sufferings, disappointments and grumblings, uncertainties, sorrows and disillusionments. I listened and observed my table companions. In nothing they said about their unenviable function as executioners of the sentences was there a note of cynicism, boasting or swagger. On the contrary, their words testified to their sense of having discharged a hard and painful duty. It was right that they should have felt as they did. I left the company greatly contented at having met them, at having had an ample dinner, at having had that impressive experience. And when on top of it all, the company cobbler delivered me my newly soled boots—I sat at the table in my socks—nothing could have disturbed my contentment on that day.

The First Death Sentences

The first two death sentences were carried out in Warsaw at about the same time. The first to be shot was a lieutenant of the Blue Police, Roman Leon Swiecicki, who was condemned for the part he played in the German Police Court, which sentenced many Poles to death. Apart from reliable evidence, the facts were generally known. The case was clear and Swiecicki richly deserved the punishment he received. As far as I remember, the Executive's investigations established that Swiecicki used to leave his home on Saxon Isle every morning and cross over to the Washington Roundabout, where he boarded a tram-car, which took him to his office. He was killed by several revolver bullets. Both the executor of the sentence and his cover withdrew without difficulty, although the incident was observed by many people waiting for the tram.

The other condemned man was Isadore Ossowski, an official of the German Labour Board, situated in the former building of the Agricultural Mortgage Bank at the corner of Mazowiecka Street and Malachowski Square. He was employed in the department dealing with Poles who avoided deportation to Germany as forced labour, whom he pursued with exceptional zeal and for the most venal motives. According to my report to the Government in London of June 9, 1943, there were 12,600 people in Warsaw alone whom the German police were seeking as guilty of that crime. Ossowski was shot dead in his home. When the sentence was read to him, he fell on his knees, begging for mercy; which could not be shown to him.

In order to keep the Polish people informed of the activities of the Underground Courts of Justice, and to frighten persons infringing the Civil Resistance regulations, the Directorate resolved to give the greatest possible publicity to the execution of the sentences. In addition to an announcement broadcast by the BBC from London, which was being listened to secretly throughout the whole country, and in addition to a special communiqué of the Directorate of Civil Resistance, published in the underground press, the death sentences were placarded in Warsaw, the place of their execution. It was a difficult undertaking. Large red posters were printed, the contents of which began with the words: 'In the Name of the Polish Republic . . .' and ended with the signature 'Directorate of Civil Resistance'. In appropriate forensic style and observing the formulas used by Polish State Courts announcing sentences for criminal offences, the posters brought to the public notice that, on such and such a day, the special Court, having tried the cases of Swiecicki and Ossowski on such and such a charge, found both of them guilty of having committed crimes under articles so and so, and sentenced them to death. The sentences of the Court were carried out by shooting on such and such a day.

For the task of sticking up the posters about two hundred people were mobilised from among the members of underground organisations within Civil Resistance, including the boy scout underground, known as the Grey Ranks. The City was divided into districts, each of which was allotted to a separate group. The most difficult part of the undertaking was the actual placarding, which could only be done during the night, when a strict curfew was in force, and when any person found in the streets without a permit would be arrested. It was not unusual after curfew for gendarmes to shoot down anybody they recognised as a Pole. In short, the placarding was done at the risk of death, all the more so as possession of a placard would have been sufficient proof of guilt.

The action was carried out with the utmost efficiency; the city was placarded with two thousand red posters, and not one of our men was captured. This took place during the night of March 4, 1943, though the sentences were passed much earlier.

Next morning, as soon as curfew was over, I left the residential wing of the Warsaw Polytechnic, where my wife and I were hiding in the apartment of Cesia, the widow of the former professor and Minister of Public Works, Broniewski, who herself became one of our most devoted underground workers. I decided to do a round of Warsaw by bicycle to see how the work had been carried out. No sooner had I started when I noticed at the corner of Basket Street a group of people standing in front of a kiosk reading a large red poster. I stopped and approached them. They stood there in silence, their eyes fixed on the poster. I wish I could describe the glances and smiles they exchanged before moving on. Under the German occupation people learned to make themselves understood by exchanging glances. Their language consisted of a quick look, a wink, a side glance, the raising of eyebrows; and on this occasion I could read in their eyes pleasure and approval at what the poster announced.

I rode on, and everywhere I observed similar scenes. Groups of people reading silently and dispersing with an expression of satisfaction on their faces. In the suburbs of Praga and Wola, the poorly dressed public went so far as to comment loudly on the cases. I could hear such remarks as, 'They deserved it', 'Every spy should get a bullet in his head', or 'Look, we have our own courts already'.

Within two hours, by the time I was returning from my

round of the City, the position had already changed. I encountered squads of gendarmes or Blue Police everywhere, acting on what was obviously a uniform order, for their procedure was the same on each occasion. They rode up to the reading public silently on their bicycles, seized one or two people, and ordered them to tear down the posters. The Germans apparently wanted the posters to be destroyed by Polish hands.

During the course of the day the posters were thus torn down in the central parts of the city, but not before thousands of people had read them; and the whole capital was seething with excitement. In the suburbs the posters remained on the walls much longer. Several years afterwards, in 1947, I was going up the footway stairs of Poniatowski Bridge. On turning from one flight of stairs to another, I beheld on the wall a shred of red poster with the words, 'In the Name of the Polish Republic. . .' on it. I am not usually given to easy emotion, but I felt my heart warm at the sight of that veteran of Civil Resistance still holding to its post after the lapse of four years.

Further Sentences

The third sentence of death was passed on Frank Rutkowski, a foreman in Warsaw's municipal waterworks, a notorious agent of the Gestapo, who boasted about it before the other workers, blackmailing and terrorising them mercilessly. The sentence was carried out on March 18, 1943, by two parachutists who came from England and joined the Executive of Civil Resistance. One of them was Philip, famed for his courage and recklessness, a young man of gigantic proportions, who on one occasion arrived at a street rendezvous with me in the uniform of a German stormtrooper, with several revolvers dangling from his belt. I told him off, for I felt as if I was in a pillory when passers-by, hearing us talking in Polish, looked at us with contempt and hatred. The other was a shy and pleasant youngster from the Peasant Youth Organisation, 'Wici'. Philip reported the details of the execution to me:

'The observer team tipped us off that Rutkowski was directing the construction of some sewers in distant Grochow. We hired a cab to go there and on the way we decided on a ruse. I had on me a forged identity card of a Gestapo agent, with my own photograph on it. I took Rutkowski aside, showed him the card, and told him that his chief wanted to see him urgently, and that we had come to fetch him. Without a moment's hesitation Rutkowski got into the cab. During the drive I told him that we had to make an arrest on our way back and that we might need his help. He again agreed without hesitation. As we were driving along in the cab, he grumbled that although he was working so hard, he could not get his children accepted in a German school. That was more than we could stand, so as soon as we reached a desolate spot, we stopped the cab, pulled out revolvers and read the sentence to him from a sheet of paper. He fell on his knees, cried and begged, but. . . .' and without concluding Philip pulled an imaginary trigger with his finger.

'Did you have any trouble afterwards?' I asked him.

'None,' he said, 'except that when the cabby saw what had happened he whipped up and drove off as fast as the horses would take him. We ran after him, as we wanted to pay him well for his trouble in driving us so far, but we would have needed a motor-car to overtake him.'

Below is a selection of other cases, which I am listing not because I relish detailing these grim and sombre memories, but to give the reader an idea of the nature of the crimes for which the death penalty was exacted.

The Special Court in Cracow: Michael Klimonczuk, sentenced to death for betraying to the German police several people who had escaped a round-up for forced labour in Germany. Execution took place on April 2, 1943. Karol Bielicki, a Blue policeman, for killing a Pole and for subservience to the Germans. Executed May 2, 1943. Frank Bubny, commissioner in the village of Dobczyce, for giving away to the Germans the location of a secret store of arms. Executed on June 5, 1943. Walenty Pawlik, Walenty Dec, Wanda and Slavomir Madrad, confidential agents of the

Gestapo, who were instrumental in causing the arrest and death of numerous Poles.

The Special Court in Warsaw: Severyn Wegorzewski, of the Municipal Tramway Company, for causing the arrest of several tramwaymen. Executed on May 1, 1943.

No sentence of death was ever passed on a Pole for having registered as a 'Volksdeutsche'. The reason for this leniency was that the problem was more complicated than it appeared on the surface. Roughly speaking, the problem bore different aspects in the various provinces of Poland. The Silesians, for instance, at the very beginning of the German occupation and in sheer self-defence, decided to register as Volksdeutsche, which in my opinion did not affect their patriotism and devotion to Poland. In Pomerania, from which district large numbers were deported to the Government General, the remainder of the population were compulsorily registered as German, and all men of military age were conscripted into the German Army. The same occurred in Posnania. These soldiers by compulsion eventually deserted from the German army and joined the ranks of the Second Polish Corps in Italy. It was only in the Government General that the Poles were not compelled to register as Germans, and cases of defection were extremely rare. The special courts never dealt with such cases.

Private justice

In the circumstances prevailing under German occupation, there were inevitably some cases of people taking justice into their own hands. They sometimes pretended to act on behalf of the Directorate of Civil Resistance, which forced me to issue a manifesto against the felonious misuse of the name of the underground organisation. At a later stage, when the Directorate of the so-called Underground Resistance (cryptonym 'Khedive'; the diversionist organisation of the Home Army), was merged with the DCR and a Directorate of Underground Struggle, headed by the Commander-in-Chief of the Home Army, was formed, of which I was a member, an additional proclamation against personal justice was issued on September 15, 1943. The proclamation pointed out that all sentences of the Underground Courts were being published in the underground press, so that they could be distinguished from cases of abuse.

There were certain cases of individuals who had been shot dead before the Special Courts were established, and such cases have never been clarified. One such case was that of the well-known film actor Igo Sym, who registered as a Volksdeutsche and became an official of the German Propaganda office for the Warsaw District. Despite the fact that he was trying to help some of his former colleagues in the theatre, which the latter always emphasised in his favour, he was shot by a person unknown to the Directorate of Civil Resistance. No doubt he deserved punishment. Knowing the practice and the code of the Underground Courts of Justice, I have no doubt that he would have been sentenced to death if he had still been alive when the Courts were set up, and if he had continued his activities. He was too well known as an actor and his treason caused too much harm for his case to be postponed until after the war.

An undoubted case of rough private justice was that of the well-known physician, Dr. Wiczynski, and also that of the famous actor, Junosza-Stepowski. They were both shot dead at a time when the Underground Courts of Justice were already functioning, and both were killed for having social intercourse with the Germans. They were punished much too severely, for that offence was within the competence of another judicial body and the special Underground Courts of Justice were not concerned with it. Junosza himself considered the punishment unmerited. After being mortally wounded he was alleged to have said:

'I am guilty, but I have been punished too severely.'

According to general opinion he maintained social relations with the Germans because of his wife, who was engaged in the risky operation of ransoming prisoners.

Judicial Commissions of Civil Resistance

Lesser offences were usually dealt with by the Judicial Commission of Civil Resistance, consisting of three Polish citizens of irreproachable character. They were really Courts of Honour and were empowered to pass sentences of infamy, censure and reprimand. The degree of harm done to Polish interests and the social standing of the defendant determined which of the three sentences was applied. Sentences of infamy and censure were published in the underground press, while reprimands were delivered to the condemned in writing. The following instances, in which well-known public figures were involved, illustrate the offences committed and the penalties imposed:

The actors Samborski, Kondrat, Plucinski and Chodakowski were sentenced to infamy for acting in a German film slandering Poland.

The conductor Dolzycki was sentenced to infamy for servility to the Germans.

The actor Dymsza and the actresses Perzanowska and Malicka were censured for maintaining social relations with the Germans.

The actors mentioned in the first instance acted in a German film as Poles maltreating Germans. The film included scenes in which the Polish police manhandled Germans. In addition to those sentenced, the Germans tried to engage a number of other actors, who, however, knew how to excuse themselves, thereby proving that it was possible to do so.

The case of Dolzycki was at the time notorious in Warsaw. Before the war he had been a conductor of the Warsaw Philharmonic. When Poland was occupied by the Germans he pretended to be a Ukrainian and flirted with them, without however going so far as to force the underground authorities to intervene; which they were particularly reluctant to do since Dolzycki was able to restore the Warsaw Philharmonic Orchestra and by organising concerts in the vast café Lardelli at the corner of Polna and Oleandry, enabled its members to make a living. This was the only cultural activity allowed by the Germans, and even then the works of Chopin, Moniuszko and other Polish composers were prohibited. The huge hall was always full; the Germans among the audience usually occupied the front seats and behaved themselves decently.

However, rumours began to circulate that Dolzycki was trying to get into the good graces of the Germans. Proofs were forthcoming that he was giving private concerts at the residence of Governor General Fischer. Finally, before the start of a concert, he allowed himself to address the Germans in the audience; speaking in German, he said that the day marked the 25th anniversary of his career as a conductor, and that it gave him special pleasure to inform his German guests that the first concert he ever conducted was in Berlin. The Germans applauded vociferously, while the Poles in the audience kept silent. This was the last straw, and Dolzycki was condemned to infamy; which meant that his concerts were thenceforward boycotted by the Polish public.

The cases of Malicka and Dymsza caused a great deal of bad blood in Warsaw. The two artists, whom the capital had given everything, success, fame and wealth, repaid it with base ingratitude. Malicka entered into intimate relations with a German officer, while Dymsza took part in drunken bouts with the Gestapo and entertained them in his residence, never suspecting that each orgy was being registered by members of the Civil Resistance living in the neighbourhood. He was also seen on several occasions driving in a cab in the company of Germans. He was severely reprimanded, which damaged his career after the war. After the occupation of Poland by the Soviet Army, he was not allowed to appear on the Warsaw stage, and when he appeared in Lodz his name was omitted from the programme. It was not long, however, before Dymsza joined the Communist Party and engaged in party activities, whereupon his past misdeeds were—at least for the time being—forgotten.

The majority of cases concerned the prohibited intercourse with the Germans, but there were also other forms of improper behaviour constituting punishable offences, such as frequenting a German Gambling Casino in Warsaw, attending the German theatre or cinemas in that city, etc.

Cases of Collaboration

The Cracow centre of the General Welfare Council, with

its President, Count Adam Ronikier, was by the very nature of its activities exposed to the danger of political collaboration with the Germans, who, from time to time, attempted to use the Council for their own purposes, especially to extort obedience from the Polish population for the preservation of public order in the country. Ronikier maintained contact with the underground authorities, and having been warned, controlled his political ambitions and his desire to play a bigger part than that of President of the Welfare Council, and shunned the slippery path of political collaboration; for, as he himself was reputed to have said: 'If I am going to be shot, I prefer to be shot by the Germans than by Poles'. As a result, the General Welfare Council kept within the bounds of charitable activities throughout the German occupation.

In 1940, considerable notoriety was given to the sorry case of Ferdinand Goetel, a well-known writer, who was accused of collaborating with the propaganda department of the Warsaw district by trying to persuade writers to register with that department and to obey its decrees. His case was postponed until after the war, mainly because he had ceased such activities by the time the Underground Courts of Justice were established, and did no further harm.

However, Goetel came into the limelight once again, after the Germans discovered the mass graves of Poles murdered in the Katyn forest. The Germans flew a delegation to Katyn to view the graves, and among the members of the delegation were Goetel, Emil Skiwski and the Reverend Trzeciak. The facts were given considerable publicity by the German-controlled press, and the underground took it as additional proof of Goetel's close relations with the Germans.

Emil Skiwski, mentioned above, and the astronomer Feliks Burdecki collaborated with the German publishing firm, 'Polish Editions', founded by the wife of the chief of propaganda for the Warsaw District, Ohlenbusch, and they edited a German propaganda periodical in the Polish language, 'Przelom'. For this activity they were condemned by the underground and attacked by the underground press; however, I do not remember if their case was considered by a special Court of Justice and I do not know if they were sentenced.

The last case of collaboration worth mentioning here is that of Josef Mackiewicz, a contributor to the German Polish-language daily published in Wilno, 'The Daily Courier'. One of the editors of the 'Courier', Ancerewicz, was shot dead by sentence of the Underground Court; and, if my memory serves me right, Mackiewicz, was also condemned by the court and the sentence published during the winter 1942/43 in 'Niepodleglosc' (Independence), the organ of the Wilno District Home Army. I should be glad if anyone of the Wilno underground would amplify my incomplete information and clarify the matter finally.

It may be asked why I have disinterred these sorry facts, which might otherwise be forgotten? I do it simply because I cannot bear to think that matters for which men and women of the Underground Courts of Justice risked their lives and often perished should ever be forgotten; nor should I like it to be thought that public opinion could be disregarded at a time when the country was suffering under the terrors of occupation.

Flogging and Hair-cutting

Apart from procedure initiated before the special Courts of Justice and before the Judiciary Commissions, there was a third method, which in the absence of a better description I would call administrative procedure, the penalties of which were flogging and hair-cutting. The latter punishment was applied to women consorting with Germans. Such penalties were applied when the case was not serious enough to be dealt with by the special Courts, and in which such punishment as infamy or censure would not act as a deterrent. The consideration of each case and the imposition of punishment were entrusted to local leaders of Civil Resistance, who were guided by instructions from higher authorities. Punishment by flogging was usually applied in the villages, for such offences as attendance at a German festival, the cutting down of timber in State forests, for misappropriation of Polish property, etc. Fortunately, such cases were extremely rare, and so was the application of punishment by flogging.

However, I remember a case in which both punishments were applied. It concerned one of the little theatres in Warsaw devoted to the muse of obscenity rather than to serious art. It was generally known that the German Department of Propaganda was deliberately lowering standards in such little theatres, in order to deprave young people in Poland. The underground authorities tolerated the little theatres for the simple reason that they provided a possible livelihood for the large number of actors who had come to Warsaw from most of the other cities. However, the underground authorities required the managers and producers of such theatres to oppose German instructions, aimed systematically at the lowering of the repertory. The appropriate department of Civil Resistance was in regular contact with the celebrated actor Stefan Jaracz, who invariably conducted himself as a great Polish patriot. He was uncompromising, and advised actors to give up theatrical work. The actress Perzanowska took the opposite view; but the overwhelming majority of actors, especially those from the Jaracz School, followed their master; they boycotted the theatre and earned their living as waiters or messengers.

In the case in question, both the manager and the producer not only disregarded the instructions of Civil Resistance, but showed an excessive zeal in carrying out German requests. I do not remember why the Warsaw authorities of Civil Resistance chose to impose the punishment of flogging and hair-shaving instead of referring the case to the Judiciary Commission, but I know that the carrying out of this punishment required a great deal of organisation and involved considerable risk; for the carrying out of such punishments was more difficult than the execution of a death sentence, since the culprits would subsequently be able to report to the police.

On the selected day, just when the rehearsal was about to begin, a dozen or so armed men invaded the little theatre. They secured all exits and windows, and several of them made for the stage. From among the terrified actors they called forth the culprits; and after reading them a complete list of their offences, they administered, in the full glare of the footlights, the prescribed number of strokes to one of them, and shaved off the other's hair. The executors of the sentence, with a lawyer at their head, conducted themselves with great dignity. News of this punishment spread throughout the theatre world and ensured obedience to the decrees of the underground.

A Warsaw Show Trial

During the second half of 1951, there was held in Warsaw a show trial of Pajor, Ojrzynski, Nienaltowski and Czystowski, during which the Communist prosecutor attacked the Civil Resistance authorities and the special courts which existed under the German occupation. According to 'Zycie Warszawy' for December 14, 1951, the indictment stated *inter alia:*

'In order to restrain the growing struggle for national liberation, the Government Plenipotentiary appointed the so-called Directorate of Civil Resistance, with Stefan Korbonski as its head. . . . Within the DCR in the capital city of Warsaw, there acted a number of experienced intelligence agents detailed for the DCR, among them Lechowicz, the accused Nienaltowski, and others. According to instructions issued by the chief plenipotentiary of the DCR, Korbonski, the principal task of the DCR was the search for leaders of the Left wing and their trial by a specially organised court, the CSC (Civilian Special Court).'

During the trial the following dialogue took place between the witness Kurczewski and the Communist Prosecutor:

Witness Kurczewski: 'The Directorate of Civil Resistance was appointed by the Government Plenipotentiary in Poland at the request of the London Polish Government. The machinery of Civil Resistance was directed against the Communist sector, against the Left.'

The Prosecutor: 'How did the Directorate of Civil Resistance discharge its task of combating the Left?'

Witness Kurczewski: 'By identifying certain persons of the Left and liquidating them.'

The Prosecutor: 'What was to happen to the persons against whom sentences were passed?'

Witness Kurczewski: 'These persons were condemned to death; they were to be executed, and were in fact subsequently executed.'

Another witness, Zborowski, deposed as follows:

'The Directorate of Civil Resistance organised in 1942 was officially directed against criminal elements. However, that was only a cover, behind which was organised the struggle against Left elements, grouped in the Communist Party and kindred organisations. The head of Civil Resistance was Stefan Korbonski, who used the pseudonym Zielinski.'

I do not think it is worthwhile to reply to these depositions, which were extorted from the witnesses by the Security Police, but I think it desirable to unmask the Communist lies. The Communist regime and its Ministry of Public Security knew from the very outset of their activities that Underground Courts of Justice had existed under the German occupation, and that special courts had functioned. To dispel all possible doubts on that score, I would mention that long before my escape from Poland, I myself described in broad outline the activities of the Underground Courts of Justice in the organ of the Peasant Party, 'Gazeta Ludowa', for July 28—August 3, 1946, Nos. 205-211. The Communist censor deleted not one word from my articles; and after they were published no objections were raised either by the Communist press or by the Communist Party against the activities of these Courts. This would undoubtedly have occurred if, for instance, the family of any one of those executed had protested to the Ministry of Public Security that the sentence of death was imposed for political reasons, in the struggle against Communists, etc. Opportunities for such a political murder were unlimited, and the fact that not a single case of that nature occurred is proof that the sentences were indeed passed for the crimes described in their contents, principally for high treason, that they were just, and that neither the Communist Party nor the Ministry of Public Security found anything objectionable in the activities of the special courts. It was only after the Communists launched their slanderous campaign against the underground, and after a series of trials directed against the underground Party organisations, the Government Plenipotentiary and the Home Army, that Civil Resistance and its special courts were attacked. Nothing, however, can alter the fact that Polish public opinion regarded the Underground Courts of Justice as what indeed they were, the legal organs of justice of the Polish Underground State, empowered to promulgate sentences 'In the Name of the Polish Republic'.

CHAPTER IV

Efforts to Maintain Liaison

The Workshop in Muranowska Street

Joey was for a long time without a place of his own to live in and without a workshop. We searched for the right hideout, but without success. In the end, Stanislaw persuaded a woman in Muranowska Street to agree to offer a room in her apartment as a workshop. The woman was queer, but safe, and made no difficulties over Joey's taking possession of a room on the first floor giving on to Muranow Square. The Street was divided by a wall, behind which extended the Jewish ghetto. From the window we could occasionally see what was going on in that hell and our hatred for the Germans turned into a grim passion. But all we could do was to send out messages to London describing the horrors of the ghetto. We gradually transported all the required materials to Muranowska Street, and Joey again took up the construction of new apparatus. The transport of every parcel involved great nervous strain because one had to pass close to several Latvian sentries, in black uniforms and steel helmets, who formed a cordon around the ghetto and shot at sight anyone who tried to get out of it, or, on the Aryan side, anyone who approached the wall too closely. Fortunately they were not interested in us, because their duties did not extend to the control of passers-by. Nevertheless, it was rather unpleasant to walk past them.

I had an opportunity to become acquainted with the landlady of the apartment, which was roomy, but neglected and filthy. The landlady was a woman of middle age, lean, chain-smoking, lively and chatty. I soon found out that she was also a reckless desperado, but full of courage and ardent patriotism. All these qualities were mixed up in her in strange proportions. No sooner had I been introduced to her when she overwhelmed me with her eloquence.

'Don't bother to tell me who you are, because I know. I can tell you I am up to my ears in the underground movement myself, and I have wide connections. My husband is a high-ranking officer in General Sikorski's army, you know,' she said, spilling cigarette ash on my knees and fixing her deep eyes on me. She flung at me masses of information and confidential confessions. The slight smell of vodka confirmed my suspicion that she had imbibed too much. As I subsequently discovered, our hostess was chronically tipsy, and as Joey put it 'moved in low gear'. As she had referred to her husband as a General, we thenceforward called her Mrs. General.

One day Joey confided to me with appreciation:

'Our Mrs. General is a real Herod in skirts. She is trading in illicit vodka, you know, and that's why she is always drunk. But what's even more interesting, she is hiding some Jews in her backroom.'

'Oh, that's bad,' I moaned. 'Too many forbidden affairs under one roof. It's as bad as at Wladek's in Lesna Podkowa.'

'But that's not all. She is also being visited by some warders from the Pawiak prison, and drinks with them. I think she must be a go-between in sending messages to the prisoners.'

I listened with genuine admiration, but did not conceal my anxiety. Mrs. General was active in too many directions at once and inviting trouble. We decided, therefore, that for the time being Joey should remain where he was, as we had no other place to fall back on, but that we would look for a more secure hide-out.

This dangerous situation was resolved only after some months. I was about to leave for a birthday party, to which I had very much been looking forward as a relaxation from our daily worries. Before leaving, however, I wanted to make sure that everything was in proper order, and called on Joey. I found him rather depressed.

'I am glad you've come,' he said, 'Mrs. General has told me

that someone's blackmailing her; but let her tell you the story herself.'

He brought Mrs. General in, and after she had seated herself comfortably and lit a cigarette, she said:

'There's a bum living in this house with his family. No one knows what he does or how he makes his living, and the tenants are all wary of him. He has always been courteous with me, for I know how to handle people. But he came to see me yesterday and said, "I know what you are hiding in your apartment, and what that tall youngster is doing there. I am a good Pole and I shall keep my mouth shut, but my wife is very ill and I have no money to pay for her treatment. I need five thousand zlotys, and I think you will lend them to me." You know, I swore that there was nothing illegal in my house, and that I hadn't got five thousand zlotys. But that bum told me to think it over, and promised to come to-morrow for an answer.'

I disliked the story distinctly. Mrs. General did not seem at all scared, and I could see that she was expecting me to pull out five thousand zlotys and give them to her. All sorts of suspicions ran through my mind, but they all boiled down to the conclusion that we had to decamp at once. I was sure that even if I had given her the five thousand zlotys, this would not have been the end, and that the blackmailer—whoever he was—would have been encouraged to ask for more. So I said to Joey:

'Pack up the quartz, the more valuable valves, the photocell and the instruments. I shall take them with me. We'll leave the remaining stuff for the time being, but in a few days we'll remove everything. Get your things and let's go.'

My quick decision made a profound impression on Mrs. General.

'Don't get so excited,' she said. 'There's no need for all this haste. I'll talk to that bum and perhaps he'll accept less. There's ample time, for he won't rush straight to the Gestapo.'

'We cannot take any risks,' I answered. 'But we should like to reserve the apartment for future use; please keep it for us.'

We picked up the parcels and said good-bye to Mrs.

General, who was visibly embarrassed. As we carried the parcels to the tram stop Joey muttered that there was something wrong about it all.

'Did you see any other way out of the situation?' I asked him.

'No,' he answered angrily, 'one can never be sure in such company, and it's safer to move out.'

We parted. Once again Joey went searching for a hide-out for the night with one of his chums, while I, carrying the parcels and a revolver, boarded a tram and went to the birthday party. But I was worried, and that evening, amidst the merry company, I was not a welcome guest.

The Workshop in Marshall Street

I was lucky enough to find a hide-out in a large tenement house in Marshall Street, close to the Union of Lublin Square. Joey was given a large room with a huge window overlooking the Mokotov Field. The furniture was truly Spartan and consisted of a large table, an iron bedstead and two chairs. The room was soon littered with equipment, as Joey liked to have everything handy, and we only kept a reserve store in the dry vaults of the Polytechnic. Joey introduced a novel signalling system by pushing a pin through the door frame. When the head of the pin was pressed, a buzzer sounded in Joey's room. He never replied to the doorbell.

Soon the workshop was producing new apparatus, and we had to make new purchases of equipment. We succeeded in purchasing a motor-driven generator, which we deposited in a hide-out in the Old City. I had to provide against the emergency of finding ourselves in an area of fighting, without any current from the grid. We then took up our old hobby, sound broadcasting, as I had succeeded in acquiring a transmitter valve with a power of one kilowatt, and Joey went ahead with the construction of a new station. Moreover, he got hold of a sound recorder, and I made plans to broadcast a programme of speeches, recorded on discs, by the Government Plenipotentiary and the Commander of the Home Army. We were spurred on by the thought of our colleagues in London and how impressed they would be when we offered them another test in sound broadcasting.

I secured a new hide-out in Mokotowska Street, which we liked very much; and we particularly liked the people who offered it to us. They were gradually all drawn into our work, especially young Jadzia, a seamstress by trade, who worked very hard to keep her aged parents and her younger brother, Bolek, still at school. They were all simple, pleasant and good people. An odd situation was liable to arise in that apartment, for in one room Jadzia might be fitting a customer with a new gown, while in another Wladek would be sending out messages to London.

It so happened that at about this time we unexpectedly came into possession of the first transmitters dropped by parachute from Polish and Allied planes. I went one day, accompanied by Joey, to the distribution point for parachute drops in Buxom Street, to collect a promised parcel of quartzes, which were always in short supply. There we met several people collecting parcels, and the functionary who was distributing them was in a great hurry, as he had to be out of the hide-out by 2 p.m. He was expecting someone and was obviously embarrassed. He turned to me, saying:

'I was expecting someone who was to collect two radio transmitters. It's now 2 p.m. and I've got to close this room at once, because some lodgers who are not initiated are due to return at that time. What am I to do with the transmitters? I don't know where to hide them.' I exchanged glances with Joey and made a suggestion:

'If you don't know where to hide them, we could take them to our place.'

He hesitated for a moment and then said:

'All right, take them. If there is a row about it, the man who failed to collect them will be responsible.'

Joey and I both checked our revolvers, wrapped the two radio transmitters in newspapers, and hurried away, to avoid the risk of an encounter with the man who was supposed to collect them. And as we were thus in possession of them, I later succeeded in persuading the authorities to allow us to keep the two transmitters for good.

Soon equipment was dropped in such quantities that we had no difficulty in obtaining additional transmitters; these had an advantage over the home-made ones in that they were very small, and everything, the transmitter, the receiver, transformers, etc., was neatly packed in a metal box. We dubbed these new transmitters 'Nelka', while the operators called them 'pipstaks'. After we had tested one of them, we remembered with pride that we had been operating on Joey's home-made stations for nearly two years.

Joey was an inexhaustible source of new schemes and ideas. One day he told me that in his spare time he had constructed two-way radio-telephonic apparatus for ultra short waves. He kept one at his place, while I took the other to my hide-out at the Polytechnic. In the evening, we made a test, and found we were able to talk to each other, though it was not easy. However, I soon put a stop to such an extravagance, for I would not accept Joey's assurances that we were talking on such short waves that the German listening posts would not be able to pick them up.

The first case of arrest

I was no longer able to reconcile other conspiratorial functions with the direction of Radio Liaison for the organisation, so I suggested to Stanislaw that he should take the latter job over, as he was a self-possessed man and an excellent radio operator. As usual, I banked on the man, and gave him considerable freedom in organising the work, reserving for myself decisions with regard to fundamental changes in the system and method, and insisting that efficiency must not be reduced. The experiment lasted for two months, and failed. With all his good qualities, Stanislaw had not the gift of improvisation, which was indispensable under conditions in which breakdowns, for a variety of reasons, were always liable to occur. Moreover, he was a rather hard-boiled professional; he worked conscientiously and reliably, but the work did not attract him, and he lacked initiative. We had to go back to the old system, and I had to run about again all over the place, as constant movement was a part of our work.

One morning I received a message: 'Stanislaw was arrested to-night while spending the evening with his wife in her apartment.' As it turned out, Stanislaw, before joining us, had belonged to some other underground organisation, which he had left. There was a slip-up in that organisation, a list of members was found, someone squealed, and Stanislaw became involved.

Greatly troubled, we met for consultation. We reminisced about our former work with him, our common adventures, and praised him for his solid qualities. All misunderstandings were forgotten and everyone thought of him with affection. By way of consolation, we were glad he had not been caught at work with us, and that he therefore had a chance of escaping death. What were we to do? He knew our hide-outs in Muranowska Street, in Silver Street, in Milanowek, and others. If we froze them all, our work would come to a standstill. I decided not to change anything, and explained my position to those present.

'I think,' I said, 'that since Stanislaw was not caught while operating a radio station but through a slip-up, the Germans will only know that he belonged to an underground organisation, and not that he worked with us. Consequently, if the worst comes to the worst, Stanislaw will only confess to having been a member of the underground. They will not ask him about our work, because they don't know of it, and besides, Stanislaw won't talk, because that would mean certain death for him.'

Everyone agreed with this, and I only ordered a suspension of three days and the abandonment of the threatened hide-outs for that period; after which the work proceeded as usual. We extended our protection, anonymously, to Stanislaw's family.

After several weeks, through our intelligence within Pawiak prison, we received the information that Stanislaw had been sent to the Majdanek camp. It will serve as a macabre commentary on the times we lived in, when I say that we rejoiced at this news, for it meant that he had not been executed.

A Slip-up on the Electric Railway

Wladek came to say that the transmitter in Milanowek had broken down. It made a lot of noise, then a flash and smoke, and it just ceased to function. Joey took it cheerfully. 'It's nothing,' he said, 'it must have been a short circuit. We must get the transmitter to Marshall Street and I'll have it repaired in no time.'

It was Saturday afternoon, and I instructed Wladek to take Helena with him on Sunday so that she could bring the transmitter to Warsaw. I expressly told him to go on Sunday, because on that day the watch for smugglers on the railways was relaxed. On Monday, I dropped in at Joey's, and when he told me that Helena had not brought the transmitter yet, I went to Silver Street to find out what had happened. There, the girl who was lodging with Helena told me that Wladek had not turned up on Sunday, but had only come early that morning, i.e., Monday, and that Helena had gone with him to Milanowek and had not come back yet. I looked at my watch; it was five in the afternoon.

'When did they leave?'

'At seven in the morning.'

'Something must have happened. I shall be back before curfew.'

I was greatly perturbed. Had Helena gone the same way as Stanislaw? I was superstitious and believed that such things never happened singly; I feared there had been another slip-up. On the other hand, it could have been negligence, and I was determined to remedy that. Together with Zosia, I went back to Silver Street at about half-past seven. The scared room-mate opened the door.

'Helena isn't back yet and I am worried about her,' she said.

Now I was almost certain that something had gone wrong, and we tried to figure out what it could be, though we still did not give up all hope. Perhaps she had fallen ill? Perhaps she had gone to spend the night with friends, having calculated she would not make it before curfew? Perhaps she might still come at the last minute? But it was by then only ten minutes to curfew hour, and we had to hurry to get home ourselves. We left, leaving a message for Helena to get in touch with us first thing in the morning.

Next morning very early we hurried to Joey's, as Helena was supposed to leave the parcel there. As soon as Joey opened the door, he asked:

'Where's Helena?'

'Never mind; get your things out, because Helena knows this hide-out. It's better to leave at once and deliberate afterwards.'

We went in the direction of Silver Street, though we realised that by now the Germans must have set a trap in Helena's apartment. In Lindley Street we chanced on an old, pre-war messenger in a red cap, one of those who were popularly known as 'bullfinches' in Warsaw. Despite the early hour he oozed with drink and was in a happy mood. As we had no other means, I wrote a conventional message to Helena's room-mate, gave the messenger a large note, and told him to bring the reply to a nearby café. The 'bullfinch' trotted off gingerly, slightly off-balance, and we followed him to keep an eye on him. When he entered Helena's house, we hid some distance away in a doorway, to see what would happen. I reproached myself for having sent the messenger on such a dangerous errand; but I could do nothing about it now.

After only a few minutes, he emerged from the house as red in the face as his cap, and almost ran in the direction of Lindley Street. We watched carefully to see if anyone would follow him, but the messenger disappeared round the corner without anyone on his tail. We went after him in Indian file, and noticed that he stopped in front of the café and looked all round him. I kept back, and Zosia went up to him.

'Are you looking for someone?' she asked.

'Yes, I am looking for a tall fellow who sent me.'

'He could not wait and asked me to meet you instead.'

'He must be a devil to send me on such an errand! The Gestapo are in that place. They opened the door, took the message, read it, hit me in the face, and kicked me downstairs. I think, little lady, I have earned another "hundred".'

Zosia gave him a handful of zlotys and the messenger disappeared into the nearby pub.

When Zosia told us what he had said we were heartbroken. Here was a second victim already, and such a brave, courageous girl! We tried to make out how she had slipped up, and if Wladek, too, had been caught. With heavy hearts we went to the contact post, where, however, we found Wladek, who knew nothing at all. He did not go to Helena on Sunday because a friend visited him, so he went on Monday morning instead. (We exchanged knowing looks, guessing that it was a woman friend. The quiet Wladek was in love with a widow twice his own age.) They reached Milanowek safely, she took away the transmitter, and left the hide-out before 10 a.m. When we told Wladek what had happened, he turned pale. It was obvious that Helena had been caught on her way back to Warsaw. When I reproached Wladek for not having observed my instructions strictly, he became so depressed that I left him alone.

Now once again we were confronted with the same accursed problem as with Stanislaw's capture. Were we to liquidate the hide-outs Helena knew, or not? They had caught her with the transmitter, and had clear proof that she was engaged in radio work. On the other hand, we all knew her to be a tough girl who would rather be tortured to death than squeal. However, Joey and his workshop were of the utmost importance to us; I decided therefore that Joey should leave Marshall Street for a time, while the equipment would be evacuated to our hide-out in the Polytechnic. Without further delay, I hired a cart, and together with Zosia, in broad daylight, I transported a heap of suitcases and boxes to Cesia's. Joey moved to some friends of his, and production ceased.

Several weeks later I received a scribbled note from Pawiak prison, written in minute letters; it reached me through an underground cell that had contact with the prison. Helena wrote:

'Dear friends,—While alighting from the Electric Railway at the corner of Zelazna Street, I was searched. I told them I didn't know the contents of the parcel I was carrying, and that I was to hand it over to a man I did not know, except by description, and who would exchange passwords with me. I said I was doing it for a fat reward. I have told them nothing, and I shall not tell them, although they are beating me. I know what you fear most, but have no fear; go on working in the old hide-outs and don't worry about me.'

We read the note with tears in our eyes. She was not thinking of herself, but of us, and of the work. Wladek, who felt guilty, was utterly crushed. We trusted her so implicitly that we transported all the equipment back to Joey's hide-out in Marshall Street.

After several weeks, in the list of people transferred from Pawiak to the camp at Majdanek, sent to us by the previously-mentioned prison cell, there was the name of Helena. And again we repeated the words of the macabre consolation: 'Thanks be to God, she's only got the camp. We are lucky in our misfortune.'

The Return of Frank

I pressed the pin-head, and presently Joey opened the door. He was smiling mysteriously as he ushered me into his room. When I entered, I could hardly believe my eyes. Stretched out on a mattress was Frank. The same Frank who had been caught during the slip-up in Downhill Road, but pitifully changed, with his hair shaved off, with a white pallor on his swollen and sore-covered face, yet nevertheless the same simple and funny boy. I welcomed him with genuine joy.

'How did you get here, Frank?' I exclaimed.

'I escaped from the transport to Majdanek,' he said, and gave a full account of his adventures. As he talked, he seemed to re-live everything all over again, and showed it by the way his voice broke here and there.

'When I entered the room, Joey had already made off and the Gestapo were standing by the radio equipment. They at once jumped on me with fury. I explained to them that Joey was a friend of mine, and that I had come to ask him if his parents would like to buy some butter I had for sale. They beat me all over my body, but I stuck to my story to the end. They put me in the Pawiak jail, and I remained there several months. What I lived through and what I saw there are impossible to describe. Do you know the Gestapo let their hounds devour people alive, and people are ordered to pretend to be dogs, to crawl on all fours and bark like dogs? Terrible! On several occasions I saw Janek from a distance; he seemed to have some function in the jail. Several days ago they drove masses of people into the prison. The crush in the cells was so great that people died of suffocation. The Germans sent out transports and put me into one. We were crowded into cattle trucks like herrings. Next to me stood a Warsaw boy, and when the train started, I suggested to him that we should try and get out of it. We examined the planks in the side of the truck and discovered that one of them was loose. One of the men near us had a knife concealed on him, and we started to loosen the plank a little more. Finally it was free, and during the night we pushed it aside and one after the other, whoever wanted to, escaped. I was lucky enough to get to a village, where I chanced on some good peasants; I told them I had escaped from a transport and they gave me food and some clothing, in which I dragged myself to Warsaw.'

I pressed his hand warmly and promised to look after him. He was not to worry but to get well as soon as possible. We had to find a safe place for him, as we could not let him go to his mother, who earned her living by laundering, because they would look for him there. I had to make it up with Mrs. General, and place Frank with her in Muranowska Street. Mrs. General did not disappoint my trust in her, and promised to look after Frank like a mother. However, after a week or so, she asked for an appointment with me, and when we met she complained bitterly.

'I just cannot do enough cooking for that hungry wolf. I buy all the things he wants, butter, lard, cheese, eggs, but the money you are paying me isn't enough to buy ham for him. And yet he's worrying me to get him lots of ham. I make gallons of soup for him, I feed him with meat, and still it isn't enough; he wants ham! I didn't know what to do, so I cooked a whole cow's head for him; and would you believe it, he devoured it all at one go. He never stops worrying me for food; I cannot satisfy his hunger. You must do something about it, because I am at the end of my tether.'

I took counsel with Joey, who found the cow's head a wonderful dish.

'Joey,' I said, 'have you talked with Frank about all this? Is it true, what Mrs. General said?'

'I talked to Frank, and it's true he complained that she wouldn't give him any ham, but I asked him, "When did you have ham in your life before, you beggar, that you can't go without it now?' He took the hint, but complained that with the money you give her, she grills steaks for herself but feeds him with cows' heads. It's a great joke, this cow's head; now I always address Frank as "You cow's head",' and Joey, greatly pleased with himself, could hardly stop laughing.

An Adventure in Chopin Street

In the course of our daily work, which continued to expand, I came to know a most interesting man. His name was Christopher, a young man of about thirty, very good-looking, with a swarthy handsome face, steely eyes and complete self-assurance. He was always groomed with the overdone elegance of a suburban gay Lothario. He put at our disposal his bachelor apartment in Chopin Street, and told us stories of his exploits.

'Last month,' he said, 'I took 500 litres of pure alcohol from the Germans and sold it. I fabricated the necessary documents, my men drove up to the depot, and the stupid Germans handed over the consignment. My God, what a stupid nation they are! All you need is a bit of effrontery, a scrap of paper with a stamp on it, and you can talk them into anything. Now I am having my meals at the Bristol on German ration cards, and all I have to pay for a dinner with wine is twenty zloty.'

He went on telling us of his many anti-German exploits of a 'commercial' nature, and finally he made a suggestion:

'If you could print German ration cards for fats, my boys would empty all the German shops.'

I ignored the suggestion, and only made use of Christopher's apartment once a week. He had just one room on the top floor, with a single window giving on to Chopin Street. Along the entire storey ran a wide balustraded ledge, which formed some sort of balcony.

On one occasion, Martin and the look-out girl Cesia, introduced by Christopher, were on the point of unpacking the transmitter when through the closed window a shadow fell across the room. Outside the window, standing on the ledge, was a gendarme making signs to be let in. Christopher did not lose his head for a moment. Just as he was, in his overcoat, he approached the window in order to conceal the other two, and whispered:

'Take everything away and run, while I keep him off.' He made signs to the gendarme that the window would not open, and that he would have to walk round to the door; and during that silent conversation Martin and Cesia had time to put the transmitter back into the bag and leave. At the door they found Joey and me: 'Turn right back,' they said, 'the Germans will be here in a minute.' Without wasting time finding out what had happened, we made for one end of the corridor and Martin and Cesia for the other. We were making for the alternative exit, which we knew existed, since, in accordance with our usual procedure, we had inspected the place thoroughly before starting work in it, and had memorised all its entrances and exits. Neither we, nor Martin and Cesia, whom we saw when we regained the street, encountered anyone. I signalled to them to make themselves scarce, while Joey and I stopped at the corner of Mokotowska and Chopin Street, to see what would happen to Christopher.

Half an hour later, several gendarmes and a German civilian left the house, without Christopher. We did not want to risk going back to the house, so we waited in the street. About a quarter of an hour later, Christopher emerged from the doorway and walked towards us smiling.

'Let's turn into a side-street, for I must give you a few things Cesia left behind.'

We entered a house, and on the staircase Christopher pulled out of his pocket some earphones, a length of rope, and a few wireless trifles, and told us what happened.

'They were not after a radio station at all. There is a German woman living in the house and she had been burgled. Naturally, she informed the gendarmerie and the men came to investigate. Someone told them that my room was empty and locked, and that it was being visited occasionally by some people. This led them to suspect that my place was a den of thieves, and that that was where they ought to search to find the thief who robbed the German woman. The gendarmes had tried to get in just before we arrived, and as no one opened the door, one of them went with the janitor onto the roof, and from the roof to the ledge to see what was in the room. The others waited in the German woman's apartment. I told the gendarme by signs that he should come round to the door, and while he climbed down from the roof, through the loft and into the corridor, you were able to get away. The gendarme didn't notice Martin and Cesia at all when he looked through the window. I also had time to hide the small things in my pockets and in the stove, and when he entered my room I treated him haughtily and showed him my papers, which are quite good. They indicate that, but for me, the entire German war production would come to a standstill. In the end the gendarme, instead of searching my apartment, told me the story himself; I gave him a cigar and we parted on the best of terms.'

Christopher was smiling contemptuously. I looked at him with admiration; I was unable to find the slightest trace of the dangerous encounter he had just had. He had nerves of steel, and I told him so. He looked surprised.

'That was nothing,' he said, 'compared with some other scraps I've had with the Germans.'

However, I gave up the hide-out; for this fresh experience had taught me that it was dangerous for several people to meet in an uninhabited apartment; it attracted attention.

I ran into Christopher a number of times afterwards, invariably finding him in the best of humours and well groomed; until he disappeared from my purview. The last time I saw him again was in Marshall Street in 1946. He looked his usual self, but somehow his self-assurance had left him. He paused for a moment in passing and said vacantly:

'Well, what have you got for all your patriotic chores? . . . dirt!'

And without waiting for an answer, he gripped my hand firmly, and made off.

Our Private Lives

During that period I had quite a number of adventures, some dangerous, some amusing.

We lived, Zosia and I, registered under the name of my cousin Ignacy Bujnicki, a former President of Kalisz, who was murdered by the Germans, at Cesia Broniewska's, in the professorial wing of the Polytechnic. The apartment was very well appointed, with many tapestries and ancient coats of arms. One morning, we were awakened by the stamping of feet on the stairs and the sound of German voices. We jumped out of bed and listened. The voices passed our floor, and a moment later we could hear them a floor higher. Cesia rushed into our room.

'They are searching two storeys higher, in Professor Smolenski's apartment. A motor-car is in front of the house and the Gestapo are watching the back entrance from Basket Street.'

This was a blow, as we happened to have a great deal of incriminating material in the house, messages and ciphers, which were too urgently needed to be burnt. But the search might be extended to Cesia's apartment at any moment. I had no time to think matters over, so I quickly made a small parcel, wrapped it in newspapers, and slipping shoes over my bare feet, and a light overcoat over my trousers and shirt only, I left through the kitchen, with the bundle of newspapers under my arm. I wanted, if possible, to leave the precincts of the Polytechnic by a little gate opening on August Street, and to take the parcel to the Staszic Housing Estate. In my pocket I kept a firm grip on a Colt revolver which I had obtained from one of the parachute drops. As soon as I emerged into the street, I noticed on the pavement in Basket Street two Gestapo men standing by the side of a car; and they had already noticed me. I could turn to the right and reach the exit into August Street by another route. But instinct made me continue in the direction of Basket Street. I came up to the Gestapo men and passed them, walking leisurely under their sharp gaze. But they did not stop me, and this once again confirmed my experience that one must not hesitate for a second, but make straight for the Germans, if one is to stand a chance. When I returned, I learned that the Gestapo had taken away Professor Smolenski's entire family, and cleared his apartment of everything worth taking. They entered no other apartment and stopped no one; which explains why the Gestapo men left me alone.

I had another adventure when I took Zosia to the Fuchs Café in Mokotowska Street. For some time now, I had made a point of never being without a revolver, as the Gestapo had already been to our previous hide-out in the Staszic Housing Estate, where we had lived with the Zarembas, and had asked about me. Moreover, they had raided my former two-room office in the Prudential Building by night and left a summons for me with the superintendent, requesting me to appear with my wife and personal documents at their Headquarters, so that I could be examined as a witness in a case involving a commercial firm. We were all greatly amused by the clumsiness of the trick, which was typical of German lack of intelligence. Joey teased me:

'Perhaps you've got a friend working at the Gestapo, who wants to let you know you are being hunted.'

I realised that I was in danger and always had my Colt on me, though I often warned others not to risk being caught in possession of a firearm. Zosia had removed a trouser pocket and sewn in a strong holster.

After a call at the radio station, I went to the Fuchs Café, where I had a rendezvous with Zosia. I was sitting there, bending forward towards her and whispering confidential information, when my Colt slipped out of its holster and dropped with a thud right on to a red cocoa-nut mat. We were both petrified for a moment, and there was dead silence in the café. I quickly grabbed the revolver, picked it up from the floor, and without putting it back into the pocket, I looked round the café. A stray German might have been present. But no one moved; so I put the revolver into my pocket, though without withdrawing my hand from it. Laughing nervously, we quickly finished our coffee and paid the bill. The waitress took the money, and gave me my change with unconcealed loathing. I asked Zosia if she had noticed it, and she explained it perfectly:

'She took you for a German.'

We met her after the Warsaw Rising at the home of a friend in Lesna Podkowa. She recognised me at once and was startled to see me there. When our host introduced us as his good friends, there were no end of exclamations and reminiscences.

I had to lead a double life, as it were. On the one hand, I moved among the leaders of the underground as the head of Civil Resistance, while on the other I descended every day into the conspiratorial depths, directing personally radio liaison and meeting telegraphists, look-out girls, and the owners of our hide-outs. I must admit that Civil Resistance gave me greater satisfaction, but radio work was undoubtedly more exciting. One met the strangest assortment of people, things and situations. Here was a riverside urchin helping Joey, there a young aristocratic girl acting as a look-out. In time this diverse throng formed one radio family. They became friends, they quarrelled or made love to each other, and frequently they gave their lives together.

It was only now that I came to know Warsaw and its suburbs, particularly the maze of the Old City and the Riverside, so beloved by Joey. I came to know Bielany and distant Grochow, and met the people who lived there, the common people of Warsaw, who risked their own and the lives of their dear ones by offering their homes as hide-outs for our radio stations.

Underground Warsaw

These were the streets of Warsaw, the alluring melody of which blended so well with the memories of our best years. It is true that at the time the melody was but a hubbub, but to-day it sounds in retrospect like a symphony to the nostalgic

ear. There rushed about the avenues and streets their undisputed ruler, the newsvendor, with a bulging pack under arm,
ragged but lively; like the tenor in a choir he added to the
hum its basic tune, as of old. But his movements lacked their
former abandon and his noted wit had acquired new and
hitherto unknown metaphors; while his voice sounded
stranely altered. The names of the journals, too, were different; they were no longer 'ABC', 'Robotnik', 'Kurjer Warszawski', or 'Gazeta Polska', but, 'Warschauer Zeitung', or
'Nowy Kurjer', which, although in the Polish language, in
fact spoke German.

The hoofs of the cab-horses continued to beat the rhythm
of the melody, but the clatter of hobnailed boots imposed
another beat. The tram-car bells continued to warn careless
pedestrians, but were silenced by fear when a grey marching
column in gleaming steel helmets crossed their tracks. Time
and again there sounded in the music of the street a false note,
a horrible screech. Above the roofs rose an alien, guttural
song, to which the streets listened paralysed with horror; to
which they were forced to listen for five long years.

Like water splashed by a passing wheel, the crowds spread
back against the walls of the houses. And right there, along
the middle of the roadway rushed an open motor-car, bristling
with the muzzles of revolvers, filled with large, black caps
with the skull and crossbones badge, and men with black ties
on brown shirts. Their eyes struck the passers-by like daggers.
The crowd replied with mute hatred. They stopped, they
jumped out, and fired their guns. And a moment later, the
deserted street hugged the dead bodies of its children. It
remembered tearfully how they had tried their first clumsy
steps on its pavements, how, when a little older, they had
hurried along them to school, and when grown up, it had
seen them sauntering along or walking gravely, not anticipating that it would soon behold their sudden and cruel
death. The Warsaw streets had a sad and hard lot to bear.

At home, in the kitchen, a mother would be cooking dinner.
The black iron pot had already forgotten the taste of meat
and was simmering with boiling potatoes. The mother gazed
at the wall with eyes blinded with tears. Sorrow had left her

face lined. That thick furrow over the forehead came in one night, when she received the news that her beloved son Andrew had been killed in the battle of Kutno. The other one, just below the first, was growing deeper every day from worry over John, who was last seen in the Carpathian mountains, crossing the Hungarian frontier. On alien soil, he was no doubt still fighting for his native land. Down the two new ones on her cheeks, nocturnal tears were wont to flow because of Bolek and Helenka, the remaining two children in Dobra Street. They were more affectionate and more solicitous for their mother, but they were rarely at home. They went their own ways, grave and thoughtful. The mother did not know, but suspected, and cried quietly, without asking questions and without attempting to stop them. She yielded to the power which took her children away from her, perhaps, one day soon, for ever. That power was Underground Poland.

Many thousand Polish mothers lived through similar anxieties, in Poznan, Krakow, Lwow, Wilno; in towns and villages throughout the length and breadth of Poland. Thousands of beloved Andrews covered with their graves their bleeding motherland, thousands of Johns fought in foreign lands for the freedom of their native country, on land, on the seas and in the air. And thousands of Boleks and Helenkas descended into the fighting underground.

And the buildings of Warsaw, which had seen the glory of ancient Poland, the kings proceeding to the Castle, in a cortege of many stately carriages, with an escort of winged hussars, the insurgents fighting the savage Cossacks generation after generation, and again the splendid armies of reborn Poland: when the fatal September dawned, the streets proved worthy of the traditions of a great city, of which they became the first line of defence. With barricades thrown across them they halted the rolling tanks, marked with the sign of the crooked cross.

The buildings in the Old City, in Buxom Street, in Raven Street, in Mokotow or Zoliborz, then stood mute and crippled, with their battered-broken walls, and their windows like empty sockets. But in their mysterious interiors something new and strange was happening. Their bodies were being shaken by the blows of pickaxes, chiselling in the walls ingeniously constructed hiding places; while the foundations hospitably received the arms and munitions which careful hands were depositing in their recesses. In the cellars the earth, hiding family treasures and heirlooms, muted the reports of revolver-shots fired for practice, while the friendly flat roofs, with their edges close to each other, helped the pursued to escape. They had their rivals, the cellars, which, when the roofs were blazing in the Rising, had to play a more responsible part; in their labyrinths almost the entire population of the Risen City was to find shelter.

But the most important function fell to the doorbells. At that time each no longer summoned its lord and master, the janitor, asleep in the stench of his lodge—with the broom, the symbol of his authority by his bed—to open the door to a tenant who was late. Instead they warned of enemies outside the door. And the janitor himself had changed. He no longer asked, 'Whom do you wish to see?' but without a word admitted into his kingdom strange, unknown men, when at dusk they slipped into the entrance hall to spend a quiet night in the house. He had already lost all respect for the register. He no longer trusted it, and shrugged his shoulders when he read in it the names of persons who never crossed the threshold he was guarding, or when the names of tenants who never left the house vanished from its pages. But when in the dead of night the doors groaned under the blows of hobnailed jackboots, and the intruders even put the muzzle of a revolver to his head to quicken his memory, he would lie without batting an eyelid to protect his own people from the vicious enemy. He knew, of course, everything that was going on in the house. But he kept his mouth shut; he watched and he warned whoever needed it, and thereby, though nameless and humble, he became a true soldier of Fighting Poland, the initials of which, drawn by an unknown hand in the dark of night, his house proudly bore on its front, like a cross of valour.

CHAPTER V

Directorate of Civil Resistance

Organisation of Civil Resistance

In the course of its development, the Directorate of Civil Resistance evolved a definite shape. It consisted of myself as its head—from its inception until the end of the war—my deputy, Krajewski, and a number of departments, the names of which indicate their tasks: the Departments of Justice, Sabotage and Diversion, Registration of German Crimes, Radio Information, Armaments, Chemicals and Legalization. As may be seen from this, the Directorate of Civil Resistance was not a corporate body, but was constructed on the principle of hierarchic dependence. In addition, the Directorate of Civil Resistance included a Delegate of the Union for Armed Struggle (later the Home Army), Piotrowski, who served as a link between the Directorate of Civil Resistance and all branches of military work.

The Government Plenipotentiary authorised the Directorate of Civil Resistance to put forward to all the bodies subordinate to the Plenipotentiary its demands concerning the conduct of Civil Resistance in the regions within their individual purviews. In the event of a difference of opinion arising, the Government Plenipotentiary made the decision; while at the lower level such decisions were made by the District Plenipotentiaries, to each of whom was attached a District Director of Civil Resistance. The work at the District level was on the whole analogous in its organisation to that of the Central body.

In its relations with the Polish Government in London, the Directorate of Civil Resistance was authorised by Plenipotentiary Ratajski to send, through its own radio network, messages describing the situation in the country, especially the terror and the counter-terror directed against the occupying power. Messages of a political nature were excepted; these were the prerogative of the Plenipotentiary and the Political Consultative Committee.

As far as the Union for Armed Struggle was concerned, the Directorate of Civil Resistance, or, to be more precise, the Commander-in-Chief's Plenipotentiary for Civil Resistance Affairs, had in theory the same powers as he had in the affairs of the bodies subordinate to the Government Plenipotentiary. The delegate of the General Staff to the DCR, Piotrowski, co-operated in the execution of all tasks. During the first phase of the struggle, this involved collaboration with the Office of Information and Propaganda of the Union for Armed Struggle; but in the second phase, there was, in addition, close collaboration with the Directorate of Diversion (Khedive), i.e., that section of the Union for Armed Struggle which, for the purpose of maintaining the current struggle against the occupying power, was excluded from the general organisation of the Home Army when the latter was formed into divisions, regiments and their relevant staffs.

The entire team of people constituting the Directorate of Civil Resistance gradually became a closely knit body, which met regularly in the hide-outs of the central direction, besides which each department had its own hide-outs. All these hide-outs were offered by brave Warsaw families, intercourse with whom infringed all the accepted rules of social conduct. Apart from the discoverer or introducer of the hide-out, who was known to the occupiers of the apartment, all the rest were complete strangers to them. There were no introductions, no small talk, no questions asked, but only formal courtesy on the way from the door to the room. No one tried to overhear or showed any desire to know what we were doing. We were surrounded by an atmosphere of friendly consideration and watchfulness; for when we were in the apartment, one of the members of the family usually took up sentry post and kept watch either outside, in the street, or inside from a window. In the course of five years I passed through scores of such hide-outs, and the main impression I have retained is of the grave earnestness that used to characterise such contacts. One knocked at the door in the pre-arranged manner, there was the click of the latch, and a pair of watchful eyes looked through the slightly-opened door. Then came the clatter of the unhooked door-chain, and a smile which meant 'I recognise you'. 'Good morning' or 'Goodbye' on leaving, comprised the whole extent of one's intercourse.

My deputy, the secretary, and one of the contact-girls usually waited for me in the room. Sometimes a specially trusted man was let in if the matter required it. Ordinary mortals of the underground were never admitted to the hide-outs of the central direction. I remember the storm which broke out on one occasion when a trusted person brought to the hide-out a 'teen-age village girl from the Zamosc district, who, with the obstinacy of a child, was determined to work in Civil Resistance. The poor thing had to go back to Zamosc; but she was given the address and the password that would admit her to the local leader of Civil Resistance.

On the table in front of Krajewski would be piles of papers and copies of underground publications, which were my pet aversion. There would follow two or three hours of conversation, reporting, decisions; then a hurried good-bye, and again the daily errands all over the City.

Our hide-outs were of various kinds. Once we had a laundry, where one arrived along with other customers, and passed into a back-room full of humidity and steam. Then we had a monastery, where once one passed the gate one entered an atmosphere of calm and peace. The silent guide, in a monkish cassock, conducted one through a maze of corridors and rooms, kneeling down in front of every little altar. Here and there a similar figure glided noiselessly over the shining waxed floors of the corridors. The silence almost rang in one's ears. My hobnailed boots made so much noise that I was embarrassed, and found myself squeezing my cap in my hand like a schoolboy. This was a different world from the one I had left outside the gate, and one could forget for a moment that there was a war, a conspiracy and innumerable worries. Then a door would open and I would again behold Krajewski over a familiar stack of printed papers. That sight alone would restore my sense of reality and I would grumble: 'You haven't got more of this stuff, have you? This accursed wastepaper will be our undoing.'

I still think I was right. The underground press was the pride of the conspiracy, but it must be owned that we over-did it. The publication of a newspaper was almost a certifi-cate of importance to even the smallest organisation, for it gave it a position in the underground world. Hence, even little groups of a dozen members endeavoured to have their own newspaper published.

A few months after the Warsaw Rising I began to feel nos-talgic for the laundry and the monastery; but I found only rubble where they once stood, and a stillness which only the twitter of sparrows disturbed. It would be beyond me to de-scribe it, but I shall be understood by anyone who has him-self crossed Napoleon Square in Warsaw, along a trail trodden over the mounds of rubble and round the water-filled craters.

We had to be constantly on our guard; for the Plenipoten-tiary's intelligence department informed us that the Germans were pursuing the Directorate of Civil Resistance relentlessly, especially since they had learned from the underground press, which was read assiduously by the Gestapo, of the Govern-ment Plenipotentiary's manifesto; the far-reaching preroga-tives with which this endowed us, caused the Germans to re-gard Civil Resistance as a particularly dangerous enemy. But fate was kind to us, and somehow we prospered. Even acci-dents were happily resolved, as when the head of the Chemi-cals branch luckily recovered after he had become infected with some of his beloved bacteria. After a series of injections he was back with his vials and filters, which contained such a terrible menace to the Germans, and to us; for the vials con-tained poison, which each of us carried on him against the possibility of being caught by the Germans.

It was towards the end of 1943 that the Germans got in a blow at us, when they caught the head of the judicial depart-ment, a Poznan barrister who had been expelled into the Government General; he was caught in a hide-out at night and murdered. I knew him only by his pseudonym, which escapes my memory.

The General Commission of Civil Resistance

The General Commission of Civil Resistance consisted of delegates of the political Parties that were represented on the Political Consultative Committee, and it was popularly called the 'little PCC'. After a time the General Commission was joined by the Civic Self-Defence Organisation (CSO), which consisted of about twenty smaller underground groups. At various periods the General Commission included Casimir Baginski, representing the 'Triangle', Urbanski, representing the 'Romb',[1] and Leszek Raabe, delegated by the 'Circle'. Assisted by Wincent Bryja, Casimir Baginski drafted for Civil Resistance a detailed code of corporal punishments, such as flogging, for lesser offences. Such punishment was widely applied in the villages. The General Commission of Civil Resistance was on the one hand an initiating and policy-making body for the various actitivies of Civil Resistance, and on the other, it functioned as an executive body, in the sense that it transmitted through the Party organisations and the COS all instructions and recommendations of the Directorate of Civil Resistance; which ensured that they reached all points at which conspiracy existed. In this way Civil Resistance had at its disposal a powerful network of liaison, not only within the Government General, but also in territories incorporated into the German Reich, and in those East of the Government General which the Germans occupied after the outbreak of the German-Russian war.

Moreover, through the General Commission, the Directorate of Civil Resistance could use the machinery of the political Parties, which played a considerable part in such mass actions as, for instance, the sabotaging of deliveries of farm products and the destruction of illicit stills.

The Clergy Commission

For the carrying out of special tasks, Commissions of clergy,

[1] the Labour Party

women and young people were appointed as executive branches of Civil Resistance within the given environment. One of the unforgettable characters was the chairman of the Clergy Commission, the Prior of the Pallotine Fathers in the Convent in Long Street. He had the ascetic look of a typical sufferer from tuberculosis, with hollow cheeks and sunken, feverishly shining eyes. When I called on him, I frequently found him in bed, and it was only the underground work he was doing that kept him alive. The struggle meant life for him; and he engaged in it with the assistance of a few young clergymen. He succeeded in creating a conspiratorial organisation among the clergy, through which he distributed the instructions of Civil Resistance. This network was of considerable importance; for although the clergy were not allowed to summon people, from the pulpit, to resist the occupying power, nevertheless lessons, parables, allusions, the tone of voice or a quotation from the Old or New Testament, would influence the faithful in their attitude. More important still were the private contacts of the clergy with their trusted parishioners, which enabled them to make the necessary communications. The Polish clergy, following the magnificent stand of that historic personality, Cardinal Prince Sapieha, conducted themselves splendidly from the point of view of Civil Resistance. The Cardinal himself maintained close contact with the underground, especially with the successive Government Pleniopotentiaries. He refused an invitation to call on Governor-General Frank, or to make any pro-German pronouncements; but, on the contrary, he fearlessly protested on many occasions against the conduct of the Germans in Poland. Moreover, he issued appropriate instructions to the clergy, and pressed the Holy See to intervene and to condemn German crimes. He became an object of veneration of the entire Polish nation.

The Women's Commission

The Women's Commission had the task of distributing instructions issued by Civil Resistance, especially concerning women, mothers and wives. As the occupying power had closed down all schools and colleges except primary ones ('The Poles are to supply only labour, and it will suffice if they can simply read and write. . . .' proclaimed Governor Frank), the instructions required redoubled care of the young, encouragement of self-tuition, and secret tuition. Moreover, remembering the splendid part women had played in the struggle for independence in the past, the instructions appealed to every Polish home to become a bastion of resistance to the Germans.

The part played by women in the underground organisation is still waiting for its historian, but I am sure he will exhaust the whole vocabulary of superlatives when writing on the subject. I can only say that as far as Civil Resistance was concerned, the general resistance of the Polish people would not have been what it was but for the courage, patriotism and self-sacrifice of Polish women of every social class.

Here I should like to mention the problem of prostitution, which has always flourished during wars and is usually the most fertile ground for 'fraternisation' between the victors and the vanquished. This did not apply to Poland during the Second World War, as the Germans themselves recognised; for they distributed among all German soldiers passing through Poland leaflets warning them that they should 'avoid Polish girls, because they would lead you into ambush, in which you would lose not only your arms, but your life as well'. Many Warsaw prostitutes served in the underground intelligence, and thus worked for the common cause. The picture would not be complete without mentioning this point.

The Women's Commission was also occupied with problems of social welfare, among others with assisting the deportees from the province of Zamosc. In this connection Warsaw set a wonderful example of national solidarity. When the news spread through the capital that the Germans were transporting by rail thousands of Polish children from that province, and that the trains would be passing through the Warsaw railway stations, the people of the capital were seized by an excitement bordering on hysteria. Thousands of men and women rushed to the stations and crossings to get the children out somehow. People who were hardly able to feed their own children were ready to kidnap, to ransom, or to take by force the peasant children from Zamosc. I know of one public utility office in which all the employees, from the director to the most humble worker, in spite of the strict control exercised by the German Treuhänder, left work and went in official cars from station to station in search of the children from Zamosc. And all this happened in face of thousands of German gendarmes, SS troops and Gestapo, in a city in which volleys of shots in the streets were as common as the ringing of church-bells elsewhere. This spontaneous, unorganised action on the part of the population of Warsaw was one of the finest manifestations of national solidarity under German occupation. Its mainsprings were hidden deep in the soul of Poland, and yet responded so easily to an appropriate touch.

I remember one peculiar adventure, which brought me into contact with the head of the Women's Commission.

One of my friends, who lived at 2, May the Third Avenue, asked me to meet a forester from Minsk Mazowiecki who wanted to communicate an important matter to a responsible member of the underground. At the appointed time, in the apartment of my friend, I met a weather-beaten young man who made me a very attractive proposal.

'Governor Fischer and various civilian and military dignitaries visit our forests from time to time for hunting. I am usually informed a week or ten days in advance of their coming, so that I can prepare everything required for the hunt. They often hunt with beaters and I personally choose the position for each hunter. I can let you know in advance when the next hunt is to take place, and hide your men in the forest. You would be able to polish off the Germans to the last man.'

At first I was very much taken by the suggestion; but common sense prevailed.

'Well, if we do it, the Germans with tear you to pieces.'

'They will not, for I shall join your people and get away.'

'I can see you've got a score to settle with them. Has anything occurred lately?'

'No, nothing; but I can't stand it any longer.'

'Now, suppose you do get away, what will happen to the beaters and the men in the Forestry administration?'

My visitor had no answer to that, and we discussed the possibilities of a different solution. As the suggested action lay within the competence of 'Khedive' the latter, with the approval of the competent authority, delegated one of its officers for it; and he attended our next meeting, during which we elaborated an alternative plan. One of the participants in the action gave me an account of how it was carried out.

'We set the ambush, not in the forest where the hunt was taking place, but in another one through which the road to Warsaw runs, the road Fischer and his guests had to take on their way back. We decided to block the road by means of a steel rope attached to pine trees on either side; this would force the cars to stop, so that we could get them under our automatics. Unfortunately, the road was frequently used by German military convoys, which we had to let pass; so we fastened the steel rope on one side of the road only and waited. It was already dark when we saw the headlights of the cars in which Fischer and his guests were travelling emerge from a clearing along the road. As luck would have it, a column of military motor-cars was just passing. When it had passed, our men hurried across the road with the steel rope; but it was too late to fasten it to a pine tree, and they were only able to loop it round the tree and hold on to it. The first car, travelling at great speed, tore the rope off the tree and continued on its journey. We opened a brisk fire, but somehow they got away. Later, when we were withdrawing, we found, several hundred yards away, two abandoned motor-cars with holed tires. Some of the Germans must have been hit.'

Several days later I met the head of the Women's Commission, who was overjoyed.

'Please convey to the underground authorities the thanks of several hundred employees of the office I work in. Our Treuhänder, apparently scared by the defeats of the German armies, attempted to establish more friendly relations with the Polish employees and wanted to arrange for a Christmas party, during which he was to make a speech. The Polish employees decided to boycott the party, in accordance with the instructions of Civil Resistance, and were prepared for reprisals and arrests. Unexpectedly the German cancelled the party himself, for, as it turned out, "Polish bandits" shot him in the leg when he was returning from a hunting party.'

From this unexpected quarter came confirmation that the action had been partially successful. Later on I learned that there had been killed in the ambush a German general who was visiting Warsaw at the time, and who was invited by Fischer to the hunting party. Fischer himself escaped. There were rumours that he had not taken part in the hunt at all; that at the last minute urgent official business had prevented him from attending it.

The Youth Commission

The Youth Commission included in its ranks representatives of young people recruited into the Party organisations which formed the Political Consultative Committee. After a time I dissolved this Commission, because it became obvious that the young people represented on it were already fully active in military organisations which were already linked with Civil Resistance in other ways, and it seemed to me desirable that this should remain so. One of the problems closely affecting young people was that of so-called 'national mourning', with which the Political Consultative Committee had been concerned. The question was whether to proclaim national mourning for the duration of the war, which would have involved a total prohibition of all entertainments and recreations. We came to the conclusion that it would not be desirable to do so, because the prohibition of all forms of amusement would weaken the psychological forces of the nation, especially of the younger generation. National mourning may reasonably be maintained for some months, but not for years. As a result, the prohibition affected only entertainments connected in some way with German propaganda efforts, such as cinemas, lotteries, gambling casinos, German festivities, etc. On the other hand, all amusements within the home, birthday parties, holiday parties, concerts in cafés, and sports, were permitted. Polish cabaret theatres were tolerated, but not the municipal theatre of Warsaw.

In connection with my work on this sector, I met a young

man who may be regarded as a classic example of the lengths to which morbid ambition can lead. He was introduced to me by Malicki, of the Information and Propaganda Department, who seemed to be his patron. The young man was in his early twenties, tall, bespectacled, and pock-marked about the face; he chose the pretentious pseudonym 'Arpad'. Whether Malicki had assured him that he would become chairman of the Youth Commission, or whether, as president of a separate organisation backed by the Information and Propaganda Department, he had such an ambition I do not know, but he was deeply hurt when this honour eluded him. It led to bickerings with Malicki, and Arpad ostentatiously threatened to resign; but fortunately the Commission was dissolved soon afterwards, and my contact with Arpad came to an end. Several years later I read the documents concerning his trial before a military court of the Home Army, which twice sentenced Arpad to death for having denounced to the Gestapo a colleague in the organisation who had competed with him for an office. The first sentence was not sanctioned by the Commander of the Home Army, and the matter was sent back to court for retrial. The military court passed the death sentence for the second time and, as I learned, Arpad was shot by an execution squad but not killed; after which he went into hiding.

In 1946, while walking down Marshall Street in Warsaw, I came across a young and smart Lieutenant-Colonel of the Soviet-controlled Polish army, who saluted me with the utmost deference. I could hardly believe my eyes: as I raised my hat, I recognised Arpad. I am sure that with his past record he must be a general by now.

Civic Self-Defence Organisation

Among the organisations co-operating with the Directorate of Civil Resistance, one of the most important was the Civic Self-Defence Organisation, known by its Polish initials as SOS. It consisted of about twenty smaller groups, of which the more active were: 'Reveille', with the lawyer Witold Rosciszewski as its leader; 'Raclawice', a village youth group under Marszalek, of the State Agricultural Bank; the 'Polish

Renaissance' group, with Kossak-Szczucka as its head; and the Polish Freedom Union. The coalition was formed primarily in order that the small groups should secure a representative on the Political Consultative Committee, which later became the National Political Representation. But it was also an attempt by the UAS to form a competitive political body; for some of the military politicians of the UAS who wanted to influence General Rowecki were dissatisfied with the policy of the Political Consultative Committee. This was probably a throwback to pre-war conditions, when the military elements had an ascendancy over the political ones; but the manoeuvre failed, because the Government Plenipotentiary refused to agree to a fusion of the SOS with the PCC; nor would he agree that the SOS should have their representative on the Committee, since the former consisted of heterogeneous groups with conflicting ideological and political programmes. Instead, the Plenipotentiary advised the SOS groups to co-operate with Civil Resistance, which offered them a wide field of action. This co-operation became not only close, but most fruitful; although the successive chairmen of SOS continued to bear a grudge against the Government Plenipotentiary and the Political Consultative Committee for having disregarded the political aspirations of the SOS. This was a typical instance of attempts on the part of the military elements to control the political activities of the Underground, and this tendency, resisted by the Government Plenipotentiary, was characteristic of the conditions in which the conspiracy developed during its early years.

As time went on, I observed a strange phenomenon within the SOS. One by one its leading men perished. Such was the fate of Bilek, Marszalek, Jakub (President of the SOS), the lawyer Jarczyk, of Warsaw, and finally Rosciszewski himself. The death of Rosciszewski threw some light on the mystery, and the circumstances in which it occurred formed one of the most fantastic episodes that can be imagined.

A Gestapo Agent at the Headquarters of the Underground

One of the members of the Executive of the SOS was the

chairman of a group calling itself the 'Association for the Union of Slavs', a tall, good-looking, olive-skinned man with jet-black hair. I met him regularly during the joint meetings with the Executive of the SOS devoted to the affairs of Civil Resistance. Right from the beginning I was struck by the fact that he was in possession of a great deal of information concerning the Gestapo, its methods of work, its network of confidential agents, etc., of which he used to tell us quite a lot. I gave his group credit for collecting all this information, and I must admit that I was greatly impressed by their energy.

As a result of the insistence of the Executive of the SOS, a meeting was arranged with the Government Plenipotentiary, Professor Jan Piekalkiewicz. After I had introduced to each other all those present, we had a prolonged discussion on the activities of the SOS. It proceeded in an atmosphere of the utmost goodwill, and the representatives of the SOS left greatly pleased. Another meeting of the Executive of the SOS, this time with the Commander, Grot-Rowecki, was to be arranged. Before it was actually held, the chairman of the Association for the Union of Slavs put forward at one of our joint sessions a proposal which I found quite astonishing; for he suggested that we should organise a large-scale underground action against the Germans in such a way that it should appear to have been carried out by the Ukrainians, who would therefore have to suffer the German reprisals. Coming from the chairman of an association for the union of all Slavs this was rather surprising; it caused me to pay greater attention to the good-looking young man. In the meantime, Grot summoned a meeting, to which he invited Colonel Rzepecki; so I communicated my doubts to the latter. Colonel Rzepecki was equally astonished, but set out for the meeting forewarned.

In the dusk of an early autumn evening we gathered in a still unfinished and uninhabited building in the suburb of Praga. The staircase had not yet been put in and we had to walk up on planks fitted with rungs. The meeting, held in a badly-lit room, was attended by seven persons, Rowecki, Rzepecki, myself, and four representatives of the SOS. The discussion followed the usual course. It opened with a report

by Jakub on the requirements of the SOS; this was followed
by Rowecki's questions, and miscellaneous matters raised by
individual members of the Executive of the SOS. As usual,
everyone present spoke in turn, in a veritable flood of loqua-
city, so characteristic of bad conspiratorial habits. When the
turn of the good-looking chairman of the Association for the
Union of Slavs came, he laid before the meeting his favourite
plan of organising an action at the expense of the Ukrainians.
Rzepecki, who listened attentively without saying a word,
looked at me meaningly, and after the chairman had finished,
asked innocently:

'May I ask of what organisation you are chairman?'

'The Association for the Union of Slavs,' he answered in a
perfectly natural tone.

It so happened that on this occasion Rowecki was in a more
expansive mood than usual, and he spoke at length on his
plans for future activities. The SOS delegates listened with
concentrated attention, as befitted their first attendance at a
meeting with the Commander-in-Chief of the Home Army.

When the representatives of the SOS departed, I stayed behind with Rowecki and Rzepecki, and the latter, made somewhat uneasy by his suspicions, drew Rowecki's attention to
the fact that he had spoken too freely about his plans in the
presence of insufficiently known persons who might talk.
Rowecki, perhaps because he felt a little guilty, retorted with
angry animation:

'If you invite people to our meetings, I am entitled to
assume that they can be trusted.'

I felt that the matter required clarification, so I arranged
a meeting with Rosciszewski, whose pseudonym was Trze-
binski. With some circumspection, since I was speaking of a
colleague of his, I told him that the suggestions of the chairman of the AUS had made a very bad impression, and asked
him who the man was before the war and what his record had
been. No sooner had I put the question, when I knew I had
touched upon a sensitive point; for after first requesting me
to treat the matter confidentially, he frankly confessed:

'Unfortunately, no one in the SOS knows who the man is.'
I was amazed.

'For Heaven's sake, how could you accept him and his group into the SOS without knowing anything about him? How did it happen?'

Rosciszewski was not able to explain it.

'Someone introduced him somewhere to someone in the conspiracy,' he said, 'and step by step he reached the Executive of the SOS.'

It was time for me to speak out, so I put to Rosciszewski the direct question: had he noticed that for a chairman of a small and unknown group the man had too much knowledge of the Gestapo? Rosciszewski, growing visibly nervous, replied in the affirmative and admitted that it had aroused certain suspicions in him that he had hardly dared to express. Towards the end of our talk he asked me not to do anything on my own as he had already arranged for the man to be shadowed, and he was sure that by joining forces with the Home Army Intelligence and the Intelligence of the Government Plenipotentiary it would be possible to discover what lurked behind the chairman of the AUS.

I did not have to wait long for results. After a week or so, I received a note from Rosciszewski requesting an immediate meeting. As soon as I met him in a little room in Chmielna Street, I had a premonition of impending disaster. Rosciszewski, imploring me to keep the matter an absolute secret, put all the cards on the table face up.

'We have ascertained beyond a shadow of doubt,' he said, 'that the man is an agent of the Gestapo.'

I was staggered. I had had vague suspicions before, but this confirmation of the worst possible surmise came as a real shock to me.

'This is a pretty mess. An agent of the Gestapo participating in a conference with the Government Plenipotentiary and the Commander-in-Chief of the Home Army, not to mention the rest of us into the bargain. We ought to arrange for a Requiem for our souls right away! What are you going to do now?'

Rosciszewski had a plan ready.

'Look here, Zielinski,' he said, 'don't you do anything. The SOS, or rather I myself, will settle the matter.'

'How?' I asked.

By way of reply he touched his temple with his pointed finger and said:

'That's how.'

Within a few days I received a report that the chairman of the AUS had been shot dead in Chmielna Street by Rosciszewski himself.

What information and what addresses the man had communicated to the Gestapo before he was shot, and how much was known by his agents, who were still alive, remained to be found out. The arrests of members of the SOS, which took place both before and after the shooting, indicated that the organisation was pretty well penetrated by German agents. However, no members of the Government Plenipotentiary's Office, of Civil Resistance, or of the Command of the Home Army were arrested. It may be that the precautions taken were effective, or it may be that the chairman of the AUS was too ambitious, and wanted to discover the entire leadership of the underground rather than present the Gestapo with any incomplete reports.

The final episode of the matter was the kidnapping of Rosciszewski. After he had killed the chairman of the AUS, he went into hiding and broke off all contacts with the Directorate of Civil Resistance. It came as a complete surprise to us when we heard that the Gestapo had hauled him out of his secret hide-out, the address of which was not known even by his closest collaborators. The Gestapo agents waited in the early morning until the milkwoman arrived, and when the door was opened, in answer to her call, Rosciszewski's fate was sealed. There were rumours that his capture was the result of an act of personal vengeance on the part of the dead Gestapo agent's fiancee, the dancer, Mann.

In this way one of the most active members of the underground met his untimely death. Though he was ideologically at the opposite pole to me, Rosciszewski became one of the closest collaborators of the Directorate of Civil Resistance. A man of fearless courage, he and his organisation, 'Reveille', were two pillars on which Civil Resistance could always depend when it came to carrying out a difficult and dangerous task.

Action against cinemas and German lotteries

Among the organisations which were linked with Civil Resistance but did not join the SOS, were the Union of Polish Syndicalists and 'Dash', which was the underground arm of that section of the Labour Party which followed Felczak and Widy-Wirski. The Union conducted energetic propaganda whose conspiratorial ideology was rather remote from reality, while 'Dash' undertook tasks that involved the use of arms.

I have already mentioned that the Directorate of Civil Resistance proclaimed a boycott of cinema theatres which exhibited only films supplied by the propaganda agencies, and which as a rule served German interests. To enforce the boycott, various methods were employed, inscriptions on the walls of cinemas pillorying cinema-goers, the scattering in cinemas of leaflets justifying the boycott, the planting of stench-producing or cloth-destroying substances, and appropriate propaganda in the underground press. It had considerable effect, but the cinemas continued to open their doors, and thoughtless people still visited them. The Directorate of Civil Resistance, decided, therefore, to aim a more direct blow at them by destroying their technical equipment. 'Dash' undertook to carry out this action. On the appointed day, and at the same hour, armed squads of 'Dash' raided the Warsaw cinemas, and after terrorising the operators, set fire to or otherwise damaged the machinery. The action succeeded in six cinemas, while in others it encountered some obstacles; the six, however, were put out of action for some time.

Similarly, in connection with the decision of the Directorate of Civil Resistance to impose a boycott on German lotteries in the Government General, the same action squads carried out, on October 28, 1943, a series of raids on the various offices of the lottery; and in six of them they destroyed all the records and confiscated large quantities of lottery tickets.

Some days later, the people of Warsaw were astonished to see, driving at great speed along the main streets, a motor-car from which three men were throwing into the air piles of leaflets. These were eagerly picked up by the populace in anticipation of some underground announcement. In fact, the leaflets consisted of lottery tickets carrying on the reverse an overprinted appeal to Poles to boycott the German lottery.

In order to carry out their hazardous actions on behalf of Civil Resistance, 'Dash' needed increasing amounts of money for the purchase of arms, which they bought from various sources, but mainly from the Germans themselves. The trade in arms flourished particularly strongly after the war had taken a decisive turn in favour of the Allies. The demoralised Germans were selling everything, but the keenest demand was for arms and munitions. This trade was concentrated in the neighbourhood of the Main Railway Station, in Chmielna and Zielna Streets. 'Dash's' demands induced me to study this particular market. Donning suitable clothes, to avoid being too conspicuous among the crowd of traders and buyers, I entered Chmielna Street from the Marshall Street end. I immediately found myself plunged into a lively street market. Men and women were standing on the pavements and in the roadway holding in their hands a variety of articles, old clothes, boots, overcoats, kitchenware, towels, linen, etc. Against the walls sat old women huddled in numerous skirts, blouses and sweaters, as it was already cold. In front of them stood enormous baskets filled with loaves and rolls of bread, or haberdashery. Amid this hubbub and noise, bargain-hunters were examining the wares on offer with the utmost care and haggling about the price. Here and there, moving silently, were German soldiers, the most important clients in this unusual market. Similar markets existed at several other points in the Capital, notwithstanding the fact that the Germans raided them regularly, confiscating the goods and arresting the men and women.

I turned into Zielna Street and, carefully watching all that was happening, I walked on quietly. I soon caught the eye of one of the men, and then of another. One of them moved closer to me, and walking by my side opened the conversation.

'What is it you're after?'

'Nothing in particular. I'm just looking round to find something worth buying.'

'If you're looking for hard or soft stuff, you've come to the wrong place. You should go to Fraternal Street and to Napoleon Square.'

My companion, who had the sort of face one sees only in a nightmare, was telling me nothing new; for in Fraternal Street, or in Napoleon Square, one could see at any time of the day a line of men standing at regular intervals, like marking stakes, and muttering under their noses, as if they were talking to themselves: 'Hard, soft, buying, selling. . . .' These were dealers in gold and paper dollars, and also in gold roubles, a trade punishable by death.

'No, that's not what I am after.'

'May be you are looking for little pipe-lengths?' my strange companion asked, looking meaningly at me.

'Have you got some?'

'Why not? What sort do you want?'

'What have you got?'

'I can offer you Walters, Vis and Parabellum.'

'New?'

'You don't expect them to come straight from the factory, do you? But they are in good condition.'

'Could I see them?'

'Are you alone?'

'Alone.'

'Well, see that house opposite? Walk up to the first floor and wait for me.'

I went into the house without hesitation. The place was safe. If an *agent provocateur* came there, he would be bumped off straight away by the arms vendors. There was no question of their robbing a client or denouncing him to the Gestapo. If any robbery were to occur, news of it would spread and put an end to the trade; and as for the Gestapo, it was out of the question, because the vendors were as good Poles as any.

After a few minutes the man arrived, accompanied by another, whom I had not seen before. We were standing on the landing. The newcomer produced a revolver from his pocket.

'It's not loaded. You can examine it.' I examined a Walter revolver in good condition.

'How much?'

'Eight thou.,' he answered.

'And what is the price of a Vis?'

'Six thou.'

'And a Parabellum?'

'Five, or six, according to the condition it is in.'

In this way I found out the current prices, which was the main purpose of my expedition. However, to keep appearances I bought a Walter with two clips, and before leaving I asked:

'Have you got any Colts?'

I wanted to find out whether American revolvers from drops had found their way into the market. They looked at me with new interest.

'No, we haven't got that article, but we would pay for it well.'

I laughed, said good-bye, and left the premises of the two-man concern, followed by a valedictory:

'Should you need more, you can always find us in Zielna.'

I was mistaken. The concern consisted of three partners; for the third was standing sentry in the doorway below.

I met the chief of 'Dash' and his right-hand man, Widy-Wirski, for the last time during the Warsaw Rising, when, as soldiers of the Home Army, they were on guard duty at the Polytechnic gate in Noakowski Street. After the 'liberation' of 1945 they soon became important figures. Felczak was appointed Governor of Pomorze, while Widy-Wirski became Governor of Posnania. Both offered their services wholeheartedly to the Communist regime.

The Socialist Fighting Organisation

The Directorate of Civil Resistance collaborated closely with the Socialist Armed Organisation (SAO), while I, personally collaborated just as closely with its chief, Leszek Raabe, with whom I struck up a genuine friendship. The position of the SAO in the underground and in the Polish Socialist Party was not very clear at first. The leading personality in the Party, Casimir Puzak (pseudonym Basil) deliberately ignored its existence. This was due to a split among the Socialists in the underground movement which divided them into two groups, one, Liberty, Equality and Independence (WRN), with Puzak and Zaremba at its head, and the other, the Polish Socialist group, of which the leadership was in the hands of Markowski, Wachowicz, Raabe, Chudoba, Osobka and others. The split had been preceded by a misunderstanding between Puzak and Zaremba on the one hand and Zygmunt Zulawski and Stanislaw Dubois on the other. At one time the WRN section of the Polish Socialist Party, represented by Puzak, left the Political Consultative Committee and were replaced by the Polish Socialist group, represented by Markowski. As a result, Leszek Raabe was delegated by them to the General Commission of Civil Resistance; after he had broken with Wachowicz, Chudoba and Osobka, who were even at that time taking a rather extremist attitude and glancing towards the East. At that time the SAO enjoyed the support of the father of Polish Socialism, Thomas Arciszewski, who regarded the organisation as a re-incarnation of the struggles, spirit and traditions of the armed revolutionary organisation of 1905.

The complicated nature of SAO's situation is best illustrated by the following episode. The Government Plenipotentiary was paying financial subsidies to various organisations for the purchase of arms, liaison and travelling. In the case of the organisations linked with Civil Resistance, the money was paid through the Directorate of Civil Resistance. After having agreed with Leszek on what the SAO needed, and after approving the budget submitted by him, I took the matter up with the Government Plenipotentiary, Jankowski, recommending that it be sanctioned. The Plenipotentiary perused the report with some embarrassment and said:

'You see, I shouldn't like to give my sanction without first consulting Basil. You know yourself that the situation within the Polish Socialist Party is rather complicated, and I shouldn't like to make a false step.'

I fully agreed with this view, and the matter had to be delayed. After about a fortnight, however, the budget was approved. When he informed me of his decision, the Plenipotentiary seemed to be amused.

'I showed Basil the SAO budget and asked him if he would

like to have a look at it and give me his opinion. And do you know what he said?'

'No,' I answered, 'but I should very much like to know.'

'Well, he told me that he knew nothing of any such organisation.'

'How is that possible? He must know of it. But what is your decision?'

'Very simple. If Basil does not recognise this organisation, we have a free hand. I have sanctioned the budget.'

The SAO specialised in railway sabotage and in propaganda for sabotage among the railwaymen. It achieved considerable results, which they reported in the most minute detail. It was a real pleasure to read their reports, giving the locality, date and exact hour, the serial numbers of the locomotives or wagons destroyed, the description of the freight in which the explosive charges had been placed, or the exact position of the destroyed shunting points or signals. The reports were frequently confirmed, unfortunately, by German reprisals. The results obtained and proofs of the efficacy of these actions were communicated to the Government in London. By way of example I should like to quote two of our telegrams:

'October 1, 1943. The German journal "Kolejowiec" complained that Polish railwaymen fasten motor vehicles in the wagons insecurely, that they do not protect the freight from shifting, and that they distribute it badly in the wagons, as a result of which axles are overburdened and rolling stock is being damaged.'

'November 9, 1943. The Official Gazette of the Cracow Railway District lists 500 wagons and 200 tankers as lost in transit, and offers rewards to railwaymen who help in tracing them.'

The Socialist Armed Organisation also maintained regular contact with the Warsaw Ghetto. They gave aid to their Socialist comrades in the Ghetto, and I know that they managed to organise the escape of a number of persons and groups, some as late as the end of the Rising in the Ghetto.

On one occasion I asked Leszek if he had not got a cameraman among his men, as the Directorate of Civil Resistance would have liked to shoot a film showing life under the

German occupation, which would be sent to London. I thought it would be a great feat if we succeeded, for instance, in filming some armed actions or scenes from the Ghetto, the horrors of which went beyond the bounds of human imagination, and which the West refused to believe. Leszek received the idea enthusiastically, and within a few days a special film unit was formed. After many difficulties a film camera was secured and a number of scenes in Warsaw were shot at first hand. A mobile platform was prepared in an old truck by cutting an opening in the back wall of the truck, and everything worth filming was shot. It was remarkable that one of the members of the film unit was a Pole of German parentage whose brother was a well-known *Volksdeutsche,* who made a fortune in illegal commercial transactions. I need hardly add that not only filming, but even the possession of a film camera was a capital offence.

I saw a showing of this film, arranged in Zoliborz. The windows were carefully covered, a white sheet was stretched on a frame, and there before us was the entrance to the Ghetto, guarded by gendarmes, behind whom appeared a crowd of wretches in rags, with armbands on their sleeves. Another scene, filmed from a window with the camera concealed by a pillow, the corner of which continually popped up in front of the lens, showed a manhunt in Zoliborz, barbed wire fences and concrete bunkers in front of German offices, and also, scrawled on pavements and walls, the initials PW, standing for Fighting Poland.

All this was quite good, but not enough to be shown abroad. I was speculating on the ways of doing something out of the ordinary when an opportunity presented itself in the Peasant Festival, during which a passing-out parade of cadet-officers of the underground Peasant Battalions was to be held in the forests of Zamosc. The camera-man attended the festival and shot a number of scenes, such as that of the cadets parading before visitors from Warsaw, who included a General of the Home Army, also Casimir Baginski and the Commander of the Peasant Battalions, Francis Kaminski. Also filmed were a field Mass, and a banquet to which a great number of peasants from the neighbouring villages were invited.

All this took place in a fine, sun-bathed clearing in the forest, though it was frequently interrupted by alerts caused by sweeps of German reconnaissance planes; for the enemy suspected that something unusual was happening in the forest.

Everybody was excited by the idea that the film would be sent abroad and exhibited there. Everyone wanted to add to it; but the most audacious offer was made by a peasant boy, the commander of a partisan detachment in the vicinity, who proposed to the operator that he would arrange for him the derailing of a German military train in broad daylight, so that the filming could take place under the most favourable conditions. The operator was ready to undertake it, so, immediately after the celebrations were over, they set out by night in several carts for the young commander's headquarters. Driving along in the dark night, they suddenly came to a crossroads where they were greeted by bursts of machine-gun fire. One man was killed, but the others escaped across the fields. It was an ambush, set by the Germans because they suspected that something unusual was going on that day. In the confusion, the film camera was lost, and with it the scenes that had already been taken. It is possible that the Germans found it, and if they did, it is also possible that the film reached a foreign country, but not the one for which it was intended.

We were disconsolate over this loss, and at our next meeting the subject was constantly referred to, especially by the operator, a young boy with a speech defect. When I met him after the Warsaw Rising, more than a year later, in the crowded streets of Milanowek, when the whole matter had long been forgotten, he still remembered it and said to me:

'It's a great pity we lost that film, sir.'

The boy had both his hands bandaged up to the elbows.

'What is the matter with you?' I asked.

'A "roaring cow" burnt my hands, and I don't know what's going to happen to them.'

Leszek recommended to me for the job of district commander of Civil Resistance in Lwow a lecturer of Lwow University, Ostrowski. He was a young and intelligent man, who made a favourable impression on me; he was particularly keen to undertake actions against the Communists, so he had to be restrained; for, although we carried on energetic anti-Communist propaganda, we were opposed to the activities of the National Armed Forces, which aimed at the liquidation of Polish Communists (and in some cases also non-Communists). Ostrowski was later appointed District Government Plenipotentiary, and I supported that appointment too. Later, during the Warsaw Rising, we received a report that when the Soviet troops occupied Lwow, Ostrowski immediately offered his services to the puppet Government of Osobka, and by the following year he was already in the high office of Governor of Cracow. In that office he distinguished himself by exerting pressure on the ailing Vincent Witos to co-operate with the Lublin regime of Osobka, and by purloining furniture from the Royal Castle with which to furnish his own apartment. When, in November 1947, I escaped with my wife to Sweden, I was informed that the Warsaw Government were energetically protesting to the Government in Stockholm against our being granted political asylum. The protests were presented by the Ambassador of the Warsaw regime in Stockholm, the self-same Ostrowski whose appointment as leader of Civil Resistance in Lwow I had signed with my own hand. This remains the only black spot in my memories of the Socialist Armed Organisation.

During one period I had a standing arrangement to meet Leszek every week, on the same day and at the same hour, at the corner of Zlota and Zielna. Should one of us be prevented from keeping the appointment, the other was to wait at the same spot the following day. One day, I came to meet him punctually at the appointed hour, but although I waited fifteen minutes, Leszek failed to put in an appearance. The same thing happened the next day. I became somewhat uneasy, so I sent a note through the underground post enquiring what had happened and proposing a new date for a meeting. This was attended not by Leszek, but by his deputy, Kaczanowski, who was greatly upset and worried. Before I could open my mouth, he said:

'Leszek has disappeared without trace. He was last seen in the "Little Horse".'

The 'Little Horse' was a small café in Buxom Street, run

by the well-known sportsman, Trojanowski, which Leszek was in the habit of using for appointments. His disappearance was a bitter blow. He was such a splendid young man.

'What could have happened?' I asked. 'You must find out through Intelligence if the Gestapo have got him in Szucha Avenue, or if he's in Pawiak prison.'

'We've already made enquiries, but we haven't been able to get any information as yet.'

Kaczanowski, a small, dark-haired man, was completely downcast. We were both trying to figure out what could have happened. The Germans were not in the habit of acting secretly; as a rule, they did everything with a great deal of noise and ostentation. If they wanted to arrest a person, they just raided a café openly, without waiting for him to come out into the street.

Some time later we ascertained that Leszek was neither in Szucha Avenue nor in Pawiak prison, but we also found out that there were a few cells in Pawiak prison for the solitary confinement of persons whose names were kept absolutely secret and not even entered in the prison registry. Was it possible that Leszek was one of them? The mystery remained.

It was never established how Leszek Raabe disappeared. But circumstantial evidence gradually accumulated indicating that he had got into the merciless clutches of the Russian NKVD, which was then already active in the underground on territories occupied by the Germans. It should be borne in mind that from the point of view of Osobka, Chudoba, Wachowicz, and their group of Socialists, Leszek was a renegade, and such heresy had to be eliminated.

Leszek was succeeded in the command of the Socialist Armed Organisation by Kaczanowski, with whom I co-operated until the outbreak of the Warsaw Rising. We both had a slightly dangerous and amusing adventure. I met him and his newly-appointed deputy in a hide-out in Marshall Street, close to Dabrowski Square. We were both in a hurry and rapidly settled all the business in hand. I left first and quickly descended the stairs . . . straight into the muzzle of a pistol in the hand of a German gendarme, whom I had not noticed standing in the entrance hall. In answer to the familiar, 'Hands up', I raised my arms; while another gendarme searched my pockets. I felt somewhat uneasy; for although on this occasion I happened to be without my revolver, which I nearly always carried in my pocket, I had on me a German aviation weekly, 'The Eagle', and between two leaves glued together, I was carrying secret messages. The gendarme, however, showed no interest in 'The Eagle', as he was obviously searching for arms. At that very moment Kaczanowski came running down the stairs, and the same thing began all over again. We were kept waiting in the hall while the gendarmes dealt with other people entering or leaving the house. We had a feeling that we might be taken to the Gestapo for examination, so, taking advantage of the fact that the gendarmes had turned their backs on us, I pulled 'The Eagle' out of my pocket and placed it out of sight on the large letter box. I breathed a sigh of relief. Kaczanowski looked around and whispered in my ear:

'There is an exit through the back yard into Szkolna Street.'

'Let's run for it,' I suggested. 'You lead!'

'Right. You follow me.'

Very quietly, foot by foot, we moved to the back of the hall, unobserved by the gendarmes, who were occupied with searching new arrivals. Next moment we were in the yard, and for a second expected to hear the cry, 'Halt!'; but nothing happened. So we crossed the yard to the gate leading into Szkolna and there, emerging into the street, we ran for our lives. People looked at us as if we were mad; but no one stopped us. We came to a halt in Hospital Street, and I started to worry again about the messages between the pages of 'The Eagle'; while Kaczanowski was anxious about his deputy, who remained in the house. He decided to ring him up. An amusing conversation then ensued:

'How are you? Wlodek speaking. How do you feel, how are things with you?'

'Are you mad? You saw me only a minute ago!'

'Never mind, I want to know if you have any visitors?'

'What visitors? I am all by myself, reading a book.'

'In that case I want to ask you to do me a favour. My companion was tightening his shoe laces in the hall, and placed a
copy of "The Eagle" . . . you know, the German aviation
weekly . . . on the top of the letter-box. Go down, but
watch your step, and if you can, get that journal, for he hasn't
read it yet. He will call for it later. I'll 'phone again in a few
minutes.'

Which Kaczanowski did.

'Well, have you got "The Eagle"?'

'I have.'

'Well, and how are things in the house?'

'How should they be? You really must be mad.'

'I can't explain it over the telephone. Bring "The Eagle"
here. We are waiting at the corner of Szkolna and St. Cross
Street.'

Five minutes later Kaczanowski's deputy arrived, and it
turned out that he knew nothing about the house being
raided by the Germans, who had been searching everyone
around. When he went down to fetch 'The Eagle', the
Germans were no longer there.

The end of the Socialist Armed Organisation, as a military
unit, came during the Warsaw Rising. At its outset, during
an attack on the Germans in Zoliborz, they were wiped out
to the last man. Kaczanowski was one of the first to be killed.

Stanislaw Dubois

One afternoon I was hurrying along Ordynacka Street in
the direction of Tamka. I was making for the 'Kazik' bar,
where I hoped to find my friend Stas Dubois, with whom I
had maintained the closest contact from the very beginning
of the underground movement. Just as Rataj had appointed
me his deputy in the event of his arrest, so Niedzialkowski
had appointed Dubois. As Niedzialkowski had informed me
of it officially when he was arrested on that memorable day,
December 23, 1939, I reported it to the leaders of the underground. However, the underground Socialist Party refused to
accept Niedzialkowski's decision, and delegated Casimir
Puzak as their representative on the Political Consultative

Committee. I was not at all surprised by this change and mention it here only to give the true facts of the matter. Later on, Stas, with the support of his followers, organised a kind of opposition in the underground Socialist Party and edited a journal entitled 'The Barricade of Liberty'. Later still, his group joined the underground Revolutionary Party of Polish Socialists.

I was looking forward to the meeting with great pleasure, for Stas was an excellent companion to have during the hard times through which we were passing. I often scolded him for taking his meals in the 'Kazik' Bar, but I understood that he did so because of the credit he had with the proprietor, who was his good friend. Stas, owing to the unquenchable thirst with which nature had endowed him, occasionally needed such credit. Reaching my destination, I found myself in front of the modest entrance of the 'Kazik' Bar. I went inside.

I was struck by the strange, desolate appearance of the place. The proprietor stood behind the bar, but apart from him there was not a soul in the place. The elderly man looked at me closely as I went up to him and asked:

'Has the Editor been in to-day?'

Instead of answering, he said:

'You are a friend of the Editor's, Mr. Stefan, I think?'

'That's right,' I said.

The proprietor hurried from behind the bar, came up to me, and although the place was deserted, whispered in my ear:

'The Gestapo took him away fifteen minutes ago, together with Imbus (Borski, editor of 'Robotnik'), another man, and two women. The editor came as usual to have dinner with his company. They had already been served when two civilians entered and sat down at another table. They ordered two glasses of beer and just sat there. As soon as the editor and his company had finished their dinner, the two pulled out revolvers, went up to the table, and took them all to the car waiting in the street. You'd better not stay here, because they may come back.'

The advice was sound and I left at once. I took the street

leading to Tamka, and on my way I met a young girl, a member of the Polish Socialist Party named Genachow, and a squat boy in a leather coat, Ferszt; both of Jewish origin. I knew them well as Stas's collaborators; they were hiding in the Aryan part of the city. I stopped them, enquiring where they were going.

'To the "Kazik" Bar, to meet Stas,' they answered.

'Stas was arrested there fifteen minutes ago; I have just left it. Come with me towards the river,' I said, noticing on their faces the familiar reaction; their eyes suddenly darkened, their faces became pale and their features drawn. The boy put one hand into his pocket. He was armed.

I passed on the story the proprietor of the bar had told me, which gave no indication of how the Gestapo had found Stas. We dispersed quickly, to alert all concerned. I went from one place to another thinking of Stas and of what we had both lived through together. He had been the youngest deputy of the Seym. Together with our friend Mieczyslaw Thugutt, we had often climbed the Tatras and skied in Zakopane. I often saw Stas at mass meetings of workers, with hundreds of eyes glued on him in admiration. I remembered the time he and I had crossed the frontier illegally to meet Vincent Witos and Casimir Baginski in Prague, on the very day of President Masaryk's funeral. On the way there and back we crossed the frontier between Poland and Czechoslovakia by night, over thickly wooded hills. . . . Now, as each door at which I knocked opened, the same scene was repeated; my ill tidings produced the same silent despair and fear. I left to others the notification of his wife. I had no strength left to face that ordeal.

Some days later we received news from Pawiak that the Germans were cross-examining Stas and torturing him. He told them nothing, and after several months of examination they deported him to Auschwitz. From there, they hauled him back twice more to Szucha Avenue and to Pawiak for further investigations. These were the most terrible days, for he was tortured again. He was finally sent back to Auschwitz, where he proved to be what he had been all his life, a real man. When Kostek Jagiello, his devoted collaborator, organised his escape from Oswiecim, Stas refused, reluctant to expose the fellow sufferers in his barrack to reprisals. According to former inmates of Auschwitz, he became the head of the camp's underground organisation. One day SS men led him to the place of execution and shot him.

Emissary Michael Strzelecki

Among the men whom our work in the underground brought closely together was Michael. I do not know where he came from or what education he had had, but to me he was a typical Warsaw working class man who had seen much and knew a great deal. He was always in high spirits, he liked good company, and he was in his element in the underground, like a fish in water. He was dropped by parachute near Lowicz, as an emissary of the Government, which gave him a respectable standing in the underground. The drop was made, through an error of judgement, not in the Government General but on territory incorporated in the Reich. Michael, together with the other parachutists, including Celt, went through harrowing experiences before they arrived in Warsaw. When crossing the frontier between the Reich and the Government General, they killed several frontier guards, whereupon the Germans organised a manhunt and issued posters offering a reward for the capture of the 'bandits from Lowicz'. This added a halo of heroism to Michael's reputation, which had many victims among the young women of the underground, to whose charms Michael easily succumbed.

We soon became friends, though I did not take his political mission seriously, which is perhaps why I do not even remember what is was. On the other hand, I remember a number of amusing episodes.

On one occasion, when we were spending the night with friends in a small apartment in which all those present could hardly find room to lie down, I found Michael in the morning in the bathroom. He was fast asleep in the bath. When I woke him up and he began to undress to have a wash, I noticed that he took off, one after the other, five shirts. Seeing my astonishment, Michael explained:

'Although I have got a permanent hide-out, I drop in there

only occasionally and I never know when I shall be there, or where I shall be spending the night. That's why I have on me several changes of underclothing.'

'But how do you manage to have a clean shirt?'

'That's very simple. When one shirt gets dirty, I put it on next to the skin with a clean one on top; and so I go on, till they all get soiled.'

Michael had a great personal interest in my radio liaison; for I frequently transmitted to London in my code his confidential reports to the Government. He knew the difficulties we had in securing safe hide-outs from which to transmit the messages, and he promised to find me a suitable apartment. When we next met, he told me triumphantly that he had found a place but . . . and here the self-assured Michael became somewhat embarrassed.

'You see, old man, the hide-out is in the apartment of a very attractive lady, whom I like very much. I wanted to show off before her, and told her that I have got my own radio station, which I use to talk with the Government in London. So you see, when we get there, I should very much like you to speak to me a little more deferentially (here Michael blushed), so that she should know I am your superior. It can't matter much to you, because what you want is a hide-out and not prestige.'

Michael was right. All I wanted was a hide-out for the radio station, and everything else was of little importance. So, the following day, in a fine villa in Mokotow, I moved about cap in hand in a beautifully appointed apartment, in the company of Michael and a really lovely lady; and as we inspected the house I glibly answered every one of his silly technical questions, 'Yes, chief . . . No, chief . . . As you say, sir!' But we got the hide-out, and kept it.

When he was about to return to England, some of us, Michael's friends in the underground, arranged a farewell party. We chose the canteen of the National Economic Bank in Fraternal Street, where only trusted people foregathered, so it was relatively safe to meet there. We met at noon, with the ladies, in a reserved room, where a well-provided table was awaiting us. Michael was placed in the chair of honour, and he was in his best form, addressing gallantries to the ladies and telling innumerable funny stories.

Towards the end of the dinner, I knocked on a glass with my knife, to warn those present that I was going to make a speech. Everyone stopped talking and looked towards me. Michael became very serious. In touching words I bade him farewell, enumerating his great deeds, beginning with 'the murder at Lowicz' and ending with the bravado with which he moved about Warsaw, swarming with Germans, although he knew that the Gestapo was looking for him. Then, with great solemnity, I concluded:

'Dear Michael! I should now like to inform you, and all those present here, that London has sent me an order which it will be an honour for me to carry out. In the name of our supreme authority I have the honour to decorate you with the badge established for parachutists who make the jump into our country. You are the first to receive this distinction.'

I then advanced towards Michael and pinned to his lapel a bronze medal. The company, deeply moved, crowded round Michael, embracing and kissing him.

In the end, Michael was not able to keep up his part. With much laughter he told the surprised gathering that an hour previously he had been walking with me down the street, when we both decided to play a joke on them. We had noticed in the window of one of the innumerable shops in Warsaw, in which the starving populace were selling out everything they had, the medal which was now dangling on the lapel of his jacket. We bought it, with the result known to all.

Everybody present was furious with me. I withstood the initial attacks, and as there was still plenty of food and drink on the table, the anger soon subsided, to be followed by a discussion, with many hostile glances in my direction, on whether the incident should be treated as a joke or a dirty trick. As the company grew quieter, the opinion prevailed that if Michael had not been privy to the plot, if he had been fooled by me, it would have been a particularly dirty trick. However, since Michael had been in it, the incident might be regarded as a joke, of course a rather lame joke, 'because Stefan can't afford a better one', because 'you can't expect anything better from Stefan', not to mention the fact that 'nothing is sacred to him'. When the discussion was over and people had a look at the medal, there was renewed merriment in the reserved room in Fraternal Street. The medal showed a fireman's helmet, surrounded by pickaxes, axes and other tools, and the proud caption: 'Twenty-fifth anniversary of the establishment of the fire brigade in Radom'.

Such was the brighter side of my connection with Michael. It should not offend anyone because of the tragic reality that underlay these episodes; for laughter was the redeeming feature that saved us from going mad. If we had not been able to laugh occasionally we would not have survived the five frightful years of occupation. There never was a time when wit flourished so vigorously as during the war. A collection of funny stories and anecdotes was published in a book of about 200 pages, 'The Germans—laugh at them', edited by Stanislaw Dzikowski. I would hazard the opinion that as long as the Poles were able to laugh and to joke they could not be vanquished.

A few days before his return to England, Michael was caught by the Gestapo and taken to Berlin. From that moment he vanished without trace. The Gestapo discovered his hide-out, which was in an apartment occupied by the parents of the first wife of Cyrankiewicz, the present Prime Minister of the Communist Government in Poland; their name was Munk, if I remember rightly; but strange to say no one in the house was harmed. The matter is still awaiting clarification.

CHAPTER VI

"SWIT", The Secret
of the Commander-in-Chief

A Mysterious Telegram

One day, late in 1942, in one of our secret hide-outs, Zosia was deciphering a telegram just received from London. She lifted her eyes from the large table littered with sheets of paper, and said to me excitedly:

'Take a look at this. It's interesting.'

I bent over the columns of figures with which Zosia miraculously juggled to extract a coherent text, and read:

'Do you listen to secret underground radio station broadcasting daily in the Polish language at 8 a.m. and 7 p.m. on the 31 metre band?'

I was astounded and surprised. We knew nothing of the existence of such a station. The only radio station broadcasting in Polish that we knew well was the BBC, which, in view of the fact that all receivers had been confiscated by the Germans, was being listened to secretly on receivers which had either not been given up or had been constructed in our underground workshops.

Long before 7 p.m. Zosia, Joey and I were eagerly waiting in Joey's hide-out in Marshall Street. Joey had turned on his receiver in good time. Exactly at seven o'clock, a strong, clear voice filled our room. It was obvious that the station was a powerful one. A few words by the announcer sufficed to make it clear to us that the station was anti-German and transmitting from somewhere inside occupied Poland. We racked our brains for an answer to the riddle. Where could the broadcast be coming from? With our hard-won knowledge of the possibilities of underground radio, we could not understand how such technical perfection could have been achieved. However, it was plain that our own fantastic hope had been turned into reality by someone else. This underground station was indeed broadcasting to us, and we could only marvel at the excellence of the transmission.

I immediately sent a telegram to London praising the technical achievement of the unknown station. I also mentioned that we knew nothing about it. We continued to listen to the station regularly, but we remained mystified.

And then one day all became clear. The mystery was solved by a telegram from London, which was classified as top secret. We were not to divulge the information to a single person in Poland: the secret SWIT radio station was located abroad— in an allied country! SWIT was seeking to create the impression that it was an underground transmitter operating in occupied Poland for two reasons: in the first place, this would lead the Western world to place greater trust in reports broadcast by it, and in the second, it would confuse the Germans and harass them with its anti-German propaganda. The telegram emphasised that we were being entrusted with a secret shared only by the Supreme Commander of the Polish Forces, who personally vouched for its safety. It went on to stress the point that the entire plan would fall through unless our own radio stations furnished SWIT with the latest information on the situation in Poland. Only if SWIT showed detailed knowledge of daily events inside Poland could it masquerade as an underground radio station.

The idea appealed to us. In a mood of elation, we vied with one another in suggesting ways of making fools of the Germans. Nor did the political significance of the idea escape us. Of course, it would be absolutely essential to provide SWIT with a steady stream of up-to-date news items. Events in Warsaw would have to be reported on the day they occurred. This was feasible, as our radio stations were in Warsaw and our chief code expert, Zosia, was always available.

All this brought into being a type of activity which was to provide us with many hair-raising adventures and narrow escapes.

Work and Ruses

Day after day I roamed the streets of Warsaw and dropped into underground meeting places in search of sensational news items which would enable SWIT to go on the air that evening. If during the night the Germans had posted a list of persons executed for one reason or another—these huge red posters were a tragically familiar sight to every Warsovian— or if they had put up one of their numerous decrees, or if something had transpired which was the talk of the town, I would return to my temporary hide-out and draft my information into a telegram. Zosia would then encipher it and take the dangerous slip of paper to the radio station.

Somewhere on Garden Street, or perhaps on Peacock Street, which afforded a view of the Ghetto beyond the wall, the loitering look-outs would give Zosia the 'all clear' signal as she hurried by with her message. A glance upwards at the window of the apartment housing the transmitter: the curtains were drawn back, the flower-pot was in the pre-arranged spot. Obviously the coast was clear. And now for the knock on the door. Two loud raps, one soft one, and again, two loud and one soft. The door would open slightly. Seated at the table with his earphones on would be Wladek or Martin— perhaps concentrating on 'getting London'; in front of him, a radio transmitter, its tubes flickering, the transformer humming; above him, the aerial high up in the room, casting a weird shadow against the ceiling. His face would be tense, as his hand beat out a staccato of dots and dashes: 'Station No. 30 calling. . . . Can you hear me?' The signal would be repeated again and again. And then: 'Over'. As he removed his hands from the key the telegraphist would become all ears. In a moment, his face would light up, and with a satisfied nod he would reach for the telegram. London heard him very well. A few seconds more and the news item for SWIT would be borne on invisible waves from Warsaw to London.

That evening we would hear the item broadcast back to us over SWIT. It would be amplified and accompanied by a commentary. It would be heard by thousands of Poles inside Poland who would be endangering their very lives by listening to it. It would be heard by thousands of Jews, sealed within the ghettos, for whom radio was the sole remaining link with the outside world; who would rather die than give up their radio set, which they had hidden more carefully than their gold and diamonds. It would be heard by Poles in Sweden and in Switzerland and in the occupied countries, such as France. It would be heard in German prisoner-of-war-camps, for in almost all of these Polish ingenuity managed to acquire or to construct a secret receiving set. The one place where Poles would not hear it would be in the country from which the broadcast originated.

The 'Nowy Kurier Warszawski', a Polish daily newspaper published by the Germans, came on the streets at about one o'clock in the afternoon. It was crammed with loathsome German propaganda, but there was always something in it that would prove of interest to SWIT, which had among its other objectives that of combating this propaganda. However, since the preparation and sending of a telegram took several hours, how could SWIT quote from the current issue of the 'Nowy Kurier Warszawski'? In the Polish underground nothing was impossible.

One day, at eight in the morning, I was standing, watchful and alert to what was going on around me, at the corner of Marshall Street and the Square of the Saviour, not far from where the 'Nowy Kurier Warszawski' was published. A moment later a familiar figure jumped off the trolley car. He looked tired and he was in need of a shave. Having carefully glanced up and down the street, we stepped into the nearest doorway and walked up the stairs. We paused and listened. No one was following us. My companion pulled a sheaf of galley proofs from his pocket, pressed them into my hand, and murmuring, 'See you to-morrow', bolted down the staircase.

I hurried to our hide-out. I was so pleased I felt like whistling. Spreading out the galley proofs, I began to scan the still damp sheets of the 'Nowy Kurier' five hours before it would be on sale. We had been fortunate in winning the co-operation of an employee in the editorial office, who promised to deliver to us early in the morning the first proofs of the newspaper. Our liaison man had just secured the initial batch from him. Working at top speed, we perused the galleys, selected our material, drafted the telegrams, and added a single word of instruction: 'Ridicule'. Soon the message was on its way to free London. That very evening Mr. Jozef Wierusz Kowalski, who because he was a Swiss citizen, had the right to own a receiving set, and who monitored SWIT's programmes for us, heard this news item come over his radio in his home in the Staszic Housing Estate.

'You are listening to Station SWIT. . . . To-day's "Nowy Kurier Warszawski" carries a decree of Governor General Frank increasing the fat rations for Poles in the so-called Government General. The stupid German thinks he can win over the population with a few grams of fat. . . .' More words of mockery followed.

Our monitor did not suspect that he was listening to a station located outside Poland. Indeed, since I had told him in advance exactly what parts of the programme I wanted him to take down, he would probably have been willing to stake his life on his conviction that SWIT was an underground transmitter.

The intelligence reports that drifted in to us advised us that the Germans were wild with rage, and were leaving no stone unturned in their efforts to locate the SWIT transmitter. Needless to say, such reports were music to our ears.

To carry out another ruse, I made an appointment in one of the countless coffee houses with which Warsaw abounded at that time, with an acquaintance who edited a secret underground newspaper. I asked him when he was putting out his next issue.

'Thursday,' he said. This was only Monday, so there was plenty of time to carry out the new idea.

'Will you be printing anything important?'

'Yes. The staff of the Luftwaffe has established its headquarters at Konstancin after its retreat from the front.'

The next day a telegram was forwarded to London with the note that the item was to be used on Thursday. Thursday morning SWIT was able to state: 'According to to-day's underground newspaper . . . the staff of the German air force has established headquarters at Konstancin, near Warsaw.' The commentary that followed discussed the significance of this fact.

We learned by listening to the BBC that this news item had been picked up by the radio and press of the whole world. It can hardly be wondered at that listeners abroad, as well as in the Polish underground, would literally have sworn that SWIT was broadcasting from inside Poland.

Inasmuch as the entire set-up was working smoothly by now, I decided that the time was ripe to give SWIT official status. A communique, signed by the Directorate of Civilian Resistance, appeared in the underground press, reporting the existence of the SWIT radio station, and giving the time schedule and wave-lengths on which it operated.

Intimidating the Germans

SWIT helped us not only to keep the world abreast of developments inside Poland, but also to intimidate the Germans, who, incidentally, carefully monitored its broadcasts. We addressed ourselves especially to those Germans who were guilty of atrocities in Poland. SWIT listed their crimes and made threats. Some of these Germans mended their ways; others made frantic efforts to be transferred to the Reich. One, the sheriff of Warsaw County, sought to justify his conduct to the underground movement through a Polish physician, whom he summoned under the pretext of illness, and to whom he conveyed his plea for mercy.

The following are samples of the type of threat we suggested be issued over SWIT:

'April 20, 1943. Broadcast a threat to Geyer, head of the German police in Kielce, who personally killed two village officials and the wife and two daughters of the village secretary during a reprisal expedition to Samsonowo. Broadcast a threat to Gestapo agent Witek in Lagow Kielecki for burning several families alive in a barn, and to railway official Vogt in Jedrzejow, who shot a passenger and railway worker Kudera without provocation.'

'October 15, 1943. This afternoon the Germans announced over the loudspeaker system the names of forty more hostages. The number has now risen to one hundred. Keep repeating the following announcement: "The Gestapo has recently embarked upon a new wave of terror. It has ordered mass round-ups of innocent citizens and the shooting of hostages, as occurred in Warsaw on October 13 and 14 of this year. The Poles cannot be intimidated by such senseless and cruel activity. In reprisal for this kind of terror, additional retaliatory measures will be taken by the underground".'

SWIT broadcast the death sentences that had been carried out against Gestapo agents by the Directorate of Civilian Resistance; it apprised the Polish population of sabotage instructions issued by the Directorate; and it appealed to the Allies for reprisals for German atrocities. It even quoted anti-German anecdotes. In brief, SWIT became a magnificent weapon in the battle against the occupying power in Poland.

Here are examples of this type of message:

'June 22, 1944. Announce that by virtue of a sentence of the special court for the Cracow district, there were executed Walenty Pawlik, Walenty Dec, and Wanda and Slawomir Madrad, who served as informers for the Gestapo. By virtue of a sentence of the special court in Warsaw, Antoni Pietrzak, a corporal in the Blue police, was executed for collaboration in the persecution of Jews.'

'April 23, 1943. Warsaw has been placarded to-day with posters carrying a proclamation by Mayor Leist, which calls for voluntary registration for work in the Reich and in the Government General. If the response is weak, forced registration is threatened. Leist promises prospective applicants they will receive the same food as the Germans, spiritual guidance, good housing, etc. . . . Call for resistance in the name of the Directorate of Civilian Resistance.'

'June 22, 1944. Near a church in Cracow, a pole supporting a loudspeaker was overturned. The pole bore the following inscription: "I have been lying for four years and am now going to confession".'

Emissary Nowak[1]

One day I received a report that an emissary of the Polish Government in London, who had secretly arrived in Poland via Sweden, wished to meet me. I nominated Malachowski Square as the place for our rendezvous. Arriving punctually, I had no difficulty in spotting the emissary among the few strollers. His behaviour conformed to that described in the report, and so did his appearance. I went up to him and spoke the password; the man gave me a knowing smile and the correct reply. I stretched out my hand to him. Everything was in order.

Emissary Nowak—for that was his alias—was a young man. He sported a short, neatly-trimmed moustache and he had a scar on his face. He eyed me with interest. 'I understand you are the director of SWIT,' he said.

'Yes, I am; but why do you ask?'

Whereupon Nowak launched into an explanation. It was with difficulty that I refrained from bursting into hearty laughter as he unfolded his story. Nowak had travelled by way of Sweden, where he had contacted some Poles who helped him slip into Poland through a German port. He learned from them that the entire Polish colony in Sweden, official as well as unofficial, listened in to SWIT. However, there was a difference of opinion among the radio audience. Some claimed that it was impossible for a secret broadcasting station to go on the air twice daily in a country under German occupation. They insisted that a few broadcasts would have sufficed for the Germans to locate it. (Those people know what they are talking about, I thought to myself.) Another group, consisting of SWIT'S enthusiastic supporters, maintained, on the strength of the subject matter of SWIT's broadcasts, that the transmitter *must* be inside Poland; for how else could it report events in Poland just as soon as they happened? To settle the dispute, Nowak promised that if he succeeded in arriving in Poland, and if he found the station to be really inside the country, he would let its listeners in Sweden know by broadcasting a pre-arranged message.

[1] At present Chief of the Voice of Free Poland, Radio Free Europe

When Nowak had finished, I said:

'Yes, it can be done. What is the message?'

The reply was something along the lines of, 'Janek sends greetings to Zosia'.

I did some quick thinking. This was Monday, I could send a telegram the following day, and by Wednesday London could surely be broadcasting the message.

'Good,' I said to Nowak, 'beginning Wednesday, SWIT will broadcast the message for three days.'

Nowak was greatly pleased. He began to heap high praise on SWIT'S splendid organisation and the heroism of those who worked for it without regard to the terrible danger that lurked on all sides. I did not feel embarrassed listening to these encomiums. After all, our telegraphers and look-outs *were* heroes who risked their lives daily.

The telegram went out, and from Wednesday on, we heard SWIT announce: 'Attention! Attention! We shall now broadcast an important message: "Janek sends greetings to Zosia".'

All doubts in the minds of the Polish colony in Sweden were resolved; but at the price of Nowak's credulity. I met him again much later, at a time when he had come to know the secret of SWIT.

'You certainly made a fool of me,' he said with a reproachful look. 'I can't hold it against you, of course, because I realise the situation demanded it. Do you know, when I got back to England from Poland I even swore to those in on the secret that SWIT was in Poland, because I had spoken with its director?'

Conflicting Complaints

Other, similar, incidents abounded. One day I arrived for a talk with a high functionary of the Government Plenipotentiary's office who was connected with the Department of Information and Propaganda, and who naturally did not know at that time that SWIT was operating in England. My interlocutor was visibly indignant and started off without any preliminaries:

'SWIT is functionally subordinate to our Department, and

I shall do my utmost to persuade the Plenipotentiary that it should be handed over to us.'

I told him in reply that SWIT was primarily an instrument of Civil Resistance, of which I was the head, and that I was not prepared to give up such a means of action. My interlocutor subsided slightly.

'In any case,' he said, 'I count upon you to take into the SWIT team some of our script-writers, and trust that you will put at our disposal several programmes a week.'

Without departing from the truth too violently, I told him that the SWIT team was complete, and that it could not function properly with two editorial centres working independently of each other.

Here my interlocutor exploded:

'If you refuse my proposals I shall get my own SWIT going within three months.'

'I doubt if you will succeed.'

'I bet you that within three months I shall be broadcasting from my own station.'

'It would be sheer robbery to accept such a bet, because I know such a thing is impossible.'

My rival-to-be was jubilant.

'Ah, I see you are afraid to accept the bet! You will see in three months' time.'

I did not see anything, either in three months, or six months, or a year; because the thing was impossible. An underground sound broadcasting station in an occupied country, going on the air daily, at the same hours and on the same wave-length, and therefore so easily able to be pinpointed by the enemy, would be madness. The utmost that could be done were short, infrequent programmes of the kind we tried in 1941. It was different with the 'Lightning' station which functioned during the Warsaw Rising. It was operating on territory held by the insurgents under conditions of full freedom.

On another occasion I met one of the leaders of my own Party. He was gloomy; he bit his lips nervously and shuffled his feet, which to those who knew him were sure signs that he had something unpleasant to say.

'My dear colleague,' he said, 'in your SWIT you talk about everything except the Peasant movement. I have read monitored reports of it and found nothing about the life of the villages, but only matters connected with the Home Army.'

I protested hotly; for I often drew upon the Peasant Party agency, 'The Village', and the underground peasant press for material for SWIT. However, I was not able to convince my Party colleague and we parted rather coolly.

By a strange coincidence, straight from that meeting I went to a meeting with Colonel Rzepecki, chief of the Home Army's Office of Information and Propaganda. I had in front of me a replica of my previous interlocutor, with the same gloomy face and all. Without any preliminaries he put his cards on the table face up.

'That SWIT of yours is broadcasting nothing except Peasant Party stuff. I am having its programmes monitored and I think the neglect of Home Army affairs is downright scandalous.'

I was greatly amused; for the two complaints cancelled each other out, and I could disregard them both.

However, recurring conflicts forced me to initiate General Rowecki into everything. His reception of it was rather mixed. On the one hand he was furious with London for not having informed him of it in advance, and on the other he regarded the organisation of the broadcasts as sensible; and he laughed at the tricks we played on the Germans with the assistance of SWIT. In conclusion he said to me:

'Of course, I cannot help feeling hurt that as my Plenipotentiary you did not initiate me into everything right from the beginning. But let's forget it. You are doing good work; so good luck to you.'

In the result, the Commander-in-Chief was able to appease the conflicting interests, and he kept the secret to the end, even from his closest collaborators.

The Zbydniow Crime

At about this time, everyone in Poland was familiar with the facts of the horrible crime perpetrated by the Germans in

Zbydniow, a country estate belonging to the Horodynski family, on June 25, 1943. The Gestapo raided the place while a wedding reception was being held there, and murdered all the guests and servants with the exception of the bridal couple, Mr. and Mrs. Wankowicz, who had left for town to have their picture taken, and two Horodynski boys, Zbigniew and Andrew, who had managed to hide in the attic.

On the basis of our telegrams, SWIT broadcast the details of the gruesome crime and the names of the victims. It also announced that an investigation would be made and the guilty punished. SWIT's listeners were shocked by the enormity of the crime: everyone waited for the underground to strike back.

Several months later the promise came true. A secret investigation revealed that the instigator of the mass murder was a Nazi official in Cracow by the name of Fuldner, if I remember correctly, who had his eye on the Zbydniow estate. After he had wiped out its owners, he lost no time in moving in himself. But he did not enjoy his new home long. One day, while he was conferring at Zbydniow with two visiting Nazis from Cracow, underground justice caught up with him. A group of armed men, led by Zbigniew Horodynski and his friend Horoch, broke into the manor house, kept the Germans covered with their guns, and read to the terrified Fuldner the death sentence that had been pronounced against him by the underground court. They then shot him in full view of the Germans from Cracow. The latter were released and ordered to relate to Governor-General Frank what they had witnessed.

We transmitted an exact account of the execution to SWIT, along with the instruction: 'For broadcast Saturday evening. The executors of the sentence will be listening.'

On Saturday, a trusted group met in the home of the previously mentioned monitor, Wierusz Kowalski. We conversed in low voices, impatiently waiting for the broadcast to begin. Our host was tuning in. Anxiously we kept looking at the door, wondering why Zbigniew Horodynski and Horoch were so late in coming. On the dot, SWIT began its broadcast. It gave a gripping description of the administering of justice to the criminals responsible for the Zbydniow atrocity.

The programme ended with the words: 'We know that those who carried out the just sentence are listening to us to-day. We pay tribute to these heroes of the Polish Underground.' We were all deeply moved. The women were wiping their eyes. But those for whom these words were intended had been unable to come. The Horodynski brothers and their friend Horoch were all killed while covering the escape of a group of prisoners from Pawiak prison. The escape had been a German provocation. Along with other Home Army soldiers, the three boys had fallen into a trap and, surrounded by German SS units, perished in the battle that raged at the Powazki Cemetery in Warsaw.

Alarums

At this time the Germans were getting wind of our Warsaw stations more and more often, forcing our people to stop their work and change hide-outs. This change of address continued to be a problem. In the first place the landlord had to be so absolutely trustworthy. In the second, very few citizens were willing to agree to the installation of a secret radio station in their apartment. And, finally, such an apartment had to answer our needs from a technical point of view.

Whenever we were unable to furnish SWIT with fresh material, it would treat its listeners to quite a performance. Halfway through a programme, the SWIT announcer would suddenly break off in the middle of a word. This would be followed by a silence of several days. Listeners would be convinced that SWIT had been raided. I would be showered with questions from the underground leaders. My standard reply was that the difficulties were only temporary. If some extra curious person enquired as to the nature of the difficulties, I had to look mysterious. I must say that I did not enjoy the role I had to play on such occasions.

Several days later, SWIT would be on the air again. The announcer would preface the programme with the following statement: 'We apologise to our listeners for the interruption. It was caused by conditions beyond our control, the nature of which we cannot disclose.'

Everyone would rejoice that SWIT had come through safely and had resumed its broadcasting. Little by little, SWIT became enveloped in an atmosphere of mystery and danger. The impression was not an undeserved one. After all, SWIT's suspension of operations was invariably due to German activities against our underground stations, which formed an inseparable part of SWIT's organisation. We acted as SWIT's eyes, while SWIT, whenever it broadcast our telegrams, served as our voice.

Hysteria also entered into the picture. One day the underground mail brought us the following alarming piece of news: 'Helena from cell X wishes to warn you that, according to her information, the Germans have learned where SWIT is broadcasting from and will raid the station in a few days'.

The Secret of SWIT

When did the secret of SWIT become known in Poland? If my memory serves me right, the Communist radio station Kosciuszko, broadcasting from Soviet Russia, began to state quite early in its career that SWIT was not operating in Poland; but no one in the country believed it, because it was generally known that Kosciuszko was a Communist station. As for the Germans, they were at a loss for a considerable time. I think it was early in 1944 that 'Nowy Kurjer Warszawski' came out with the information that SWIT was broadasting from England.

As far as the authorities of the Polish underground were concerned, the secret was prised open some time after General Sikorski's death. It was then that information was received, through military channels, about the location of SWIT, its organisation, the conflicts of its Polish personnel with the English authorities, etc. As long as General Sikorski was alive, the secret of SWIT was well kept. Until the day of his death it was—in the words of his own telegram—the secret of the Commander-in-Chief; and as far as we were concerned, he took upon himself full responsibility for this war-time ruse.

CHAPTER VII

Civil Resistance

The Sabotage of Deliveries

The German's plans for their war economy allotted the territories of occupied Poland an important part, primarily as a storehouse from which they could draw grain, meat, dairy produce, timber, etc. This was to continue also in the future, after the German victory. The Directorate of Civil Resistance set itself the ambitious task of frustrating these plans, and proceeded to organise the boycott and sabotage of all delivery quotas imposed on Polish farmers.

Special appeals were issued and appropriate propaganda was launched. This campaign was carried out mainly by the underground Peasant movement, through its numerous newspapers and by its armed forces, the Peasant Battalions, with which I was closely connected during the initial period of the war, when I held the rank of major in them. Special instructions were issued to the effect that deliveries of meat, dairy produce, grain, etc., should be sabotaged. The slogan was: 'As little, as late, and as bad as possible'. Naturally, it was not practicable to impose a total prohibition of all deliveries; for this would have been a foolhardy act for which the villagers would have had to pay with rivers of blood. The Germans were in complete control, and a total boycott would have certainly been broken by frightful reprisals. Such a boycott was proclaimed only on the eve of the Warsaw Rising in territories East of the Vistula, and during the Rising in territories which were still in possession of the Germans. Carefully prepared instructions told the peasants how to hide foodstuffs and how to prevent their deterioration. We tried to silence arguments between the villages—which, as is usually the case in times of food shortage, were better off than the cities, filled with their hungry masses—by constantly urging the peasants to supply the cities with foodstuffs at low prices. For this, the slogan was: 'As little as possible to the enemy, and all that is available to the population of the cities'.

The Directorate of Civil Resistance recommended that railway warehouses and wagons should be soaked with petrol, that wagons should be opened in transit and the grain poured out, and wherever possible, armed raids on food transports and the seizing of anything feasible, such as cattle for instance. Here are some of the telegrams I sent to SWIT concerning these activities:

'October 6, 1943. On the line Kocmyszyn-Czyzyny a train was held up and the quota cattle being transported to Germany let loose. On the line Warszawa-Siedlce wagons carrying quota grain were opened and the grain spilled. Please encourage such actions.'

'October 6, 1943. In the vicinity of Przeworsk, the executive of the DCR ejected a commision sent for the inspection of quota cattle, killing the chairman, a *Volksdeutsche*, and disarming the gendarmes. Describe this action as an example for emulation.'

The Polish villages rose to the occasion and responded in full to the appeals of the Directorate of Civil Resistance. This was especially the case with the peasants; for they were less easy for the Germans to control than the large estates, which had to keep books and were frequently managed by a *Volksdeutsche*. The ingenuity shown in discovering ever new methods of avoiding deliveries was extraordinary, and included such ruses as the bribing of officials, followed by the fictitious delivery of the same grain a number of times; the forging of receipts for alleged deliveries of grain and cattle; the concealment of cattle before registration; and the false branding of concealed heads. When partisan detachments began their operations in the country, a new procedure was evolved. The partisans would requisition, say, two pigs from a manor, and give a receipt for six. The Germans were furious, but had to accept the receipts as genuine. This served both the partisans and the estate owner; for he would then be able to kill the four pigs for his own consumption, or for sale on the black market.

The Germans tried to maintain deliveries by every possible means, including reprisals; during which villages went up in smoke and peasants were murdered; but taking the country as a whole, they had only limited results. Sabotage assumed such proportions that the Germans were helpless. For our own part, we took counter-action, as may be gleaned from the following telegrams that I sent to London, either reporting to the Government or requesting SWIT to broadcast appropriate instructions:

'August 26, 1943. Emphasise that it is prohibited to burn grain in stacks, barns, etc., or to destroy threshing machines, but that delivery quotas should be destroyed at German collecting points.'

'October 9, 1943. The collection of quotas, their transport and delivery in the Government General now takes place under the protection of military detachments and gendarmes, and also of armed German civilian officials. The Germans have mobilised all their forces.'

'October 20, 1943. In the village of Samsonow, in the district of Kielce, German gendarmes summoned all bailiffs and members of the local quota commission and beat them up severely for non-delivery of quotas. At about the end of September the Germans surrounded the town of Skaryszew, in the Radom district, killed five people, beat up and robbed the population, and took away 150 cows as punishment for non-delivery of quotas.'

'June 24, 1943. Threaten Dr. Schoen, Kreishauptman in Sochaczew, who is setting fire to farms for non-delivery of quotas.'

'November 5, 1943. A communiqué of the DCR of October 30 states that on September 13, in the village of Szarpsko, in the Opoczno district, our detachments wiped out a punitive expedition consisting of ten gendarmes, who had seized quotas and maltreated the population.'

The crowning achievement in the sabotage of delivery quotas consisted in the burning of all documents on quotas throughout the Government General. These documents were kept in village offices, where they served as a basis for fixing the quotas. The Directorate of Civil Resistance realised that if the documents were destroyed, general confusion would ensue, and it would take the Germans months to reconstruct them. In short, the destruction of the documents would lead to complete disorganisation in this field. A detailed plan was elaborated, emphasising the need for sparing other documents, such as registries of peasant farms, which included the peasants' title deeds. However, instructions permitted the burning down of village offices in cases where it was not possible to destroy or to remove the quota documents. Orders were issued for a simultaneous attack on the offices, so that the Germans would be given no time to dispatch armed garrisons to those threatened.

By way of supplementing this action, the Directorate of Civil Resistance ordered the burning down of timber mills and distilleries, and the immobilisation of dairies, so as to prevent the destruction of Polish forests, the use of grain for the production of alcohol for German consumption, and the export of Polish butter to Germany. While the campaign was being carried out, and the principle of surprise no longer applied, I requested London to have both SWIT and the BBC, which were listened to in all country districts, repeat the order in the following message:

'August 26, 1943. Emphasise that it is necessary to burn down timber mills and distilleries, and to immobilise dairies by removing and concealing essential parts of machinery, or, as a last resort, by burning them down.'

The carrying out of this order took several weeks. In each region the local commander of the Peasant Battalions or of the Home Army alerted as many armed squads as there were village offices in his region; which were then all attacked on the same night. Those who tried to resist were terrorised, and all the documents concerning delivery quotas were seized and burned; wherever this proved to be impossible, the whole village office was burned down. During the later weeks of the campaign, the squads encountered armed guards of gendarmes and Blue police. In such cases the village office was stormed, both sides suffering casualties. The campaign spread far and wide all over the country and yielded the desired results. My telegrams to London may give an idea of its dimensions; and also of the results of another action, aimed by Civil Resistance at Labour Exchanges, to enforce the boycott of compulsory labour.

'May 21, 1943. In accordance with the general instructions issued by the Directorate of Civil Resistance, documents and files concerning delivery quotas have been burned in the majority of village offices in the district of Pulawy. Other documents were removed to a place of safety. After the carrying out of this action the Germans amalgamated twenty village offices into four, in Pulawy, Naleczow, Opole and Kurow.'

'June 7, 1943. In carrying out the instructions of the Directorate of Civil Resistance, we burnt or removed to a safe place the files, lists and documents needed by the occupiers in connection with drafts for compulsory labour and delivery quotas in nearly all villages of the Pulawy district, in many villages in the districts of Lubartow, Janow, Lublin, Krasnystaw, and in some of the villages in the districts of Siedlce, Radzyn, Sokolow, Wegrow, Wloszczowa, Kielce and Nisko. In addition, documents and files were destroyed in several Labour Exchanges in the districts of Warsaw and Jedrzejow, and in Losice, District Kielce; and a timber mill was burned down near the railway station in Pulawy. The action continues.'

'June 10, 1943. The destruction of files in village offices has been extended to the district of Lukow. The Labour Exchange in Biala Podlaska and the district office and Labour Exchange in Radomsk were also destroyed.'

'July 16, 1943. Communiqué of the Directorate of Civil Resistance: "In execution of the instructions of the DCR the campaign for the destruction of documents and files on delivery quotas has been extended to village offices in the following districts: Tarnow, Ilza, Opatow, Sandomierz, Stopnica, Pinczow, Piotrkow, Radomsko, Lancut, Krahow, Jedrzejow, Warszawa, Garwolin, Wysokie Mazowieckie".'

It seems to me that the successful sabotage of delivery quotas, though less spectacular than fighting the enemy arms in hand, represented a substantial Polish contribution to the struggle against Germany, though it has never been fully appreciated. I would venture the opinion that if a balance-sheet could be drawn up it would be found that it was worth at least several divisions fighting at the front.

The Provisioning of the Cities

The provisioning of the cities with foodstuffs and the ex-change of commodities with the villages represented a reverse task for the underground movement. The occupation authori-ties fixed starvation rations for the Poles. They were not big enough to live on, but they just prevented people from dying. The daily calorific value of the rationed foods in Warsaw, according to our calculations, amounted to 863 calories in January 1941; 1,119 calories in January 1942; 552 calories in March 1942; and 468 calories in April 1942. Mortality in-creased fourfold, and the number of births fell below that of deaths.

On September 22, 1943, the occupation authorities an-nounced new scales of food rationing for Poles. According to these, the standard monthly ration, as from October 1, 1943, was to consist of: bread, 20 lbs., or, in lieu of 2 lbs. of bread, 1 lb. 11 ounces of flour; cereal, 12 ounces; coffee, $3\frac{1}{2}$ ounces; sugar, 10 ounces; jam, 14 ounces; meat, $11\frac{1}{2}$ ounces; potatoes (annually), 220 lbs. The monthly ration for children under 14 years of age was 11 lbs. of bread and 14 ounces of other rationed foods.

The gap between the normal requirements of the human body and the scales set by the occupation authorities was filled by Polish smugglers, who did their job so well that they de-serve a monument to perpetuate their memory. It would be impossible for me to describe within the scope of.this book all the means which the genius of the smugglers devised to feed the cities and to provide the villages with indispensable com-modities; the subject would need a book to itself. But I should like to mention the almost legendary pig that was conveyed in a railway compartment dressed up as a peasant woman, with a shawl covering its dead snout. When it was discovered by the gendarmes, even they, bereft though they were of all sense of humour, nearly died of laughter. I must also pay my tribute to the Warsaw women costermongers, who provided the city with meat and fresh bread, baked in the vicinity of the capital, where according to German calculations there were more than 2,000 illegal bakeries in operation.

I myself would not have survived the occupation but for their motherly help. They moved like pillars, carrying and transporting by rail or carts tons of foodstuffs in little bags sewn into their underskirts and blouses. Never before have I seen such over-sized busts as in Poland at this time. But when a gendarme approached, the women would run like stags, beating all speed records and leaving only a trail of flour or a broken egg as evidence of precipitate flight. Sometimes the courage of these women outmatched the most valorous fighters of the underground. I once saw in the open market one such amazon hitting a gendarme on the head with a basketful of eggs, because he wanted to take it away from her. Swearing and cursing, the gendarme left rather hurriedly, having noticed a squadron of other amazons hurrying to succour their comrade. No one else would have dared to treat a gendarme in such a fashion. I may add that in time all the gendarmes learnt at least two Polish expressions coined during the occupation, 'na lewo' or 'leftish', i.e., illegally, and 'lipa', or forged. It was amusing sometimes to hear German gendarmes shouting themselves hoarse, and interspersing their vituperations with two Polish words, 'na lewo' and 'lipa', which were so characteristic of the occupation.

I also remember one of the most refined ruses by which the Germans were cheated. It was related to me by a tough young man, Wiktor Lipinski, during the hungry days of the Warsaw Rising:

'I was trading on a very large scale in anything I could lay my hands on, using for the purpose trucks registered in the name of firms under German management. And since I was a soldier of the Home Army, I occasionally transported arms and munitions dropped into Poland by parachute. All that, however, was too risky, even with German passes, forged or authentic. So I tried to think out something exceptional, and eventually hit on a good idea. I got a well-equipped unit of the underground to print me a new type of German pass for "urgent" shipments. They had a broad band printed diagonally in green, which gave them an authentic appearance, and they had perforated vouchers which were to be torn off by the gendarmerie posts the transports had to pass. When the time came, the same unit also fabricated a circular from the Governor General, instructing the gendarmerie that transports travelling with that type of pass, a specimen of which was attached, were urgent and were not to be examined, but on the contrary their rapid transit had to be facilitated. The circulars, multi-graphed on appropriate stationery from the Governor-General's office and bearing beautifully forged signatures and seals, were addressed and dispatched to the various gendarmerie posts in the province of Lublin.'

'After the lapse of a week, I dispatched a trial truck with flour, equipped with the new type of pass, from Lublin to Warsaw. The idea worked. Wherever the gendarmes stopped the truck along its route, they released it immediately on being shown the pass, and they even gave the driver friendly hints as to the state of the roads and the safety of transport. Further transports were soon carrying, in addition to ordinary freight, arms and munitions. No slip-up ever occurred. I stopped using the passes only when the time came for the return of the vouchers to Central Headquarters; a date which I had myself fixed in the circular.'

In 1946, the same Lipinski was hauled before a Communist military court in Warsaw for having taken delivery, on the basis of forged documents, of about ten tons of tin, which the regime had imported into Gdynia for industrial purposes. Cross-examined by the Prosecutor on the motives for his action, Lipinski neither attempted to defend himself nor did he ask for mercy; he simply said:

'I was engaged in economic sabotage against one invader and continued to do so against another.'

He was condemned to death, and the Communist press reported that the sentence was carried out.

A revealing light on conditions in the Government General was thrown by an official report on a paper prepared by a

German economist for Governor Frank in Cracow, and for a number of German dignitaries in the Government General. I read the report with great relish. Having enquired into German economic policy in the Government General, the German economist, with some sense of humour, stated frankly and clearly that official German economy in the territory was dwelling in a world of make-believe. If the annual balance-sheet showed a turnover of several hundred million marks, the unofficial or black market turnover was several times higher. Everything official was fictitious, such as prices, wages, etc. The legal commercial transactions of modest dimensions were only a cover for an immense unofficial trade. The German economist ascertained that all transport vehicles, railways, trucks and the innumerable horse-drawn vehicles, were carrying, besides official cargoes, larger illegal ones, usually covered by authentic German documents. All this was being illegally consumed by the Polish population of the Government General. He pointed out that on week-days the streets in the cities of the Reich were empty, because everybody was at work; while in the Government General the streets were swarming with young men and women. Yet whenever a passer-by was stopped, he was able to produce German documents stating that he was employed in a German factory, or in an office under German management. The real currency circulating in the Government General was the dollar or gold rouble. The larger illegal transactions were conducted on a dollar basis. The official currency of the Government General, the zloty, was only an auxiliary medium of circulation.

The economist concluded his frank but, to his German listeners, painful paper by stating that besides the political underground, there existed in the Government General an economic underground, which inflicted irreparable damage on the war economy of the German Reich.

This was undoubtedly true. An implacable struggle was being waged against the occupiers on the economic front, and its intensity increased as the German economy began to totter. This war was waged by men of a special type, a type that, by our pre-war criteria, I would not hesitate to call American. These men had courage and the capacity to take great risks;

they were animated by a peculiar kind of patriotism, and knew how to combine the interests of their country with their own self-interest.

Sabotage of Compulsory Labour

According to German war economy plans, next to food the commodity that Polish territories were to supply was man-power, which the Germans needed for their war production. The requisitioning of this particular commodity was under-taken with the utmost ruthlessness. A series of decrees was issued introducing general compulsory labour, not only in Poland, but in the German Reich as well, which involved the compulsory deportation of labour to Germany. A network of special offices was set up, the so-called 'Arbeitsamt', charged with the task of supplying manpower from the Government General to Germany, and having at its disposal both the gen-darmerie and the Blue police.

The Directorate of Civil Resistance was entrusted with the task of counteracting this operation, which was of such im-mense importance to Germany. It is sufficient to remark, in this connection, that every worker deported from Poland to Germany freed a young German from a factory or farm for service in the armed forces. The DCR began its campaign with widespread propaganda for the boycott of every kind of compulsory labour in Germany; it issued appeals, declara-tions and instructions, explaining the means to be employed for this purpose. These instructions were circulated through-out the country with the assistance of SWIT or the BBC, through the underground press, and through the various underground organisations.

For instance, the DCR appealed for a complete boycott of the *Baudienst*, and warned employers not to apply the so-called 'German tariff ordinances', which reduced by 20-30 per cent the starvation ration scales of the workers; this was calcu-lated to force them to volunteer for labour in Germany. The DCR issued a prohibition, supported by sanctions, on the acceptance by any Pole of the post of labour recruiting officer for Germany, and it prohibited employers from undertaking the selection of employees for deportation to Germany, or even from giving their opinion in the matter. Moreover, the DCR threatened with reprisals any functionaries of the Blue police and the labour exchanges who took part in labour round-ups. It also issued a proclamation appealing for the sabotage of deportations to Germany of young people, girls as soon as they reached the age of 18, and boys from the age of 17.

Here are some of the telegrams on the basis of which SWIT and the BBC broadcast their appeals for the boycott of various local actions:

'April 25, 1943. An appeal was posted to-day by Burgomaster Leist for voluntary enrolment for labour in Germany and in the Government General, with the threat of compulsory measures should it fail. The appeal promises the same food rations as for Germans, religious observance, comfortable living quarters, etc. Appeal for resistance in the name of the DCR.'

'June 4, 1943. I secured a copy of a poster issued by the commander of police and SS in the district of Bialystok stating that those mobilised for labour had failed to report, and announcing that 100 persons had been arrested and would be held responsible if those mobilised failed to report within a week. The poster also appeals to the population not to submit to the terror of the Directorate of Civil Resistance, which is spreading unrest and lies. On behalf of the DCR, please express our gratitude to the population.'

'May 8, 1943. Warn the district of Lublin that classes from 18 to 20 inclusive are to be mobilised for compulsory labour. The DCR prohibits observance of the ordinance. The same applies to the districts of Lwow and Bialystok. Confidential: we managed to obtain copies of posters printed by the Germans in Lublin.'

'June 26, 1943. Threaten Stadthauptmann Kremer in Cracow, who forces employers to deliver personally to the camp in Narrow Street 20 per cent of their workers for deportation to Germany. He moves about under armed escort.'

Our Special Courts decreed reprisals against functionaries of Labour Exchanges and the Blue police, and, as already mentioned, the first sentence of death was carried out on Isidor Ossowski.

On the other hand, the DCR tolerated work in factories, undertakings and institutions taken over by the Germans, as it was not possible for a general abandonment of all labour, a kind of 'national withdrawal of labour', to be enforced. Instead of a boycott of labour, 'petty sabotage' was introduced, consisting in reducing the speed of work, etc. Instructions were issued recommending the damaging of machinery by negligence, such as inadequate oiling, the waste of raw materials, and the destruction and removal of raw materials and finished products from the factories whenever possible. Instructions were also issued on how to disorganise work, transport, etc.—in short, how to pour sand into the gears of the German war machine. All these instructions were readily obeyed. From valuable light metals used in the production of aeroplanes, illicitly cigarette lighters, cigarette holders and other trifles were manufactured to flood the market in the Government General; and, better still, high quality steel was used for the manufacture of automatic pistols for the Home Army.

The boycott of labour in Germany assumed the character of a mass movement, and between April 1940 and April 1942, the Germans were able to deport to Germany not more than 68,000 men and women. During these two years in Warsaw alone the Labour Exchanges were looking for 12,600 people who had escaped compulsory labour. Actually, anybody who stood the least chance of avoiding such labour did so. To get out of it, people lived in the cities without registering, they entered wrong birth-dates on their documents, produced forged employment-cards wholesale, used forged medical evidence to prove their incapacity for work, and many other such ruses.

In the countryside, apart from similar dodges, people completely and absolutely ignored all German summonses. The whole underground machine worked to make the boycott effective. As in every other sphere, practical jokes furthered the aims of the underground. When walking along Nowy Swiat one day, I saw a huge German poster showing a group of workers preparing to be transported to Germany, with a caption underneath: 'Come with us to Germany'. An unknown joker had climbed to the height of an entire storey to alter the caption to read: 'Don't come with us to Germany'. Such tricks were quite effective. On one occasion, the Germans put up posters announcing a number of executions signed by the commander of the SS and the police, von Moder; whereupon men of the underground altered the name to Mörder (murderer), and the Germans had to remove the posters.

The Germans replied with all kinds of reprisals, such as punitive expeditions into the villages, during which they massacred and executed large numbers of men and women, or mass manhunts for the rounding up of all who shunned work in the cities, during which they simply kidnapped men and women in the streets, and deported them to Germany. This induced a large number of young people to escape into the forests, which helped to intensify partisan fighting throughout the country.

The Directorate of Civil Resistance undertook energetic action to frustrate the German measures; simultaneously with the steps taken against the village offices, we struck at the Labour Exchanges, ordering them to be burned down without exception. This was more difficult to accomplish, as the Exchanges were located in the cities and towns. It was carried out by larger units and with much greater hazards; and though the results were not as great as we would have wished, they were satisfactory. About twenty Labour Exchanges were successfully fired, which put them out of action for a long time, as the destroyed files and card-indexes made compulsory recruitment impossible.

We were not able, however, to destroy the Labour Exchange in Warsaw, situated in the Agricultural Credit Bank building at the corner of Mazowiecka Street. The unsuccessful action had a fatal outcome.

Towards evening on the appointed day, after the office had been closed, there was a knock at the door. The German sentry on duty opened the peep-hole and saw a Gestapo man accompanied by a civilian. He let them in immediately;

whereupon the Gestapo man, speaking plausible German, enquired how many people were still in the office. On hearing that there were only one or two, he ordered the sentry to take him to them. When they were all together in one room, he pulled out a revolver, terrorised them, confiscated the sentry's revolver, and ordered everyone to lie down on the floor. Leaving the armed civilian in charge, he then withdrew to the back of the building.

In the meantime, a dozen men, equipped with containers filled with petrol, entered the yard by the back-door entrance in Mazowiecka Street, and waited to be let into the building. They knew that the door would be opened from the inside, but they did not know who would be doing it. After a minute or two, the door duly opened; but there stood a tall Gestapo man who, in loud German, invited the hidden raiders come in. Nerves were taut. Not having been warned that they would be admitted by a man in the uniform of a Gestapo officer, and hearing him speak in German, moreover, they suspected treachery; so, pulling out their revolvers, they fired at him and made off, leaving the petrol cans behind. Rosciszewski, who was directing the action, was barely able to drag the gravely wounded 'Gestapo man', who was a member of 'Pobudka', into a car waiting in Malachowski Square and to escape too. Just as he was being put into the car, German soldiers approached, enquiring what had happened. They were told that the man had been wounded in a skirmish with 'Polish bandits', and departed.

Rosciszewski, who reported the incident to me, was stricken with grief. He blamed the nerves of the incendiary squad, but had to admit that the alleged Gestapo man had been carried away with bravado, and had overplayed his part by addressing them in German. Had he done so in Polish, the incident would not have taken place. He was a native of Poznan or Pomorze. He succumbed to the wounds he received.

A Meeting with Andrew No. 2

The campaigns against delivery quotas and Labour Exchanges remain in my memory inseparably connected with

Andrew No. 2, Jozef Wiacek, the successor to Andrew No. 1, Wladyslaw Jasinski, of Mielec, the fallen partisan commander in the province of Kielce, whose pseudonym became the popular nickname for his detachment, who were known as the 'Andrew boys'.

One morning I received a message informing me that Andrew No. 2 had arrived in Warsaw and insisted on being introduced to the head of the Directorate of Civil Resistance. I gladly agreed, as I wanted to see what this redoubtable partisan leader looked like. On the appointed day I went to Ujazdow Park; I entered it by the Piekna Gate, turned to the left, and counted the benches. It was a fine sunny day, but as the hour was early there were a few people about. As I approached the fifteenth bench, a young man of about thirty, with a typically Polish mop of fair hair and the healthy complexion of a weather-hardened man, rose from it. I noticed his clean, open-necked shirt. He recognised me from the description he had been given. I looked at him with a kind of envy. He came from a land of freedom, so different from that in which we lived in Warsaw, doomed to meet the Germans at every step and living a life of perpetual fear. As usual, the conversation opened with banalities, but Andrew soon took up the matter he had in hand. He had come to Warsaw to offer himself and his partisans to the Directorate of Civil Resistance, for the work appealed to him. He did not want to fight the Germans on his own, but preferred to take part in organised warfare. By way of a beginning, he had brought with him detailed reports of all his exploits, a statement showing the loot he had taken from the Germans, and the expenditure he had incurred on behalf of his partisan detachment, requesting that the statement should be checked. I was rather surprised by his offer, attractive though it was, and I had a feeling that there was something more behind it than had so far emerged. I enquired cautiously what his relations were with the local Home Army, and asked him why he had not turned to them for leadership. I seemed to have hit the nail on the head; for Andrew explained to me frankly that his relations with the local Home Army command were not good. He had tried to join them, but had been treated rather high-handedly as a non-commissioned officer, and had been told that he would have to yield the command of his detachment to an officer appointed by the Home Army command. His partisans would not hear of it, and Andrew was devastating in his mockery of the whole idea.

'Partisan warfare cannot be learned from books,' he said, 'or in a military academy. One has to learn by hard experience, step by step, and right from the beginning. An inexperienced commander could bring about the doom of his detachment within a few days.'

In my own mind I knew he was right. Discipline in the underground was based on a tacit understanding between the commander and his men, on their freely subordinating themselves, and not on a rigour imposed from above. To Andrew's volunteer partisans it was a matter of life and death whether their commander knew how to lead his detachment in the field, whether he knew how to conduct himself in the open, amidst forests and fields, and whether he was popular with the local villagers, which was a fundamental condition for the effectiveness and survival of every partisan unit.

To gain time, I questioned Andrew about the organisation of his detachment and about his future plans. He told me he maintained a permanent nucleus of partisans in the forest. Whenever needed, numbers were made up by a muster of men living in the villages and leading a normal life. They answered every summons. The detachment had adequate quantities of automatic arms, which they had captured from the Germans; and they also had motor-cars and motor-cycles. He trained his partisans so that each knew how to handle the arms and machinery. They attacked and dispersed detachments of gendarmes when they arrived in the villages to make requisitions, they killed all Gestapo men, wherever and whenever it was possible, they destroyed transports, and they fought for the release of prisoners, etc.

I then resumed the main subject and told Andrew that I accepted his offer, but only within the sphere of authority of the Directorate of Civil Resistance. On the other hand, I advised him to come to terms with the Supreme Command of the Home Army during his visit to Warsaw, for they were the regular Polish Army; and I offered to facilitate everything for him. Andrew agreed, and with Piotrowski's help matters were arranged. Andrew was given the rank of a lieutenant of the Army and approved as commander of the detachment, while two junior officers were detailed to assist him, and to gain for themselves experience in partisan warfare.

During my last meeting with Andrew I told him, half-jokingly, that I would have loved to spend a few days with him in the forests, for I needed a rest from the nerve-racking life of Warsaw. Andrew received this with enthusiasm.

'You simply must come. We have a nice little house in the forest, where you will feel comfortable and safe.'

'But how shall I get to you? The Germans are bound to catch me on my way there.'

'From the moment you leave the train,' he said laughingly, 'I shall be responsible for your safety, and I guarantee that no harm will come to you. I shall be waiting for you at the station with a cart. You will find not a single German at the station, or on your way to the forest.'

'How will you do that?'

'No trouble at all! I shall simply forbid the gendarmes to be in the railway station or near the road we'll be taking for two days.'

'I doubt if they would obey your orders.'

'What? You evidently don't know that I imposed a curfew on them, and that after the curfew hour none of them dare remain in a village for fear of a bullet. At first they wouldn't observe my order, but I killed so many of them that to-day all the gendarmerie patrols withdraw their outposts from the villages before the curfew sets in, and none of them ever dare go out before morning. The night belongs to us.'

Before we parted, I initiated him into the various ruses for sabotaging deliveries and forced labour, inviting him to do his bit. The way he assured me that he would try to do what he could was very promising. That he kept his promise may be seen from the following telegram addressed to the Government in London:

'June 10, 1943. Andrew's partisan detachment, acting on instructions issued to him directly by the Directorate of Civil

Resistance, burned during one night the files and documents in all the villages of the district of Sandomierz. They subsequently took possession of the town of Busko, where they burned down the District Governor's office and the local Labour Exchange.'

In 1946, under the Soviet occupation, a relative of Andrew's visited me in Warsaw and told me the sad news that the Security Police had arrested him, and that all attempts to get him out of prison had failed. Such was the Soviet's reward for his struggles against the Germans.

The Government Plenipotentiary, Professor Jan Piekalkiewicz

The news that the Government Plenipotentiary, Professor Jan Piekalkiewicz, · had been arrested spread like wildfire throughout underground Warsaw. All were horrified that the Gestapo should have been able to lay their hands on the political head of the Polish Underground. It was a heavy blow indeed, and one which released an avalanche of precautionary measures, such as changes of hide-outs and pseudonyms, which were the usual steps taken in such circumstances. Investigations showed that the Plenipotentiary had boarded a tram-car in Rakowiecka Street to attend a meeting in Piekna or Basket Street, but that he did not reach his destination. He disappeared from the tram-car en route and without trace. Such slender hopes as still lingered were finally dispelled when our intelligence discovered that he was in the Gestapo prison in Szucha Street, and that in spite of being tortured he was holding out firmly during cross-examinations; we also learned that he would not agree to other political prisoners cleaning his cell. Some time later the news arrived that he died on June 19, 1943, under torture, without betraying anyone or anything. Before the war I knew him well as a politically not very active member of the Peasant Party. He was a quiet and modest man, a professor of statistics, and had not pushed himself forward in the Party leadership. When he was appointed Government Plenipotentiary he became even more contemplative and tactiturn. He was weighed down by the heavy burden of responsibility. It was evident that he looked upon his appointment as a great and unusual distinction, and tried to live up to it, in which, I think, he fully succeeded. During his period of office, the underground was further consolidated and developed, for which a great deal of credit was due to him personally.

Prior to the appointment of Professor Piekalkiewicz as Government Plenipotentiary, Jozef Niecko had made a fresh attempt to seize control of radio liaison with London.

When Plenipotentiary Ratajski resigned, Niecko invited me to a talk. He had advanced rapidly to a leading position in the conspiratorial hierarchy of the 'Triangle', though someone else was head of the underground executive of the Party. He was then advanced in years, and rather squat; as was his custom, he approached the real purpose of our talk by a roundabout way. I knew him well, so I talked calmly on a variety of indifferent subjects, knowing that it would be some time before Niecko showed his cards. That was his nature. After about an hour, the question of Ratajski's recent retirement came up. Niecko pretended to deplore it, but actually he approved of it, mentioning Ratajski's advanced age and his inability to adapt himself to a life of conspiracy. When he finally mentioned casually that it would be necessary to look round for someone younger and more energetic to take on the office of Government Plenipotentiary, I pricked up my ears. I could see which way the wind was blowing. Niecko, however, again casually, turned the talk to the subject of radio liaison, enquiring how my radio stations operated, and whether they were safe; and recommending that they should be guarded at all costs, because to have our own radio liaison with London was extremely important. By way of reply I just kept muttering meaningless data, waiting patiently to see what he was really after. At last he blurted it out:

'Our Party,' he said, 'is to submit a candidate for the office of Government Plenipotentiary, and from my knowledge of the situation in the Political Consultative Committee, I feel sure that our candidate will be accepted. I am looking around for a nominee, but I cannot see anyone suitable. I have been thinking of you, but you are doing good work already, and it would be a pity to take you away from it.'

Niecko stopped and looked at me enquiringly. I said nothing, waiting for what was still to come. Knowing his method of conducting such talks, I knew that it would be a mistake to show even the slightest interest in the prospects unfolded by him. Niecko, too, remained silent; but seeing that I was not biting at the bait, he continued with evident dissatisfaction:

'The position is difficult, very difficult indeed. On reflection I think I would put forward your candidature; but we would have to reach some kind of an arrangement by which you would not feel lonely when matters of paramount importance are to be decided. Besides, you would no longer be able to run the radio stations personally, because it would be too dangerous, and inconsistent with the high office of Plenipotentiary. But I think I could help you out over that, too.'

I had to smile up my sleeve. This was one more attempt on the part of Niecko to seize control of radio liaison with London. He had tried it many times before, but I had been able to repel all his efforts. Now he wanted to kill two birds at once: to gain control of radio liaison, and to run the office of Government Plenipotentiary from the sidelines. As the talk went on, Niecko suggested a definite arrangement to me. He would put forward my candidature for the office of Government Plenipotentiary, while I would agree to accept his political guidance and hand over to him personally, and to no one else, radio liaison with London.

Now that the cards were on the table, I told him with perfect and unruffled composure that even under his experienced guidance I would not feel strong enough to discharge such responsible functions as those of Government Plenipotentiary; that in any case Civil Resistance and radio liaison fully satisfied my ambitions; and that I was not looking for a change of responsibilities.

We parted after another half-hour of talk; for the ritual required that withdrawal from a fruitless conversation should be effected under a smoke-screen.

At that time the candidature of Professor Piekalkiewicz was accepted. Had I listened to Niecko, it would have been I and not Piekalkiewicz, whose body was exhumed and re-interred one gloomy morning at the cemetery of Brodno in Warsaw, under the watchful eyes of the Communist Security Police.

It may be asked whether Piekalkiewicz submitted to Niecko's conditions. There is evidence that he did not, supported by the rather notorious incident between Plenipotentiary Piekalkiewicz and Jan Domanski. Domanski became Chancellor to the Government Plenipotentiary, a position next in authority to the Plenipotentiary himself. After only a few weeks this vigorous and energetic man suddenly resigned his office for health reasons. We all understood that there was something more substantial behind this conventional form of polite withdrawal. It soon transpired that the 'tactful' Domanski, on assuming office, told the Government Plenipotentiary that although he was officially the Plenipotentiary, nevertheless, lacking political experience, he should follow his, Domanski's, advice, because he represented 'Tata' himself, which was Niecko's nickname in his Party. In reply, the Plenipotentiary told him that there was not enough room in the office for both of them. Niecko was sufficiently aware of the position to know that he could not provoke a crisis because of Domanski, so the latter resigned. Strangely enough, after this incident, Domanski did in fact suffer from various complaints, as if his health were taking its revenge for having been involved in an unsavoury affair. However, in 1943 he was flown from a secret airstrip in Poland to England, where he became a member of the National Council, under the pseudonym, Bartnicki. He returned to Poland in 1945, and is to-day one of its Communist dignitaries.

All this took place in a country under a terrible enemy occupation, where the firing of execution squads never ceased, where the smoke from the ovens of the crematoria belched forth day and night, where towns and villages were being destroyed by fire by way of pacification. I must add, however, that such strife between rival factions was not confined to one Party alone. The same was true of the other Parties. Men in the underground, like men everywhere, were competing for a place in the sun; which frequently proved to be a place under the gallows.

After the arrest of Piekalkiewicz, Jan Jankowski was appointed Government Plenipotentiary, and the underground at last received the leader it needed and deserved. Politically experienced, a man of independent mind and great character, he was a true personality. He knew how to maintain his position and authority, especially in his dealings with the Home Army, which was not an easy matter at all. He became a real head of the Underground Polish State.

CHAPTER VIII

The Death of Joey

Joey received clear proofs that the Gestapo were still after him, and that the case of the Downhill Road raid had not been closed. His numerous friends from the Riverside and Grochow warned him that the Gestapo had released from Pawiak prison a youngster who knew him well, and that this young man was now calling on their mutual friends trying to find out Joey's whereabouts. Joey's reaction to all this was that instead of one revolver he now carried two. It was clear that his one-time friend had been released from prison on condition he helped by betraying Joey, who for his part was determined not to be taken alive. Unfortunately on one occasion Joey unexpectedly ran into his colleague; he was recognised by the latter, but was able to jump on to the platform of a passing tram, and thus shook off his pursuer. But he became still more watchful and avoided the streets as much as possible.

Early one day we were awakened by a telephone call for Zosia. When she came back, I knew at once that something had happened, and I was not mistaken.

'Joey was to have spent the night in Good Street, but didn't turn up. Neither did he spend the night in Marshall Street.'

'We must get in touch with Marshall Street at once, and find out what time he left, and if he left any message.'

In Marshall Street they explained that Joey had left the house the day before in the afternoon, but had left no message, either in writing or by word of mouth. Worse still, a Blue policeman had called early that morning to check whether Joey was registered there, mentioning the false name, Tomaszewski, which Joey had assumed. When the landlady asked him what the matter was, he would not say, but departed somewhat disgruntled.

I was oppressed by an evil foreboding. I tried to check the fear which was growing in my mind, but I sensed more calamity hovering in the air.

Without delay I got in touch with a Civil Resistance officer who, on instructions from the organisation, was serving in the Blue police, with the rank of Inspector. I called on him at his office in the police station, full of shabby office furniture. I told the Inspector what had happened and enquired about the significance of the Blue policeman's visit that morning. The Inspector reassured me.

'I am sure Tomaszewski has been detained. I shall find out at once. If he is in the hands of the Blue police, we shall be able to let him go somehow.'

The Inspector picked up the telephone and proceeded to put calls through to various police stations. I listened anxiously to his questions, to which several of the stations were unable to give any answers. At last he said:

'Is that station No. 11? Inspector J. speaking. Have you got there a youngster by the name of Jozef Tomaszewski? All right; I'll wait.'

The Inspector turned towards me:

'They are checking up and will let me know.'

He was waiting, with the telephone to his ear, while I shook with impatience and fear. Finally he spoke:

'Yes, yes! I am listening! What? Killed? . . . Where? How?'

The Inspector listened, looking at me with astonishment in his eyes as he repeated the report he was receiving:

'Yesterday, at twenty-one hours, at the corner of Kopernik and Ordynacka Streets. Shooting it out with the Germans. Some others were killed. . . .'

I was staggered and felt paralysed. From the outset I had had a foreboding that something like this must have happened, but now it had become a certainty. Joey was dead. I was overcome by grief. What a terrible blow! And once again, as so many times before, one's heart was oppressed and one's mind a blank. But the Inspector would not let me remain plunged in despair. He strapped on his belt, put on his peaked cap, took me by the arm and led me outside.

'Call back in an hour's time. I am going to Station No. 11 to find out all the details.'

I went to the rendezvous with Zosia and saw her from a distance, approaching with an air of anxious expectation.

'Zosia, you must be prepared for bad news.'

'Don't spare me. What's happened to Joey?'

'Joey is dead.'

I took her by the arm, and we walked on aimlessly and silently. Zosia controlled herself, but tears were running down her cheeks. When she calmed down a little, I told her what the Inspector had found out, and in utter despair we wandered in the streets for more than an hour. But new worries rescued us from our painful thoughts. The question imposed itself: had the workshop in Marshall Street been raided or not?

I called on the Inspector again, and he reported:

'In Ordynacka Street, close to Kopernik Street, there is a restaurant for Germans. Just before curfew an SS man, on leaving the restaurant, noticed a youngster running away from Nowy Swiat. This hurry seemed suspicious to him, so he stopped in the middle of the road and called out: "Halt!" Instead of stopping, the young man pulled out two revolvers and fired. The SS man returned the fire, and so did other Germans, who came running out of the restaurant at the sound of shots. The shooting continued on both sides, and the Pole was killed on the spot. A German was killed, too, and a number of passers-by were wounded. The SS man emerged unscathed and what I am telling you is based on his depositions.'

'Thank you, Inspector. Do you think the Germans are interested in the identity of the killed, and especially in the place where he lived?'

'As a rule, if a man is killed in a street fight, they are not interested. If he is in possession of a fire-arm, they may enquire, but not at once. They leave the body and the formalities to the Blue police, and only later, when the Blue police send the file to the Gendarmerie, do they study the case and sometimes order a new investigation and search. However, it will be at least two days before the Blue police can forward the file.'

'There are various objects in the room where the dead man lived which we must get out.'

'You have two days in which to do it. If you let me know, it will be possible to keep the matter in the hands of the Blue police a little longer. I was told that so far none of the German authorities had enquired about the matter.'

'And what is going to happen to the young man's body?'

'It will be taken to the morgue in Oczki Street, and if it is not claimed by the family, the city will have to inter it at its own expense.'

This was no time for mourning, for the workshop had to be saved at all costs. Zosia fetched a parachutist, the commando Philip, whom I have already mentioned. I put the fateful question to him.

'Can you and your men evacuate our workshop? It is possible that it is already in German hands. The place is close to Szucha Avenue, and if it comes to fighting it out the venture will be very risky. Besides, there is so much equipment that you will need a motor-car.'

Philip knew the nature of our work and did not keep me waiting for an answer.

'It shall be done. I shall be ready in two hours. We'll manage everything at such speed that the Gestapo in Szucha Avenue won't even suspect what is happening, and won't interfere. I'm glad to have this chance, because my men have been grumbling recently about nothing happening; a little job like this will do them good.'

We fixed the rendezvous for 5 p.m., at the corner of Field Street and August 6th Streets. The date was May 10, 1943.

The hours dragged by unbearably slowly. Unable to remain idle, I went back to Zosia; we roamed the streets, went to a café, and tried to read the newspapers; but we just could not sit down quietly, so we resumed our wanderings. Except for a cup of coffee, I had had nothing all day; but I could not even think of food.

At half-past four I went to have a look at the building in Marshall Street; but I stopped dead. From a distance I could see that the road in front of the building was swarming with Gestapo men, gendarmes and civilian agents. They were loading on to a truck the suitcases, boxes and packages that were so familiar to me. On either side of the house were stationary motor-cars, and in the near one I could see the muzzle of a machine-gun aimed down Marshall Street. I guessed that there was another machine-gun mounted on the car at the farther end, and that the approaches from Union Square and from Field Street were well covered.

I retraced my steps and hurried to the rendezvous. It would have been murder to attempt the rescue of the workshop under such conditions. I could see in the distance Philip and groups of youngsters approaching in two's and three's, carrying small packages and leather cases. Close by, at the tram stop, Zosia was waiting, completely worn out. I signalled to Philip, and we went along Polna Street in the direction of Union Square.

'Philip, I am calling off the expedition. Both in the building and all around it there are swarms of Germans, and the approach to the house is guarded by two machine-guns. We would only endanger our men without being able to salvage the equipment.'

'Why? We shall manage. The men are itching to go in. There are ten of them armed with three automatics, revolvers and hand-grenades from the drops, all in excellent condition. We also have a motor-car.'

'Where did you get it?'

'It was no trouble at all. A chauffeur was waiting in his car. Two of my boys went up to him with their automatics, ordered him to drive them here, and there he is.'

He turned round and pointed with his finger. By the kerb stood a large private car, with the motionless chauffeur at the wheel. A boy was sitting on the running board, smoking a cigarette. Suddenly a voice behind us said:

'Philip, some people are watching us suspiciously. We musn't delay. It's time to begin.'

I hesitated no longer. I thanked Philip, and ordered him to disperse his men. Profoundly disappointed, Philip hurried to the rendezvous, grumbling.

'We must at least kidnap one of their agents by way of consolation.'

Some time later, when I was on my way to keep an appointment in Honey Street, I noticed a cordon of gendarmes blocking the exit from Honey Street into Cracow Suburb Street. From the direction of Long Street I could hear intermittent firing.

'This has been going on for nearly two hours,' whispered an elderly, well-dressed man standing near me. As the firing continued, I decided not to keep the appointment.

A few days later, I learned that three of our men had been killed: Philip, the youngster from 'Wici', and another parachutist; they were carrying out a task in a *Volksdeutsche* restaurant in Long Street. They succeeded in terrorising all the Germans present, but they did not notice a waitress slip out into the street through a basement window; she raised the alarm shouting, 'Bandits', which alerted the police. The shooting went on for several hours, with tragic results.

But that was not the end of the affair. After several more days, I again met the friendly Inspector of the Blue police. He was worried.

'Just imagine,' he said, 'In the shooting in Long Street we lost one of our best men in the underground police organisation, the troop-leader L. He was with his squad at the police station, when the alarm came that bandits were robbing a restaurant in Long Street. As you know, we have instructions from the underground authorities to deal with bandits as we did before the war. What a calamity! L. was killed on the spot. I have since found out that it was a task being carried out by the underground, and not a bandit raid. It's terrible that a man of the underground should have perished at the hands of the underground. Something must be done to prevent such a thing happening in future.'

The inspector was right. It was true that the underground authorities had issued an order that the increasing wave of banditry should be suppressed; for in 1943, the Gestapo conceived the idea of extending its protection to bandits, and encouraged them to carry out armed robberies. The Gestapo were trying to discredit the underground by accusing it of acts of banditry, and thus turn the nation against it. As a result, a special body was formed for the suppression of banditry, and a number of death sentences were in fact carried out on bandits.

The attitude of the underground authorities towards the Blue police was hostile, because as a body it had become a tool in the hands of the German police; but a number of policemen, such as the above-mentioned Inspector, were members of the underground, and frequently carried out most dangerous instructions. The Blue police were aware that the underground authorities had ordered the suppression of banditry, so they were always glad to take a hand against them.

I felt quite helpless. I could see no possible approach to the problem of preventing similar tragedies to that in Long Street. Under conspiracy conditions, when everything had to be kept secret, it was impossible to warn anyone in advance of planned actions, so as to distinguish them from actions carried out by common bandits.

Joey's Funeral

So Joey was dead. A splendid, talented boy, with a brilliant future had perished. I had fondly thought that after the war, in a free Poland, Joey would have been able to study and to develop his extraordinary technical abilities. I had not doubted that he would become a scientist and an inventor. An SS man's bullet put an end to all this.

Why did Joey run? There were two possible reasons. He was either anxious to get to his hide-out before the curfew hour, or he was running away from his old friend who was spying on him. I never succeeded in finding out what actually happened.

How was it that, contrary to the opinion of the Inspector, the Germans rushed to Marshall Street so soon? I can only assume that their suspicions were aroused by a magnificent chronometer watch of foreign make, brought for me from England by Philip, which I had given to Joey to wear, as he had admired it beyond measure. He never parted with it and always wore it on his wrist.

We could not reconcile ourselves to the thought that Joey's body should be interred anonymously by the City Refuse

Works. On the other hand, I was convinced that the Gestapo had instituted a watch on the body, in the justifiable belief that his comrades would want to pay their last homage to a dead hero. I knew of actual cases in which people had been arrested at funerals, so I issued a strict order that no one was to visit the morgue; though I myself hated the thought that I should never see Joey again.

Two young women helped us out in our sorrow. They were detailed by the underground for service in the morgue. One performed the macabre duties of a morgue sweeper, the other those of a secretary. Undertakers, too, were brought into a unique underground organisation, the object of which was to purchase from the Germans the corpses of murdered men and women, so that they might be decently buried. The Germans accepted a bribe and issued the necessary documents; whereupon the undertakers supplied a coffin and made all the arrangements for the funeral and burial.

I could not make out why the Germans never tried to find out from the undertakers who paid for the funeral; but when Zosia asked the undertaker about it, he would not divulge anything.

'I don't know who you are,' he said to her, 'and I don't want to know. If the Germans came here to make enquiries, I would give them the name you gave me for the receipt. But they won't come.'

Zosia communicated with him with the utmost circumspection, as she had been warned by the two women attendants in Oczki that the morgue was under observation.

A few days later the undertakers notified us that the funeral would take place the following day. I would not allow anyone to attend it, but we lingered individually along the route the hearse was to follow; and in this way we bade farewell to Joey, who, in a lonely hearse, made his last journey through the streets of the city of his birth, and of his death. We gazed at the hearse, and each of us must have wondered whose turn would come next.

I confided to Zosia how grieved I was not to have seen Joey after his death, but I felt somewhat relieved when she said:

'I am sorry to have acted contrary to orders, but I went to

Oczki and managed to see him. He lay there, calm and with no trace of suffering in his features. The bullet had penetrated his heart; he was killed instantly. No one paid any attention to me, as there were a lot of corpses there and I pretended to be searching for some one, examining each corpse with equal attention. There they lay, one close to the other, covered with blood and wounds, in that dark and sombre hall, with weeping and terrified people moving among them. I shall not forget the sight as long as I live.'

Joey was buried in Powazki Cemetery under the name of Jozef Tomaszewski; but a sealed bottle with his real name, Jozef Stankiewicz, had been placed in his coffin. Many a judge and lawyer in Warsaw will remember an elderly secretary of the Supreme Court, hard of hearing and with large whiskers, whose name was Stankiewicz. Joey was his son.

CHAPTER IX

Liquor! Liquor! Liquor!

Under the occupation, the Polish people drank more liquor than before the war. People drank more to forget their worries. The desire to escape the grim reality, uncertainty about the future, and the feeling that death might come any day produced an atmosphere of hopelessness which was overcome by heavy drinking. Lack of recreation and amusement contributed to this atmosphere, especially among those engaged in the underground movement, who lived in constant danger and under permanent tension, which required a certain relaxation from time to time. Liquor supplied the indispensable relief. The consumption of vodka was so great that the Occupation Monopoly was unable to meet the demand; and throughout the whole country countless illicit secret stills were in operation, the liquid product of which was called 'bimber', no one knows why or by whom. To a Pole, however, the word had a pleasing sound, like the clinking of glasses; it must have been invented by a musical drunkard.

The quality of 'bimber' varied greatly, from a bluish, cloudy liquid, which sometimes caused blindness in those who drank it, to a nearly pure neutral alcohol, produced by pre-war specialists using the most 'modern' equipment which the extraordinary ingenuity of the Poles under the occupation was able to produce.

I visited two such illicit stills. One was installed in a windowless room in the Prudential building in Napoleon Square. On a large table a complete 'pocket' distillery had been erected, with piping of glass, copper and rubber, and with gas burners under bulging containers, from which emanated a strong smell, the most dangerous enemy of a secret distillery.

The whole looked like a university laboratory, and all that was missing were men in spectacles dressed in white coats, with the mark of learning on their thoughtful faces. Instead, there was the bibulous red face of the proprietor, as he proudly explained to me the working of the installation, adding modestly that his output was not big, but sufficient for home consumption and for some of his closest friends. He invited me to try one of his specialties, consisting of a mixture of 'bimber' and raspberry juice, which he called 'mum and dad'. To refuse would have been ungracious, and I must admit it was not bad at all. It tasted like Potocki's cherry brandy, to which a small quantity of kerosene had been added by mistake.

The second illicit distillery I visited after the Warsaw Rising. It occupied the cellar of a villa and represented a large-scale, almost legal undertaking; for it paid a regular tribute to the local German gendarmes. The latter consumed this tax only in part and sent quantities of it to Germany, where vodka was worth its weight in gold. After entering through a camouflaged door, I found myself in a veritable underground factory, constructed with an almost prophetic vision of future atomic wars. There were huge vats, containers, pipes, filters, and an enormous furnace with many burners. The handful of workers regarded me in silence. Production ran into hundreds of litres a day and was of a high quality, which I was invited to test for myself. The product reminded me of Bulgarian plum brandy.

The number of illicit stills in the Government General ran into thousands. In the villages, liquor was manufactured and consumed locally. In the cities and towns there were innumerable restaurants and cafés in which it was sold openly. But there were also many restaurants and bars in Warsaw where it would have been regarded as an insult to ask for 'bimber', or to suspect that one's drink was anything but genuine monopoly vodka. In such places everything to eat and drink was still obtainable, at a price, of course, and by infringing the innumerable prohibitions of the occupation authorities, which carried heavy penalties, including the death penalty. The three leading hotels in Warsaw, the Bristol, Europejski and Adria, were requisitioned for the exclusive use of the Germans.

Restaurants and bars during the German occupation were strange places. The proprietors themselves, with their casual attitude, gave them a most unprofessional atmosphere, for they were men and women who had never dreamed of running a restaurant before. They were mostly people who were well known and respected in Warsaw, and the public used to go to restaurants and bars not only for a meal or drink, but to see and talk to them. If one went to the Actresses' bar, which opened in Pius XI Street and later moved to Mazowiecka, it was because one wanted to see the great Polish actresses, Cwiklinska and Roman, serving tea, coffee and pastries. 'Cwikla', as she was popularly called, reigned supreme, ordering the guests about, telling them where to sit, and what to order. On a visit to SIM one went to see and hear the great actor Maszynski, whose wife served at the bar, and also to hear the exquisite playing of Panufnik and Lutoslawski on two pianos. The old guard used to go to the Chestnut Café, in the yard of the Deaf and Dumb Institute, to refresh their memories of the good old times in chats with the now ageing musical comedy star, Lucille Messal, who had also a great reputation as a cook. The bright young things, whom no enemy occupation could ever wipe out, congregated at the 'Fregata', where the large number of ladies serving as waitresses created the atmosphere of a social function rather than that of a restaurant. The soup grew cold while flirtations flourished.

From the 'Fregata' it was only a stone's throw to the 'Nectar' in St. Cross Street, which was well known in the underground; for on one occasion, bribed Gestapo men dropped in there for a bite with a prisoner, Mr. R., whom they were escorting from Gestapo headquarters to Pawiak prison, and allowed him to escape by the back door. I once had to meet someone there, and my attention was attracted by four men in the corner, who sat silently having a drink. Their behaviour contrasted with their whole environment, at least to an experienced eye, so I discreetly asked a waitress, whom I knew well, who they were.

'They are Englishmen,' she told me, 'who have escaped

from the Germans and are hiding in Warsaw.' I was not at all astonished. The preceding Easter holiday I had visited some friends, and had found there an Australian pilot who had escaped from German captivity and was being sheltered by the Underground in Warsaw. He learnt to speak Polish tolerably well. The Underground in Warsaw sheltered scores of escaped Allied prisoners-of-war, and a special unit was formed to look after them. Unfortunately, it so happened that one of them was captured by the Germans, and talked, giving the names of people and the addresses where he had been hiding. As a result, the entire Olszewski family, who had played an important part in that unit, was wiped out.

I wanted to know more about the four Englishmen, so I asked the waitress:

'Do they speak Polish?'

'No, but they understand it a little.'

'They must be mad to sit here, in a restaurant, where any minute someone may ask them questions.'

'I know; but they won't stay at home, because they get bored. So they come here, where they get everything at a reduced price; for we charge them only half the regular prices.'

On the way from the 'Fregata' to the 'Nectar', one passed a bar called 'Behind the Curtain', which was once the scene of a grim episode. It was said to have been established by the Gestapo, and it became the meeting place of its agents and those who had been drawn into the spy networks. When the Underground learned of this, they made short work of it. One day, several young men, pretending to be customers, pulled out their automatics from under their overcoats, and shot the entire staff. Unfortunately, during the shooting, a casual customer was killed, a deportee from Poznan and a member of a prominent family there.

A few steps from the 'Nectar' brought one to 'The Shilling', in Marshall Street. Here one found a noisy crowd, as in the old days. The menu was as good as the best before the war. The tables were loaded with plates and dishes. Vodka flowed in streams. It was a restaurant for the new rich; and like so many other bars and restaurants, it paid a heavy tribute to the Germans to ensure that they did not see what was served at the tables. Here, war millionaires celebrated their illegal transactions with glasses of vodka.

An entirely different atmosphere was to be found 'At Grzedzik's', in Heron Street, which was quiet and peaceful. It was the rendezvous of gourmets, who spent the remnants of their pre-war wealth to satisfy their palates. During the Warsaw Rising, both Grzedzik and Grzybowski, in Ordynacka Street, conducted themselves splendidly. They opened their doors to all, and fed hundreds of people free of charge, until they had used up all their reserves of food.

Here, or close by, one was sure to be accosted by a drunken woman who was known throughout the centre of Warsaw. Hunched and bent, she would scuttle up to her victim's side and cry in a heart-rending voice, 'A crumb of bread for my children, I im*plore* you'. As soon as she was given anything, she would turn on her heels and go straight to the nearest bar, for a glass of 'bread' for herself. One could also see shady characters everywhere, wearing overcoats and suspiciously stout at the waist, whispering hoarsely, 'Vodka, vodka, vodka'. These were street vendors of 'bimber', offering their wares.

Crossing Jerusalem Avenue one entered the coffee-bar quarter. 'Zusanna' in Wspolna, with 'Magarogype' on the opposite side of the street, 'The Little Horse' in Buxom Street, 'Fuchs' in Mokotow Street, 'Under the Palm' in Prus Street, 'March' in Three Crosses Square—dozens of them, sometimes very tastefully decorated, and always provided with magnificent cakes and pastries.

Coffee bar . . . black coffee . . . how inseparably it was all linked up with conspiracy in Warsaw! One remembers so much that took place within their walls. Warsaw was still starving when the coffee bars began to appear, like mushrooms after a good shower of rain. Cosy and attractive, they became meeting places for all the world. I can still hear the orders: 'Large black', 'Small black', 'small black in a large glass' . . . the last being given in the hope that a small portion would be poured out more generously into a large glass. The wits were ordering 'A large small coffee'. Coffee was expensive and every drop had a price. The coffee bars became regular conspiratorial institutions, often serving as 'letter boxes', but primarily as meeting places for conspiratorial consultations. The manageress and the waitresses in these cafés were usually the wives, sisters or sweethearts of military men. They were all fully aware of what was going on around them, and they were all 'safe'. Their husbands, brothers and fiancés were either in captivity or abroad. The atmosphere was altogether peculiar. Everyone talked in whispers, and watched everyone else; though on the whole they knew each other, at least by sight or reputation. Sometimes scraps of papers circulated under the tables in an exchange of correspondence or radio bulletins. The café was filled with regular customers. A stranger would immediately attract attention. A waitress would lean over the table as she served the coffee, and whisper the warning, 'Watch the table in the corner to the right'. Sometimes amusing situations arose. Colonel Horak of the Home Army was 'on duty' for hours every day at a table in a coffee bar in Sienkiewicz Street, where the waitresses regarded him as a great seducer. Among themselves they called him 'Bluebeard', because he was visited there every day by two or three contact-girls. 'He whispers to each of them so affectionately,' one of the waitresses said to me, 'and he looks at them with such loving eyes.'

We had a large number of hide-outs, but we had to use them sparingly, and only for permanent and regular contacts. One would not give the address of a hide-out to a man whom one met only once in a few months. It was better to meet him in a café, in a park or square, or simply in the street. I often used this method, and arranged meetings at the 'Sim', which was frequented by German officers from the city command (Für Deutsche erlaubt). The place was not included in the boycott, and the Germans had so little imagination that they never suspected that conspirators might be sitting at the next table, discussing the text of messages to be transmitted to London, or ways of carrying out of a death sentence.

In time, however, the Germans began to suspect what was going on in the coffee bars. They started to raid them, to check the personal documents of visitors, to make searches, and to arrest people. It was in this way that a member of the National Party, the lawyer Jazwinski from Kalisz, was arrested, when the Gestapo raided a coffee bar in Napoleon Square. In another raid, on a bar in Filter Street, they arrested a former deputy to the Seym, Sacha, of the same Party, and a number of other people.

As the German occupation continued, the spread of alcoholism became a serious problem, one with which the underground authorities had to deal. A number of slip-ups occurred, due to people blabbing when drunk, and this speeded up the necessary counter-measures. In the first place, internal instructions were issued prohibiting or restricting members of the underground in their consumption of alcoholic beverages. I was present at a meeting at which the problem was discussed, which resembled a gathering of teetotallers rather than the dreaded leadership of the underground. In addition, the Directorate of Civil Resistance undertook a campaign for the elimination of drunkenness in the villages, where it assumed even larger proportions than in the cities, and where the problem ceased to be one of the physical and moral health of the population, and became one of the security of the underground organisation. For in the countryside the organisation had become a mass movement, and there were districts in which the Peasant Battalions numbered many thousands of young boys. The danger arose from the fact that the Gestapo knew that in the villages illicit stills had become something in the nature of social centres, where people used to meet and gossip; so they began to organise a network of spies around them.

We came to the conclusion that appeals in the press and a whispering campaign were not enough, and that it was necessary to strike at the illicit distilleries in order to destroy them. The decision was put into effect by units of the Peasant Battalions, which constituted an excellent instrument for Civil Resistance action in the villages. In addition, groups of the Home Army proceeded to liquidate stills throughout the whole Government General. As a rule, the proprietor of an illicit still was visited during the night by a number of armed young men, who destroyed the equipment. If the proprietor objected and resisted them, they destroyed everything and punished him by flogging. If he behaved quietly, they spared all that part of the equipment which could be used by the household, such as barrels and boilers, but destroyed everything else. This action was carried out smoothly and almost without casualties; there were only a few cases in which nearby gendarmes intervened.

I was present at Civil Resistance headquarters when the final results of the action were being checked, on the basis of reports received. There was general satisfaction when it was established that about two thousand illicit stills had been liquidated, for no one had expected such spectacular results. But when somebody proposed that the occasion should be celebrated by a drink, we all agreed sorrowfully that 'it wouldn't do'. Such was life, in which there were no roses without thorns.

Zofia Korbonski
(ca. 1939–1945).
Courtesy of Zofia Korbonski.

Stefan Korbonski
(ca. 1939–1945).
Courtesy of Zofia Korbonski.

Zofia Korbonski,
July 1939.
Courtesy of Zofia Korbonski.

Zofia and Stefan Korbonski
on a truck after escaping
from the Gestapo, 1942.
Courtesy of Zofia Korbonski.

Józef Stankiewicz, "Joey," SWIT radio operator.
Courtesy of Zofia Korbonski.

Joey on the balcony of his apartment on the Vistula River in Warsaw.
Courtesy of Zofia Korbonski.

Left: Joey in front of his workshop on Rycerska Street in Old Town, Warsaw.
Below: Joey on the bank of the Vistula River.
Both photos courtesy of Zofia Korbonski.

Left: Joey and a friend at the Warsaw Mermaid statue.
Courtesy of Zofia Korbonski.

General Stefan Rowiecki, "Grot."
Courtesy of Zofia Korbonski.

General Tadeusz Pełczynski, "Grzegorz."
Courtesy of Zofia Korbonski.

Janusz Gryf-Kwiecinski.
Courtesy of Zofia Korbonski.

Maciej Kataj.
Courtesy of Zofia Korbonski.

Colonel Franciszek Kaminski,
commander of Bataliony Chlopskie.
Courtesy of Zofia Korbonski.

Above: The bombing of the Prudential Building in Warsaw. Courtesy of the Piłsudski Institute.

Right: Photo shows some of the destruction of a building after bombardment. Courtesy of Zofia Korbonski.

Left: Nowy Swiat Street during the Warsaw Uprising, August–October 1944.

Below: Zankowy Place, King Zygmunt's column during the Warsaw Uprising.

Both photos courtesy of the Piłsudski Institute.

Polish insurgent's grave in the street.
Courtesy of Zofia Korbonski.

German appeal to Poles to cease resistance.
Courtesy of Zofia Korbonski.

German Propaganda.
Above: An anti-British German propaganda poster.
Left: German propaganda newspaper printed in Polish.

Courtesy of Zofia Korbonski.

"Poland will win!"
Courtesy of the Piłsudski Institute.

"We'll avenge Pawiak"
(a notorious German prison).
Courtesy of the Piłsudski Institute.

Above and below:
Polish soldiers during the
Warsaw Uprising,
August–October 1944.
Courtesy of Zofia Korbonski.

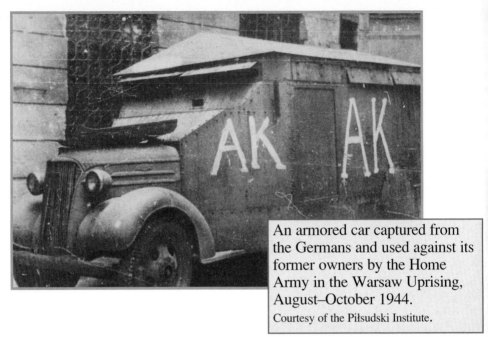

An armored car captured from the Germans and used against its former owners by the Home Army in the Warsaw Uprising, August–October 1944.
Courtesy of the Piłsudski Institute.

Polish soldiers of the Warsaw Uprising.
Courtesy of the Piłsudski Institute.

German prisoners of war.
Warsaw Uprising,
August–October 1944.
Courtesy of the Piłsudski Institute.

Lieutenant General
Tadeusz Komorwoski
(General Bor) in civilian
clothes, leaving German
headquarters after surrender negotiations.
Courtesy of the Piłsudski Institute.

Stefan Korbonski after the war.
Courtesy of Zofia Korbonski.

CHAPTER X

The Jews under the Occupation

Messages and Warnings

It began with my sending to London several messages, one after the other, with the information that on July 22, 1942, the Germans had begun to liquidate the Ghetto. In Stawki Street, 7,000 people were loaded into freight wagons and transported to Majdanek, where they were all killed in gas chambers. I was extremely astonished when the BBC made no use of my messages, and ignored them completely. I dispatched a special telegram, demanding to know the reasons for this silence. My astonishment grew when this urgent inquiry received no reply either. I would not give up; hurrying to the station, I ordered the radio operators to demand a reply to all my messages, every time they were in touch with London. They did so for several days, and apparently the daily bombardment caused the Government in London to reply at last. But the reply did not clear up the mystery; for it simply said: 'Not all your radiograms lend themselves to publication.'

I could not make out what it meant. Here were the Germans deporting and murdering 7,000 people every day, and London did not think it lent itself to publication! They must have gone mad, I thought. It was not until a month later that the BBC broadcast the news, based on our messages; and many months later still, a Government emissary who was parachuted into the country explained it to me:

'Your messages were disbelieved. Neither our Government nor the British would believe them. They said you were exaggerating for the sake of anti-German propaganda. But after the British received confirmation of it through their own channels, they were filled with dismay, and the BBC broadcast your information.'

While the liquidation of the Jews in Poland was proceeding, we simply inundated the Government in London with telegrams giving the facts, and we also informed them that Jews from the Balkan countries, Hungary, Holland, and elsewhere, were being transported to Poland. We requested that the Jews in these countries should be warned by radio that they should do their utmost to avoid being deported to Poland, where death was to be the end of their journey. This time the BBC and, later on, SWIT regularly broadcast our warnings. However, when trains from the various countries continued to arrive, and when here and there Polish railwaymen were able to whisper a warning to the unfortunate Jews, they were not believed and were laughed at, especially by those Jews who travelled in passenger trains with their luggage and bedding; who were convinced that they were being transported to some labour camp, and that they would be able to survive the war by working hard.

Towards the end of July 1942, I was summoned to attend a meeting with a person named Kowalski, who was to supply me henceforth with information about the Jews. Up till then I had gathered all I could from my own observations and from Civil Resistance sources, but I lacked direct information from the Jewish community, so I was glad to attend the suggested meeting.

In the Staszic Housing Estate, I knocked at the door of a rather large building; the door opened immediately, and someone standing in the dark corridor motioned me into a room. When I went in and saw a man standing by the window, I could not help laughing. The mysterious Kowalski had turned out to be my good friend Wolinski, a counsellor at the Office of the Prosecutor General in Warsaw, a man with the distinguished head of a philosopher. He looked at me through his thick spectacles, visibly moved.

'Ah, you are that mysterious Mr. Nowak who is in contact with London! I am so glad it is you. But what is that outfit you have got on?' he said, admiring my top boots, worker's jacket, and peaked cap of an employee of the Warsaw Power

Station. I was pleased too, for I had a great liking for Wolinski. In those sad days it was a pleasure to meet a pre-war friend whom one had not seen since long before, and to know that he was still alive.

From that day began our collaboration. Wolinski was in charge of Jewish affairs in the Office of Information and Propaganda, and supplied me with current information, which he received by the underground channels from the Jewish organisation in the Warsaw Ghetto. On the basis of what he gave me, I composed the telegrams transmitted to London. Here are two samples:

'June 20, 1944. As from May 15, the Germans have been carrying out mass murders in Auschwitz. The first to die are the Jews, followed by Soviet prisoners-of-war and the so-called sick. Hungarian Jews are being brought here *en masse*. Thirteen trains of 40-50 wagons each arrive daily. The victims are convinced that they are going to be exchanged for prisoners-of-war, or settled in the East. The gas chambers are working day and night. The corpses are being burnt in crematoria and in the open. More than 100,000 people have been gassed up till now.'

'July 19, 1944. The mass extermination of the Jews in Auschwitz is being supervised by its commander, Hoess, or Hess, and his aide, Grabner.'

Appeals of Civil Resistance and Sentences

On September 17, 1942, the Directorate of Civil Resistance issued an appeal concerning the liquidation of the Jews. It was published in all the underground newspapers and broadcast in the Polish language by Allied radio stations. Here it is:

'In addition to the tragedy through which the Polish people are passing, decimated by the enemy, there has been taking place in our country, for nearly a year, a monstrous, planned slaughter of the Jews. These mass murders are without parallel in the history of the world, and all the cruelties known to history pale beside them. Babies, children, young people, men and women, Catholic Jews and Jews of the Hebrew faith, for no other reason but that they belong to the Jewish race, are being mercilessly murdered, poisoned by gas, buried alive, thrown out of windows on to the pavement, suffering before death the additional torture of dying slowly, the hell of humiliation, torment and the cynical sadism of their executioners. More than a million victims have already been massacred and their numbers grow every day.

'Unable to oppose these crimes, the Directorate of Civil Resistance, on behalf of the entire Polish nation, protests against the crime being perpetrated against the Jews. All Polish political and social groups join in this protest. As in the case of Polish victims, the executioners and their henchmen will bear direct responsibility for these crimes.

The Directorate of Civil Resistance.'

Six months later, on March 18, 1943, the DCR issued another declaration, this time aimed against those who co-operated with the Germans in the persecution of Poles who were protecting Jews:

'The Directorate of Civil Resistance makes the following declaration:

'The Polish people, though themselves the victims of a terrible reign of terror, is witnessing with horror and profound compassion the murder of the remnants of the Jewish people in Poland. It has issued a protest against this crime, which has reached the ears of the entire free world. It has also given effective help to Jews who have escaped from the Ghetto or from the extermination camps, which has caused the occupation authorities to publish a decree threatening with death all Poles who help Jews. None the less, there are individuals devoid of honour and conscience, recruited from the criminal world, who have discovered a new source of profit for themselves by blackmailing Poles who protect Jews, and the Jews themselves.

'The DCR issues the warning that every case of such blackmail will be recorded and punished with all the severity of the law, whenever possible now, and at all events in the future.'

With the declaration were issued instructions imposing the death penalty for such crimes. On this basis, the special courts passed a number of death sentences, which were subsequently carried out. Here are the names of some of the executed: Boguslaw, vel Boris Pilnik, Warsaw; Jan Grabiec, Cracow; Tadeusz Stefan Karcz, Warsaw; Antoni Pajor, Dobranowice; Janusz Krystek, Grempkow; Jan Lapinski, Warsaw; Boleslaw Szostak, and Antoni Pietrzak, a corporal of the Blue police in Warsaw.

The above did not exhaust the problem of the protection the Poles and the underground extended to the Jews in Poland. A full description of this aspect of the struggle does not fall within the limits of these reminiscences, but it may be said that, thanks to the efforts of the Polish people, about 300,000 Jews who took the risk of refusing to enter the Ghetto survived the German massacres. And it should be borne in mind that the occupying authorities had issued a decree, mentioned in the proclamation of the DCR, which threatened with death every Pole who gave any protection or help to a Jew.

A Friend from the Ghetto

One day, before the liquidation of the Ghetto began, I set out for the District Court in Leszno, which was the only place in Warsaw where Poles and Jews were able to meet, which they did while attending cases in the Court. Access to it from the Aryan part of the city consisted of the roadway only; this was separated by a fence from the sidewalks and buildings, which were within the confines of the Ghetto. On the other side the Court was accessible from the Jewish quarter. I was at once lost in a throng of people who were engaged in transacting every kind of business, except that of the Court. A trade in jewels flourished here. The fine new building, which I knew so well, was hardly recognisable for the dirt and litter. The corridors were crowded with couples talking in whispers, with bowed heads, watching out for the gendarmes. As a rule, one of the two carried an armband with the Star of David, while the other was Polish. Here, Pole communicated with Jew. Unexpectedly, I noticed a familiar face. It was that of the barrister Rozensztat, a colleague of mine from the Barristers'

Council in Warsaw. I shook him by the arm.

'How are you, dear colleague?'

'Ah, it's you, colleague Korbonski. How glad I am to be still able to see you.'

I took him aside, and in the privacy of a window-recess, we chatted for more than two hours. Rozensztat had a sober view of the situation, and had no illusions as to the ultimate outcome of it all. He was resigned and had no thoughts of escape, though I tried to persuade him to do so, quoting the example of a number of our Jewish colleagues, who were in hiding in the Polish sections of the city. We did not discuss the Germans, as we had nothing new to say on the subject. However, he told me a great deal about the conditions prevailing in the Ghetto.

'Imagine our life with its two extremes! On the one hand, a group of fanatical chauvinists, who say that for the first time in a thousand years the Jews have regained something in the nature of independence, with their own government and territory, though under the protection of a foreign power. They rejoice in the Ghetto self-government and in the institutions run by the Jews, and they imagine they are nearer a Jewish State. On the other hand, scum of the worst kind are coming to the surface, who think realistically and anticipate a speedy end. The Jewish police would sell their fathers and mothers to the Germans to survive, and to have a chance of saving their skins. Between the two extremes are the mass of resigned and wretched people, who are daily dying in their hundreds from hunger and disease.'

We took a sad farewell. I tried to cheer Rozensztat up by a conventional, 'Au revoir, after the war'. But he shook his head:

'Not in this world, dear colleague, not in this world.'

And he was right.

Jewish children

One evening I returned with Zosia to our hide-out on the Staszic Housing Estate. While turning in, we heard from outside a child crying, 'Mame, mame. . . .' I opened the window on the frosty night and listened. From the verandah of the neighbouring house, separated from ours by a garden, there came a stifled cry and the voice of another child: 'Shut up, or a German will come'. The warning had no effect and the pitiful voice continued to whine 'Mame, mame'. It was easy to guess that these were Jewish children who had escaped from the Ghetto. Dozens of them were roaming the city, begging and hiding from the police. Zosia leaned out of the window and whistled. The crying and the voice stopped at once. In a low and gentle voice Zosia called: 'Children, listen to me, children. . . .' There was no answer, and only after repeated summoning, a frightened voice asked:

'Who is it?'

'Don't be frightened. Someone will take some food to you presently. You won't be frightened, will you?' This time a weak voice replied:

'Yes, lady.'

Zosia gathered together everything that was available in the kitchen. I took an American military blanket of the indestructible kind used in the First World War, and slipped quietly through the front door, so as not to waken the landlady, who slept on the ground floor, and who had no idea what dangerous tenants we were. Because of her, and because of our own precarious position, there could be no question of taking the children in. As curfew was on, I moved like a shadow along the walls of the darkened houses to get to the other side of the block.

When I reached the little gate I asked in a low voice:

'Children, are you there?'

'Yes, sir,' a voice answered from the other side of the gate.

When I reached the verandah, I found four little children, of whom the eldest was about nine and the youngest five. They stood in a row, shivering with cold.

'Have you come from the Ghetto?' I asked.

'Yes, sir,' answered the eldest of them.

'And what happened to your parents?'

'They are in the Ghetto. They sent us out hoping we should find some food.'

'And when you do find it?'

'When we get a little food, we shall take it to our parents.'

I had no reason to doubt them; for it was a fact that the children used to come and go, crossing the walls of the Ghetto somehow.

'Here is some food for you, and here is a blanket. Wrap yourself up and sleep. All the time you're here I shall bring you some food each evening.' More voices chimed in:

'Thank you, thank you, sir. . . .'

In the early morning we again heard the muted voice:

'Lady, lady!'

'What is it you want, children?' Zosia answered, leaning out of the window.

'Could we get some hot water? Or a little milk?'

Here another voice spoke indignantly:

'Are you crazy? Perhaps you'd like a cup of hot cocoa too?'

Zosia looked at me:

'I have a little cocoa and milk. I shall prepare it right away.'

When Zosia returned after fifteen minutes, she was in tears.

'As long as I live,' she said, 'I shall never forget it. If you had seen how they drank that cocoa and how they thanked me!'

For the next few days we saw the little company in other parts of the Staszic Estate. The youngest was covered in the huge blanket, which trailed behind him on the ground. Some days later the blanket disappeared. I asked the eldest boy:

'What happened to the blanket? The little one is freezing.'

The boy blushed.

'We took it to the Ghetto, so that our parents could sell it. They are very hungry.'

Later on they no longer spent their nights on the verandah, though they continued to move about the Staszic Estate, more cheerful and better looking. In passing them on one occasion I asked them:

'Why don't you sleep on the verandah?'

The oldest boy blushed; he wanted to say something, but hesitated, and at last he said evasively:

'We are better off now.'

Zosia accidentally discovered the truth of that betterment. A childless woman who kept a shop in Filter Street took care of the children. At night she hid them in the shop, and gave them something to eat. During the day they had to fend for themselves.

One day Zosia returned from the shop terribly upset.

'Just think of it! The woman is crying all the time. Yesterday, in broad daylight, the children came across a German patrol and were shot on the spot.'

The Rising in the Ghetto

On April 19, 1943, a rising broke out in the Ghetto. The whole of Warsaw, despite the frightful terror overhanging it and the daily deaths by violence of hundreds of Poles, was electrified, stunned, helpless and . . . proud. The news spread all over the city that above the walls of the Ghetto the Polish and Jewish flags had been hoisted.

We did our best to get as close to the Ghetto as possible, and we organised a special information service concerning the Rising. Gradually, at the Directorate of Civil Resistance, news from all sources about the fighting in the Ghetto was being collected, and a steady flow of telegrams was being transmitted to London. One of our stations was operating in a house in Marshall Street with a view of the Mokotow Field. From the roof one could see the smoke and fire issuing from the Ghetto, and hear the sound of explosions. Zosia, Joey, who was still alive then, and I observed what was happening from behind a chimney stack, and afterwards sent a telegram:

'From the house our station is operating from fire and smoke can be seen over the Ghetto, and artillery bombardment can be heard. It is a frightful scene.'

Several hours later, we listened to SWIT broadcasting a programme based on our telegram, designed to make it seem as if the announcer were describing his impressions as he looked out from the window of the radio station, and saw the blaze and smoke and heard the roar of cannon. While monitoring this programme we were deeply moved by the announcers' dramatic story, and he, too, judging by the emotion in his voice, was gripped by what he was saying. We looked at each other, feeling a kind of sorrowful satisfaction, till Zosia said:

'It will be easier for them to die with the knowledge that the world hears how they are dying.'

All the teams at the station were deeply conscious of their responsibilities at this period. The whole organisation worked with devoted efficiency. Cold calculation warned us that we were overdoing it, and that the Germans were bound to locate us and catch up with us. But our run of luck held, and all that happened was that we had to 'freeze' two hide-outs which the Germans approached too closely with their mobile interceptor units, which, however, were fortunately observed in time. As a result, SWIT was able to broadcast daily news of the fighting in the Ghetto, together with impressive appeals and protests prepared by the London team.

Here are samples of the telegrams, the tragic eloquence of which needs no comment from me:

'April 21, 1943. Resistance in the Ghetto is continuing. Gunfire and explosions can be heard all night and day. Occasional conflagrations.'

'April 28, 1943. The fighting in the Ghetto continues. The Germans are setting fire to house after house.'

'May 7, 1943. "The Republic" of May 6 has published a declaration by the Government Plenipotentiary in Poland denouncing the latest German crimes in the Ghetto. It expresses admiration and compassion for the Jews who fell fighting, and it calls on the Poles to help those Jews who have escaped from the Ghetto.

'May 15, 1943. A horrible massacre of the remaining Jews in the Warsaw Ghetto has been in progress for the past three weeks. Under the command of the Jewish Fighting Organisation, the Ghetto has been heroically offering armed resistance. The Germans have used tanks and artillery in the battle. Jewish fighters have killed over three hundred Germans, and have wounded about a thousand. The Germans have removed, murdered, or burned alive tens of thousands of Jews. Out of three million Polish Jews no more than 10 per cent remain. The rest have been murdered by the Germans.'

'May 22, 1943. German rumour has it that Dr. von Sammern, the Gestapo chief, who was recalled from Warsaw, has been sentenced to death for the disgrace that the Ghetto's armed resistance has brought upon the Germans.'

'June 9, 1943. The underground Economic Bulletin of May 15 states that in the Warsaw Ghetto there have been burned down or blown up 100,000 dwelling units, 2,000 industrial establishments, 3,000 commercial establishments, and a score of factories. In September 1939 only 78,000 dwelling units were destroyed in all Warsaw.'

'June 29, 1943. The Ghettos in Stanislawow, Lukow, Wegrow and Zolkwia have been completely wiped out. In Warsaw, some 2,000 Jews are dying in cellars and amid the ruins. Skirmishes still occur during the night. At Sobibor railroad station the Germans welcomed with music Jews arriving from other countries.'

During the Ghetto rising I set out one day for my usual weekly meeting with the Government Plenipotentiary, vice-premier Jan Jankowski (now in a Moscow prison serving an eight-year term as one of the 'convicted' leaders of the underground). A man of about 60, bald, tall and slender, and wearing spectacles, he greeted me with his customary friendliness. He observed me attentively from behind his thick lenses while I made my weekly report on the activities of the Directorate of Civil Resistance. As I was about to leave, he suddenly said to me as a kind of afterthought:

'By the way, I have some news for you. The Jewish Fighting Organisation in the Ghetto has requested the representatives of Jewish organisations to convey their thanks to me for the SWIT broadcasts on the fighting in the Ghetto. I am passing it on to the proper quarter.'

On page 7 of his remarkable book, published in New York under the title 'The Wall', describing the history of the Warsaw Ghetto, John Hersey wonders why the hero of the story, Levinson, on whose alleged diary the book is based, failed to mention SWIT. He writes:

'With all his thoroughness, Levinson must have had some prejudices or blind spots. How else account for some of the omissions from his notes? For instance, he never mentions the underground radio transmitter, which broadcasts even at the beginning of the final battle in the Ghetto under the call letters SWIT. He must have known about it. He must not have wanted to write about it. Why?'

The fact that Hersey speaks of an 'underground radio transmitter' seems to indicate that his astonishment was based on the conviction that SWIT operated in Poland, and that the alleged chronicler of the Ghetto, Levinson, ought to have known and written about it.

When Hersey's book appeared in 1950, and I read the paragraph quoted above, I sent him for perusal the story of SWIT. In a letter dated June 14, 1950, Mr. Hersey wrote:

'Dear Mr. Korbonski,—Many thanks for sending me your article about SWIT, which I read with much interest. I certainly was under the impression—and many people still are—that this underground station was inside Poland.'

This shows that in his painstaking research into the enormous material on which he based his book, he never discovered the secret of SWIT. But his research confirms the fact that SWIT was listened to during the Rising in the Ghetto.

CHAPTER XI

P.P.R.— The Paid Lackeys of Russia

The Two Brothers—Hitler and Stalin

In the early days of the German occupation Stas Dubois communicated an interesting bit of news to me:

'Wanda Wasilewska is in Warsaw. She is being driven around in a lush German car and accompanied by smart officers of the Gestapo. She has been trying to make contact with her former friends in the Polish Socialist Party, but has had no luck, because most of them are in hiding under assumed names, for one thing, and for another, they don't want to see her. She has found only a few among the older generation, who were friends of her father's, and the news comes from them.'

I wasn't as impressed as Stas seemed to be; for I had already seen in the 'Berliner Illustrierte' pictures of Stalin and Ribbentrop shaking hands, and Soviet and Nazi officers doing the same on the river Bug, where they were delineating the frontier. However, I wanted to know why she had come to Warsaw.

'What is it exactly she's come for?' I asked. 'I am sure it wasn't for a cup of coffee at the Adria?'

Stas was well informed.

'She came for purely commercial reasons,' he said. 'She wants to sell a house she inherited from her father. The Germans are helping her in the sale.'

In a few days the whole of Warsaw was talking about this new proof of Soviet-German friendship. And it was so typical of Warsaw that, because Wanda Wasilewska's father had been chairman of the Frontier Commission which, together with the Soviet delegation, delineated the Polish-Russian frontier at the conclusion of the Riga Peace Treaty in 1921, the saying was coined: 'What the father gained, the daughter gave away.'

The Communists slowly began to be active, but so ineffectively that it was obvious they had neither proper organisation nor leadership. The dissolution of the Communist Party by the Kremlin before the war had evidently liquidated the core of the Party, and everything had to be started up afresh. The first signs of their activity were reported by the railwaymen. These old and experienced Socialist workers soon noticed that it was the Communists who were propagating among them slogans for the efficient transport of supplies, mainly crude oil and foodstuffs, from Russia to Germany. The Communists counted on the radicalism of the railwaymen, and advanced the view that the war had been provoked by Western imperialists and capitalists in order to enslave the Germans, and that for this purpose they made use of the silly Poles. That slogan, however, did not work; on the contrary, railwaymen were joining the Polish underground in increasing numbers. They carried on their famous sabotaging activities, such as placing time-bombs in freight-cars, set to go off after the transport reached German territory.

A little later, the prison guards in Radom and other cities reported still more interesting news:

'The Gestapo are using Polish prisons to house transports of prisoners *en route* from Russia to Germany. These people, who talk German, are trying to establish contact with the outside world; they say they are German Communists who escaped to Russia after Hitler came to power. Now the Soviets are handing them over to Hitler.'

I must admit that I could not believe these reports. I knew through our underground intelligence that close co-operation existed between the NKVD and the Gestapo, *inter alia* with regard to the exchange of information and evidence concerning the Polish underground, which led to arrests; but that Communists should hand over to Hitler their fellow-Communists I could not believe. Stas, however, through whom the information came, soon convinced me:

'You've been in Vienna yourself and you've met former members of the *Schutzbund*. Of those who escaped to Russia almost all have been liquidated. The same thing happened to other foreign Communists. Don't you remember the Communist deputy to our Seym, Dabal, and what happened to him? Yet at first they were naming streets after him. . . . If they were capable of doing that, why shouldn't they hand over German Communists to Hitler? What better proof of friendship could they offer?'

After the war many documents were brought to light confirming the truth of that monstrous iniquity. A few German Communists who, like Margarete Buber, miraculously survived the hell of German concentration camps, have written books in which they fully confirm the facts. The world was amazed; but soon forgot. To-day, after the liquidation of Beria, the world would not be astonished if it learned that Khrushchev, the party leader, had liquidated Khruschev, the Ukrainian nationalist.

By the end of 1940 and the beginning of 1941, Communist whispering propaganda, which now had as its slogan the mutual destruction of the Fascist-Capitalist world, was in full swing; and it was turning also against the Polish underground, which it alleged was subordinated to the 'Fascist' Polish Government-in-exile in London.

The outbreak of the Soviet-German war on June 22, 1941, brought all such activities to an end. After the Agreement concluded on July 30 between the Polish and Soviet Governments, a sort of truce in Communist propaganda against the Polish Underground ensued. The Polish Communist Party was reorganised under the name of the Polish Workers Party (PPR), which proceeded to develop its own anti-German underground. However, right until the end of the war it remained rather feeble, and incapable of undertaking actions on a large scale. Suffice it to say that throughout the entire period of occupation, the PPR kept boasting about an 'armed action' it had organised which consisted of the throwing of a hand-grenade from the crowded street into the Café Club in Warsaw, in which German soldiers were having a cup of coffee or a glass of beer. The man who threw the hand-grenade risked no more than the scores of passers-by, among whom he immediately found a safe refuge. The Home Army never undertook any action in which innocent passers-by would be exposed to such a risk. But the Communists continue to glorify the action against the Café Club as a symbol of heroic daring; whereas to underground Warsaw it became an object of derision.

A Meeting with Marshal Zymierski

While a Communist Underground was being formed in occupied Poland, one of my friends in the Peasant Party came to me with an interesting proposal:

'Wouldn't you like to meet General Zymierski? He wants to join our underground and would like to talk to you about it.'

I remembered the affair in which Zymierski had been implicated before the war, when his name became notorious in Poland; I had no great opinion of the General, and frankly said so to my friend. He was ready with his defence:

'You are thinking of the "Protekta" affair, and the imprisonment of Zymierski? Forget it! Some months ago Zymierski requested three well-known public figures to form a court of honour, and to consider his case again. They issued a verdict absolving Zymierski of any guilt whatsoever. They came to the conclusion that the Court which sentenced him had acted under pressure, and that the judgement was not fair.'

Nevertheless, I refused to meet Zymierski; and I would not mention the matter here, but for the fact that in 1946, under Soviet occupation, I called on Zymierski, accompanied by the above-mentioned friend, to ask him to put on the list of Military Court barristers a number of barristers belonging to the Peasant Party, so that they would be able to defend members of their Party tried before Military Courts for political offences, which were the only ones competent to deal with such cases. To save our people, I had to force myself to visit Zymierski.

We arrived in Klonowa Street and entered the building of the Inspectorate General of the Army, which by then had been fully reconstructed after the damage it suffered during the war. There were sentries posted everywhere, and crowds of officers in uniform, trying to look smart, at a time when it was the fashion of Communists to show negligence in their appearance. There were shining floors, carpets, pictures and old coats-of-arms on the walls. Looking closer at this display I came to the conclusion that most of it must have been loot from the newly-acquired Western provinces.

After a young aide had announced our arrival, the doors leading to the 'Marshal's' study opened at once; but before we entered, three 'generals' filed out, including Zawadzki, chief of the personnel department. Zymierski, in a Marshal's uniform, came to the door to welcome us and to motion us in.

When I informed him of our request and submitted to him a list containing the names of the barristers recommended, he at once agreed to do what we wanted, asked us to regard the matter as settled, and opened a political talk. In the course of it, my companion, by way of return for the speedy and favourable decision, and to my great dissatisfaction, complimented the Marshal by saying that the peasant movement was most favourably disposed towards him, and that he was sure the Marshal reciprocated these sentiments. Zymierski was extremely pleased.

'I have always been most friendly disposed towards the Peasant Party. Do you remember the time when I wanted to join your Peasant Battalions? You wouldn't have me then, and you would not even see me. Others, too, did not want me. What was I to do? I, a General, during a war in which my country was fighting against an enemy? I joined the PPR; and that's how I reached this place.' With a wide sweep of his arm, Zymierski indicated what had once been the study of Marshal Rydz-Smigly, Commander-in-Chief of the Polish Army at the outbreak of the war.

Such was the authoritative explanation of how the PPR gained one of its leaders, and the People's Army it's beloved commander, 'the legendary General Rola'.

However, the barristers, members of the Peasant Party, were never accepted as military defence counsels. It was obvious that Zymierski had no influence in such matters. The decisions rested exclusively with the Ministry of Security.

Katyn

The situation underwent a drastic change in the spring of 1943, when the scales of victory turned in favour of the Soviets, and their plans to grab the whole of Poland began to take shape. From then on events moved rapidly. On March 1, 1943, the Union of Polish Patriots was formed in Moscow to counter-balance the Polish Government in London. On April 13, 1943, the German radio announced the discovery in Katyn of the mass graves of murdered Polish officers. The whole country was shaken with horror and despair. Thousands of men, the flower of the nation, had been murdered in a most bestial manner. The whole of Poland went into mourning, and throughout the length and breadth of the country a great weeping went up.

The question arose at once: who was responsible? The Germans were making frantic efforts to supply, as quickly as they could, the most convincing answer. Delegations from various prisoner-of-war camps, representing many different nationalities, were taken to Katyn, and people from Poland, too, were taken to see the mass graves. German-controlled Polish-language newspapers published daily reports of the discovery of more graves. It all impressed us as authentic; but because it was the Germans who were saying it, we had to treat it with the utmost reserve. Day by day I sent a stream of telegrams to London reporting everything the Germans announced, including the names of people they had sent to Katyn, and their statements printed in the newspapers. Notwithstanding the fact that everything was being done by German initiative and under German control, a comparison of the reports received from the families of the victims, and of the dates on which the correspondence of the prisoners with their families suddenly stopped, the position of the front line at the time, etc., all the circumstantial evidence indicated that the crime had been committed by the Russians. However, absolutely reliable news was still lacking, and the suspicion remained that it could, after all, have been an exceedingly clever German propaganda manoeuvre.

When I met the Government Plenipotentiary, it was decided that I should myself get in touch with one of the people who had been to Katyn and secure first-hand information. We considered the names of all those who had been there, and we resolved to choose one who could be fully trusted to be veracious, impartial and safe to talk to. We excluded at once Jozef Mackiewicz and Ferdinand Goetel, whose pro-German sympathies were notorious. The choice fell on Casimir Skarzynski, Secretary General of the Polish Red Cross. He had been taken to Katyn by the Germans because of the position he occupied in the Red Cross.

Skarzynski and I had a mutual friend in Wierusz-Kowalski, who undertook to organise a meeting; and the following day, in a private room in the offices of a Bank in Jasna Street, where I called as a customer, I had a conversation with a tall, greying and extremely good-looking man.

I shall not try to reproduce the conversation, except to say that his lengthy, dispassionate and objective information, based on observed facts, admitted of no doubt that the murderers were Russians. In the presence of Skarzynski and others, graves were opened which it was obvious had not been disturbed for a long time. In their presence, letters and notebooks were taken out of the pockets of the uniforms in which the victims had been buried. The written documents showed that the murdered prisoners were in Russian custody to the last. I listened to Skarzynski's story shaken to my very being, and I cursed the Russians with all my heart.

After the conversation, I hurried to the Government Plenipotentiary. Though he anticipated what my report would be, he wrung his hands in unbridled passion, despondency and grief, as sentence by sentence, I repeated to him all that I had learned. When I had finished, he asked me to transmit to London as much information as the safety of the radio station permitted.

Leaving the Government Plenipotentiary, I went straight to the station, where I found ready waiting for me Zosia, the telegraphist, and the look-out girls, who had been warned in advance that there might be urgent telegrams that day. Looking at them with almost frenzied eyes—as I was told later— I cried:

'The murderers of Katyn are the Russians! I have spoken to a man who was there. To work everyone! No matter what the risks, we must send off a full report.'

During that day and the next, long telegrams embodying the report were sent to London, on the basis of which SWIT accused the Russians for the first time of being guilty of the Katyn crime. After the Polish Government had applied to the International Red Cross in Geneva, with the request that the Katyn murders should be investigated, the Soviets, on April 26, 1943, broke off diplomatic relations with the Polish Government.

By way of an epilogue to my reminiscences, I should like to mention that Casimir Skarzynski appeared as a witness before the United States House of Representatives Committee to inquire into the Katyn mass murders, and that in his depositions he referred to the report he gave me in 1943.

The NKVD in Warsaw

On Soviet orders, the PPR changed its attitude completely, and instead of fighting the Germans took up the struggle against the 'internal enemy' in the 'London' underground. From that moment all activities against the Germans were carried out by Soviet partisans only, who were aided by parachute drops of men and arms, and also small groups of the Peoples' Militia, subsequently named the People's Army. On the other hand, the PPR, as a party and as an underground organisation, was charged with the task of struggling for the soul of the Polish people. This struggle was carried on by means of the underground press, by whispering propaganda and so on, supported by unlimited funds and technical assistance, under instructors schooled in Russia who were either dropped into the country by parachute or passed through the fluctuating battle front.

In addition, the PPR was allotted the task of spying on the Polish Underground, of preparing index cards of its members, its organisations, etc. In charge of this particular task was a Soviet cell of the NKVD, which was by then operating in Polish territory still held by the Germans. Under its experienced guidance this aim was achieved; to the extent that when the Soviet Armies entered Polish territory, the NKVD, which followed up behind the front, had in its possession all the necessary material to effect the arrest of thousands of members of our underground.

I may add that the first blow to fall on the Directorate of Civil Resistance came not from the Germans, but from the NKVD. The office of the Government Plenipotentiary had its intelligence branch, which tried to unravel the secrets of the Gestapo, just as the intelligence service of the Home Army tried to get possession of military secrets. Our intelligence constantly protested that I was being seen about too much in the streets, and prophesied that I should not escape arrest. I was of a different opinion, and pointed out that the Gestapo made many more arrests in secret hide-outs than in the streets.

One day, my eighteen-year-old contact-girl, Ela, a nice blonde with a slight stammer, who was most devoted to her work, was sent to the hide-out of the 'Cripple,' a member of the Intelligence Service of the Government Plenipotentiary's office in Poznan Street, and vanished without trace; just as, with one exception, everybody else vanished who went there on that day. The one who came back told us later that after knocking in the pre-arranged way, the door opened and she found herself facing several civilians armed with revolvers, who took her into the room where the 'Cripple', Ela, and several other people were being detained. To her amazement, the civilians were not Germans, and the man who cross-examined her spoke to his companions in Russian. She succeeded cleverly in explaining away her visit to the house, and as nothing incriminating was found on her, she was allowed to go, after several hours of cross-examination. All the others, including my contact, Ela, and the 'Cripple', disappeared for ever; they were most probably taken out of town and murdered.

Subsequent investigations revealed that this action was carried out by the Russian NKVD at a moment when our struggle against the common German enemy was at its highest pitch.

The A-Cell

It may be asked what sort of counter-action was undertaken, and how much truth there was in the Soviet accusations that our underground murdered Communists. Anyone who lived in Poland during the years of the German occupation will know that our anti-Communist campaign, the campaign of that underground organisation which obeyed the orders of the Government Plenipotentiary, was limited to counter-propaganda in the press, scribbled slogans, and nothing more. We all remember the large letters daubed on walls and fences: 'PPR—Paid lackeys of Russia', which proved to be a very effective slogan all round. It was as late as the summer of 1943 that the Government Plenipotentiary appointed a special anti-Communist cell, the so-called A-Cell, entrusted with the task of co-ordinating this action. Its head was Francis Bialas, whom I met for the first time when I attended a meeting of the A-Cell. Several meetings were held, in which I took part, and during which methods to be applied were discussed. One of those present proposed that the Communists should be liquidated as a reprisal for their collaboration with the Gestapo during the first period of the war, a collaboration which had many Polish victims. In the discussion which ensued, only that one person supported the proposal; all the others, including myself, opposed it, and the proposal was rejected as inevitably leading to a 'fratricidal war'. It was decided that the A-Cell should rely on propaganda and leaflets, of which several were printed and distributed. Such was the 'murder' of Communists by the Polish Underground.

To-day, when I reflect on all these matters, I have no regret that we adopted such an attitude. At least we were able to prevent an internal struggle, which would not have affected the future in any way. In support of the truth of my account, I may refer to the following facts:

During the Warsaw Rising all the leading Communists, with the exception of Bierut and those who joined the Lublin Committee or remained in Moscow, were within our reach, which means at our mercy. No one would question the fact that the Home Army and the Government Plenipotentiary held undivided sway over the capital, and they could have had all the Communists arrested and liquidated without any difficulty, and without any fear of reprisals. But such an idea never entered anyone's head, and the PPR had no need to hide from our underground; it functioned with full liberty.

We may be quite sure that in similar circumstances the Communists would have acted very differently in relation to their opponents. This has been proved by what happened in the cells and prisons of Wilno, Lwow, Luck and other Polish cities. In all these prisons, the NKVD, as they retreated before the advancing Germans, murdered all political prisoners.

CHAPTER XII

New Men and New Tasks

Civil Engineer Richard

In the slip-up in Marshall Street we lost all the transmitters under repair, nearly 300 valves of all kinds, the new sound transmitter under construction, a recording machine, a mass of instruments—in short, we lost everything except the transmitters kept in the hide-outs from which they were operated and the equipment stored at the Polytechnic. The stations were working and maintained uninterrupted contact with London. However, they often developed defects which had to be repaired, and we needed a skilled radio technician. While Joey was alive, all such troubles were easily overcome. He had an infallible instinct, and with one touch he was able to remove a defective part and ensure the working of a transmitter.

I was looking for another technician, and I got in touch with Richard, an engineer employed by the municipal waterworks. I called on him at his office in Lindley Street, and thus made the acquaintance of a gentleman past his sixties, but in full vigour, despite his strikingly pale, parchment-like face. With his lively movements and keen eyes he impressed me as a most energetic man. He had been advised of the purpose of my visit and we soon came to an understanding. Without beating about the bush, I asked him if he knew how to construct a radio transmitter on his own, and if he disposed of the necessary tools and means. He assured me that with the assistance of a technician he knew, he would be able to do it. I was somewhat put off by the tolerant smile with which he answered my queries. But I continued to question him.

'Where did you work before the war?' I asked him.

'In many places. In South America, in Indo-China, and in Africa.'

Noticing my surprise the engineer added:

'I studied in France and England, and I have spent most of my life constructing power stations in many different parts of the world. I arrived in Poland shortly before the outbreak of war.'

Engineer Richard started to work for us, and after a few weeks he delivered the first transmitter of his own construction. I named it 'Dick'. Though of small dimensions, it developed 50 watts and, as my telegraphists told me, its construction and operation were very simple.

I discovered with pleasure that Richard displayed considerable initiative, and that there was no need to hurry him. He was also scrupulously punctual, which was an invaluable quality in a conspiracy. Unpunctuality in underground work is simply criminal.

As time went on, we met frequently and became quite intimate. I was greatly touched to find Richard treating me, and Zosia even more, in an almost fatherly way. We both felt that he had come to like us very much, and we reciprocated his sentiments. He was most solicitous about our safety, and used to say:

'You must be very cautious; and remember that you must live until Poland is free again. Stick to me, I bring luck to people.'

New men open new opportunities, and Richard secured the services of a radio telegraphist, Mirek, a student at the Polytechnic, a young, somewhat haggard-looking, fair-haired young man of extraordinary courage and audacity, which I frequently had to curb. Mirek was able to find his own hideouts, and established his main base in an apartment in Lower Street. He worked with London as station No. 71. He had to work hard; for as a telegraphist he was an inexperienced amateur, but he made up for his shortcomings by his enthusiasm and devotion.

At about the same time I met a young, somewhat clumsy and nervous man with a pleasant and gentle face, who implored me to engage him for some underground work.

'Give me any work that's going. I'll do anything you tell me to do. I can work as a contact, messenger, floor-sweeper, anything. I've been wanting to join the underground so much, but I've never met anyone before who would introduce me.'

I could not refuse him, so I entrusted him with the task of finding safe hide-outs. Miet, for that was his pseudonym, was very much impressed by his new function, and at once started to comb the city for likely hide-outs. After a few days he found one.

'I've got a safe apartment. Do you know where? With a professional radio-telegraphist!'

'Do you think he would be willing to work with us?'

'He would like nothing better; but I did not dare to suggest it to him on my own.'

We soon recruited the new telegraphist, whom I called Gene. He was a tall, fair-haired man of middle age, with an emaciated face, as nervous and as keen as Miet. He wanted to start work as soon as possible. When we put him on to London, he stayed all night long at the station, which was designated No. 50. I was critical of his excessive eagerness, but I became reconciled to it, because the station on which Wladek and Martin worked disposed of only three hide-outs, while Mirek, as a beginner, worked as a relief in two hide-outs. At about that time Poland suffered a great loss. General Sikorski was killed in the tragic disaster in Gibraltar. It fell to us to deal with an extraordinary flow of telegrams from and to London, and the work was done mainly by Gene, who handled piles of incoming and outgoing telegrams with efficiency and relish.

We discovered at this period a new talent in the person of Ralph, mentioned earlier, a workman of middle age, with a finely featured face. He was a quiet man of great self-control. In dealing with him one was impressed by his reliability, and his most serious attitude towards the problems that every Pole had to solve for himself under occupation conditions. He joined us as an observer, but on his own initiative he was also searching for hide-outs, he helped me in innumerable other matters, and he extended his protection to Wladek and Martin, who were strangers in Warsaw and not always able to manage things on their own. The three became great friends and worked most efficiently together. I appreciated this, and after sounding Martin and Wladek, I appointed Ralph to be head of the radio station, which was designated No. 43.

We had, therefore, a new workshop at Richard's and three stations working independently of each other. The men operating one station did not know the men operating the others, and each worked in separate hide-outs unknown to the rest. All the teams were most enthusiastic in their work, each man was a patriotic Pole, and all were animated by a desire to fight the Germans. It was at this period that we achieved the highest degree of organisational and technical efficiency, which we were able to maintain in spite of further blows, up to the time of the Warsaw Rising. London appreciated this in its reports concerning radio liaison, which we received by parachute drops, and in one it stated that 'the best station we are working with is No. 43'.

How the stations worked

There was always an exciting atmosphere at the radio stations. I was not a technician, and the magic of being able to communicate, with the help of a small box and a piece of wire, with a great city a thousand miles away, which was the centre of political and military decisions in the prolonged war, always held me spellbound. I used to spend a great deal of time at the stations, not only because it gave me pleasure, but also because it cheered up the operators, who disliked being alone in the room. I always sensed a certain tension as the hour approached for work to begin, and when, after tuning in, the telegraphist put the earphones on and placed his fingers on the key. I used to get as nervous as the operator himself when he could not hear London calling or replying. I cursed as much as he did when, turning to me with his earphones on, he shouted, as all telegraphists do when wearing earphones: 'That beastly fellow is late again. He isn't there yet'.

Our stations worked with the utmost punctuality, and it

was only rarely that the London operator was late, or, if he worked with another station, would not reply to our call. But when it did happen, our men would be wild.

'The bum's probably gone for a drink, or taken his girl-friend to the pictures—that's why he's late. When he arrives, he'll take off his gloves (this imaginary action always made him most indignant), sit down in front of his apparatus, and get through his few hours of work, while we here have to slave day and night. There is nothing worse than an official who works for a regular salary.'

But as soon as London called, his anger would subside at once. His London colleague would then explain why he was late at great length, till our man would mutter to himself, 'It's all right, its' all right', and take up the work in hand. But woe to the London man if he failed to apologise! The first question he would then hear would be: 'Why are you late? In future, please start punctually! . . .' and a nice little string of uncensored abbreviations would follow into the ether.

The transmission of telegrams was a heavy and laborious job. The telegraphist had in front of him columns of figures grouped in series of five each. He was frequently obliged to repeat the whole, or parts, of a message two or three times, before London confirmed its receipt. In the meantime his ear-phones would be crackling, and he would say, 'Ah, I can hear the *gonia* trying to pinpoint me'. I attached the greatest im-portance to the telegraphist's mood. They were always excited by their work, and when in addition they knew that they were being pursued by mobile interceptors their excitement was enhanced by fear, of which no man in their place would have been free. They worked very hard, for it was an exhausting task and required a great deal of concentration; when their spell was over they frequently got up wet with sweat.

I had to take care that the stations did not operate for too many hours. We tried to limit each session to not more than two hours, during which a telegraphist was able to send out two or three hundred groups of figures and to receive consider-ably more. When I discussed these matters with experts after the war, they could hardly believe it, and told me that French underground radio stations were not allowed to operate for longer than fifteen minutes at a time. Our limited output capacity did not allow us to satisfy the requirements of the underground authorities, and much bad blood was caused by it. I protected the liaison as best as I could, because I was convinced that if we were in fact to send out as many telegrams as we were requested to do, all our stations would soon be knocked out, and that would have been the end of them. The average member of the underground, though he appreciated the dangers threatening the radio stations, did not realise how great and how sudden they were. I forced myself to be completely ruthless in opposing all unnecessary verbosity, and I was fortunate in having the support of each successive Government Plenipotentiary, who understood what was involved.

However, when a message was of special urgency or of exceptional importance, all restrictions had to be thrown to the winds. In such cases we would take every risk, including the loss of a station and of the men operating it. I would then inform all concerned in advance of the absolute necessity for the telegram to be sent without regard to possible dangers, and with Zosia as a look-out in the street, I would keep vigil at the station.

Our work was greatly facilitated when London organised the so-called 'transmission into the ether'. At a pre-arranged time, London would begin to broadcast its telegrams on a powerful transmitter, sending each group of figures twice, at a slow speed. We simply tuned in the receiving apparatus only, and without giving our call signs, received the telegrams. At the next normal session, we would confirm receipt of them, and if there were any sections our telegraphist had not been able to hear, he would request a repetition. Naturally, such reception involved no risks.

If the apparatus had no defects, if audibility was tolerable, if the look-out girls did not raise an alarm, and if, at the London end, a good telegraphist was at work (our men could distinguish skilled operators from the very first signals), in short, when the four 'ifs' were in order, we were always able to send out and to receive most urgent telegrams.

After the work was finished, the telegraphists would bid each other farewell endlessly, and in everything that the London operators said our men could feel a genuine solicitude for their safety, and appreciation of their work and courage. Their faces would beam and, completely disarmed, wiping the sweat from their brows, they would take down on a pad: 'Thank you very much. It was a pleasure to work with you to-day. My cordial greetings . . . I shall call you up to-morrow at the same time'.

At Christmas, New Year or Easter, our teams would receive from London such affectionate telegrams of good wishes, such warm appreciation, that they would be deeply moved. On such occasions Martin was usually the first to master his emotions, and he would say in his drawling borderland accent: 'Nice fellows, those Londoners. Let's go and have one to drink their health'.

The Messages

Our stations served the Government Plenipotentiary, the Peasant Party and, by request, other Parties and organisations as well. We would receive their telegrams, encoded in their own ciphers, which we did not know, and we in turn delivered to them any messages received for them. But on the whole our unit served primarily the Directorate of Civil Resistance, and as I performed the functions of Director of Civil Resistance and director of our radio liaison, this was only natural, especially as the concentration of functions in one hand simplified and shortened the DCR's contacts with the stations. It made it possible for us to keep London, and therefore the whole world, up to date with what was happening in the capital and in Poland as a whole.

A typical example of the kind of information supplied to London were my telegrams transmitted from Warsaw at noon on January 15, 16 and 17, 1943, which enabled the Polish Government in London to inform correspondents of London and overseas newspapers of the man-hunts taking place on those three days in Warsaw, Praga and Saska Kepa. In the evening of each of those days, both the British radio and SWIT broadcast our information to the whole world, and we listened to it in Warsaw with profound satisfaction.

Our speed record, consisting of receiving a telegram from London, deciphering it, preparing a reply, encoding and transmitting it, was one hour, and it was established in the following circumstances.

On that particular day our station was operating in an apartment close to the corner of Tamka Street and Kopernika Street. London began to send out an urgent message. Zosia, who was present at the station, immediately copied the columns of figures as they were being written down by the telegraphist, and at once deciphered them. The urgent message asked whether the parachutists, who included the Government courier, Bronek, had reached Warsaw. London had received no information from the proper military cell concerning the matter, and as the parachutists had been dropped into Poland several days before, they were anxious about them.

It so happened that I had already met Bronek that very morning, so I immediately dictated the reply:

'Bronek, safe and sound, together with the other parachutists, is already in Warsaw.' The telegram was enciphered within a few minutes, and sent out at once. The same evening we received a telegram thanking us for the lightning speed of the information.

As may be seen from the above, in many respects we enjoyed privileges denied to other members of the underground; for we were able to see the results of our labours almost immediately. That was why, whenever the Allied press and radio published news based on the DCR's telegrams, all our workers were profoundly gratified. The telegraphists, who knew that they had been transmitting the basic telegrams, were particularly happy. 'We like this job,' they would say. 'The whole world knows what is happening here. The Huns must be raging; they must be mad with fury.'

The DCR's telegrams constitute a veritable chronicle of the occupation. They were believed and trusted abroad, and were circulated by the press and radio of the whole world, which was shocked by the horrors and deeply indignant at the happenings in Poland. I think I am entitled to assume that they influenced the Allies to establish a registry of

German crimes. We kept them informed of innumerable acts of terror, not only those which the Germans themselves publicised by means of posters, but also those perpetrated in secret. The DCR received information about these through underground channels, from such places as Pawiak prison and the camps at Auschwitz and Majdanek. We sent out telegrams describing countless arrests, executions, murders and torturings. Our unit distinguished itself especially during the terrible massacre that took place from October 1943 to March 1944, in the course of which several thousand men and women were publicly executed in the streets of Warsaw, which became red with the posters announcing the names of the murdered victims. During a period of over four years we sent out many thousands of telegrams and received many thousands more. I remember three telegrams particularly well.

One morning Cesia handed me a letter from a woman-prisoner in Ravensbrück. I held the piece of paper, which was almost charred from being heated to bring out the invisible ink, with a feeling of reverence. With some difficulty I read the secret message and was paralysed with horror. In a quiet, matter of fact manner, the writer described the experiments which the Germans were making on women, adding the names of the victims. I at once sent a telegram to London on the 'guinea pigs' of Ravensbrück, and returned the letter to the Government Plenipotentiary, for it to be sent to London as well.

On another occasion I met an employee of the power station in Pruszkow, who told me how he had overheard a conversation which the 'Treuhänder' of the power station, the *Obergruppenfuehrer* S.A. Fuehrer, had with an unnamed German friend. The conversation sounded most interesting. Fuehrer was speaking.

'I want you to let me have your car to-morrow, for mine is out of order.'

'For how long do you need it?'

'For at least two days, for I have to drive three hundred kilometres to the North-East, where the roads are very poor.'

'It's not very convenient for me.'

'But you must let me have the car. I am going to the Fuehrer's Hauptquartier (Hitler's headquarters) on an important errand.'

'Oh, in that case it's all right.'

That was enough for me. I telegraphed the entire conversation word for word to London, and London was glad to have the information. After the war one could inspect a city of underground bunkers in the forest near Ketrzyn, situated in the direction and at the distance indicated in the telegram.

Finally, through Civil Resistance channels, I received information, which was repeatedly confirmed over a period of time, that in a region from which a part of the population had been evacuated, missiles were falling and exploding with tremendous power. After each explosion gendarmes would arrive and collect up all the fragments and splinters. The conduct of the Germans indicated that these were their own missiles, with which they were making some experiments.

I sent out several telegrams concerning this matter, without suspecting that the missile was the V2 rocket bomb, which played such an important part in German plans.

CHAPTER XIII

Unity in Struggle

Directorate of Underground Struggle

In the autumn of 1942, I read in the 'Information Bulletin' a communiqué describing an anti-German action and signed 'Directorate of Underground Resistance'. My surprise was not a pleasant one. The name of the organisation resembled that of the Directorate of Civil Resistance. The difference between 'Underground Resistance' and 'Civil Resistance' was only slight. (In Polish.) The new name, by its very similarity to that of the Directorate of Civil Resistance, had too obvious an appearance of 'unfair competition'. Within a matter of hours I learned that the communiqué had been issued by the High Command of the Home Army, and described an action carried out by 'Khedive'.

This fact caused a certain amount of misunderstanding, not only among the public but also in the underground itself. How did it come about that besides the Directorate of Civil Resistance, which had already been in existence for over a year, a new centre of underground leadership had arisen? When not long afterwards another communiqué appeared, concerning the carrying out of a death sentence passed by an underground Court, and signed by the Directorate of Underground Resistance, the confusion increased. The underground newspapers were now publishing communiqués on the execution of death sentences with two different signatures, that of the DCR and that of the DUR. I may add that the emergence of the new centre and the new name came as a complete surprise as much to the office of the Government Plenipotentiary as to myself.

It became necessary to straighten the matter out. I went to General Rowecki and reminded him that I had been appointed Plenipotentiary for Civil Resistance affairs in the first place by him personally, and only afterwards by Plenipotentiary Ratajski; and that the Directorate of Civil Resistance was as much an organ of the Home Army as of the Government Plenipotentiary; and, this being so, the Plenipotentiary should have been consulted, and I should have been warned. Rowecki was greatly embarrassed. He tried to evade the issue, but I would not be put off, and demanded an explanation. He then told me with complete frankness:

'There was a near mutiny among my staff because of the Directorate of Civil Resistance. I admit that it came into being as a joint organ of the Home Army and the Government Plenipotentiary, but you have civilianised it to such a degree that even the men who were transferred to it from the Home Army lost all spiritual contact with their military units, and became enthusiastic Civil Resistance men. (Here Rowecki mentioned several names.) I appreciate your work very highly, but the notoriety it acquired, enhanced further by your communiqués published in the underground press and broadcast by the Allied radio, caused a great deal of trouble with the commanders of "Khedive", whose actions are passing unobserved and unknown to the nation. For this reason I appointed a special Directorate of Underground Resistance, which will henceforth direct the activities of "Khedive" and underwrite them.'

I was not at all convinced, and objected that the High Command as such could easily have signed and published the necessary communiqués, and that there was no need to invent a new name for the command of 'Khedive', and one so obviously directed against the DCR. Without standing on ceremony, I declared that I saw in it an attempt to belittle the DCR by the creation of a rival centre, and all this looked too much as if the High Command were trying to monopolise control of all underground activities. General Rowecki kept denying any such intention, but without much conviction.

When I next submitted the matter to the Government Plenipotentiary, Jankowski, he fully agreed with my opinion;

and as the continued existence of such a duality as the DCR and the DUR might cause serious harm, he decided to demand from General Rowecki that he liquidate the DUR.

Not long afterwards I was summoned by the Government Plenipotentiary for a talk. I could see at once that he was worried. Without preliminaries he came to the point right away.

'From my talk with Grot I have come to the conclusion that you are right. Unfortunately Grot refused categorically to liquidate the DUR, and suggested instead a fusion of the DCR and the DUR into one body under his direction. It would consist of five people, of whom you would be one, as my representative and Director of Civil Resistance, which would be renamed National Resistance. You would continue your activities without any restrictions, except that they would be within the framework and under the name of the new centre, to be known as the Directorate of Underground Struggle (DUS). What do you think of this suggestion?'

'Mr. Plenipotentiary,' I replied at once, 'you realise that, of the organisations comprising the Plenipotentiary's office, the direct struggle against the Germans is being waged solely by the DCR; just as in the Home Army it is being waged by "Khedive". If you should relinquish control of the DCR to the Commander of the Home Army, this would give the military a complete monopoly of the struggle. Do you think that the masses forming our underground, which is in effect the nation, will gain anything if all successes in the struggle are credited to the High Command of the Army? Moreover, we ought to remember the past and think of the future.'

'I agree with you,' the Plenipotentiary answered, 'but nevertheless, I want to accept Grot's proposals; for by paying this price, and at the cost of yielding in relatively lesser matters, I want to ensure that matters of considerably greater importance for our future shall be safeguarded. As you know, as soon as the underground movement began, the military people proceeded to organise a so-called "replacement administration", in other words, cadres of officials who would take over the administration of the country after its liberation. For many months now I have been demanding of Grot that he surrender this administration to the Government Plenipotentiary's office, for the matter is really outside the competence of the High Command; and, moreover, we are already organising our own cadres for the future administration and for the judiciary. I want to put an end to this dangerous duality. Unfortunately the negotiations up till now have not been conclusive. In my opinion it would be more dangerous for the country if its civil administration after liberation should be militarised than that the struggle against the Germans should be directed by the military. I want, therefore, to suggest to Grot that in return for the transfer of the replacement administration to the office of the Government Plenipotentiary, I should agree to subordinate the DCR to his command. I did not want to proceed without consulting you.'

What could I do? The Plenipotentiary was right. He who controlled the administration of the country after its liberation would also govern it, and organise the elections. And that was that.

After Grot had accepted the Plenipotentiary's proposal, the Directorate of Underground Struggle came into being; and the nation was informed of it by a joint manifesto of the Plenipotentiary and the Commander-in-Chief of the Home Army, issued on July 5, 1943.

I hesitate to record these details of back-stage intrigues, and I am sure I shall be criticised by all those who consider that everything connected with the history of the Polish Underground should be presented in the most favourable light. For my part, however, I think that the Polish Underground in the late war discharged its tasks so magnificently that it will suffer no harm to its reputation if I reveal how the actors conducted themselves off stage. The truth can only enhance the fame of the Polish Resistance, and the truth is what really matters. Above all, our rivalries—and it was often rivalry for a place in front of an execution squad—did not prevent us from reaching an understanding for the more effective waging of the struggle against the cruel enemy.

The Activities of the DUS

It was in this way that I found myself a member of the body

that might be called the brains of our entire struggle against the Germans from the middle of 1943 onwards. It consisted of five people. At its head was General Bor-Komorowski; for to everyone's grief Grot-Rowecki was captured by the Germans on June 30, 1943; they seized him in one of his hide-outs in Spiska Street, 14, and immediately transported him to Berlin. They were afraid the underground might in desperation risk everything to liberate him. I personally felt the blow very acutely; for I had a great liking for that manly, courageous and amiable personality, whose career in the underground movement I had followed from beginning to end. He had often found himself in difficult situations. For instance, when the former Commander-in-Chief of the Polish Army, Marshal Rydz-Smigly, asked him for a meeting, having escaped back to Poland from his internment in Rumania, Grot was torn between loyalty to the hapless Commander-in-Chief and anxiety lest such a meeting might spoil his relations with the then Commander-in-Chief, General Sikorski, and undermine the latter's confidence in the Home Army. He followed the voice of reason and refused the meeting, which I think was the right thing to do. It was being said in Warsaw that Rydz-Smigly wandered about the city unrecognised, all day long, accosting strangers and asking their opinion of him. They were mostly uncomplimentary, and it was said that this killed him. He died in Warsaw and was buried there in secret. It all makes a tragic picture: the former Commander-in-Chief wandering disguised in the streets of the devastated capital, moving from one scene of his former glory to another. Perhaps the shadow of Pilsudski followed him, whispering accusations. Rydz-Smigly and his unhappy return from Rumania is still waiting for an inspired historian.

As for General Bor, I met him in 1940 in Cracow, during one of my rare excursions to that city. He was dressed plainly and looked drab and inconspicuous; there was nothing to distinguish him from any of the other men in the hide-out, where I first met him. In the DUS he was always a suave and tactful chairman; he never lost his temper, and he had an unfailing instinct for choosing the right proposition from among several possible ones.

Next to him in the hierarchy was the Chief of Staff of the Home Army and Deputy Commander-in-Chief, General Pelczynski (pseudonym Gregory), who has received insufficient mention so far, as one of the military leaders. He was an excellent organiser, a co-creator of the Home Army; he had a clear mind and quick intelligence, and he readily understood my 'civilian' approach, which was invariably different from that of the military men; discussion with him was thus easier than with the others.

Next to him was General Nil (pseudonym), Commander of 'Khedive', swarthy, with black hair and the fine features of a Highlander, taciturn, and always ready to receive orders. He was soon to be replaced by Lieut.-Colonel Radoslaw (Jan Mazurkiewicz), one of the bravest commanders among those I met in the underground.

The fourth military member was Colonel Rzepecki, a good organiser and a man of fine intelligence, with an obvious flair for politics, more of a military politician than a soldier.

Finally, I have to mention myself, the only civilian among soldiers, treated with that courtesy with which a well-mannered and congenial company treats a stranger. At least, such were my beginnings with them; for later on, many weekly meetings, of many hours' duration, infused much warmth into these relations, which developed into friendships that endure to this day.

This body was responsible for the most important decisions, which, reduced to orders and issued to 'Khedive' and 'National Resistance', yielded magnificent results; such that the Polish Underground outdistanced that of any other occupied country struggling against the Germans. It is not my intention to record the history of the fighting underground as directed by the DUS, but I should like to mention some of its activities, such as railway diversion, i.e. the derailing of troop trains, transports of arms and munitions, the blowing up of railway bridges, etc. For instance, in November 1943, by way of reprisals, ten trains were blown up and shot up, with the destruction of six engines and 26 wagons. German casualties amounted to 1,000 killed and wounded. In February 1944, again by way of reprisals, 17 railway trains and 78 wagons; German casualties: 540 killed and 1,000 wounded. In addition, the DUS decreed, as a reprisal for the displacement of Polish villagers, especially in the province of Zamosc, an action against German settlements in the Government General. As a result, the settlements were burnt down and German settlers liquidated. Another of the actions decreed by the DUS was the mass liquidation of Gestapo agents and gendarmes, and during the period July 1943 to June 30, 1944, it was responsible for the killing of 1,616 Germans.

This last action was crowned by the killing in Warsaw on February 1, 1944, by order of the DUS, of the Police and SS General Kutschera, head of the Police and Gestapo for the Warsaw district. This was a reprisal for the public executions begun in October 1943 and preceded by the issue of the German decree on the 'Safeguarding of the work of reconstruction in the Government General'. In these executions in the streets of Warsaw and other Polish cities, before the eyes of the entire population, several thousand Poles were shot, the majority of them having been rounded up at random. Here, I must also mention the actions undertaken for the liberation of prisoners, in the course of which several hundred prisoners were freed from more than a score of prisons. In conclusion, mention must be made of the innumerable verdicts on individual German criminals. Here are some of the telegrams concerning these cases:

'October 11, 1943. Communiqué of the DUS No. 16. On October 1, 12,05 hours, in Warsaw, killed by shooting, SS-Sturmman, Ernst Wepels, the cruel oppressor and executioner in the Women's Prison in Pawiak.'

'June 21, 1944. In the period June 2-10, by order of the DUS, 136 Gestapo agents and spies, including Willi Holtze, August Gering, and Kammertentz, were executed in the provinces of Warsaw, Lublin and Kielce.'

'June 22, 1944. By order of the DUS, killed by shooting at the corner of Crane Street and Three Crosses Square, on June 12, Peschel and Leitgeber; and in Zoliborz on June 15, Jung and Hoffman.'

'July 19, 1944. By order of the DUS, killed by shooting

in Rzeszow on May 25, Gestapo men Pottebaum and Flaschke, exceptionally cruel oppressors of the people.'

The Directorate of Underground Struggle was often confronted with situations requiring extremely far-reaching decisions. The fundamental purpose of the underground movement, to carry on the struggle against the Germans, was never lost sight of. On the other hand, the tactics of that struggle were being constantly adapted in accordance with the international situation and with the position at home. In time, a vicious circle was created. By way of reprisals for German bestialities, perpetrated from the very outset of the occupation, the underground launched actions which inflicted losses on the Germans in killed and wounded. In their turn the Germans increased the terror to intimidate the underground; to which we replied with more reprisals; and so the terror steadily grew, and thousands of people were being put to death. The terror reached its greatest intensity in the period from October 1943 to February 1944. To-day, it might be asked if there was any sense in it as far as we were concerned. To which I can only reply that from the very beginning of the occupation the leaders of the underground, and later the Directorate of Underground Struggle, were constantly preoccupied with that problem. Attempts were made to find out whether the Germans would desist if the underground suspended their reprisal activities for a time. The results were entirely negative. The Germans, systematically pursuing their aim of destroying the core of the Polish nation by exterminating its brains, as represented by the intellectual class, and all the elements of national resistance, concentrated mainly in the cities, drowned them in a sea of blood, murdering without reason thousands of men and women. When the attempts failed, there was nothing left but to exact an 'eye for an eye and a tooth for a tooth'.

Conference of the Leaders of Civil Resistance

I summoned the district leaders of Civil Resistance to a conference in Warsaw, which took place on July 30-31, 1943. Without exception, they all came, including the head of Civil

Resistance for the district of Lodz, Boleslaw Scibiorek, who was killed in 1946 by the Communist Security Police; the head of Civil Resistance for the Lwow district, Ostrowski, mentioned previously, at present holding a high diplomatic post under the Warsaw regime; and W. Winkler, head of Civil Resistance for the Warsaw district, at present living in the United States.

The conference was held in a quiet villa, where we reviewed the results of our activities and discussed future plans. After I had made a survey, in which the problems of the war were linked with particular Civil Resistance campaigns, each of the heads of the central departments reported on his own problems, and the heads of the district organisations reported on the situation in their territories, and submitted their own observations and demands. None of those present knew the names or the pseudonyms of the others, and they eyed each other with great curiosity and listened to each other with special attention. From all the reports there emerged a picture of a deadly struggle, carried on with considerable success.

During the first day of the conference we deliberated all day long, taking our meals in the villa, and relying on our liaison girl-officers to provide them. We dispersed shortly before curfew hour; everyone was to spend the night in a different hide-out.

The second day of the conference brought a surprise. Without saying why they should do so, I told everybody present to take a walk over a definite section of New World Street, where I also went myself.

At one o'clock in the afternoon a loudspeaker attached to a pillar suddenly emitted a popular Polish marching tune. Passers-by, among whom were my collaborators, slowed down in their stride and listened with surprise. Then the music broke off and a clear young voice launched a patriotic address, appealing for a life-and-death struggle against the Germans. The street witnessed strange events. Ever larger groups of passers-by stopped and crowded round the loudspeaker, listening with solemn attention, and glancing about to be sure a German patrol was not coming. Everywhere people stood with smiles on their faces, An occasional German civilian passing by looked at the swelling crowd with astonishment, but without comprehending what was happening. Finally, after completing a news bulletin, the sounds of the national anthem, 'Poland shall not perish', blazed forth from the loudspeaker. The multitude bared their heads and stood there in motionless solemnity. The casual Germans in the street only now began to betray some anxiety, and to look about to see if gendarmes or the military were in sight. However, none of them dared to offend the crowd. Before anyone showed up, the anthem came to an end, and the rejoicing and excited throng rapidly dispersed.

An hour afterwards the conference met again for its final session. The district leaders were tremendously impressed by what they had seen and heard. They thanked me for the programme, which had been organised by specialists among the 'Grey Ranks' at the request of the DCR for the occasion of the conference. Everyone of them was enthusiastic about arranging a similar programme in his city. Ostrowski was particularly excited and begged me to send such specialists to Lwow immediately. Not because of his keenness, but because of the importance of Lwow, I agreed to recommend the 'Grey Ranks' to go there. As fate would have it, the little slip of paper written in this connection nearly cost me my life.

CHAPTER XIV

Emissary "Salamander"

I first read of him in the weekly report of our Intelligence, which said that 'The Gestapo is searching for a Government emissary using the pseudonym "Salamander" '; later I met him and was introduced to him. A man of about sixty, who jumped by parachute into an occupied country, he impressed me tremendously by his exploit, all the more so as someone who was present when he came down told me that the Doctor ('Salamander' was Dr. Jozef Rettinger) was suffering from night blindness, and that it was necessary to take him by the arm and lead him like a blind man. I thought all this was a poor recommendation for a secret parachutist-emissary, but proof of extraordinary courage.

I set out for the meeting with mixed feelings. I knew of the close ties Salamander had with General Sikorski, but there were certain rumours circulating in the underground as to the real character of his mission in Poland. In order to gain a clear picture, I sent out a message to London: 'Salamander is regarded here to be both your emissary and also an envoy of the British Government. Please clarify.' I waited several weeks for a reply, but none came, which naturally did not conduce to a better understanding of the position. Writing this to-day, I realise that before my telegram could reach its addressee, it had to pass through the British censorship; and I am not sure whether it did actually pass.

As soon as I set eyes on Salamander, I could immediately appreciate all the advantages his appearance gave him. He was of medium height, the malicious would say small, thin, and altogether drab; dressed in a 'Polish' lounge suit, carefully fabricated in England, he did not attract attention by his appearance, and that was already a lot. He at once touched my weak spot by inquiring about radio liaison and praising it highly. When I answered his direct question about what our monthly budget amounted, he amazed me by saying:

'Your entire unit costs as much per month as the wages of two messengers at the BBC.'

Salamander was greatly impressed by some reports on sabotage activities which I had on me, and which I showed him. It was unedited, primary material that he perused, received straight from the field, and the reports had the stamp of authenticity and truth.

He requested me to arrange a meeting for him with Dr. Henryk Kolodziejski, a former director of the Seym Library and a prominent freemason, who both before the war and during the occupation was the 'eminence gris' of Polish public life ('making and unmaking Governments'). I was not at all surprised at this request. I myself frequently called on Kolodziejski, a man of impressive intelligence, though as the years of Soviet occupation were to prove, little spirit, to listen to his wise and sober opinions. Everybody used to visit him, and in his apartment I have run into such luminaries of the underground as Puzak and Jozewski. Towards the end of the German occupation I was told the amazing news that Kolodziejski had been visited by the Gestapo, but that after a talk they had left. Under the conditions prevailing in Poland at the time, this was a most unusual occurrence, which might perhaps be explained by the great influence freemasonry exerted internationally.

When taking Salamander to Kolodziejski's apartment I never thought I should live to see, after the opening of the Warsaw Seym in the winter 1947, in a finely restored Chamber, and under the watchful eyes of the Soviet Ambassador, Lebedev, none other than Kolodziejski propose Boleslaw Bierut as a candidate for the office of President of the Polish Republic. Such are the times we live in!

The meeting between Salamander and Kolodziejski was not a success. It was neither one thing nor the other. The talk was too obviously desultory. I made ready to leave, so as to let them talk without a witness, but Salamander seized the opportunity to take leave himself, and departed together with me.

We began to meet more frequently, and under better auspices; for we met not in underground hide-outs, but in cosy little semi-conspiratorial restaurants. The temptation was too great and the companion excellent. I should say that during the time Salamander stayed in Warsaw the average consumption of alcoholic drinks per head must have increased by a good few per cent. He was indeed a man without fear, with a proclivity to inviting hazards for the sheer fun of it. On one occasion, when I told him about some of 'Khedive's' magnificent actions, he begged me most earnestly to make it possible for him to see the exploding of a German troop train. I reported his request to the DUS, who agreed; and arrangements were made for Salamander to be taken on such an expedition.

At the pre-arranged time, accompanied by a young officer from 'Khedive', I walked along Pieracki Street, where Salamander had a rendezvous with us. We walked up and down the street, becoming increasingly nervous at the delay. The rules of conspiracy required that an appointment in the street should be kept with absolute punctuality. After waiting half an hour, we left, each going his own way. Salamander had failed to appear, but that very night a German troop train exploded near Celestynow.

A few days later, at a meeting with the Government Plenipotentiary, Jankowski, I got a rap over the knuckles.

'Don't you ever again organise any risky expeditions with Salamander. Quite unintentionally he let drop that he was going off somewhere to see the exploding of a troop train, and I forbid him categorically, not only to take part in the expedition, but even to keep his appointment with you; for I feared he might be tempted at the last moment. All we need for our happiness is that something should happen to him during such an expedition. Who would be held responsible for it? In the eyes of the Government, I would be responsible; and I would have nothing to say in justification.'

I agreed that the Plenipotentiary was right, and I renounced for ever all expeditions with Salamander, except those to the nearby bars of Cyranka and Grzedzik.

The day came when, after an affectionate farewell party, Salamander departed for the base from which an Allied plane was to take him back to England from a secret airstrip. His mission, which to my mind had consisted in the examination of the situation on the spot, both as regards the country in general and the underground movement in particular, was completed, and it was time for him to return.

My amazement was boundless, therefore, when several weeks later I was summoned to one of the Warsaw hospitals, where, in a separate room and under an assumed name, I found Salamander. He lay there, like Lazarus, aged, haggard and miserable. By his bedside stood a table bearing bottles of medicine, and other liquids which did not look as if they served that purpose. I greeted him jocularly:

'I can hardly believe my eyes! Aren't you perchance the grandfather of my friend, Dr. Salamander, who not so long ago left by plane for England?'

Salamander, however, was not in a mood for joking.

'Don't Stefan,' he said. 'Come closer, the matter is serious.'

I sat down on the bed. Salamander poured himself a tumblerfull of some medicine; I took a remedy from another bottle, with a more promising label, and asked:

'What has happened?'

I was curious to know, so Salamander, propped up by pillows, told me the story.

He was taken to a Home Army base, and there he patiently waited for the arrival of the plane, which, as may be imagined, was a risky and difficult operation. At last, after several days, he was unexpectedly alerted, put on a cart, and driven at great speed in the direction of the airstrip, on which the plane was at any moment to land and, for reasons of security, immediately start back again. As they approached their destination, Salamander saw before his eyes the welcome sight, but with the sequence reversed, like a film shown backwards. A plane emerged above the tree-tops, not to land, but to fly away; and off it soared into the air, alas without Salamander. The Home Army officer who accompanied Salamander was very upset.

'We were late. Confound it!'

The cart was turned round, but—misfortunes often occur in two's—while it was being driven rapidly away from the airstrip, where a German expedition might have arrived at any moment, the cart lurched into a ditch and Salamander was thrown out into ice-cold water. His body was not used to that kind of close contact with liquids, and reacted with an inflammation of the nerves; so here he was, back in Warsaw again, seriously sick and in the worst of moods.

Towards the end of our talk, the conversation was not bereft of dramatic moments. Salamander suspected that the delay before he was taken to the airstrip and the crash of the cart into the ditch were not accidental and this, together with his sickness, made him see everything black. He pulled a fat envelope from under his pillow and, handing it to me, he said:

'Except for yourself, I have at this moment no one I can trust. This envelope contains a letter to the Prime Minister in London. I have described in it everything I have seen and found out. It also contains a kind of last will and testament. Will you promise me that if I die or get killed, you will deliver it to the Prime Minister?'

The matter looked serious enough, so I took the letter; and, having received from Salamander more details of the unsuccessful expedition, I brought the matter up at the next session of the DUS. I first presented the case as seen by Salamander, and asked for an explanation. The Commander-in-Chief and the other members were unable to give any, except that the departure of Salamander had not taken place because he was late at the airstrip. I decided, therefore, to exaggerate the case and said, half seriously and half jokingly:

'If we came to the conclusion that from our point of view, Salamander's departure for England was undesirable, it would be better to lock him up somewhere, and keep him here till the end of the war. But it does not make sense, first to stage such incidents as being late at the airstrip, or to apply hydro-therapy according to Father Kneipp, and then send him back to England. I can imagine what he would have to say about us there.'

Thereupon the Commander-in-Chief made a firm declaration, which put his good faith above all suspicion.

'Salamander,' he said, 'will be sent back to England by the first available plane. I have already promised the Plenipotentiary.'

And that was what happened soon afterwards. Before he had even fully recovered and before he could even walk, Salamander was carried into a reserved compartment in a crowded train, 'For Germans only', and travelled to a point near the secret airstrip. His transportation was in its way a masterpiece of organisation, involving the preparation of a number of forged documents, the paying of bribes, etc. Everything went smoothly, and the emissary from England, for whom the Gestapo had been searching for many months, sick, moreover, and on a stretcher, travelled in comfort on a German train like any Nazi dignitary; while the representatives of the 'master race' were squeezed into crowded compartments, or had to stand in the corridors and eye with respect the closed doors bearing the notice 'Reserved'.

This time Salamander reached his destination safely. I intended to keep his letter and return it to him after the war. The letter survived the Warsaw Rising, but, after a peripatetic existence, it was burnt by me in 1945, together with a part of my archives, just as the Communist Security Police were surrounding that part of Lesna Podkowa in which I was hiding.

I am almost ashamed to admit that I never read the letter I had with me for so long. Having spent since then several years in exile, amidst politically active emigrés, I realise that I have been guilty of an unpardonable crime. Why, Salamander's confidential report to the Prime Minister might have yielded incriminating material against many a person, maybe against the Prime Minister himself. I am sure I acted with intolerable thoughtlessness—at least in the eyes of some emigré politicians.

CHAPTER XV

Blows at Liaison

Wladek's Last Adventure

At one of the periodic meetings of the DUS someone asked me:

'Will you describe to us the organisation of your radio liaison, more particularly the methods by which you safeguard its security, as we should like to compare them with our own methods?'

I explained at length all the ruses we employed in our system. The group of higher officers listened with great attention, and when I had finished the Chief of Staff, Gregory, said:

'Your methods hardly differ from our own. Nevertheless, all our stations operating in Warsaw have slipped up.'

I was greatly surprised at this frank admission and wanted to know more details.

'Were they uncovered by spies or located by German interceptors?'

'There cannot be any doubt but that they were traced by radio interception. The stations were pinpointed one after another, and although those arrested at one station knew nothing of the other stations, they were all caught one after another.'

This painful admission made me think. I was unable to account for the fact that our precautions proved adequate, especially as far as street observation was concerned, while in the case of the military stations they did not. I was inclined to think that Home Army liaison was much more widespread than ours, and attracted much more attention on the air. Moreover, it was easier for German intelligence to get at it, owing to the large number of operating units, employing a considerable personnel. I was so impressed by all this that I summoned the men in charge of our stations, and after telling them all I had heard, recommended them to observe the utmost care and caution. They were as impressed as I was, but they too were unable to arrive at a clear view of the situation.

A month afterwards, in the evening of November 10, 1943, I was hurrying with Zosia to a meeting with Ralph, who, as was his daily custom, was to bring us the incoming telegrams and collect the outgoing ones. We were in good spirits, for that afternoon we had been visited by Speaker Rataj's daughter, Hanka Stankiewicz, and her husband, and we had spent some pleasant hours together. It was raining, the evening was dark, and we had to look sharply at each passer-by. Ralph had a regular beat in Buxom Street ,between Poznan and Marshall Streets, on the even-numbers side.

Soon, two shapes emerged from a dark doorway. I recognised Ralph and Martin. Ralph grabbed me by the arm:

'A terrible thing has happened. Wladek was arrested a few hours ago.' I was petrified. A blow always falls when it is least expected. Our turn has come, I thought, and I grieved for poor Wladek, whose behaviour lately had seemed to suggest that he had a foreboding of what was to come. Ralph and Martin, both trembling with emotion, drew us into a side street, and Ralph told us the story.

'Wladek was working in Trench Street to-day. As usual, look-outs were on duty in the streets and also in a nearby apartment. The landlady of the hide-out, who kept watch from the window, with only a dressing-gown and slippers on, descended into the courtyard, intending to call at a nearby shop. No sooner had she emerged into the courtyard, when she was stopped with a 'Hands up!' And there stood a group of armed civilians, who talked Polish among themselves. They had broken in, through a wooden fence, from the house next door, which they had entered from another street. They detained everyone who appeared in the courtyard. The woman stood against the wall with other tenants of the house and noticed a number of civilians, one of whom had a cord dangling from his ear, climbing the stairs to her apartment. Fearing that this would be the end of her, the woman risked sneaking into a passage, from which she ran into a grocer's shop, and thence into the street. The street was clear and our look-out girls were quietly patrolling it, unaware of what was going on in the house. In this way the woman escaped in what she stood up in, and warned her husband not to return home after finishing work; while the look-out girl warned me. I immediately went in the direction of the house, but all was over by then. The house was quiet, and no enemy was in sight. I enquired cautiously what had happened. People living in the apartment next to our station told me that the armed civilians came and banged on the door of the apartment, and that Wladek himself had opened the door. They immediately seized him, handcuffed him and took him away in a motor-car. Apparently Wladek had the earphones on and must have thought it was the landlady, and that she had banged on the door because he hadn't heard her knock; so he opened it without fear. The worst thing is that he can't have had time to hide the transmitter and the ciphers, so that everything must have been seized.'

Ralph and Martin were full of despair and lamentation because of Wladek and the loss of the station. I was stunned myself, but some of the details in Ralph's account surprised and puzzled me. Why were they civilians? Why did they talk in Polish? Was there no German in uniform? What was the meaning of it all? Could these be the same men as the ones who stole the sound transmitter? Could it have been an internal diversion? If so, Wladek's life was not threatened. A glimmer of hope arose in my heart. I questioned Ralph:

'Are you sure they were Germans? It seems incredible that Polish-speaking civilians should have seized the station!'

'The neighbours were certain they were Germans. Although they spoke Polish, wore top boots and altogether had the appearance of men from the underground, they behaved like Germans. You know, cock-sure—they acted so openly, and afterwards drove off in a motor-car.'

'Many things are still not quite clear to me,' I said. 'We must investigate the matter. I suppose Wladek knew all your hide-outs?'

'He knew them all.'

'In that case you must suspend all work at once, freeze the hide-outs, and keep away from them.'

'We must do something for the landlady and her husband. She is stranded without shoes and without a dress, and he has only got what he had on in the morning, when going to work.'

'Zosia, can you help?'

'I'll try to get all she needs by to-morrow.'

'In that case, let us all meet at eleven. I'll bring some cash, Zosia some clothing, while you, Ralph, try to find out as many details as possible.'

Curfew hour was approaching. We had to part hurriedly, as we had another meeting, with Mirek of station No. 71, in a nearby street. He came punctually as ever, with a parcel under his arm, and I told him what had happened. Though he did not know Wladek, he was sorry for him; but there were some details about the slip-up which he, too, found strange. I warned him that he would have an urgent message to send out to-morrow; to which he replied calmly that he would be ready in good time.

We returned for the night to the little room which was our hide-out, soaked with the rain, chilled and prostrate with grief. Apart from Wladek's terrible fate, we had lost the station, and with it the ciphers and telegrams. There was still the question of whether it was the work of the Germans or of Polish diversionists; but on the whole, the Germans seemed to be indicated. In any case, the station was lost, and no matter who had got hold of it, it was necessary to cancel the ciphers and all operational details at once. Those who had seized it might possibly resort to the ruse of pretending to be us, and with the help of our ciphers, might cause a great deal of confusion by altering data, hours of work, etc. I drafted an appropriate telegram, which I was determined, notwithstanding the risk involved, to send out from Mirek's station in Lower Street, which contacted London daily at 1 p.m. Gene's station could not be used, as he had had difficulty in finding a hide-out and would not be able to work the following day.

My talk with Ralph next morning yielded nothing new. He too was not so sure that the raid had been made by Germans. In the end, however, we came to the conclusion that for the purposes of our work we should assume that it had been the Germans, and draw appropriate deductions.

A Slip-up in Lower Street

On November 11, 1943, at 12 o'clock noon, I boarded a tram-car and proceeded to Lower Street. Our station was on the top floor of the block, to the right from the Pulaski Street staircase. I alighted at the nearby tram-stop, and though there was still an hour before the work was to begin, I reconnoitred Pulawska Street, Lower Street and the neighbouring streets, without noticing anything suspicious. At a quarter to one, Zosia arrived with the look-out, Irena. They took up their positions in the street, while I went to the hide-out where Mirek had his station, intending to keep watch from the window. Mirek was already sitting in front of the transmitter, tuning it in. I went to the window. It gave on to the back of a little church in Pulawska Street, and allowed a wide view over the open ground below. I studied this view for some time, but found nothing to worry about. In the room I noticed two revolvers and some hand grenades on a table by the wall, and I knew that Mirek was prepared to face sudden danger, and if necessary, to fight. That reassured me. I called him away from the transmitter and handed the telegram to him.

'Mirek,' I said, 'this telegram invalidates all the operational data for the station which was raided yesterday. It must be sent out to-day, at all costs.'

Mirek must have noticed my excitement and anxiety, for he said reassuringly:

'Don't worry! If conditions are tolerable, I shall get it out inside half an hour.'

It was by then 1 o'clock and Mirek, calm and alert, sat down and called London. London replied immediately that it was ready for reception, and Mirek started to send out the telegram, while I went back to the window.

After about twenty minutes, I noticed just over half a mile away a plane approaching from the direction of the Vistula, and flying towards Okecie. The plane looked like a Junkers.

I motioned to Mirek to stop and come to the window. When I pointed to the plane, he only shrugged his shoulders.

'They come and go all day long, making for the Okecie aerodrome. It has nothing to do with us.'

I felt reassured, for it was true that the plane was heading in the direction of Okecie. I continued to watch from the window, and suddenly noticed under the rails surrounding the little church, two heads close to the ground. I hesitated whether to call Mirek or not; but to make sure, I did so. He rose reluctantly, but studied the two heads carefully.

'It's nothing—those are bums who come here to play cards. They must be playing pontoon there. I know them. . . .'

'Have you still got much to send out?' I asked.

'No, only a few more groups and corrections.'

I approached the window again, and noticed that the two heads had disappeared. The work was drawing to its end and with it the tension gradually subsided. But I had to continue my observation from the window and suddenly . . . I rushed to Mirek and pulled his hand away from the key. At that moment, from just above the roof, came the roar of an aeroplane engine. It had appeared unexpectedly from behind the church, close to its roof, and passed directly over our house. My heart stood still. Mirek became deadly pale. There could be no doubt that it was a German radio interception plane, which had taken precise measurements of our location, and that we would soon be surrounded by German mobile interception cars, which were in constant radio contact with the plane. There was no question about it, we had been trapped!

At that moment the doorbell rang three times. It was Zosia. Mirek rushed to the door. Zosia's face betrayed the utmost tension, though she made an effort to control her voice.

'Take what I must tell you calmly,' she said. 'Little groups of civilians are cruising about in the streets. They look like Germans, and I noticed one of them go behind a wall and put something to his ear. I ran here at once, and passed on the steps outside one of the civilians I had just seen in the street. It looks very suspicious.'

'I have just finished the telegram,' said Mirek.

'Mirek, give the telegram and the ciphers to Zosia. Leave

everything else behind, for there is no time to put it away. Let's go. There is not a second to lose. The Germans are here.' 'I'll just put my boots on. Don't wait for me. Go! I'll follow you. Wait for me at the corner of Pulawska. It will be better if we leave separately.'

I had to agree that it was better to disperse. We went out on to the staircase; but no sooner had we descended the first few steps when Zosia, who was in front of me, said horrified:

'Jesus . . . they are coming!'

Through the staircase window I looked into the garden, and saw a file of civilians advancing with automatics and re-volvers at the ready. The leading men must have already entered the building, for I could hear stamping down below.

Zosia turned back, threw herself at the nearest door, and knocked. The door opened at once, and on entering the apart-ment we found several horror-stricken women, who must have seen what was happening through the window.

'If anyone asks what we are doing here, tell them we are looking for an apartment,' Zosia said to them imploringly. A young girl advanced towards us and angrily refused.

'Get out of here, at once! I have seen you hanging about the house for more than an hour. Get out!'

She shut the door in our faces. We had no choice, and started to descend the stairs. We were stopped by a furious 'Hands Up!' and raised our arms. On the stairs below were about ten men with revolvers and automatics. One of them, standing in front, shouted: 'They came out of there!' and pointed to the door of the apartment from which we had just been ejected. Several Germans entered the apartment imme-diately, and a few seconds afterwards, all the women emerged on to the landing with their hands above their heads. We looked at what was going on as if spellbound. We were in for it. This was the end. Our turn had come. Our lips were dry, our eyes took in everything and everyone, especially the civi-lians with revolvers in their hands. A young, good-looking fair-haired man was in command. When I looked at his face, I no longer had any doubts. He was a German, an officer. He looked at us sharply and motioned us to stand against the wall. The civilians knocked at the doors of all the apartments on that floor, entered them, and from each led out little groups of people with their hands raised. Only Mirek's door would not open. I heard a voice calling in Polish: 'Don't look out of the windows! Don't move!'

The commanding officer came up to me and asked:

' Do you speak German?'

I shook my head, denying it—and at that very moment remembered I had in my pocket a copy of the German 'Warchauer Zeitung' for that day.

The commanding officer spoke a few words to one of the civilians, who then came up to me, searched me all over and, taking my hat off my head, examined my hair carefully. (It was not till many days later that I realised he was looking for the impression of earphones on my hair.) I took advantage of the incident and said with pretended annoyance: 'What do you want? I have my papers in order. Here they are.' And I held out an authentic employment card of the Power Station, which was included among the war industries, issued in a false name, but with a photograph of me and all the necessary seals. The civilian replaced the hat, rejected my card, and said in tolerable Polish: 'This has nothing to do with it'.

On her part, Zosia raised her voice most appositely:

'What is going on here? What do you want from us? We don't live here; we only came in to enquire for an apartment to let. What is going on here?'

This created a good impression, and I joined her plaintive queries, pretending to be a frightened man from the street. Another of the civilians pushed Zosia aside, and speaking in Polish, said impatiently: 'You had better keep quiet. You have nothing to do with it'.

All the tenants living on that floor were now on the landing, except Mirek, whose door would not open. Two Germans went up to it and kicked the lock with their boots. With a bang, it gave way, and at that moment a series of shots from an automatic came crashing through. The horrified Germans leapt aside and aimed their weapons at the doorway. A deadly silence ensued. A moment later, two of them, creeping cautiously step by step with automatics in hand, entered Mirek's apartment. The tension was unbearable. We waited for

Mirek's hand grenade to explode. Instead, after a few seconds we heard the triumphant and joyful cries of the Germans: 'We've got everything. He's dead!'

The men on the staircase relaxed, and while some rushed into Mirek's apartment, two of them shepherded the crowd of tenants into the kitchen of the apartment on the right. From the room in which Mirek had operated his radio station we could hear the guttural voices of the Germans.

We found ourselves in the kitchen among about a score of people, who were almost demented with fear. They gazed at us without saying a word, and the young girl's glances were hostile. I had no doubt that if the Germans were to cross-examine us, she would give us away at once. I had already recovered from the initial shock and I could see that Zosia too had regained her composure. Well, we could do nothing about it. We were trapped. For four years we had been lucky; now the end had come. I proceeded to examine the contents of my pockets, while Zosia searched her bag. I pulled out all the papers I had on me, including the identity card I had thrust at the German. I opened it and inside found a receipt:

'Two thousand zloty, being travelling costs of the loud-speaker unit to Lwow. Henryk.' It was a receipt signed by the leader of the 'Grey Ranks', who had cut in with a Polish pro-gramme over the German loudspeaker network during the Conference of the Civil Resistance leaders. The unit was to travel to Lwow in order to carry out a similar exploit there. I put the receipt into my mouth, and chewed and swallowed it. I should have had it if the German had in fact examined my identity card. Zosia took from her bag a pile of telegrams, ciphers and secret correspondence, looked round, and ap-proached the large kitchen stove. An elderly woman removed a pot, and without uttering a word, helped her to burn the papers, in the presence of the whole scared crowd of people, who looked on wide-eyed at what Zosia was doing. When all the incriminating papers had been burnt, we took leave of each other. We had no doubt that being strangers in the apart-ment house, we would be arrested and separated. We had sufficient self-control to do the parting calmly. By then every-body was regarding us with sympathy, and the elderly woman was wiping away the tears in her eyes. In the street and on the staircase a great deal must have been going on, for we heard the sound of motor-cars and the stamping of heavy boots. Raising myself on tiptoe, I could see through the window German officers in air-force uniform arriving. Then, through a crack in the door, I could see men carrying parcels from Mirek's room. This must have been the transmitter. Next, they brought out of the apartment a body wrapped in a white sheet. We muttered a silent prayer. At that moment the door opened, and the officer and the two civilians who had handled us before came into the kitchen. We all knew that our fate would now be decided. The officer looked over everybody sharply, and his eyes rested on us.

'Who are these?' he asked, pointing his finger at us.

'Oh, they came here quite by chance,' one of the civilians answered, waving his hand contemptuously. The officer turned on his heels and left, followed by the two civilians. We looked at each other with utter amazement. Was it possible that we had escaped our doom?

The hubbub on the staircase subsided as the Germans departed, and through the crack in the door I could see a Blue policeman; and I heard the voice of the civilian I already knew saying: 'See that no one enters the room. The corpse will be removed presently.'

A few seconds later the Blue policeman came into the kitchen.

'It's all over,' he said. 'You can go back to your apartments.'

The crowd shuffled about; some of them rushed to us, urging us to 'Run, run at once!'

The elderly woman threw herself on Zosia's neck, and kissing her, said:

'The Lord saved you, but for heaven's sake run!' I turned to the people present and said:

'Please let us stay a little longer. I can't believe it can all end like this for us.'

A boy hurried out on to the staircase and came back presently.

'Run! There is no one on the stairs or in the yard.'

I took Zosia's arm, and somewhat dazed, hardly able to

believe we were free, we hurriedly descended the stairs, expecting at any moment to hear a terrifying 'Halt!' But no one stopped us, and we walked briskly to the entrance door, which was unguarded. On our way out we passed the dead body wrapped in a sheet. Zosia crossed herself, and said: 'Poor Mirek'.

Thus, within two days, two of our radio stations had been liquidated. Wladek was in the clutches of the Germans and Mirek was dead. These were indeed hard blows. I dispatched my men to reconnoitre, and by next day I was already in possession of the facts. Before the Germans entered the house in Lower Street they had posted sentries all round it, and when Mirek, at the moment the door of his room was being broken in, went out on to the balcony to escape by letting himself down the rainpipe, as he had always planned to do, he was shot by a burst from the automatic of a German sentry standing at the back of the little church in Pulawska Street. I now knew the significance of the warning we had been given not to look out of the window; and I knew whose heads I had seen down by the railing.

Mirek's body was already at the morgue in Oczki, and Zosia had again to arrange for a funeral, with the same undertakers as those who had secretly buried Joey. They received her with genuine compassion, and treated her with confidence as an 'old customer'. A few days later Mirek was buried in the Powazki cemetery under the assumed name of Arciszewski, and the undertakers handed over to us his windjacket, and a photograph taken after his death. The blood-soaked windjacket had innumerable bullet holes; Mirek must have been killed by a dozen hits. In the photograph his face looked calm and thoughtful. Like Joey, he must have died on the spot, without suffering.

I have analysed our conduct and come to the conclusion that it was impossible for all three of us to have escaped with our lives. One minute's delay and the Germans would have found us in Mirek's room, and that would have been the end of us too. On the other hand, it was not possible for Mirek to put on his shoes and come with us before the Germans arrived. And even if he could have made it, the Germans would have stopped all three of us on the staircase, and found out that Mirek was registered as the tenant of the apartment containing arms and radio equipment. Had we tried to dismantle the radio station and hide it, the Germans would have surprised us at it. It was obvious that the man Zosia had passed on the steps must have already located the station as operating on the top floor, for the Germans did not even pause at the lower floors. There could be no doubt that Zosia and I had been saved simply because the Germans did not see us leaving Mirek's apartment, but only as we came out of the one next door, where the women would not let us stay; and because of this they treated us like all the other tenants. It was literally the few seconds which saved us.

CHAPTER XVI

A Meeting with the Man from Minsk

At one of our meetings in 1943, the Government Plenipotentiary asked me to call at one of the small hotels in Chmielna
Street, where an underground emisarry from Wilno had arrived, and he asked me to talk to him on his behalf. I was
given all the necessary data, and was told that the emissary
had come from Wilno legally, with travel documents issued
in his own name. Without any difficulty or risk, I found his
room in a shabby and dark corridor of the hotel, and knocked
at the door. It was opened by a man of about forty, who welcomed me as if I had been his oldest friend. I was at once
impressed by his pronounced borderland accent and by the
warmth of his welcome. He seated me in a comfortable easy
chair, poured out a drink, and offered me a meal. His manner
was so warm and friendly that I took a liking to him even
before we had exchanged a single word on the subject which
brought us together. After I had explained in what capacity
I had come to see him, I enquired:

'How are things with you in Wilno?'

His answer came as a complete surprise to me.

'My dear sir, I have not come from Wilno, but from Minsk.
I am a man from Minsk. Now that the Minsk province is under
German occupation we can get in touch with people in the
motherland. I have come to Warsaw as the representative of
the ancient province of Minsk to ask the Polish Government
not to forget our country, so that after the war the Minsk territories may be reunited with the motherland. It has been a
Polish land for centuries, and wherever you go you'll find evidence of it. There are Poles still living there, and they are
dreaming of reunion. And the White-Ruthenians, too, dream
of Poland as their deliverer from the Soviet hell.'

I remained speechless, while he went on talking to me for nearly an hour. I come from the Western part of Poland, from the district of Kalisz, and I did not know the Eastern borderlands. While I listened to the man from Minsk talking with his sing-song intonation, I felt as if I were witnessing the clock of history being turned back. I knew of cases in which Poles from Soviet Russian territories occupied by the Germans had clandestinely come over to Poland, bringing their families with them. But a delegate from the Minsk province was something altogether different. I realised that I was not the right person for such a conversation, and that in a matter of this kind no one should deputise for the head of the underground state. After thanking the man from Minsk effusively, I told him that I regarded our conversation as a preliminary exchange of views only, and that he would soon meet the right people.

When I left him, I was profoundly moved; for I suddenly beheld the spirit of Poland as a force, and one whose power I had not realised to the full before. But as fate would have it, the land of Minsk was not reunited with the motherland; instead, both Poland and Minsk found themselves enslaved under a common Soviet yoke. Poor Man from Minsk!

CHAPTER XVII

A Slip-up in the Directorate of Civil Resistance

In the central office of Civil Resistance we employed a young man from Poznan; of middle height and ginger hair, he was a taciturn and industrious worker, and always very well groomed. If I am not mistaken, he was studying law. I do not remember his ever being absent whenever I called at any of our headquarters hide-outs, and he was always watchful and ready for service. He functioned as a sort of secretary of the Directorate of Civil Resistance, and when talking of him to other people I simply called him 'Ginger', as I knew neither his name nor his pseudonym.

Early in 1944 our central office had a hide-out in Concord Street, near Hop Street, in the apartment of a university lecturer in Botany, Wiszniewski; or rather in the apartment of his father-in-law, a 'White' Russian, who before the war had been editor of a Russian emigré journal in Warsaw. He frequently opened the door to me when I arrived, but we never exchanged a single word all the time our office was there. In time, Wiszniewski worked for us and hid our papers in his herbarium. He had several thousand folders containing dessicated plants on his wooden shelves, which we used as our temporary archives. Wiszniewski told me that his father-in-law kept away from those 'White' Russians, and their organisations in Poland, who collaborated with the Germans, sometimes for no other purpose than to get better food rations. His father-in-law considered, on the contrary, that having enjoyed Polish hospitality for so many years, the Russians, while on Polish territory, should not follow a policy opposed to the interests of their hosts. Perhaps he had other reasons, such as reluctance to support Germany against Russia, even against a Sovietised Russia; but what mattered was that, thanks to that Russian, we had a hide-out in his apartment.

One day Ginger told me in confidence that he had unexpectedly run into an old acquaintance in the street, a Pole, L., who was now a notorious agent of the Gestapo. L. would not leave him, but enquired what he was doing in Warsaw and where he lived. He had great difficulty in getting rid of him, and had felt in danger ever since; especially as he had forged personal documents, and had been wanted by the Gestapo for over two years as a member of an underground organisation that had slipped-up early on in its existence. He was sure L. would do his utmost to expose him and 'fix' him. I became worried. It was true that we were all wanted; the Gestapo was constantly raiding my pre-war apartment in Friends Avenue, my two little rooms in the Prudential Building, and my apartment in the Staszic Housing Estate, the last fortunately several months after I had left it; nevertheless I was worried that an agent of the Gestapo should have come into direct contact with an employee of the central office. However, since L's role as an agent of the Gestapo was beyond doubt, I made a quick decision, which, in the times we were living through, was almost routine.

'We must notify the proper quarters,' I said, 'and get L. out of the way. Make out a slip with the necessary order. I'll sign it and you will deliver it yourself. As from to-morrow, you will keep away from this place; and you had better leave Warsaw, or at any rate change your hide-out. Besides, keep in touch with us only through a contact-girl. We'll give you all the assistance the altered circumstances require.'

Ginger lay low, and every few days the contact Dusia reported that he was well and safe. But one day the contact snapped, and Ginger vanished without trace. We at once cleared and froze all the hide-outs he knew, and this caused a great deal of trouble, because Ginger knew everything. Our intelligence ascertained that Ginger had left his new hide-out never to return. I had a talk with Wiszniewski, and requested him and his family to leave their apartment, at least for a time, and go into hiding. I offered him money, forged papers, etc. However, Wiszniewski refused, saying that if Ginger had been arrested, he would not squeal, for he was a tough man of sturdy character and, moreover, his father-in-law and his wife firmly refused to leave the apartment. Besides, all the incriminating documents had been removed and the Gestapo would find nothing.

I was not convinced, for I would guarantee no one's— not even my own—stand against torture. How could anyone know? But since they would not budge, I could do nothing. Perhaps Ginger had not been arrested at all, and had only gone into hiding in the countryside? I had so much on my mind, so many things to settle in connection with Ginger's disappearance, that I forgot the apartment in Concord Street.

A few days later came bad news: the Gestapo had raided the apartment during the night and arrested all the people living there. They had, at the same time, raided an old hide-out in Leszczynski Street on the Vistula side, where they arrested an old woman, the tenant of the apartment, whose son saved himself by escaping through a window on to the roof.

In the fourth year of the war our minds had long since become numb to such horrors, and no one felt it as acutely as in the early days of the occupation. Not even the stereotyped consolation 'they've got it to-day, our turn will come to-morrow' made much impression. We were fighting a war, and people had to risk being killed in war. Nevertheless, my heart sank when one morning I scanned a red poster listing the names of people publicly executed, and noticed the name of Wiszniewski and his father-in-law. I could hardly believe my eyes, and had to look twice to make sure. I was not prepared for such a sudden end to these people. There cou'd be no doubt about it. There it was, in black letters on the red paper: 'Wiszniewski'.

In this tragic way, in the backwash of our struggle against the Germans, a young and promising scholar perished, and with him a big-hearted Russian. As for Ginger, he vanished without trace.

CHAPTER XVIII

A Game of
Hide and Seek

Alfred and Emily

I held consultations with Richard, Ralph and Gene, who now took over the entire burden of the work, and who, without further mishap, sent out the telegram concerning Mirek's slip-up and the cancellation of his operational data. Greatly upset, we discussed once more all the details of the disaster. It now became obvious to us why so many military radio stations had been uncovered one after another. The Germans had adopted an entirely new system. The men stalking the stations were specially chosen, they spoke good Polish and dressed like the young people in the underground, and they were equipped with pocket directional receivers. We were no longer up against aeroplanes and motor-cars, which could easily be observed, and with which we were able to cope, but something entirely new.

I issued instructions that all look-out girls were to be fully informed, and told to pay attention not only to aeroplanes and motor-cars, but most of all to men; that all work should be reduced to a minimum, with frequent changes of location and of operational data; that new telegraphists were to be recruited; and that all should try to find out where the German interception unit was housed.

I was able to find a professional telegraphist, a man of medium height, well over forty, shy and modest. He had not been engaged in conspiratorial work so far, but was keen to do so. He was highly recommended to me not only as a skilled operator, but also as a discreet and courageous man; in short, he had all the qualities required for a good conspirator. I gave him the name Jan; and I little thought at the time that we had acquired for our work a real ace, someone who would become a pillar of our liaison system during the most critical times. Jan found several hide-outs for himself, with his friends in Warsaw, and operated the station with frequent changes of location.

I was also introduced to a telegraphist whom I named Alfred, who was employed as a technician by a Germanised radio firm in Warsaw. He was a good-looking young man with jet black hair and a sporting temperament. He treated the work rather nonchalantly, but he was able not only to operate the station, but also to repair any defects in the apparatus. I decided to organise, with his help, a separate station, and Alfred undertook to find at least three hide-outs for himself; he also volunteered the services of his fiancée as an observer. I met her and received a most favourable impression. Emily was a tall blonde and a highly intelligent girl. It was obvious that she was superior to her fiancée, who kept rather silent in her presence and agreed with everything she said. Emily was of a serious turn of mind; she spoke concisely and to the point, and I instinctively addressed her rather than Alfred. As Warsaw was already overburdened with secret radio stations, I readily agreed that the new station should operate from nearby Piaseczno, where they both lived.

In this way all the gaps were made good, and our work went on as before. But we continued to mourn Mirek and worry about Wladek, who was still in prison; though we knew he would meet with the same fate as Mirek. I was not surprised, therefore, when one day I saw on a red poster Wladek's real name: Wladyslaw Rozalski, from the province of Kielce.

An Encounter with 'old acquaintances'

During Jan's turn of duty I went to Starch Street, to check up on the functioning of the look-outs. I had passed the Police Station and was approaching Crow Street, when I noticed from a distance that the look-out girl was walking in my direction, smiling innocently. But what was worse, I noticed behind her back, above the house in which Jan was working, an aeroplane diving noiselessly from a height of about a thousand feet, and turning steeply on one wing. I greeted the look-out girl courteously and whispered venomously:

'Instead of giggling, you'd do better to watch out—a plane is pinpointing the house.'

The girl looked up, and with a suppressed cry rushed into the house. I looked around but noticed nothing suspicious in the traffic of the street. I walked away from the house, and turned into Crow Street; but at the corner of Cool Street I beheld a sight which froze the blood in my veins. A hundred yards away from me, close to the kerb, were two motor-cars, and close by them the Germans I remembered from Lower Street. I turned on my heel and went back to Starch Street; I turned into Iron Street, and saw Jan come out of the house and walk in my direction. The look-out girl had already disappeared. Before I could reach Iron Street, one of the motor-cars drove up, and moving at a very slow pace, advanced in the direction of our hide-out. Although I was dressed differently from the time of the Lower Street slip-up, I was so scared that I did not even dare to look at the slowly passing car; all I could do was to walk on, seemingly unconcerned. I stopped at the corner, and Jan came up to me. I pointed out the car to him with a nod: 'Those are the Germans from Lower Street. Jan looked at them with great curiosity, unable to take his eyes off them. We hid in a doorway and continued to observe what the Germans were doing. The car moved very slowly; it passed our house without stopping, turned round, pulled up again, went on, turned round again, and continued to patrol Starch Street for half an hour, before it finally sped away. We heaved a sigh of relief.

'They had located me all right,' said Jan. 'I was lucky; you came just in time.'

I at once informed all the stations of the Germans' new ruse, explaining that their planes now climbed to a considerable height several miles away from the station and then, with the engine cut out to mislead our look-outs, they glided down over the station. It was a clever ruse.

The Radio Interception Team Unearthed

'We've got them!' Miet exclaimed, pressing my hand, all excited, with his face flushed, eyes shining.

'Whom? 'I asked, anticipating important developments.

'The interceptors. I know all about them. They are billeted in the YMCA in Prus Street, and they also keep their cars in a garage there; and it is from there that they start when they set out to raid a station.'

'Sit down and try to tell me all the details calmly. Where did you get the information from?'

Miet could hardly sit still. As he made his report he became more and more excited, and kept getting up and sitting down again while he talked.

'I've got a girl friend who works behind the bar in the YMCA. You may know that although the YMCA is reserved for Germans only, the waiters and all the staff are Polish, though they have to know a little German. I asked my friend who the Germans were who lived there, and she told me there were all sorts of Germans, officers, officials and, lately, business men as well. But they were rather strange business men, for although they were registered as such, and some of them were joined by their wives, they frequently left in motor-cars, armed, and stayed away all day long. Their motor-cars were garaged in the Insurance Company Riunione Adriatica di Sicurta, and the men usually returned very exhausted. On one occasion, a German general came to inspect the place, asked to see the list of tenants, and was very angry that business men were living in the YMCA, which was not intended for them. One of the business men went up to him, took him aside, and showed him some papers; they whispered something to each other, after which the general shook his hand, saluted him and apologised.

'When she had told me all this, I asked her to try to find out more from one of the wives, when they come to visit their husbands. My friend is a cute girl; she treated one of the wives to a glass of good liqueur at the bar and commiserated with her over her husband's having so much work, for he often came home worn out; but he was probably making a lot of money. She must have touched on a sore spot; for the German woman, who by then had had several drinks, retorted bitterly that her husband was not earning as much as those party members whose wives were wearing diamonds; and each had several fur-coats. He was not earning enough, for he was in the service. My friend pretended to be greatly astonished, for business men usually worked on their own account. The German woman then said unsuspectingly that they were not business men at all, but Gestapo agents and experts from a German factory, and that they were after Polish radio stations. My friend cleverly disguised her interest in the matter, and now she is well in with the German woman. I think they are doing a little trade with each other.'

I was overjoyed. Perhaps—I thought—our run of bad luck was over, and a more auspicious star was to guide us. It was a most extraordinary and heaven-sent chance that one of our men had been able to find out where our most dangerous enemies had their lair.

'Miet, you have no idea of the service you have rendered to our cause. Is your friend a reliable person?'

'Like a rock. She is a good Pole and she will do anything we ask of her.'

I thought hard, with all sorts of ideas passing through my mind. Our problem was greatly simplified. Miet remained silent, waiting for my response. I hesitated, unable to decide on anything definite. At last I had an idea that would ensure the liquidation of the Germans, but the means which would have to be employed were doubtful. I hesitated again; but came to the conclusion that any scruples would be misplaced. They were not observing the rules of war, dressing as civilians and pretending to be Poles. Under such conditions, were we bound to observe the principles of chivalry? And what with Auschwitz, Majdanek, Palmiry, the Ghetto. . . . I could hesitate no longer but made my decision.

'What do you think?' I asked. 'Would it be possible to poison them?'

'It's a good idea. I'll try to find out.'

'Thank your friend for all she's done for us, and ask her to get the numbers of the German cars, and the hours of their departure; also how many of the men live in the YMCA, what their names are, and where their wives live. Let her get anything that concerns those Germans.'

A few days later Miet handed me a sheet of paper with all the information I had asked for written down. He was very happy and told me:

'The number-plates of the cars are changed every two or three weeks. In addition, the cars which go out for longer periods, probably away from Warsaw, are given different number-plates. The cars are equipped with radio interception instruments, and the garage is under strong guard. There is also a sentry in front of the YMCA day and night. There are about thirty Germans in all and they work in two shifts. Their hours are more or less regular. If anything should be changed, we can get the information by telephone. On the sheet of paper you will also find the addresses of some of the wives and girl-friends. My friend got all this by hard drinking with their women, and she is carefully observing all departures and everything that is happening. However, more important still, some of the Germans are disguising themselves as railwaymen or clergymen. Others again, when they leave put on leather helmets or cover their faces with scarves, as if they were suffering from a toothache. Under the helmet or scarf they have something in their ears which is connected to their pockets by a thin wire. When I told my friend what was involved, and said that her information meant life or death to us, she became so enthusiastic that I had to restrain her. I don't think she will slip up, for everyone in the YMCA is studying these business men with great interest.'

'And what are the chances of poisoning them?'

'None. Neither beer nor vodka may be served uncorked. My friend tried to offer one of them a sweet, but he politely refused. The Polish staff receive the same food as the Germans. The Germans are extremely wary, except for their women-folk. The women are always willing to have a drink.'

Miet's information took my breath away. Now we should be able to get going. Perhaps we should be able to revenge Wladek and Mirek. In the first place, however, we had to hamstring the new and undoubtedly clever, almost un-German, methods that had been adopted by the radio interception team. Without delay I communicated all the information gathered so far to the Home Army, and to all the men in charge of our radio stations. Each of them received a slip of paper with the registration numbers of the motor-cars and the hours of their departure. They were amazed, and immensely keen. Now I invariably concluded my instructions with the words: 'Watch out for clergymen, railwaymen, and men with their faces wrapped up, with caps covering their ears, and with their collars upturned.' All my men reacted in the same way; their eyes shone, they smiled, and took on new eagerness for the struggle. Our chances had improved, and the game was starting all over again.

As for myself, I too felt tremendously encouraged. My brain worked better and new ideas came to me more easily. I thought it would be necessary to strike decisively at the German team, and to destroy it completely. It was not worth while to liquidate the agents individually, while they were visiting their wives or their girl-friends; for they would then know that they had been uncovered and would change their headquarters, and perhaps their methods too. It occurred to me that it would be possible to set up a radio station on the outskirts of Warsaw under a strong covering guard, lure the Germans into raiding it, and then have them surrounded and exterminated to a man? Or perhaps it would be better to storm the YMCA by night? I felt, however, that the executive detachment of the DCR, which I had at my disposal in Warsaw, had not had enough experience in this kind of action, so I decided to approach the commander of 'Khedive', Colonel Radoslaw.

I first put the matter before the DUS, and the decision was taken to liquidate the radio interception unit. The carrying out of the decision was entrusted to 'Khedive', and Colonel Radoslaw introduced me to one of his officers, a young man in his twenties, who was appointed to command the action. I had a number of meetings and talks with him, during which we considered all the possibilities. We also surveyed the future battlefield, first from behind the garden of the Deaf and Dumb Institute, and then from the Frascati side. There were many open spaces in the neighbourhood, and it looked as if it would be possible to withdraw the detachment into Rozbrat Street. We walked along the front of the YMCA several times, but the sentry paid no attention to us. The young officer considered and calculated the chances, and made his decision.

'We'll finish them off here, in the building,' he said. 'That seems to be the best way for us.'

A Game of Hide and Seek

Ian was now working occasionally in our old, good, hide-out in Peacock Street. It was located in the apartment of a deported Pomeranian, a former sailor in the German Navy. He was an elderly man who had seen the world, and a great talker, who liked to discuss politics with me whenever I visited the station. He spoke perfect German and was thus able to get on with the gendarmes who patrolled the Ghetto wall in Peacock Street, which was divided by it into two sections, a Jewish and an Aryan one.

The sailor, to whom I gave the pseudonym Pawinski, together with his unassuming and quiet wife, acted as a look-out when the station was operating in his apartment. From it we were able to watch through the window all the horrors of the Ghetto, the shootings and executions, the pursuit of those who tried to escape, and similar exploits of the German 'supermen'. The most terrible sight I saw there was that of a mad old Jew, with a beard covering almost his entire face, who by some miracle climbed up to the top storey of a gutted house; and there, out of the reach of the Germans, he made signs to the passers-by on the Aryan side, pulling faces and chanting for hours on end. This dreadful performance lasted for several weeks, till one day he disappeared, most probably starved to death.

On another occasion I witnessed a different scene. The gendarmes in Peacock Street suddenly vanished, and a crowd of emaciated Jewish 'teen-age boys appeared on the wall. Presently, an open truck pulled up from the Aryan side, loaded with bags and carrying several men of a distinctly criminal type. Then, over the Ghetto wall, amidst much shouting and shuffling, was hauled a fine, black grand piano and some expensive pieces of furniture; while the sacks from the truck found their way into the Ghetto. Within fifteen minutes the truck was gone, the Jews with the bags had disappeared, and the gendarmes were back in the street.

The good Mrs. Pawinski and her husband had their own method of keeping watch. They used to lock the telegraphist in from the outside, using a huge padlock to assure any visitor that there was nobody inside the apartment. Mrs. Pawinska would then make herself comfortable on a chair in front of the house, and chat with the ladies from the neighbouring houses; or she would stroll up and down the road, and from time to time visit the nearby streets in which our look-out girls were on duty. In the meantime, Pawinski would engage one or another of the gendarmes in endless talks.

One day Mrs. Pawinska, panting as she undid the padlock, rushed in and alerted Jan.

'There is a motor-car in the next street with one of the numbers on the slip of paper,' she said.

Jan stopped at once, concealed the transmitter in the oven, and went out into the street. He was curious to see what the German mobile interception unit looked like, and moved in its direction. He had hardly taken a few steps when he came across . . . a clergyman. Holding a copy of the 'Nowy Kurjer Warszawski' in his hand, this man was going from one house to another, checking the numbers and comparing them with something in the newspaper, as if he were looking for a particular number.

Jan, who had been informed of all the Germans' ruses, suspected the clergyman at once. But he first wanted to set eyes on the motor-car, being convinced that it must have been the interception unit. He hurried round the corner into Watchmakers Street, and there he saw the car with the incriminating number-plate, with some civilians sitting inside. But he was amazed when the clergyman with the newspaper, whom he had noticed in Peacock Street, came along and got into the car; for although he had been warned, here it was, actually happening before his very eyes.

It was in this way that we were able to check the reliability of the information we had received, and we were particularly hot on clergymen. But shortly afterwards we had a report that the Germans had given up this disguise, and were now masquerading only as railwaymen. This information prevented a slip-up by Ralph's station; he told me the story himself:

'My wife Kazia, when on look-out duty, frequently visits a woman who runs a food-stall, and from there she watches the neighbourhood, as there is a good view from the stall. Not to arouse the woman's suspicions, she visits her at other times too, and not only when the station is operating. They were sitting in the stall a few days ago, when a Polish railwayman came along and asked for a glass of "bimber" and a sausage sandwich. He had a glass, and while eating the sandwich he engaged the women in conversation.

'Do you know of any vacant apartments round here? I like the neighbourhood and I wouldn't mind moving in here,' he said.

Kazia, a clever woman, was a match for him.

'Where do you come from, Mister,' she said, 'that you should find such slums attractive?'

'I was deported by Germans; I come from Poznan and have no roof over my head. I should like to make my home here till the war is over.'

And would you believe it, the scoundrel took a handkerchief out of his pocket and pretended to wipe away his tears.

'Well,' said Kazia, 'it won't be easy to find accommodation here; there are no vacant apartments. But if you come again to-morrow at the same time, I'll find out from my husband if he knows of any going.'

The following day, in good time, I went with Kazia to the food-stall, and presently the railwayman arrived. I had a good look at him and noticed nothing peculiar about him. As for the apartment, I told him there was none vacant in that part of the city.

But would you believe it, two days later I saw that scum again, this time not in the disguise of a railwayman, but in a smart sporting outfit, walking along the street and examining the houses. It was now clear to me that he was a German. After wandering about for nearly an hour he left. I followed him, and just imagine, three streets away he got into a German car that was waiting for him there.'

Miet, on his part, reported that the Germans had given up disguising themselves as railwaymen and that they were now going about as road sweepers. A few days after I had received this warning I was with a look-out girl peeping from behind the corner of a house in Mokotow Street, and saw just such a municipal road sweeper standing in the middle of the road; he wore a tarpaulin overcoat, with the collar turned up, his face was wrapped in a scarf, and he moved his shoulders to the right and left. His broom and dustcart were standing close to the kerb, while he remained in the middle of the roadway, turning slowly in all directions. The station had already been warned, so I was not worried about the man, but my companion was shaking with emotion.

'Why does he keep turning round?' she asked me.

'That's obvious. He has a directional aerial sewn into the shoulders of the coat, and as our station suddenly went off the air, he thinks he's lost its bearings and is trying to find it again. He won't succeed this time.'

Ralph's Duel with the Interceptors

Ralph's favourite hide-out was in a factory building which had offices on the ground floor and staff apartments on the upper ones. In one of these apartments was the radio station, usually operated by Martin, who had been able to find some kind of employment in the factory. The entire complex of factory buildings was fenced in, and a German sentry was posted at the gate; for the factory was 'wehrwichtig', or important to war production, and was under German management. The hide-out thus had a great advantage: the radio interception unit and the gendarmes were bound to regard a building with a German sentry in front of it as a German building, and therefore beyond suspicion.

The hour for going on the air was approaching and Martin was tuning in; while Ralph put up the aerial. There was a knock at the door, and Ralph, not suspecting anything, replied 'Coming', closed the door to Martin's room, and opened the one leading to the corridor. Standing there was a friend of his, who whispered:

'Some Germans have arrived; they are in the manager's office, and they are setting up some instruments on the table. Come and see what they are up to.'

'Just a second,' Ralph said, realising what was happening. He returned to Martin.

'Hide the transmitter! I think the interceptors are here.'

Martin immediately put the transmitter away and dismantled the aerial, while Ralph went down, collected some papers, and together with his friend, walked slowly past the offices on the ground floor.

'Look,' whispered Ralph's friend, pointing to a small window in the door. Ralph glanced through it, and saw a group of civilians standing round a table, on which some apparatus had been erected. One of the Germans had earphones on and was manipulating the knobs. Ralph's heart sank. There could be no doubt that it was an interception unit already listening in, as the hour for our station to contact London had come. Unnoticed by anyone, Ralph quickly left the corridor and returned to Martin, wiping the cold sweat from his brow.

'Martin, it's a miracle we didn't slip-up,' he said, and told him what he had seen on the ground floor. Martin was amazed; but soon recovered and suggested that a glass of vodka would be appropriate to celebrate the occasion and fortify their nerves. When I met them that evening, they were both in high spirits. Ralph completed his report:

'Martin left at once, and no one at the gate stopped him. That means that they didn't suspect our building, but only wanted to use it as a listening post. I had another look into the manager's office, and you can imagine how bucked I felt, seeing them all watching the one with the earphones, who was turning the knobs and shaking his head. He must have been upset not to hear anything. There are only two of them there now. One is manipulating the apparatus, while the other is asleep in an easy chair. The others left by car.'

I fully concurred with Ralph's opinion.

'It's obvious that they had you located correctly, but it

didn't even occur to them that a radio station could be operating in a building guarded by a German sentry. Such suspicions could never arise in the dull Teutonic mind. However, they were right in assuming that the station must be operating very close by, and that it would be possible to pinpoint it accurately from your factory building. But let's see! How far is it from that building to your other hide-out?'

'It's a kilometre, more or less.'

'Do you think you could move the transmitter there?'

'I shouldn't dare do it to-morrow, but I should the day after. The sentries from the Werkschutz are already "squared"; they don't search us.'

'In that case, from the day after to-morrow, start operating the transmitter from the new hide-out. The Germans will be completely confused then.'

Everything went smoothly, and Martin resumed work in the other hide-out, carefully guarded by the look-outs, while Ralph watched the interceptors in the old place, and had a good laugh, seeing how excited the Germans became when they discovered the station on the air, and how they argued among themselves when they found that it was operating in a different direction and from further off.

After several weeks, Ralph's station was moved back to its old hide-out and continued to operate. Kazia patrolled the streets, calling occasionally at the food-stall. She concentrated her attention in the street, without bothering much about the open ground, where people worked on their small allotments. No motor-car could have approached from that direction, and any newcomer would have been visible from a considerable distance.

One day, however, glancing casually in that direction, she noticed two men with long poles in their hands. Their movements indicated that they were making a survey of the plots. Kazia, however, was a trained look-out and knew that she had to keep her eyes on them until she had made sure that they were, in fact, surveyors. She soon noticed that one of the men kept taking something out of his pocket, raising his arm, and releasing a kind of metal coil, which glittered in the sunshine. At the same time, the man slowly turned round. Kazia did not waste any time, but withdrew, observing all precautions, and alerted the station. When the transmitter had been safely put away, she and Ralph went to the window and from a safe distance watched the movements of the two men; as soon as Martin had taken his hand off the key they had begun to display great nervousness. They kept turning round and gesticulating as if they had been attacked by a swarm of wasps, and they kept on holding up the glittering coils in various directions. This went on for nearly quarter of an hour, until finally they threw away the poles, and tramping over the allotments, stalked off in the direction of the street.

Ralph quickly descended into the street and followed them. They crossed a number of streets, and entered a square; and there, Ralph, by then trembling with excitement, noticed a stationary open car, in which were seated some Germans, whom the two men he was following joined. Behind the car stood two trucks packed with gendarmes with steel helmets on their heads and rifles in their hands.

In this way I received confirmation of our earlier assumption, that the German method was designed not only to locate the building in which a radio station was operating, but to pinpoint the exact apartment. The Germans knew that the transmitters would be hidden away, and that the telegraphists would be able to produce authentic identity cards, if they failed to surprise the station at work; if, for instance, they were to surround a block of buildings, or even a single building, a search might yield no results, and the station would move out never to return. They were stalking us, therefore, on the quiet, inconspicuously, and if they failed to discover the exact apartment, they withdrew discreetly without attracting anyone's attention.

I was also confirmed in my conviction that it was best to employ as look-outs members of the family of the telegraphist, or the tenants of the apartment in which the hide-out was located. They would never fail in the hour of danger, and, even at great personal risk, they would always alert the station. Kazia provided a good example in this respect.

One day I was able to see with my own eyes that the Germans were determined to get Ralph's station, and that they had resorted to their earlier method after the new one had failed. I was particularly anxious about that station, and while it was on the air, I used to go out to control the functioning of the look-outs. Both Ralph and Martin were in good spirits and would not interrupt their work, on which they were very keen. They fortified themselves by frequent visits to a modest bar in Marshall Street, where they relaxed their nerves, strained by the excitements of the day. They took a great liking to each other and became almost inseparable.

On this occasion, I went with Zosia to inspect the look-outs of their station when it was operating in Regal Street. As we approached the corner of Marshall and Regal Streets, we noticed that Kazia was keeping watch nearby. At that moment we heard the roar of an engine, and above the ruins of the Bourse building, a plane appeared, making straight for the house in which Ralph was operating. Before Zosia could reach Kazia, the latter had already disappeared through the door of the house. At the same moment, out of Saxon Gardens came an open car, in which we recognised the Germans from Lower Street; with automatics in their hands, they studied the street closely. The car slowed down, and we promptly turned our backs on the roadway, and studied a shop window with great interest. The Germans passed close by without recognising us, and pulled up in front of the canteen in the IPS building. As soon as Kazia returned from alerting the station, I sent her to Marshal Pilsudski Square, to find out what the Germans were doing. She was back in fifteen minutes, and told me that one of the Germans was sitting in the car with the earphones on, while the others had gone into the canteen. In the meantime, Ralph arrived from the station to join us.

'You know,' he said, unemotionally and rather serenely, 'I heard a constant buzzing and knew that a plane was circling around. Consequently, I was watching the sky rather than the street, and before the plane appeared above the house, Martin went off the air. By the time Kazia came up, the transmitter was already in its hiding place.'

I put Ralph's station out of action for a time, to avoid overdoing it; but when the other stations proved unable to cope with the flood of telegrams, he returned for the third time to his old base, and continued to operate from there; but only during the night. We withdrew the look-outs from the street, and the only precautionary measure observed was for Ralph to climb on to the roof after dark; there, in the stillness of the night, he could hear not only the hum of passing motor-cars, but also the footsteps of passers-by. Whenever he noticed anything suspicious he pulled vigorously at a thin cord fastened to Martin's wrist.

This method—a length of hemp cord against the most modern German measuring instruments—worked perfectly, and proved most effective. Ralph's station continued to work at night without any interruption, right up to the outbreak of the Warsaw Rising.

The State Treasury Pays a Debt

The next alarm came from another quarter. Ralph called on me greatly worried.

'It seems,' he said, 'that the Germans are on James' trail— you know, that fellow in whose apartment Wladek was captured. We gave him forged papers and a weekly allowance, as he daren't show his face where he was employed, and he was hiding with some friends. Once the Blue police enquired about him, but fortunately he was not at home; and now he is homeless again and doesn't know where to turn.'

'Would cash be of any use?' I asked. 'Perhaps you could approach the Blues, find out what's what, and, if necessary, pay them off?'

'I'll try,' Ralph answered. 'But the worst of it is that James' wife is pregnant. That fellow has been making up at home for the job he lost in the factory. What shall we do with the three of them when the babe is born?'

'Don't meet misfortune half-way. Who knows, you may be invited to be the godfather of twins.'

But, joking apart, I was somewhat perturbed; for in my experience it sometimes happened that one got out of a tight corner, only to slip up because of some trifling complication.

However, shortly afterwards, Ralph, smelling strongly of 'bimber' and in fine mettle, reported:

'I have just been entertaining a sergeant of the Blues. The whole thing is too silly for words. James owed an old hag two thousand zlotys, and when he disappeared after the slip-up, the woman swore she'd find him and get the money out of him. And she did find him. When she discovered that he had adopted a new name, she went to the Blue police and told them that James had changed his name to hide from her, and to get out of paying his debt. What a dreadful woman! To do a thing like that for sheer love of money! The sergeant was quite friendly. I poured a lot of booze into him, and he is willing to help James. I think he suspects that the matter is in some way linked with the underground; he suggested the woman should be given her money back, while he, on his part, would see to it that she withdraws her complaint. He wasn't interested in James' new name and said that didn't concern him at all. What do you think we can do?'

I couldn't help laughing, and Ralph laughed too, though he still cursed the woman.

'To-morrow I'll let you have the two thousand zlotys, and a little extra, so that you can invite the sergeant to another vodka party.'

'That will be useful, for James lives in his precinct, and we may need the sergeant again.'

Soon afterwards Ralph proudly handed me James' bill for two thousand zlotys, which the woman had returned to the sergeant. But this was not the end of the matter. The underground State Audit sanctioned the expense of entertaining the sergeant, but refused to sanction the repayment of James' private debt. It would need another volume to describe the prolonged dispute I had with that venerable institution over this matter. In the end it was submitted to the Government Plenipotentiary, who resolved it in my favour. He would not permit radio liaison with London to be endangered for a paltry two thousand zlotys.

A Tragedy in Piaseczno

Alfred, who functioned not only as the head of a station, but also as its telegraphist, already had a number of hide-outs, and was testing 'Dickie', a transmitter constructed by Richard. Alfred was in such an ebullient mood that I asked him what it was that made him so happy.

'Emily and I are getting married the day after to-morrow,' he said. 'We are at last in a position to make a home for ourselves.'

I congratulated him warmly, glad to see him so happy. A few days later, I was able to congratulate Emily as well, now a happy bride. The young couple spent their honeymoon with the capricious 'Dickie'. They operated in Piaseczno, and Emilys' cousin acted as a contact between them and the central office. It was that contact-girl, who with tears in her eyes brought the evil news.

'Alfred and Emily were captured yesterday. Emily was at home, and Alfred had gone to the market to buy some food. As soon as he returned, the Germans drove up and surrounded the house; a few of them entered it and started a search. Unfortunately the transmitter and all the papers were hidden in a cradle, under the baby belonging to Alfred's landlady. The Germans lifted the baby up and found the transmitter. They were so overjoyed they held a drinking bout on the spot to celebrate their success. Then they took Alfred and Emily away, and drove back to Warsaw.' The girl burst into tears again.

'Now they are lost, lost for ever! And they had only just been married!'

This was indeed a tragedy, involving the loss of a charming and happy couple, and the loss of another station. Such was the sad lot of our people.

As was my custom, I immediately proceeded to examine the circumstances in which the slip-up occurred. What seemed very strange was that Alfred and Emily had not been captured while the station was on the air. Could they possibly have been pinpointed previously with such precision? But if they had been, why had the Germans not raided the station there and then? It occurred to me that this might have been the work of an informer.

I expressed my misgivings to the contact-girl, who seemed to have similar doubts. She was determined to probe into the

matter, and within a few days she told Zosia that she suspected the Germanised firm which had employed Alfred previously; she believed that one of the staff, a German who had
a personal dislike for Alfred, putting two and two together,
must have come to the conclusion that if Alfred had given up
working for the firm, he must have done so for some hidden
reason. The German had probably reported this to the
Gestapo. However, it was only circumstantial evidence, and
it proved impossible to discover anything more in the matter.
Nevertheless, from her talk with the contact-girl, Zosia came
back with a new hope.

'Emily's cousin,' she said, 'met a German woman, whom
she knew before the war as a decent sort of person, and who
seems to have considerable influence here. The German
woman definitely promised to see to it that Alfred should be
sent to a concentration camp instead of being shot. As for
Emily, she would be deported to a concentration camp anyhow. The German woman requires 50 thousand zlotys for
expenses, payable after the matter is settled.'

I should not have agreed if the German had asked to be
paid in advance, but she had not, and this was already 1944
and the Germans were doing many strange things. The
Government Plenipotentiary at once agreed to the payment
of the required sum, as soon as I had ascertained that Alfred
was in a concentration camp. Several weeks later, the German
woman informed Emily's cousin that Alfred had already been
sent to one. Despite some lingering doubts, we rejoiced that
his life was spared. It was therefore a cruel blow when we
learnt from her cousin that Emily had been executed. This
was a terrible and unexpected development. How was it possible that Alfred, the head of the station and its telegraphist,
should be in a concentration camp and a mere look-out girl
executed? We could not make it out, until an underground
report from Pawiak prison clarified everything. What had
happened was that the Chief of the SS and Gestapo, Himmler,
arrived in Warsaw and issued an order that several dozen of
the more heavily incriminated women should be shot. The
German woman spoke of Emily in superlatives. 'She was a
lion-hearted woman. She took all the guilt on herself. During

her cross-examination she declared that as she was an educated woman and Alfred an artisan only, she was the dominant partner, especially as Alfred was in love with her; and that she had recruited him for the underground, and persuaded him to work in the radio station, overcoming his reluctance. In short, she did everything possible to save Alfred, and this was her own undoing.'

Several months later, Emily's cousin brought us a postcard. I read it, hardly able to believe my eyes. The postcard carried the official stamp of the concentration camp in Stutthof and read:

'Ich bin gesund und fühle mich wohl. Ich küsse meine liebste Frau and Verwandte und bitte um die Nachricht. Wladyslaw Fox.' (I am in good health and feel well. I kiss my beloved wife and family and request news.)

The German woman had been as good as her word; and we too carried out our part of the bargain. The postcard remained the last trace of the light-hearted, good-looking and enamoured Wladyslaw Fox, for such was Alfred's real name.

A Radio Station in a Forest

Gene was suffering from increasing nervous tension, and in addition to real dangers he had delusions of non-existent ones. He would then stop the work unnecessarily, and upset the look-out girls by unjustified demands and ill temper. As a result the station functioned badly and its output was exceedingly small. I found a way out of the quandary, thanks to the fact that Boleslaw Scibiorek, the head of Civil Resistance in the Lodz district, put at my disposal a small partisan detachment, well equipped with American arms, dropped by parachute, which operated in the wooded country-side near Skierniewice. I seized the opportunity for dispatching Gene to them, and within a few days he had established contact with London by means of a transmitter powered by a hand-operated generator. I was greatly pleased; for the liquidation of a radio station operating in a forest was not an easy matter for the Germans. Directional measurements could not be relied upon in such circumstances, as the trees deflected the radio waves, and the station could not be raided except by the employment of considerable forces. Against that, the partisan unit had a widespread intelligence service covering the entire region, and it would not allow itself to be encircled or taken by surprise.

Gene was glad to leave Warsaw for the forest, and the matter was settled. Liaison with the sylvan station was to be maintained by an aged and retired railwayman, who could always rely on his connections in order to get through, even if railway transport was denied to Poles. The old pensioner was a bigoted Catholic, and always carried a prayer book and a rosary wrapped round his wrist. I was not at all discouraged by this, but on the contrary, when I looked at that white-haired candidate for paradise volunteering for underground work, I was absolutely certain that no German would ever suspect him to be an underground courier carrying messages. I gave him all the necessary instructions and advice, while Gene, with a twinkle in his eye, explained to him how he was to find the secret letter-box in Skierniewice.

'You must first of all go to church. After you have said your prayers, you will come out of the church and you will see right in front of you a little shop, where the letter-box will be ready for you. You will have to wait two hours for the train back to Warsaw. The only thing you can do to while away the time is to go to church again and pray.'

The old man took the instructions with great seriousness, repeating them word for word.

The new set-up went like clockwork. The old railwayman was not only most conscientious, but scrupulously punctual. He travelled to Skierniewice every other day and there delivered and received the messages at the contact point. A messenger from the unit maintained liaison between the forest and the letter-box. Later on, they made direct contact, just outside the town, and exchanged the material. I arranged that the reception of telegrams, being absolutely safe, would be dealt with by the stations in Warsaw, and that all our telegrams, except the more urgent ones, would be handled by Gene, who was able to operate his transmitter twice daily for several hours running. This put a great strain on him, but he seemed to thrive on it; during his service with the forest unit he gained considerably in weight.

The Directorate of Civil Resistance took the unit on to its pay-roll, which helped to supply it properly with provisions. I placed in it a brother of the look-out girl, Jadzia, a thin and lanky boy, whose sister and parents were worrying about his safety in Warsaw. I also met the commander and the doctor of the detachment, who came to Warsaw to arrange for the supply of various things the unit needed. One of the diversions in connection with this partisan unit was supplied by Gene. He conceived the ingenious idea of communicating with me via London. In time, he had the cheek to inform me by means of a telegram sent from the forest to London at 6 a.m., and which London relayed to Warsaw at 8 a.m., that he wanted to see me at 1 p.m. on the same day at our favourite meeting place at the corner of Basket and Marshall Streets. He used to overwhelm us in this roundabout way with telegrams on all sorts of trifling matters, such as, for instance, that he had not yet got the leather coat which had been promised him. Perhaps it helped; for he received the coat, though not the one he dreamed about, but a second-hand one.

When the German armies were retreating, during the Warsaw Rising, considerable German forces passed through the Skierniewice forest, and the partisan detachment, together with the radio station, withdrew into the forests near Piotrkow. I was informed of this via London; for just before the capitulation of Warsaw, Gene specified Piotrkow as the new contact point. Miet and the two Pawinskis managed to reach Gene's station after the Germans had evacuated them from Warsaw, when the former occupied some sections of the city. The three of them got to Piotrkow homeless and starved, and there they accidentally ran into Gene, who took care of them. Unfortunately, just before the Germans left, Miet fell into the clutches of the Gestapo, and the station was scattered to the four winds. The partisan unit which had given the station its safe cover was dissolved by Scibiorek as soon as the territory was occupied by Soviet troops.

Decorations for Gallantry

After an unconscionable delay, I received from the High Command of the Home Army the information that Joey and Wladek, whom I had recommended for decorations while they were still alive, and also Martin, had been awarded the Cross for Gallantry. The first two did not live to receive the decoration, but Martin happily continued in his dangerous work. Without telling him of the honour that had been bestowed on him, I arranged a meeting with him in Ujazdow Park. I arrived a little earlier than arranged in the company of Major Frank, an officer of the High Command. It was springtime, the sun was up, and the park was in blossom. We delighted in the brightness and the green lawns, comfortably seated on a bench, basking in the warm sunshine. Then Martin arrived, and after I had introduced him to Frank, the latter stood up and rather solemnly, but in a natural manner, and without pathos informed Martin of the award.

'Mr. Martin,' he said, 'in recognition of the courage you have shown as a telegraphist, the High Command of the Home Army has awarded you the Cross for Gallantry.'

Thereupon, the Major handed Martin an excerpt from the Order of the Day, written out on a narrow strip of paper, and kissed him on both cheeks. Martin was extremely surprised and reciprocated by kissing the Major effusively, unable to utter a word. We were all three moved, especially Martin; and for a minute or so we kept silent, while only the birds twittered on. I was thinking of Joey and Wladek, who had not lived to see this day. I could see them both before my eyes, exactly as I had seen them for the last time. But I pulled myself together, shook Martin's hand, and congratulated him.

'My warmest congratulations, Martin. You well deserve that Cross. Joey and Wladek have also been decorated, but we can only let their families know.'

'I am so glad the poor fellows were not forgotten,' said Martin sadly. 'The crosses on their graves came to them first.'

'And now, Martin, chin up, and let's go and celebrate this day.'

We threw all precautions to the wind, as it was a festive day for the station; and unmindful of the German patrols, we hurried along the streets, straight for our destination, a modest apartment in which Zosia had organised a reception for the men and women from Ralph's station. The entire team was already waiting for us, and they all embraced Martin and congratulated him; while he seized the opportunity joyfully, kissing all the look-out girls in turn. His susceptibility to female charms was well known to all of us. He never tried to conceal it, and to-day he was untiring in paying his compliments to the ladies, who on this occasion received them more graciously than usual.

We sat down at a well-provisioned table, with Martin in the seat of honour and the Major on his right, having on his left the look-out, Irene, whom he adored. The atmosphere, which was most auspicious from the outset, improved with each toast, all of which were drank to 'Martin's permanent health'.

Martin, flushed with happiness, and the Major soon discovered that they were both natives of Lwow, and when it transpired that one came from the Upper and the other from the Lower Lyczakow, there was no end to their reminiscences. This made Irene jealous, and she claimed in her guttural voice that Martin should pay more attention to her.

Zosia was deeply involved in a talk with Kazia, who was hopelessly in love with Ralph, and was unable to talk of anything but him. We learned on this occasion that Ralph had a fine voice, and that he was a master on the guitar. I was sitting next to him. He was well groomed and rather grave in manner. But after three large glasses, each drained at one draught, he raised his finger, looked me straight in the eye and solemnly announced: 'Now I feel better'. I knew the answer to that, and promptly poured a fourth glass for him. After he had drunk it, we plunged into talk about the radio station. Ralph could not stop talking. He recalled with great emotion all his adventures with the radio interceptors. He talked about the men, the work, the hide-outs, of the many worries and ideas we had had; and all he said was centred on the radio station. When he spoke of his approach to our work, I could sense his straightforward, utterly honest nature, and I listened to him with genuine satisfaction, mixed with admiration; for Ralph was a working class man, and yet many people much higher on the social ladder might have envied him the depth of his feelings and thoughts.

In the meantime, the whole company felt better for the many drinks they had imbibed. In the general hubbub, Martin's voice predominated, as he entertained the ladies with his Lwow stories and jokes.

But all good things come to an end, and we had to think of the daily chores awaiting us. Once more, amidst general rejoicings, we all embraced Martin before we left. He shook my hand with great warmth.

'It was lovely, Chief; I never expected to live to see such a great day,' he said.

Supplies by Parachute

We had been receiving transmitters and receivers for some time by parachute drops, but not in such quantities that we could dispense with our own products. I endeavoured to equip each hide-out with at least one transmitter; for this saved us transporting them each time from one hide-out to another, which, owing to frequent raids and round-ups, increased the risk considerably.

On one occasion, for instance, when Cesia and Zosia were carrying a transmitter to Peacock Street, they overlooked the tramway stop at which they were supposed to alight and jumped off the moving tram. Cesia fell, bag in hand, right in front of a gendarme, who first told her off and afterwards helped her to her feet, shouting all the time in German. Neither of the two women understood German, and they were convinced the gendarme was arresting them. Only after the conductor of the tram, which stopped on account of the accident, had explained to them that they were required to pay a fine of 20 zlotys, did they realise they were not being arrested. They were glad to pay the fine.

I myself was once carrying some radio equipment from one hide-out to another, and as the tram was full, I stood on the step of the platform. In New World Avenue, at the St. Cross

Street tram stop, someone pulled me down sharply on to the pavement. Turning round, I saw it was a gendarme. With his eyes bulging under his steel helmet and his face flushed, he shouted at me at the top of his voice. I stood there without saying a word, but the parcel in my hand felt like a red-hot lump of lead. In the end, the gendarme pulled out a pad, tore off a receipt, and handed it to me saying, 'Five zlotys fine'.

The situation improved with the winter of 1943. Parachute drops increased in quantity, and nearly all of them brought some supplies for us. By then each hide-out had its own transmitter, and they were moved only if they needed repair.

I once came into direct contact with such a parachute drop. A friend in the conspiracy, whose duty it was to receive the drops, was without a hide-out and asked me to help him out. I offered him one of ours, and was prepared for some novel experiences. To my surprise, a cab pulled up at the door, packed with suitcases of all sizes, and carrying an elderly and rather stout sergeant of the Blue police, accompanied by a miserable-looking civilian. When they had carried the heavy luggage into the room, almost half filling it, I realised how dangerous such a transport was.

'Aren't you afraid a patrol might stop you?' I asked the elderly sergeant. 'Moving all this by cab in broad daylight?'

'It's never happened yet, as my presence here testifies. The stupid Germans think I'm taking confiscated goods to the police station, and it never occurs to them to stop me.'

'But what if they did?'

'For such an emergency we have this,' he said, and they both pulled out splendid, brand-new American Colts, which were supplied from parachute drops.

'Are you both in the Blue police?' I enquired.

'Not at all,' the stout sergeant replied. 'I only put this uniform on when transporting such equipment as this.'

When we unpacked the bags, we found brand-new radio transmitters, both large ones, which we called 'Minka', and smaller ones, which we named 'Nelka'. There were also books, films, etc. We could hardly take our eyes off all the stuff, which had come from that distant free world. There was a pile of photographs of Polish airmen, at which everyone grabbed to see. We looked at them, deeply moved. The liaison girl Irene was weeping. 'How wonderful they are, how handsome!' she said. There was a photograph of General Sikorski addressing a meeting of the National Council. I recognised some faces in it, and pointed them out to our little group with appropriate comments.

When everything was unpacked, checked, divided up and receipted, we said good-bye to the stout policeman and the thin civilian. Before they departed, they praised our hide-out.

'I like this place,' one of them said, 'and we shall be glad to deliver everything here.'

I had to damp their enthusiasm.

'You won't do anything of the kind. This hide-out is serving an altogether different purpose.'

We were particularly interested in one of the transmitters. It was contained in a small attaché case, which one could safely carry about without fear. I found from the enclosed instructions that the transmitter was of American make, so I named it the 'American beauty'. Jan fell in love with it at first sight. He kept badgering me, without telling me outright what he was after.

'What's the matter, Jan?' I asked him. 'Is anything worrying you?'

'No; but I want to ask you to allot the "American beauty" to me. I love it.'

'You can have it.'

Subsequently, Jan operated this excellent transmitter during the whole period of the Warsaw Rising.

Before the Rising

The rumours circulating in the capital caused Zosia and I, one fine, sunny July afternoon, to take a walk across Poniatowski Bridge. There, a heavenly sight was spread before our eyes, a sight we had dreamed about during the long years of occupation. On the roadway, an endless column of German soldiers was slogging along wearily, in a state we had never seen them in before. They were in rags, dirty, many without arms, and without boots, on foot, on bicycles and carts, in a disorderly retreat, frequently without any officers. Among them were many wounded with bandaged heads or arms in slings. It was an unforgettable spectacle, and the July sun shed so much light on this procession of misery that one could see every hole in the uniforms, every stain on the bandages, every spot of rust on the rifles.

Holding hands, and with difficulty restraining our joy, we could only draw each other's attention to the more interesting details of the grand spectacle by an increased pressure of the hand. There were many other promenaders like ourselves on the bridge. The people of Warsaw crowded to it, pretending to be out in the fine July afternoon to enjoy the cool breeze over the Vistula; but in reality greedy to feed their eyes on the sight of the defeated Germans. They exchanged furtive smiles, while the mob of demoralised German soldiery streamed by in an endless column, pursued by the dull roar of gunfire, booming from the direction of Radzymin and Otwock.

There could no longer be any doubt that the front was approaching Warsaw. For some time we had been able to observe among the Germans symptoms of disintegration and fear. They had been selling out their recently-acquired properties for a song, and were going back to Germany with furniture they had stolen, the pictures, pianos, jewels and fur-coats. Those of them who were prevented from running away were trying to find a Pole who would give them protection in case of need. The soldiers were willing to sell anything. In the street markets, German military nurses were selling openly watches and cigarette cases they had purloined from the wounded soldiers in the hospitals. In my telegram of July 3, 1944, I informed London of the extraordinary case in which German soldiers had sold a car-load of new parachutes at a railway station near Krakow. At about this time I sent several telegrams to London describing the execution of German deserters in the prisons within the Government General. A friend of mine told me of another extraordinary case.

'I've been contacted by a German sergeant,' he said, 'who offered to sell me three truckloads of blankets, sheets, and hospital linen; on condition that I also took the three trucks, which his drivers would dismantle and help me to dispose of. I asked him why he wanted to get rid of three trucks without asking any payment for them. So he explained. If the deal were clinched, he said, he would, in collusion with his drivers, report that the trucks had been bombed by enemy planes with incendiaries, and burnt out with the entire contents. So the trucks had to vanish too.'

During July 1944, the fever among the Germans rose to its all-time high. Offices were being evacuated, the *Volksdeutsche* had run away, and scared and excited patrols hurried along the streets, shooting at passers-by for the slightest reason, or no reason at all. My own mother-in-law was the victim of such a shooting, while she was riding on the rear platform of a tram-car. A motorised SS patrol swept the tram-car with a burst from an automatic weapon, and the elderly lady was taken to a hospital in Chalubinski Street with a bullet in her hip.

The underground movement, too, was passing through a phase of great excitement. We sensed the approaching hour of decision. During the month of July, I took part in several meetings, held in the presence of the Government Plenipotentiary, Jankowski, of the military and civilian leaders of the underground. We discussed the existing situation and tried to envision the shape of things to come. The discussions showed clearly that a Rising was inevitable. An armed Rising in Warsaw was considered an indispensable part of 'Burza', the code word for action at the crucial moment. The events in Wilno, Lwow, Lublin, and Kowno, where the Polish Underground had gone into action behind the collapsing German front to succour the Soviet armies, had to be re-enacted in Warsaw. It seemed unthinkable that the Home Army, numbering in Warsaw 40,000 officers and men, should stand passively by and not attack the retreating and demoralised German armies. National dignity and pride required that the capital should be liberated by the Poles themselves, and that was accepted without any discussion. Moreover, we had to think of what the Western world would say if the Russians were to capture Warsaw unaided. In that event Stalin would have no difficulty in convincing the Allies that the Home Army, the underground Government, and the Polish underground movement as such were a fiction. What kind of an army would it be, what sort of a Government, that, being in the capital, failed to take part in the battle for the liberation of the city? It would be obvious, then, that they simply did not exist. Finally, the Germans themselves were spreading the report that on Hitler's order Warsaw was to be razed to the ground whatever happened.

For the sake of objectivity I must say that the first three considerations were regarded as the more important ones. The question of an armed action in Warsaw on the approach of the Russians was taken for granted. At that time no one could possibly have foreseen that the Russians might deliberately halt their offensive, and stop the attack on Warsaw on the day the Rising broke out. Vague reports had already reached us from the High Command, mentioning that the units of the Home Army which took part in the liberation of Wilno and Lwow had been disarmed by the Russians; but even if we had had full and definite information on the subject, I do not think a decision to abandon the idea of any armed action in Warsaw could have been taken. No one has ever yet thought of a way to prevent a volcano erupting, and during July 1944, Warsaw was indeed a volcano on the point of eruption.

The date of the Warsaw Rising, however, was decided subsequently, during a secret session of the High Command of the Home Army, which had to take into consideration an additional factor, namely, that the Germans had placarded the city with posters summoning all males, except young boys and old men, to report for the building of fortifications. What the Germans were really aiming at was the liquidation of the entire Home Army. In the course of the High Command's secret sessions, views were also expressed opposing the Rising. The Intelligence Department in particular warned against an armed Rising. However, at a meeting with the Commander-in-Chief on July 31, 1944, at 6 p.m., the Government Plenipotentiary approved the final resolution of the High Command. Everything was now happening at such a pace that, either because of the haste, or because of an exaggerated fear that the secret might be prematurely disclosed, neither the office of the Government Plenipotentiary nor members of the Council of National Unity were informed of the date of the outbreak. I myself learned of it from . . . Zosia; in circumstances described in the next chapter.

CHAPTER XIX

The Warsaw Rising

The Outbreak

Zosia was hurrying along Marshall Street to meet me, and from the expression on her face I knew that something must have happened.

'I've had extraordinary news! Lewis called on me at 11 a.m. to say good-bye. He said that at five o'clock this afternoon the armed Rising will begin, and that he will be taking part in an attack on the cavalry barracks.'

'Don't talk nonsense, Zosia!' I answered. 'Don't you think I would know of it?'

But I was not so sure myself, and leaving Zosia in the street, I hastened to the hide-out of the central office of the DCR. If it were true, the central office would know by now. A notification of the exact date should have been sent there. But why so late? The only surprise was the zero hour; for I had known that the armed Rising would soon take place. On July 30 and 31 I had sent the following telegrams to London:

'July 30, 1 p.m. We can hear the roar of guns in Warsaw. German civilians have left. There remain the troops and the Gestapo. After several days of panic the Germans are keeping quiet. It is reported that the Russian troops are only 20 km. away.'

'July 31. The situation in Warsaw remains unchanged since yesterday. Contrary to the BBC announcement, the suburbs are not being bombarded by the Russians. The underground authorities are inconspicuously taking over institutions abandoned by the Germans. The "Nowy Kurjer Warszawski" and the "Warschauer Zeitung" were not published this morning.'

My deputy, Krajewski, was on duty at the office, together with one of the contact-girls. I took him aside.

'Have you heard anything about the Rising starting to-day?'

'Of course I have. I was waiting for you, to talk it over with you. I heard about the Rising from friends in "Bastion" group. The whole regiment has been mobilised for the last few days, and action will begin to-day.'

'Have we received official notification of the matter?'

'No. I have just looked through to-day's mail, but found nothing about it. But you can take it from me that the Rising will begin to-day.'

I looked at my watch, feeling that I had to do something. I was furious; though I knew it was useless to get excited. I could not make out why we had not been notified, except for a piece of unpardonable negligence on someone's part. I wondered what we should do about the radio interception unit. All the plans for its liquidation were ready down to the last detail, all the men who were to take part in the action had surveyed the battleground, and the attack was to take place in three days time. Were the interceptors to escape unscathed? It was now one o'clock in the afternoon, and I had made no preparations. I arranged with Krajewski that he should meet me daily in the hide-out of the DCR, and hurried to Zosia, who was waiting anxiously in the street; I signalled to her from a distance that the news about the Rising was true.

We parted without a moment's delay. Zosia hastened to alert Ralph's station, while I went to look for Jan, who was to call up London from the Peacock Street station at 4 p.m. I searched for him till 2 p.m., when I at last found him, and told him about the armed Rising. Jan just had time to run home for his bag, before going on at once to Peacock Street, to fetch the transmitter. We arranged to meet at 4 p.m. at the corner of Basket and Marshall Streets; for I had not been able to make up my mind where to make my headquarters, and my one worry at that moment was to be on the Polish side of the city after the Rising had started.

When Zosia returned, she told me that Ralph would be at the corner of Buxom and Marshall Streets in a few minutes. I hurried there, and arrived just as Ralph was paying off the ricksha in which he had travelled. I motioned the ricksha man to wait, and though I was in a preoccupied huddle with Ralph, I was struck by the man's behaviour; he winked at me understandingly, turned round, and pulled up saying, 'You must hurry, gentlemen.'

I took Ralph aside.

'Ralph,' I said, 'at five o'clock this afternoon the Rising starts.'

The news made a shattering impression on him. He breathed hard, looked up and muttered, 'Thank heaven it has come at last.' We arranged to meet daily at twelve o'clock noon on the same spot, and if we were cut off from each other, we should try to communicate via London.

I returned to the rendezvous in a state of tremendous excitement. Would the Rising break out or not? Would it succeed or not?

The streets were unusually animated. The tram-cars were crowded with young boys, who unconcernedly occupied even the front platform, reserved 'Nur für Deutsche', without the Germans present doing anything about it. On the sidewalks, women in twos or threes were walking along briskly, with obvious haste, carrying heavy bags and bundles. 'They are transporting arms to the assembly points,' I muttered to myself. A stream of bicycles flowed along the roadway. Boys in top boots and wind-jackets were pedalling as hard as their legs could go. I noticed that one of the boys carried a rucksack from which protruded something resembling a walking stick, wrapped in a newspaper and tied with a piece of string. Anyone could see it was the end of a rifle. Here and there was a German in uniform, or a German patrol, proceeding on its beat without seeing anything, and without knowing what was happening around it.

On my way I passed numerous men scurrying, grave and purposeful, in all directions, and exchanging glances with me full of tacit understanding.

While I was walking up and down Basket Street, near Marshall Street, I saw a young boy and girl come out of a gate. She put her arms round his neck and kissed him affectionately. It was a moving sight. The boy glanced at my top boots and greeted me with a nod of his head. I returned his salute, showed him my watch, and said: 'It's time'. He gave the girl another kiss, hurried away, and jumped on to a passing tram-car.

On the other side of the street I noticed an old acquaintance from my college days. He was of Jewish descent; I used to meet him occasionally in the street and talk to him. I knew he was in hiding outside Warsaw. He was walking along calmly, holding a young woman by the arm, and greeted me. I knew that if he fell into the hands of the Germans he would be murdered. I was in a quandary. I had to warn him, but I could not give away the secret. So I motioned him to cross over and said:

'Leave Warsaw at once. In fifteen minutes a large scale action is going to begin, and no one can foresee its outcome.'

Without wasting time shaking hands, he called out, 'Thank you,' and ran. I saw him jump into a ricksha and disappear round the corner of Marshall Street.

I met him in Milanowek after the Rising. He fell on my neck.

'You saved my life! I knew you would survive; for my fiancée, her parents, and I myself all prayed for you every day. We just caught an electric train at Nowogrodzka Street. On the outskirts of the city we could already hear heavy firing. The Germans wanted to stop the train out in the open, but with great presence of mind the driver pretended not to see them, and increased speed; and that's how we escaped. It was the last train to leave Nowogrodzka. I can imagine what my position would have been had I been stranded in a part of the city occupied by the Germans.'

At last Jan arrived, perspiring under the weight of a heavy bag, which he carried on his back; and soon after him came Zosia. Jan was completely exhausted; for he carried in the bag not only the transmitter, but also the transformers, which were heavy; and the tram-cars were crowded. He was helped by the young boys, who warned him, 'Hurry up, Mister! With an outfit like that you won't be in time!'

By then we could hear the first shots being fired, somewhere in the direction of Mokotow Field; so we quickly made for

Marshall Street, where, on the top floor, I had a room with a private entrance. In this hide-out Zosia and I made our home, and no one in the underground knew its address. Adjoining the room was a larder, the ceiling of which was much higher than that of the room. In the larder, close to the ceiling, was a ventilator leading to a loft. With the help of the trusted janitor, the entrance to the loft from the staircase was walled up, and in this way I had a wonderful hiding place, which could be reached only through the larder by way of the ventilator. In it I kept reserve transmitters, and a large quantity of valves and arms supplied from parachute drops. I climbed up there, followed by Jan, who was unaccustomed to the acrobatics required for getting into the loft, and dropped into it from the ventilator like a ripe coconut. Without delay, he assembled the transmitter, while I listened to the chatter of machine-guns and the infrequent single shots close by. From the yard below rose the voices of passers-by, who were taking shelter there. They consoled each other by saying that the firing would soon cease, and that they would be able to reach their homes before curfew. But before the firing did cease, many of them had waited, sheltering in our house, for two months.

There, too, I witnessed a scene which I shall remember as long as I live. I heard the tramping of feet on the stairs at the other side of the house, and into the courtyard came a young boy in civilian clothes, with a military cap bearing the Polish eagle, and the star of a second lieutenant. Covered with dust from head to foot, he held a rifle in his hand. He was followed by several other boys, two of whom were armed with revolvers and the rest with hand grenades. They rushed to the door, and presently I could hear isolated rifle shots. It was a detachment of the Home Army from Pius Street, which had penetrated into Marshall Street by using the lofts and roofs on the houses between.

Suddenly there was a deafening explosion and shock; followed by another, and then a third. It was a tank, which had driven from Pius Street into Marshall Street, and was fighting a duel with the solitary rifle firing from the front door of our house. Men and women were shouting and running into the cellars, while a cloud of dust hid everything from view.

The hour for going on the air arrived, and by the light of a candle Jan called London from the dark loft. The telegram about the outbreak of the Rising was ready to be sent out. Unfortunately, London replied:

'I am sorry, I cannot hear you at all,' and postponed the exchange till the next day.

We were greatly upset. It was obvious that the loft, surrounded as it was by tall buildings, was not suitable for radio transmission. However, for the time being we were not in a position to look for another hide-out; this could not be done until it became clear which sections of Warsaw were in the hands of the Home Army. We sat down to a frugal meal, rather discouraged. Zosia was worried about the problem of feeding us, as we had no stocks of provisions; while I felt depressed because I had lost contact with the Government Plenipotentiary and the High Command of the Home Army. Uppermost in my mind was the anxious question of the success or failure of the Rising. When would the Soviet Army reach Warsaw? I had had no time to reorganise our network in accordance with the new situation, and the whole liaison service was limited to Jan and the equipment we had in my hide-out. The three of us discussed all these problems endlessly, and it was not until the small hours of the morning that we were able to snatch some sleep.

The house we were in was in Polish hands, in the literal sense of the word; for the two boys with red-and-white armbands on their sleeves, to whom I talked in the evening, had no weapons at all. I asked them why they had none, and what they told me was not at all reassuring.

'We had hand grenades,' they said, 'but we gave them to our colleagues who went into action.'

I went out into the street, which was dark and deserted. Only in the doors of the houses, were hushed people whispering to each other, and was the glow of a cigarette to be seen here and there. I asked the two boys where the German positions were.

'They are surrounded in the Telephone Exchange in Pius

Street; from there a tank comes out and fires its gun into Marshall Street. There are no other Germans here, and their nearest positions are beyond the Square of the Redeemer.'

We went up to our room, and Zosia took the boys down a new Belgian revolver with two clips. They were overjoyed.

On the following day we were awakened by the sound of the tank's gun; being blocked by a barricade thrown across Pius Street during the night, the tank moved as far as it could and fired at random. Life in the house was more or less organised by now. The passers-by, who had been cut off from their homes, were taken in by the tenants of the house, who shared their meagre rations of food with them. All of them knew by now that this was an armed Rising, and that it would be necessary to wait a few days (!), until the Soviet troops entered Warsaw. In the cellars, pickaxes were at work breaking a way through from one house to another. This was the beginning of a maze of subterranean corridors, through which, as the fighting continued, one could pass from one end of the city to the other.

I set out for my meeting with Ralph. Passing from one cellar to another and from courtyard to courtyard, I reached Raven Street, and from there, protected by barricades raised during the night, Buxom Street. I reached the corner of Marshall Street, and, cautioned by the sentries, I peeped out from behind a barricade.

An uncanny sight met my eyes in that great avenue, which used to hum with life. There was not a man to be seen, and the stillness almost rang in one's ears. A derailed tram-car lay there, and torn electric cables were hanging loose from their pylons. From the Post Office building in Nowogrodzka Street came the reports of infrequent shots, echoing in the dead silence. Ralph was nowhere to be seen, and I started shouting, 'Ralph! Ralph!' Echo answered from Poznan Street, 'Ralph-Ralph', which almost frightened me. Echoes reverberating in the desert of Marshall Street seemed to proclaim the end of the world. But Ralph did not answer, and the sentries at the barricade began to get nervous.

'Don't shout so much, Mister! Can't you see there isn't a living soul in the street?'

On that first day of August, 1944, Ralph's splendid activities came to an end. Many months afterwards I learned that on the first day of the Rising Ralph and Martin had been trapped in a section of the city occupied by the Germans, that they miraculously escaped being shot by Ukrainians serving with the Germans, and that they were then transported via Pruszkow to the West of the country.

From that barricade, in a depressed mood, I went to meet Krajewski in the old hide-out in Wspolna Street. The landlady opened the door; she was crying.

'There is no one here,' she said.

'But why are you crying?' I asked.

'My son and daughter left with the Home Army, and I have no news of them.' She was gazing at me with tears in her eyes, waiting for a word of comfort. But what could I say to her? I kissed her hand and ran down the stairs. On that day I failed to establish contact with the staff of the DCR, or the Government Plenipotentiary, or the High Command of the Home Army. I did not know at the time that they were all located in the Old City. When I at last established contact with them, I was instructed by the Plenipotentiary to remain where I was.

During the second day of the Rising, London was still unable to hear us, so we moved the transmitter into a large apartment one floor below, and from there we stretched the aerial across the courtyard. The effect was instantaneous. London replied that it could hear us quite well, and Jan immediately sent out a telegram describing the outbreak and progress of the Rising.

When the work was finished, I set out with Jan for Basket Street, hugging the walls of Marshall Street. We were going back to Jan's apartment, where he had a store of provisions. We found several pounds of flour and a small bag of potatoes, which was a real treasure. Jan gazed sadly at his clean and cosy home, as if he knew he would never see it again. On our way back, we ran into Richard in the doorway; he was so covered with mud that I hardly recognised him. We fell into each other's arms, patting each other on the back. It was indeed a happy and unexpected encounter.

'What's happened to Zosia?' Richard enquired anxiously.

'She is very well; we are working as usual and you will be a great help to us,' I answered.

'I have been trying to reach you for two days, since I left Mokotow. I could not bear the thought of being separated from you, so I risked a break through, across the German lines. I did not know where to look for you; but I remembered Jan's address, so I came here on the off chance of finding someone I could talk to.'

He came with us, and a few minutes later he was joyfully greeting Zosia, for whom he had a great fatherly affection. Without wasting any time, he went with Jan to find a more suitable place for the radio station; while I resumed my wanderings in search of the Government Plenipotentiary and the High Command of the Home Army.

That same day we moved to 7, Raven Street, and established ourselves in a house with a huge courtyard. Jan placed the American transmitter by the window, while Richard pulled the aerial to the top of the neighbouring house, which was much higher. He went through his baptism of fire on that occasion; for hardly had he put his head out of the window on the top floor, to fix the aerial, when a burst from a machine-gun hit the window frame, and fragments of plaster fell on our heads. Richard remained cool, crouched under the window, and pulled the aerial in under continuous machine-gun fire. When everything was ready, Jan called London, and with a sigh of relief, scribbled down on the pad: 'We can hear you three plus'.

An Englishman Among the Insurgents

I met him in Raven Street on a fine August afternoon. The bombardment had ceased, and over the broken glass and rubble in the street people were streaming towards the narrow gaps in the barricades. Some of them were trying to cross to 'the other side' of Jerusalem Avenue, others were just taking advantage of the lull to take a walk. From the windows of the corner house, where a detachment of the Home Army had its billets, I could hear community singing and laughter.

'Stefan! How are you old man?' I heard someone shouting.

I turned round and recognised my friend, Captain Tom. He was in the company of a young man of middle height, snub nose and pleasant face, who was leaning on a stick. On his forage cap he had the two stars of lieutenant.

'Let me introduce . . . Lieutenant Ward, an Englishman escaped from a prisoner-of-war camp . . . Mr. Zielinski,' said Tom.

I shook hands with Ward and asked him, in Polish, how he came to be in Warsaw. He answered in tolerable Polish, though with a strong foreign accent, that he was a British airman, and that more than two years before, he had escaped from a prisoner-of-war camp in Poznania and made his way to Warsaw, where, with the help of the underground, he had remained in hiding. He had learned Polish while in the capital. After an exchange of civilities we each went out separate ways.

The next day, German tanks attacked along Pius Street, in the direction of Raven Street. In front of the tanks the Germans drove a crowd of women, who, when they approached an insurgent barricade rushed forward to reach the Polish side, unmindful of the Germans' fire. This unbelievable, but nevertheless true, act of German cruelty shook the population of the sections occupied by the Home Army, and infuriated the insurgents.

It occurred to me that Ward might draft and sign a telegram, which we could send out to London. I feared that if we ourselves reported this incident, so inconceivable to civilised men, the Allies would not believe us, and might think it was exaggerated Polish propaganda; as they had done before, over our telegrams describing events in the Jewish Ghetto. I found Ward and told him what I wanted him to do. He readily agreed, and said that he had seen what the Germans did with his own eyes; for it so happened that he was in the Pius Street sector at the time. We both went to the hospital in Mokotowska, to interview the unfortunate women, whom we found still shaken by what they had gone through. The doctor took Ward round, and he was able to question the women about their experiences before the attack itself. They told him hair-raising details, their voices still quivering.

From the hospital we went to the radio station; all the way there Ward cursed the Germans in his native tongue. At the station he drafted a telegram in English, and signed it with his name and service number. For greater speed Jan sent it out *en clair*.

In the evening of the same day, the BBC broadcast the news, based on Ward's telegram; and the following day the entire British press gave it great prominence. We also received a telegram for Ward, signed by Colonel Perkins, in which the latter requested him to telegraph personal details, such as date of birth, names of parents, his address in England before the war, etc. The British authorities evidently wanted to check Ward's identity. He immediately supplied the required data, and enquired if he might be allowed to send out telegrams on the progress of the Rising; for, as he observed philosophically, authority all the world over was the same, and expected to be asked for permission. Very soon afterwards I received two more telegrams for Ward, one from his parents, who were overjoyed to have had news of their son at last; and the other, which impressed not only Ward, but also Zosia and me, was signed by the British Secretary for Air, Sir Archibald Sinclair, who informed Ward of his pleasure at the knowledge that a British airman was fighting in the Rising in the ranks of the Home Army. The Secretary for Air gave Ward permission to send telegrams and concluded: 'Your telegram strengthened our conviction that Warsaw is still fighting.' We were amazed to read this; but it soon became clear to us, for the Germans had already announced to the world that 'the armed bandits' of Warsaw had been suppressed. The Russians circulated similar statements about the suppression of the fighting in the capital. The Allies gave full credit to Polish sources of information only after they had been endorsed by a Britisher.

I put the radio station at Ward's disposal, and he became a chronicler of the Rising, as it were. He sent out messages on the fighting taking place, on the positions held in the city by the Germans and Poles respectively, on the mass executions in those sections of the city occupied by the Germans, and on the burning of Warsaw; and he demanded insistently that help and arms should be supplied, arms at all costs. At the request of the British Air Force he indicated the exact positions where parachute supplies should be dropped; he went everywhere to see things for himself and to report to London what he had seen. The girls were enciphering his messages for hours on end, and Jan, the only telegraphist we had, never left the transmitter, working for eighteen hours a day. We had to force him to take short periods of rest. Our messages were being repeated by the press and radio of the world as coming from an Englishman, an officer of the Home Army.

We received a telegram for Ward from the London 'Times', offering him a post as their Warsaw correspondent, and asking for a daily message of so many words. Ward gladly undertook this work, and after I had established contact with the Government Plenipotentiary and the High Command of the Home Army, he had interviews with Plenipotentiary Jankowski and General Bor.

Ward was a courageous, easy-going and friendly man. He never had enough sleep; for during the night he accompanied detachments of the Home Army on various expeditions, or went with the commanders to inspect advanced sectors of the front.

One day Ward's visits to the radio station ceased, and when I went in search of him, I found him in a cellar with a wound in his leg. He was lying on a miserable bed, but was receiving most careful medical attention. A bullet had hit him in the leg when he was crossing Pius Street under the cover of a barricade; but fortunately he was not seriously injured, and was able to continue drafting his messages. He co-operated with us until the end of the Rising. After the capitulation, Ward would not report to the Germans, though it would have meant only returning to his status as a prisoner-of-war. We succeeded in evacuating him with the Home Army hospital to a place near Warsaw, and when he had recovered, he joined one of our detachments in the Kielce region. After the Soviet troops had driven the Germans out of that part of the country, he reported to me in Lesna Podkowa. I informed London of his whereabouts, and within a few days we received a telegram for Ward, ordering him to report to the

Soviet authorities, who promised to send him to England through the British Embassy in Moscow.

During a farewell meal in a little semi-private restaurant in Lesna Podkowa, at which were present Ward, Zosia, myself, and the new Commander-in-Chief of the Home Army, General Okulicki, the latter rose from his chair and addressed the Englishman with great solemnity:

'Lieutenant Ward. For your courage and your brave conduct in battle you have been awarded the Cross of Gallantry.'

Ward jumped to his feet, and with equal solemnity thanked the General for the award. However, he was somewhat embarrassed, and we soon found out why. While the General was engaged in conversation with Zosia, Ward leaned towards me and whispered:

'I have already received a Cross of Gallantry from Bor during the Warsaw Rising. . . .'

When in turn Zosia talked to Ward, I told the General that Ward had already been decorated by Bor.

'Damn it!' said the General. 'They never told me that,' and then to Ward, unperturbed:

'Of course, I meant a *bar* to your Cross of Gallantry.'

'Thank you General, for the Bar,' said Ward, chuckling with pleasure; while Zosia, sensing a certain embarrassment suggested:

'Let's drink to John's bar.' Whereupon we all laughed, and in this pleasant mood we bade farewell to the Englishman who had been through such hectic times with us.

At the Polytechnic

We had been working in Wilcza Street for about ten days, when the electric current was suddenly cut off. We did not know whether this was due to a stoppage at the power station, or whether the supply line had been severed by a bomb. While we were frantically searching the city for a new source of electricity, Cesia told us that the Polytechnic had its own small power station, which we could use.

We at once collected all our equipment and belongings, and, loaded like pack mules, we waded through rubble-covered streets, past barricades, and across a trench in Noakow-ski Street, and reached the precincts of the Polytechnic.

Cesia led us straight to the Polytechnic workshops, where we had to arrange for the supply of electricity. The Polytechnic was an advanced bastion and under enemy fire from three sides. We wound our way through the vaults, and rejoiced at the sight of what was going on there. All the workshops were busy producing equipment for the insurgents. We received a friendly welcome from the professor, a small, stooping gentleman, who looked at us with great sympathy over his spectacles. Together with his assistants, he was responsible for the production of radio equipment for the Home Army. Everything was being done openly now. Zosia and I exchanged looks of self-commiseration. For nearly a year we had been hiding in the Polytechnic, and we had not known that close at hand were such splendid installations. Our mutual condolences were interrupted by a young man who had been observing our little group for some time.

'I know you well by sight,' he said. 'You were lodging with the widow of Professor Broniewski.'

'That's right. And we never even suspected that you people here were working in the same business as us.'

'That's true. We produced many transmitters for the Home Army here.'

'What a pity I didn't know that before. We were in such dire need of a proper workshop.'

Here I told him of all our troubles, and Joey's, and the tall engineer, whom I knew as Roman, was genuinely sorry for us.

'Had we met earlier,' he said, 'Joey could have worked here with us in relative safety. The Germans occasionally took a look round here, but in this jumble of instruments and laboratory equipment they weren't able to make out what was what.'

With the help of the radio engineer, Roman, the transmitter was soon assembled, and Jan hard at work sending out our daily telegrams; while we rested and were treated to mugs of cereal by the young H.A. women auxiliaries, who were in charge of the kitchen in the vaults of the building. The grounds of the Polytechnic had many lawns, and in the warm sunshine we pretended to be on a picnic. Our sixty-year-old 'youngster', Richard, fancied some tomatoes, and set out for the kitchen garden; but instead of tomatoes he brought back a bullet hole in his jacket. Roman visited us several times a day and helped as much as he could. He and Richard became great friends. And though the Polytechnic was surrounded by the Germans on three sides, all was quiet for the time being; except that one had to watch out for an occasional bullet when crossing from one building to another.

We could not stop Richard in his restless activities, and he was always on the look-out for something new. He would talk to anyone he met, and as his age gave him a certain prestige, he got by somehow. On one occasion we visited a single-storey building opposite the hospital in August the Sixth Street, the further side of which was held by the Germans. When we went in, a young man with the badges of a lieutenant rose from his couch. Richard addressed him rather abruptly:

'Who are you?'

The young lieutenant looked at him for a long while in a not too friendly manner, but answered courteously:

'Have it your way. I am in command of this sector.'

'But what do you do in civilian life?'

'I am a teacher of biology.'

'That's no good then. We're sorry to have disturbed you. We're looking for a convenient place for a radio station; but you don't know anything about radio.'

'That's all right. But who are you?' queried the lieutenant, a little worked up by now.

'I? I am an engineer.'

'Then you know nothing about biology.'

'Of course not. But go on resting; we've got to find a place for our radio station.'

The lieutenant shrugged his shoulders, apparently convinced that he was talking to an old eccentric, and stretched himself out on the couch again.

Some time afterwards I was informed that the Government Plenipotentiary had crossed from the Old City to the Central Borough, and that he wanted to see me. We at once packed our belongings, and left the Polytechnic. Roman promised to visit us occasionally.

Crossing over to the Central Borough

Loaded with equipment, we set off in Indian file in the direction of Marshall Street. It was already getting dark when we plunged, carrying little torches, into a labyrinth of vaults. Still in single file, we shuffled half-bent along the passages. It was stiflingly hot and dark, and only here and there, in patches of dim candle-light, could one see men and women preparing for another night in the vaults. Every now and then we emerged into a courtyard, in which the sentries, lurking in the dark, enquired where we were going, and directed us to the right passage. Approaching Jerusalem Avenue we found the vaults crowded with a long queue of people loaded with bundles, awaiting their turn to cross. The exits from the vaults on either side of Jerusalem Avenue were protected by barricades; the roadway itself was open to German machine-guns and tanks which kept up a steady fire from the Main Station and from an emplacement in the Bank of National Economy. I had a pass which entitled me to priority in crossing. I showed it to the sentries, and we squeezed through the crowd, who at the words 'gangway for the radio station' readily made room for us. At last we arrived in front of a closed door. The corridor was dimly lit by electricity supplied from batteries, and the emaciated and tired faces of the waiting men and women seemed in that light tense and taut. The heat was unbearable. I touched the wall and found it was burning hot.

'Why is this?' I asked the sentry.

'The house over our heads is on fire,' he answered.

The door suddenly opened, and a man wearing an armband and a military cap shouted:

'The next five, quickly!'

We rushed forward, the door behind us slammed, and we found ourselves in a pitch-dark cellar, in which one could see the faint outline of an opening in the wall: this was the passage into Jerusalem Avenue, hacked through the brickwork.

The man in charge, on whose judgement scores of people depended for their lives, instructed us:

'Keep all your bags ready. Stand one behind the other close to the opening. At the command "three" run as fast as you can to the other side.'

We took up our positions. I was in front, Zosia next, and then Jan, with Richard bringing up the rear. In the street three grenades exploded one after the other. The traffic controller raised his hand:

'One!' he shouted, and a long burst from a machine-gun spattered the roadway.

'Two!' he shouted; and there was a two second silence, followed by two short bursts from the machine-gun.

'Three!' And I leapt from the passage, followed by the others. I ran in long leaps, with the rucksack on my back swinging from one side to the other; until I sprawled on the ground within the safety of the opposite barricade, gasping for breath. Beside me I could hear Zosia breathing heavily, and then Richard rushed in and dropped down next to Jan. In a second we could hear behind us the explosions of three grenades, and then a long burst from a machine-gun, kicking up a cloud of dust in the roadway.

In the darkness a voice close to me commanded:

'Free the passage! Quick!' And while we were entering the doorway of a burnt-out house, we could see the leaping shadows of the next five, followed by the explosions of the grenades and a long burst of machine-gun fire.

We spent the night with friends, and in the morning we separated. I set out in search of Major Frank, whose office was in the Post Office Savings Bank; the others went in search of premises for the radio station. While I was with Major Frank, a soldier of the Home Army rushed in, gasping:

'The H.A. gendarmerie has arrested your wife and a man named Jan in Szczygla Street. They passed me as they were being taken to the station and your wife asked me to find you here and tell you what's happened!'

At first, both Frank and I burst out laughing; but we remembered that the gendarmes had the reputation of not wasting their time, and that we had to move quickly. Fortunately, we found the Chief of Staff of General Monter, who commanded the operations in Warsaw, and within a few minutes I had an order signed by him for the release of our team, and a permit to operate the radio station. At the gendarmerie station I met a courteous officer, who read the order, introduced himself to me, and said:

'They have already been released. I telephoned to Monter and he explained everything. I am very sorry this happened, but you will realise that I cannot blame my men for hauling down from a roof people who were putting up an aerial and could not produce a permit.'

Though I recognised the justice of this, and made an attempt at courtesy, I really disliked the gendarmes. On my way back I saw an unusual sight. Two gendarmes were carving up a huge pig, while a number of their colleagues were looking on, their mouths watering in anticipation. I suddenly felt hungry and could not help envying them. The yellow-necks never lack anything, I thought. But where could they have purloined a pig?

A New Appointment

I found Plenipotentiary Jankowski much thinner than before and weary from strain. I asked him how he had fared in the Old City, and in his quiet manner he described a few incidents of hair-raising horror. A sea of fire and bombs had swallowed up a square kilometre of ancient, dry-rotted buildings, packed with tens of thousands of people. Now I knew the nature of that gigantic pall of smoke which had been hanging over the Old City for weeks. The Government Plenipotentiary escaped that inferno by a miracle and reached the Central Borough through the sewers. I looked at him with compassion and admiration. I could imagine that sixty-year-old man wading up to his neck in the odious, dense, fetid mud, in a sewer without air, full of the groans and cries of men and women drowning in the liquid filth.

I asked him what he thought of Soviet help, and he replied concisely:

'They are monstrous felons.'

The Plenipotentiary then told me why he had summoned me.

'Baginski has resigned his office as Director of the Department of the Interior on becoming a member of the Council of National Unity. I should like you to take over from him. It will be hard and responsible work, for you will have to do everything humanly possible to lighten the lot of the population. Problems of Civil Resistance are less urgent now and you can deal with both offices.' After a few supplementary questions had been clarified, I accepted the new appointment and got to work at once.

In the first place, I had a talk with the underground President of the City of Warsaw, Sowa, an old and experienced city official; I confirmed that the administration of the city and the responsibility for its proper functioning would remain in his hands, and that I should content myself with the part of counsellor and controller. Sowa accepted this clear definition of our respective authority with considerable satisfaction, but requested me to co-operate with him in his daily tasks. We agreed to hold regular meetings every two or three days with the delegates of all the boroughs, at which current questions and problems could be settled. These meetings continued till the end of the Rising, except that, unfortunately, the boroughs of Zoliborz and Mokotow were not able to send delegates, as they were cut off from the Central Borough. Each delegate reported on the needs of his borough, and described the situation in his precinct, which was invariably difficult, and as the struggle went on became tragic indeed. We often held our meetings under artillery fire and aerial bombardment, which some stood well, others rather badly. On one occasion we met in the building of the publishers, Gebethner and Wolff in Concord Street, just as an air raid was taking place on Marshall Street, only about a hundred yards away. Our building was shaken by the explosions, and the blasts smashed in the window panes. I did not want to go down into the cellars before Sowa arrived, because we might have missed the delegates who were still to come. We stood in small groups in the four corners of the room, chatting to while away the time. But one of the men present could not stand still, and kept pacing the room nervously. Someone asked me my views on the war situation; so, in order to forget the dangers lurking everywhere, and while the bombs crashed down and Marshall Street was already in flames, I entered into a long exposition to prove that the Germans would presently have their flanks turned by the Soviet armies in the North and South, and would have to abandon Warsaw and run. At that moment the man who was nervously pacing the room, and who had heard only the last words, rushed at me and shouted angrily:

'It's all very well for you to say "run"! But where can we run to? Tell us where to run to!' Though none of us was in the mood for merriment, we all shook with laughter. The man looked at us as if we were mad, tapped his head with one finger, and resumed his interrupted walk.

At last Sowa arrived, the raiders passed, and we opened our deliberations, amidst the crashing of the houses burning in Marshall Street and the shouting of the men and women trying frantically to rescue their belongings.

The Agues of Insurgent Warsaw

The insurgent municipal administration, with President Sowa at its head, was divided into sections comprising the territories occupied by the Home Army, i.e., Mokotow, Zoliborz, The Riverside, and the Central Borough, each with its own office. Lower down in the organisation came commanders of blocks, and finally commanders of individual houses, aided by house committees. All these authorities were in daily contact with each other and also with the authorities of the Home Army, as the functions of civic and military authorities frequently overlapped. The City was in the fighting line, it *was* the front; and General Monter was as much interested in feeding the population as the President of the City and I were interested in the military operations that were being carried out in one part of Warsaw or another. The Government Plenipotentiary himself and General Bor were also drawn into these matters, as was the chairman of the Council of National Unity, Casimir Puzak, who was always unruffled, self-possessed and unafraid.

The problem of provisioning overshadowed all others. The Germans had left a number of food dumps in various sections of the city held by the Home Army. Considerable consumers' co-operative stores were also found, and the population in general had their individual food stocks; but all this meant very little in view of the urgent needs. It was necessary, in the first instance, to safeguard supplies of food for the Home Army and the hospitals. But one must remember that when the Rising broke out, at 5 p.m. on August 1, tens of thousands of men and women were caught away from home. They sheltered in the houses nearest to them when the fighting began. Those whose homes were in the German-occupied sections had to remain in their temporary shelters throughout the entire period of the Rising, and had to be supplied with food from communal kitchens established in each house. The sacrifices of the population were extraordinary; the communal kitchens were provisioned from the stock of food available in each house. This was supplemented from public kitchens and from German and co-operative stores, especially in respect of coffee, sugar, wheat and barley.

Water supply presented a most difficult problem. The municipal waterworks were held by the Germans, who cut the water off; so that it was necessary to dig wells in the courtyards of the houses. Research and enquiries were made, and to begin with, old disused wells were dug up which had been abandoned many years before and filled in. This work of sinking wells was carried out mostly by German soldiers captured by the Home Army. Around these wells there shuffled all day long queues of men and women, running into hundreds, exposed to bombing from German planes and to bombardment by artillery. Many a man and woman were killed while waiting for water, but the queues went on. The wells were guarded by sentries, and a priority was observed, with the hospitals and the Home Army at the head of the queue. A barter trade in water developed, and as money had no value during the Rising, it was replaced by cigarettes and articles of food.

On one occasion I had a talk with German prisoners digging up a well in Raven Street. When I addressed them in

German, they stood to attention. I enquired about the circumstances of their capture. They answered obsequiously that they had been seized by young boys, who had charged like mad. Noticing an airman among the infantry men, I asked him how he came to be there. His story was simple:

'I was walking along the street at five o'clock in the afternoon, when I was hit on the head by something hard; and when I regained consciousness I found myself in this courtyard.'

One of the Germans asked permission to put a question to me. I nodded and he said:

'What will happen to us?'

'When the Soviet army arrives, you will either remain in captivity with us, or you will be taken over by the Soviets.'

'Shall we not be shot?'

They all looked at me with anxious eyes.

'No. If you were going to be shot, you would have been dead long ago.'

That seemed to reassure them, for they thanked me with great joy, clicking their heels.

Later, I often saw the oldest of the German prisoners digging to deepen a temporary latrine. I asked him whether he had much work to do. He straightened his back, leaned on the shovel, and pointing with a dramatic gesture to the full latrine, groaned:

'They have nothing to eat, yet this is always full! I dig and dig and there is never an end to it. . . .'

The supply of electricity continued for the relatively long period of several weeks, thanks to the heroic efforts of the employees of the Riverside Power Station. The Power Station not only supplied current to those sections of the city occupied by the Home Army, but also served as a bastion in the defence of the Riverside, which was under constant fire. Teams from the Power Station worked day and night to repair cables torn by bombs and grenades, and many of the workers were killed. Finally, after heavy bombardments, the Power Station ceased to function, and soon afterwards the Station and the entire Riverside were captured by the Germans. We were reduced to accumulators, which were re-charged in the insurgent factories by means of automobile engines. Light from these batteries was reserved for surgical operations in the hospitals, for the more important institutions, and such passages as the underground tunnel beneath Jerusalem Avenue, which was dug towards the end of the Rising.

The state of Warsaw from the sanitary point of view was surprisingly good. There was no outbreak of any serious epidemic, in spite of the hot summer, and the lack of water and soap; in spite of the open latrines dug in the roadways, and the cemeteries in the courtyards, with their shallow graves, and the thousands of decomposing corpses in the ruins of destroyed houses. The doctors running our health service were pleased, for they had anticipated the worst. The insurgent health service had several hundred doctors and a dozen or so hospitals, set up in the cellars. After every air raid or artillery bombardment, long lines of wounded borne on stretchers moved slowly over the rubble. Operations never stopped day and night, the surgeons working in shifts.

The organisation of fire-fighting was of primary importance. Each house organised a day and night fire watch and a supply of sandbags, pickaxes and hooks. Wherever a fire broke out, everyone went into action; and frequently the fires had to be fought under continued air raids or artillery bombardment. Hundreds of men and women lost their lives in this way, among them Judge Mateja, director of the underground Welfare Department, and the barrister Ignacy Grabski, who were shot by a German machine-gun while they were fighting a roof fire. The people of Warsaw showed extraordinary courage and contempt for death in fighting the fires, and during the first half of the Rising most of them were successfully dealt with. Later, when it became clear that the Rising had been left to its fate, people became resigned to the destruction, and the number of unfought fires increased.

The state of public security in the city was good, thanks to spontaneously maintained general discipline. Property was respected, and only abandoned or ruined houses were carefully searched, primarily for food. Cases of illegal requisitions were on the whole rare.

During one of the sessions of the municipal administration,

we resolved to send telegrams to the Mayors of New York, London, and Moscow, appealing for help for the perishing Capital. Mayor La Guardia replied at once, followed by the Lord Mayor of London; but nothing was heard from Moscow. Naturally, the replies expressed sympathy and admiration, but that was all we received.

A Meeting with Generals Bor and Gregory

Accompanied by Zosia, who wanted to visit her friends among the Women's Auxiliary Services, I called at the Post Office Savings Bank building, where the High Command of the Home Army had its headquarters. Walking along Bright Street in the direction of St. Cross Street, we were stopped by a friend who was taking advantage of the lull in the bombardment to come out on to his balcony for a breath of fresh air. Looking up, we enquired about mutual friends and received sorrowful replies; this one was killed, another was buried under debris, yet another was wounded. After two hours we passed the same spot on our way back. Where the house had been there remained only smoking debris, and not a trace of our friend.

In the Savings Bank building we had to pass a large number of sentries, to whom we had to explain our business; but finally the doors of the stronghold opened and we were ushered into a large marble hall, from where we were to be taken by an H.A. orderly, whom we happened to know, down to the nethermost vault. It was rather dark, but I noticed a candle flickering in one corner. By its dim light I could see an old woman crouching on the floor, and gazing at the flame with unearthly eyes. There was something about the scene that made me lower my voice.

'Who is that woman?' I asked my H.A. guide.

'Oh, it's an unusual story. That woman is a German from the Reich, who came here to visit her son, an SS man serving in Warsaw, and was caught by the outbreak of the Rising. The SS man was captured by our men and that woman, in search of her son, by some miracle crossed the fighting line and managed to get in here.'

'Why here? And what of her son?'

'Our military court is trying him right now in the next room.'

I had no need to ask further questions. Soldiers of the German army were being treated strictly in accordance with international law, but not so captured SS men. Their units had murdered the population in Wola, and in the Old City they had killed all the wounded in the hospital, together with the nurses and doctors. SS men and gendarmes were as a rule sentenced to death. It was enough to find out in which unit they had served to know what massacres they had taken part in. Paradoxically, however, the majority of prisoners taken by the Home Army were killed by German bombs. German airmen, noticing considerable groups of men in some courtyards, bombed them eagerly, thinking they were bombing units of the Home Army.

We made our way down into the vaults. Through an open door leading from the stairs one could see a large hall with hundreds of wounded lying on improvised beds. There was a frightful stench. Everywhere the white bandages, bed-sheets and white hospital overalls were stained with blood. On the beds, packed tight together, were young boys; I could see their faces, some pale, some bloodshot, some calm, others contorted with pain. There was much shuffling in the entrance hall, where the wounded were being brought in and the dead carried out in a procession of death.

At the lowest level were more sentries, and some familiar faces. Zosia remained here with her girl friends; while I went on, and was soon shaking hands with General Bor and General Gregory, glad to see them in good shape. General Bor looked his old self, except that he was much thinner; Gregory, however, seemed to be rejuvenated and full of energy. We discussed innumerable topics, in which both military and administrative questions were involved.

I complained about the trouble I had had in penetrating to their headquarters, and Bor promised to give me a document which would open all doors to me. Before I left the vault, I received the identity card of a lieutenant of the gendarmerie, which subsequently saved me a lot of trouble.

I also visited the chairman of the Council of National Unity, who had taken shelter in the adjacent vault. Puzak too seemed unchanged, with the same drooping moustache, thick lenses and undisturbed composure. He was a man of iron. We greeted each other with great cordiality. He too had passed through the inferno of the Old City. As we talked, I gradually succumbed to a disturbing influence in the shape of three small cans of stewed beef. I had not tasted such food since the beginning of the Rising, so I resolved to try my telepathic powers on Puzak. Hypnotising him with my eyes, I kept repeating to myself, 'Give me one can, give me one can. . . .' It worked; but without full effect, for before I left him, Puzak apologised for his apparent lack of hospitality.

'I should have liked to offer you some canned meat, but there is nothing here to cook it on, and it would be dangerous to eat it uncooked.' I nodded without enthusiasm and took my leave. This was the first and last time I set eyes on a can of meat during the entire period of the Rising.

By now we were all perpetually hungry, hunting for food and seizing every opportunity for putting something into our stomachs. As a result, food became a standing subject of conversation, and even now I have vivid memories of some unexpected windfalls. I remember, for instance, the gift of three herrings from a friendly fishmonger; and a quantity of fish oil, which was served out by the spoonful every morning for a week by an actor friend of the Home Army theatre unit, which continued to perform during the Rising. I also remember with pleasure my meetings with Papa R., a pharmacist.

One morning, after a night's labour, I dropped in at a billet to get my spoonful of fish oil. I found in the room a mummy of an old man, neatly dressed in an old-fashioned morning coat. The old man held a bottle in his hand and dazzled me with his proposal.

'Sir, will you have a glass with me?'

'What? Now, at eight in the morning?'

'What's the difference? Has the doctor told you not to drink in the morning, but wait till the afternoon?'

At that my actor friend came in.

'Have a glass, Stefan,' he said, 'and for a bite you will get a spoonful of fish oil.'

'And some bread crust,' added the old man. 'I've got a bag of bread crust which I've saved up, as I haven't any teeth and cannot eat them. Now you can have some. . . .' We sat down and had a round consisting of a glass of vodka, a spoonful of fish oil and a piece of bread crust. . . .

Papa R., as everyone called him, was a charming and utterly unruffled old man. He had considerable funds in cash, and in between air raids he would roam the city in search of liquor; and he always succeeded in hauling some in. He ate next to nothing and disliked intensely imbibing without company. So he used to startle people with offers of a drink at the most unexpected hours and in the most extraordinary situations.

After the Rising I met him in Milanowek. It was a real pleasure to hear a familiar voice behind me saying:

'Ah, dear Mr. Stefan! Let's have one at the corner.'

I also remember September 3, on which day I received an urgent summons to meet the Government Plenipotentiary in the Bank of the Co-operative Union in Bright Street. I left at once, and on my way was caught by an air raid. As the summons was urgent, I sprinted from door to door through scenes of a kind that can never be erased from one's memory. Amidst the howl and roar of engines, explosions shook the air, and houses collapsed, throwing up clouds of dust, smoke and flames. Human beings were lifted high into the air, like feathers, and close by me fell the naked body of a young boy, with his arms and legs torn off. Covered with a layer of dust from head to foot, I reached the Bank, where, in the shelter of a deep vault, normal insurgent administrative business was being transacted, I went up to the Government Plenipotentiary and handed him the summons I had received. He looked at me with compassionate eyes.

'Thank you very much, but there must be a misunderstanding somewhere on the part of the secretariat; for I did not summon you at all. But please be seated and let us have a chat.'

Return to Raven Street

We had been working in Blackbird Street for some time, in the more than modest apartment of a recluse, who would have done anything for us; he kept Jan company from early morning till late at night. But the situation was becoming desperate. There were hourly air raids, and the enemy's artillery was bombarding the city day and night. It was difficult to go out into the streets; for bricks were flying about, and the dust and acrid fumes in the air blinded one's eyes. Houses were collapsing one after another. The cellar of the house in which we were billeted, to which we used to descend for shelter during air raids, was dimly lit by a candle, and there a demented woman, who spouted hysterically snatches from the Litany, made us desperate with her shouting.

I was also worried about Zosia. The one and only time she had sat down to a game of bridge, blast from a bomb had flung her against a wall and left her painfully bruised.

I felt instinctively that the Riverside would suffer the same fate as the Old City, so when the Government Plenipotentiary decided to move to the Central Borough, I assembled my team of four, and told them we should be going back to our old haunt. On September 5, we moved to the other side, without hindrance but under most difficult conditions. There was by now only one way left to get from the Riverside to the Central Borough, across Pieracki Street, which was under constant shell fire. When we reached it, we stumbled over a number of corpses, those of people who had been killed while crossing. We moved on in a sea of flames extending as far as the eye could reach. Warecka Street, Bright Street, Sienkiewicz, Moniuszko, and part of Hospital Street were burning. Flaming timbers were flying through the air, and red-hot pieces of roofing were raining down. Covered with soot and dust, we at last reached the crossing and passed to the other side of the Avenue, where it was still relatively quiet.

No sooner had we begun to operate in Raven Street, when the Germans started to bombard the station. Fortunately, Jan was working in a little house shielded by the tall buildings around it, and thus protected from direct hits. But within a few days all the windows and doors had been blown in. We had no choice but to stick it out where we were.

We were visited there, in what was becoming a heap of rubble, by Major Frank, who invited us to move, with the station, to his house in Basket Street. He was an incorrigible optimist by nature, and assured us that the house in Basket Street was safe. I knew it well, for I had visited him there many a time, and I promised to come next day to examine its suitability for radio work.

The following day I set out with Zosia. We arrived in Basket Street, but somehow we could not find the place; until we noticed Frank climbing over mounds of rubble to meet us.

'How are you Frank?' I said. 'We are just on our way to your place, to see what the house is like, but we can't find it.'

'You're a bit late,' he said, slightly embarrassed. 'The house is gone, and I myself am looking for a roof over my head.' In the outcome, we offered hospitality to Frank, who was not fated to be our host.

At about that time we had an unexpected visit from Roman, the engineer from the Polytechnic. We welcomed him with great joy, but noticed that he was looking rather haggard. The news he brought was far from cheerful.

'The Polytechnic has been stormed by the Germans. You were lucky to leave it just in time. They took us by surprise, and I only succeeded at the last moment in escaping through an underground passage. I am without a job now and if you want me, I am free to join you.' We were glad to have him with our team, and Richard found in him not only an able assistant but a confidant and friend, whom he engaged in never-ending talks.

We had no current from the grid for a long time now, and the radio station was operating on batteries, which were being recharged by an automobile engine in the Home Army workshop. Sabotage was already at work, and one evening the Pomeranian who was in charge of the workshop warned me:

'Last night someone poured sugar into the petrol tank of the automobile.'

The fire directed against our station in Raven Street intensified from day to day, and Jan had to work under conditions of increasing danger. So once more we had to look for a new hide-out, and a soldier of the Home Army, Janusz Kurowski, at present living in the United States, helped us to find one in the former Bulgarian Embassy in Ujazdow Avenue, right in the front line. The company commander readily agreed that we might remain with him, and assured us that the sector was quiet. So we installed our transmitter, and Jan resumed his work. Next morning, however, things began to happen, and the hitherto quiet sector came until violent artillery fire. We knew why this was so, but we kept our knowledge to ourselves. It was obvious that German radio interception had located our position, but the bombardment caused us little harm, and Jan, well protected, continued to send out messages as usual.

It was there that we received telegrams from London informing us that American planes would drop supplies by parachute. This had nerve-racking consequences for us. I received two identical telegrams addressed to the Government Plenipotentiary:

'To-day American planes took off with supplies for Warsaw. Anticipated fly past fourteen hours your time.'

This was, of course, a secret message, but owing to someone's indiscretion the news spread through beleaguered Warsaw like wildfire. At fourteen hours everybody was going about with upturned heads; but there was no sign of the planes. In the afternoon I received a telegram which made me gnash my teeth as I read it.

'The planes had to turn back owing to bad atmospheric conditions.'

At last, on September 18, on a fine sunny day, an unfamiliar, deep and powerful hum of engines reached the tortured city. Before the planes could be even seen, German anti-aircraft batteries put up a terrific barrage. Over burning Warsaw, over the heads of its population, crying with emotion and raising their arms to heaven, high up—unfortunately too high up—soared the gigantic, shining, silvery planes, and from them hundreds of multi-coloured parachutes floated down . . . most of them on the other side of the insurgent lines. Jan shook my hands with tears in his eyes. I seized the code book, and within minutes Jan was telegraphing to London: 'At this very moment American planes are dropping supplies by parachute.' He switched over, and with a happy smile scribbled on the pad: 'OK, OK. Many thanks.' Then he looked at me greatly pleased.

'We have established a new speed record to-day. The drops are still going on, and yet London has already confirmed receipt of the news about it.'

The Death of Richard

Units of the Home Army attacked the Pasta Building, and I observed the action at close quarters while helping to assemble a petrol pump, one of the most frightful weapons in the hands of the insurgents. After the enemy's position had been drenched with petrol, a hand grenade was tossed over, and everything was burnt to a cinder. The besieged Germans retaliated by discharging 'braying cows', which were aimed at the surrounding houses. Time and again one heard the clatter as they were launched, and everyone scurried to find shelter before the 'cow' exploded.

It was there that Richard found me, at a moment when I had just heard the characteristic sound, like a rusty spring in a gigantic clock. As soon as the noise stopped, I grabbed Richard by the arm, and jumped through the door of the garage standing close by. There was a flash, an explosion, the smell of benzol, and the garage collapsed, together with the doorway through which we had just passed. We lay crouching in a corner, while everything around us blazed. The thought flashed through my mind that we should be burned alive. Further down, I noticed a ray of light. I pulled Richard, who was choking with smoke, towards it, and in two leaps we were through a hole and in the courtyard of the adjoining building; while the garage behind us was burning like a torch. We were still holding each other by the hand and trembling, when people emerged from the vaults and gathered round us. They helped us to beat the dust off our clothes, and congratulated us.

'You were lucky we'd made a hole in the garage wall. Otherwise you would have been roasted alive!'

Poor Richard did not enjoy this fortunate escape for long. It was Roman who, covered with dust from head to foot, rushed unexpectedly into the station hide-out, shouting:

'Richard has been gravely wounded by the explosion of a "cow". He is in the Mokotow hospital.'

Together with Zosia I rushed to the hospital at once. Zosia carried a well provided first-aid bag, which she always kept by her. In Mokotow Street we were stopped by cries of 'Halt! Halt!' and two gendarmes of the Home Army confronted us threateningly.

'Follow us to the doorway!'

'But look here,' I pleaded, 'we are in a hurry. A gravely wounded man is waiting.'

'No excuses! You must be searched.'

'Is that so? Show me your identity cards!'

They produced the cards and showed them to me condescendingly; at which, with my blood already roused, I produced the identity card I had received from the High Command.

'Well, you see, there will be no search and no spoils. But what right have you to stop ordinary passers-by?'

'Why don't you wear the badges of your rank?'

But we were in a hurry to get to Richard and had no time to waste arguing. It was obvious that discipline was cracking; I was sure the two gendarmes were after Zosia's bag, in which, however, they would have found nothing of any value to them.

We arrived at the vaults in Mokotow Street. The corridors were dimly lit by electricity from batteries. In the heat and stench the wounded were lying by the walls groaning, with their minds wandering deliriously. Casualties were being brought in continuously. We scanned the faces of the wounded, but could not find Richard anywhere; until a nurse we knew led us to the operating theatre, and there he was lying on the floor. I knelt down by his side and looked at his pale face and his wide open eyes. He took my hand and held it. He was fully conscious and moved his lips. I had to bring my ear right down to his mouth to hear what he wanted to say.

'My shoulder blade is smashed, and they want to amputate

my arm. Tell the surgeon not to do it, because my arm is sound. Look . . . I can move my fingers. . . .' I could see he was able to move his fingers, so leaving Zosia by his side, stroking his head gently and whispering words of comfort to him, I looked about for the surgeon.

The operating theatre was a dimly-lit vault without floorboards. In a pool of blood stood two large wooden tables, on which the surgeons operated. Two men in blood-stained aprons were manipulating the instruments, and the nurses held in their hands headlights which were almost as dim as ordinary bulbs. I asked one of the nurses who would be operating on Richard. She sent me to a man in a white apron sleeping in a hammock.

'Wake him up, for we've nearly finished here.'

I shook the doctor by the arm; he got up at once, and I told him what Richard wanted. He had already examined him and would not even listen to what I was saying.

'Look here,' he said, 'it's a waste of time. I must not only amputate his arm, but remove the entire shoulder blade as well, for it is completely crushed. He's got the best part of half a brick there. He is an old man and there is very little chance that he will survive. Start taking his clothes off.'

The doctor pointed to a young boy on a stretcher, who was talking quietly with two Home Army soldiers who were bending over him.

'That's a tragic case. His liver has been torn to shreds, but he is fully conscious; and that's why they brought him here, to let him think he's going to be operated upon. In ten or fifteen minutes he'll be in a coma, and die.'

I went back to Richard, and without telling him anything, I took off his torn jacket and the other parts of his clothing. He was laid on the table, and all the time he held my hand with his sound one and looked into my eyes. I did not look away, but kept on repeating, 'It will be all right, it will be all right. . . .' The surgeon would not let me stay.

'You can't do anything here. Come back in the evening to find out how he is.'

Zosia and Roman were waiting in the corridor, talking to a nurse we knew. I offered her a cigarette—she took several—

and begged her to look after Richard. I then remembered her husband, and before leaving asked her, 'How's Andrew?' She answered, with a stony calm, looking straight into my eyes:

'He was killed in the attack on the Gestapo headquarters in Szucha Avenue. I am pregnant. The child will have no father.' And she withdrew into the vault.

That same evening we visited Richard. He was lying at the end of the corridor, unconscious and with a high temperature; and so he remained the following day. In the morning of the third day it was all over. The nurse again accepted a few cigarettes and advised us to arrange for his interment without delay, otherwise he would be buried in a common grave. He had died during the night and his body was in the morgue.

Richard's Funeral

Together with Jan I dug a pit in the little garden of a house in Mokotow Street, where there were already a great many graves, at least three hundred, I thought. I was surprised to notice one grave with a Soviet star over it. Here was buried a Soviet lieutenant of a tank regiment, a prisoner-of-war captured by the Germans, who had joined the Home Army. Poor fellow! He had failed to sense what Stalin's policy was towards the Rising, and had given his life for a cause he regarded as worth dying for.

We found the digging heavy going; for the ground was hard, the sun was oppressive, and we ourselves were already weakened by hunger. Every few minutes we could hear a dull hum and a powerful explosion. The Germans were bombarding Warsaw with a gigantic railway gun. We pulled off our shirts and dug on to the depth required by the overseer of the cemetery. We heard another dull hum, but this time coming in our direction. We crouched down in the grave, just before we were struck by the blast from a powerful explosion close by; while something flew over our heads, hitting the wall of a nearby house. Jan went to see what it was.

'You ought to see this splinter. It's nearly a yard long. If we hadn't ducked in the grave, it would have torn us in half, and the grave would have been ours for keeps.'

We buried Richard decently, in a wooden coffin. The carpenters received a pint of vodka and a hundred cigarettes. Zosia traded a watch for the vodka and I got the cigarettes—which were worth their weight in gold—for nothing, from one of the women commanders of the Grey Ranks. Richard's body was in the morgue, among corpses terribly burned by petrol bombs. He was as yellow as wax and desperately thin. We wrapped his naked body in a sheet, and placed it in the wooden box. A priest came to say a prayer for the dead. I stood by his side and regarded the haggard faces and the emaciated bodies of my team-mates. They were all terribly thin. We had a last look at Richard, and nailed down the lid. The priest led the way. Carrying the coffin on our shoulders, we stumbled through mounds of bricks and rubble, joining up with other groups to make one funeral procession. In the opposite direction came another procession, carrying to the hospital those wounded in the latest air raid. We laid Richard to eternal rest among several soldiers of the Home Army. Before departing, I placed on the grave a cross with the inscription:

'Engineer Richard Pojawski, soldier of the Home Army, gave his life for his country on September 17, 1944.'

The Soviets and the Rising

The Government Plenipotentiary had his new headquarters in the Central Borough-South, at first in Mokotow Street, and later in Basket Street. Members of the Council of National Unity were also gathered there; and when, on September 4, the Post Office Savings Bank was destroyed by bombs—the Chief of Staff, General Gregory, was gravely injured there—the High Command, too, moved into Central Borough-South, occupying the newly conquered Pasta Building in Pius Street. In this way all the authorities of the underground came together, except for the headquarters of General Monter, who remained in the Palladium Cinema in Golden Street. I visited him there on one occasion, and was pleasantly surprised to set eyes on a man, not in an ill-fitting civilian suit, but in the smart field uniform of a general. From now on I took part in all the meetings of the Council of National Unity, attended as a rule by the Government Plenipotentiary and General Bor. At each session I reported on the problems of insurgent administration. The sessions took place every few days, and though we were all depressed, everyone was calm and unconcerned about the ever-present dangers. Everybody looked haggard and shabby, but inspired with unshakable determination. Our discussions were dominated by the problem of the continuation of the Rising and Soviet inactivity. The Government Plenipotentiary was making plans for the future, in which he reserved a special function for me. On one occasion he took me aside, and in strict secrecy, told me that in his opinion, though he did not believe the Soviets would relieve the Rising, it would not be politic to exclude such a possibility altogether, considering the tremendous pressure which the Western Allies were exerting on Stalin. Against such an eventuality the Plenipotentiary was preparing to remain on the Soviet side, together with the Ministers, as his and their names had already been made known by the Government in London. He wanted me and some of his staff to withdraw to the West, and, as his deputy, direct the underground on such territories of Poland as might remain under German occupation. At that time the Plenipotentiary did not anticipate that the Germans would be retreating in panic, but reckoned with the possibility that the occupation of the Western territories might continue for some time. He requested me to prepare and to present to the Council of National Unity a suitable scheme. This I did, and the Council approved the plan, except that the Plenipotentiary insisted that my name should remain secret. These plans, however, were not realised, because the Soviets never came to our rescue.

Ever since the outbreak of the Rising, the people of Warsaw had been living by listening, listening to hear the Soviet guns. When these ceased firing and a dead silence ensued, our people hoped that this was due only to some momentary difficulties, and went on listening. They all remembered the July broadcasts of the Soviet 'Kosciuszko' station, appealing to the population of Warsaw to rise. Moreover, the participation in the fighting of platoons of the Communist People's

Army and of the semi-Communist Polish People's Army indicated that the Communists had taken a positive attitude towards the Rising. During the initial period it never even occurred to anyone that the Soviets might deliberately stop their offensive, so as to enable the Germans to destroy the City of Warsaw. As far as the military forces of the People's Army were concerned, they amounted to next to nothing. As I was interested to find out the truth, I requested one of the officers of General Monter's staff to supply the relevant data. The information I received was convincing.

'The People's Army sends in requests for food and other supplies for about three hundred men. As is generally known, for the purpose of receiving provisions each unit reports a larger number of effectives so as to have a surplus, and we estimate their actual effectives at 200 to 250 men.'

As far as the Polish People's Army was concerned, its headquarters were located for some time in a house in Marshall Street, in which I frequently used to spend the night. They were just a mob disguised as colonels, majors, etc.; and judging by their appearance they looked like criminals.

An early sensation was the arrival of a Captain of the Soviet Intelligence Service, Constanty Kalugin, who reported to the High Command of the Rising. On August 5 he sent, via London, a telegram to Stalin asking for help. I also read his appeal to German units formed of Soviet soldiers who were taken prisoner-of-war, urging them not to take part in the fighting against the Rising under threat of death. The telegram Kalugin sent to Stalin received no reply, and when he swam across the Vistula towards the end of the Rising and reached Rokossowski,[1] all trace of him was lost. He probably paid with his life for that telegram in which he seemed to oppose Stalin's plans.

Our eyes were finally opened by telegrams from the Government in London, which informed us that the intervention of the Allies with Stalin, requesting his help for fighting Warsaw, had been ineffective. The Soviets, moreover, denied Allied planes permission to land on Soviet airfields when they dropped supplies for Warsaw by night. Thus, instead of being able to use fields which were only a few minutes' flying dis-

[1] A Russian Marshal in command of the advancing Soviet army.

tance from Warsaw, they had to fly back a thousand miles to Allied bases, which increased their losses enormously.

I once stood on a roof following with my eyes the shadows gliding across the sky, amidst the hum of engines and the hellish din of the anti-aircraft batteries. I stood there with bated breath when a flash turned into a flame, and the plane plunged towards Praga, from where a pillar of fire and the echo of an explosion proclaimed its destruction. People on the roof wept and recited a prayer for the dead.

At about that time, we received a telegram from London informing us that the Soviets had arrested the crew of a British plane that had made a forced landing on the Soviet side after dropping supplies over Warsaw. Thanks to energetic British intervention the crew was sent back to England; but Moscow announced that in future all such crews would be detained in Russia, and interned for the duration of the war. When I handed this telegram to the Government Plenipotentiary, and he in turn showed it to the members of the Council of National Unity, they all gave up the last faint hope of speedy relief.

A change occurred on September 9 when late at night I received an urgent message from London: 'Inform Government Plenipotentiary that to-day Marshal Stalin promised help for Warsaw.'

My people at the radio station rejoiced, while I rushed through the dark streets, stumbling over the rubble, to Mokotow Street. There I found Plenipotentiary Jankowski, Puzak, and their staff—all lying on the floor in the corridor, covered with blankets. After I had read the message an animated discussion ensued, in which each of those present expressed his suppositions. I did not wait to hear it; for I wanted to be back with those closest to me, and together with them to dream of a speedy victory over the Germans.

The following day we were awakened, not as usual by German dive-bombers, but by the roar of Soviet fighter planes, which circled over the city in twos. We breathed with relief, because at last there would be no German bombs. Unfortunately, on September 19, the Soviet fighter planes vanished from the sky, and the bombing raids began again. That was all the help the Soviet air force gave to the Rising.

During the night of September 13/14 Soviet drops of food and arms began, but, as if they wanted to mock us, without parachutes. Everything they dropped was smashed to smithereens. It was obvious that these were purely propaganda drops, which would enable the Soviets to tell the West that they were helping the Rising, while in fact they were not.

On September 14, Rokossowski captured Praga, and his troops took up positions opposite the fighting city along the entire bank of the Vistula. Between September 14 and 18, two battalions of Berling's Polish army under Rokossowski's command crossed the Vistula and reached Czerniakow, thus proving that it was possible to send help across the river. Later on I talked to officers of the Home Army who were at Czerniakow at the time. They told me sorrowfully that the two battalions had been attacked and destroyed at once, having been left without any support. The soldiers in those two battalions were raw recruits, mobilised barely a week or so before, from the peasants of the Cracow district. They had had no battle experience, they did not know how to seek cover in the ground, and they were decimated like flies. Later, it was said that Berling had acted on his, allegedly without Rokossowski's knowledge; that he had been arrested and had vanished for a year, and was not restored to his command. The two battalions were deliberately sent to their doom by Rokossowski, and only very few stragglers were able to withdraw across the Vistula.

The Warsaw Rising is often described as the most heroic episode of the last war. The Soviets' conduct during the Rising, on the other hand, should be branded as the greatest crime of that war, a worse crime even than Katyn, for two hundred thousand men, women and children paid for it with their lives.

We Return to Raven Street

German howitzers were bombarding the Bulgarian Legation more frequently and for longer periods. The company commander came to me and said, with some embarrassment: 'There cannot be any doubt that the Germans have got you pin-pointed, and that is why they are concentrating on us. I am very sorry, but I must ask you to move from here. I fear the Germans may storm our sector in order to destroy the radio station, and we are not in a position to defend ourselves. All told, my company has only got a few rifles and a dozen revolvers.'

My first impulse was to object.

'You want us to go somewhere where the civilian population will be killed by the barrage, because you, soldiers, are afraid?'

The captain took no offence.

'I am sorry, but I cannot help it. This is a sector of the battle front, and I cannot endanger it because of you.'

I left him where he stood, without saying another word; but on reflection I had to admit that he was right, and we moved back to 7, Raven Street.

In September 1948, I was sitting in a Paris café near the Luxembourg Gardens. I was enjoying the sunshine and peace over a cup of coffee. Not far from me sat a gentleman whose face seemed familiar to me; but try as I might, I could not remember where I had seen the man before. He too was observing me attentively. Finally he got up and came over to my table.

'Don't you recognise me? My name is Berezinski. Do you remember the Rising and the Bulgarian Legation? We had an argument about the radio station there. But you were wrong. . . .'

I entered into the argument again; and in this way, four years after the Rising, we concluded in Paris a conversation begun in the Bulgarian Legation in Warsaw.

Charged with Diversion

Night after night Soviet planes roared over the roofs and dropped arms and provisions. As before they dropped everything without parachutes, and in the morning the streets were littered with cereals and macaroni. Men and women flitted like shadows in search of this food. Their sunken eyes shone with hunger. I had already had a report of the death from hunger of two elderly women, who were too weak to leave their abode and beg for some food. All the horses had long since been consumed, and the turn of the dogs had come.

I received a visit from Bolek, the brother of the look-out, Jadzia, who was attached to the station in the forest. He had arrived in Warsaw on the eve of the Rising with a letter for me, and had been unable to return. He was now serving in a Home Army unit, and was at the front. He was feeling uneasy, because his unit had hardly any arms. In the evening, the soldiers scattered all over the city in search of rifles, which they tried to borrow from friends serving in other units that had been withdrawn from the front for a rest. Bolek too had a friend who lent him a rifle for the night; but the friend was so afraid of losing it that he used to spend the nights with Bolek's unit and take the rifle back in the morning.

Bolek was a good-natured fellow, and he came to invite us to a meal.

'Please do come, both of you, to our unit for dinner. We lured a large dog over from the German side, and it will be served to-day *en casserole*.'

However, we had not yet been reduced to the state of eating the poor dogs, and so refused the invitation.

Zosia and I were at that time spending the nights in our 'eagle's nest' on the top floor of the house in Marshall Street. One night we were awakened by a dull thud. We listened, straining our ears, but could hear nothing except the hum of a Soviet plane. We fell asleep again; but after a few minutes I woke up once more. I jumped out of bed, hearing footsteps in our secret hide-out above.

I climbed up to the ventilator, and after the usual acrobatics emerged into the loft, which was lit by the beams of two electric torches. I switched on my own torch, and found two men, who looked at me suspiciously. All over the place were valves, instruments, and other radio equipment.

'This is my hide-out. What are you doing here?'

'The drop fell on the roof, penetrated it, and fell in here.'

By the light of my torch I could see a mass of spilled kasha.

'Well, collect up what you can find here and let's go to bed.'

They swept the kasha into bags, dust, sand and all; but they left reluctantly, muttering something to each other. For my part, I was angry that the hide-out had been discovered.

That night we were fated to be denied any sleep. Hardly had I gone back to bed, when there was a banging on the door.

'Who's there?' I shouted, really furious this time.

'Gendarmerie for a check up. Open the door!'

How was that, I thought. Were nocturnal visits by gendarmes becoming a normal feature of our life? I got up and opened the door to three men with armbands on their sleeves and with revolvers in their hands, which they at once aimed at us.

'Don't move, or you'll be shot. Now we've got you. Search him!'

'Stop! Don't you dare search anyone here!' Disregarding the revolvers I pulled out the identity card issued to me by the High Command of the Home Army. They read it with unconcealed disappointment and tried to be nasty.

'You've got a fine nest here! And a girl too!'

'Get out, or I shall alert the detachment on the ground floor and have you arrested!'

They left, cursing us under their breath and banging the door as they disappeared.

We again lay down, but unable to sleep we only dozed. Another knock at the door sent me into a frenzy. I got up again and called:

'Who the hell is there?'

'Gendarmerie for a check up. Open the door!'

'We've had the gendarmes here already. You go to hell and leave us alone.'

'We don't know anything about that. Open the door.'

I let in three young boys. To one of them with a sergeant's badge I handed my identity card without saying a word. He read it carefully, saluted, sent the two others out, and apologised:

'I am sorry, but there must have been some misunderstanding. What happened here?'

I told him of the drop falling through the roof. He laughed.

'The entire gendarmerie has been alerted. We received information that a store had been discovered here, in possession of a German diversionist. We were sent here to check up, and if true, to take you away and shoot you.'

A Quest for the Golden Fleece

Towards the end of the Rising the Government Plenipotentiary confided to me that one of his worries was lack of money. Many buildings housing secret deposits in Warsaw had been burnt down; the Treasurer of his cabinet had been wounded, and was in a hospital that had been captured by the Germans, and it was doubtful if he was still alive; while his deputy had been killed by a bomb. The situation was as bad as it could be. I was talking about money to K., a former official of the Government Plenipotentiary's office, and he remembered that some time before he had helped the Treasurer to make a secret caché in Mokotow Street, in which he had placed several pouches packed with dollars received from parachute drops. He thought the hiding-place might not have been disturbed. I informed the Plenipotentiary accordingly, and he requested me to visit the house, accompanied by K., and ascertain the position on the spot.

We set out from Raven Street for Mokotow Street, which abutted on to Mokotow Field. As luck would have it, the Germans shelled that part of the city particularly heavy that day, and we escaped by the skin of our teeth. As it was, we had to fall on our faces in many a courtyard and corner, and we were covered with dirt and dust by the time we reached the house, which was right in the front line. K. knocked at the remembered door and was welcomed by a stout, elderly gentleman, who took us straight into the kitchen. There, three other gentlemen rose from the table holding cards in their hands.

'Ah, you are playing bridge!' K. said enviously, being himself a well-known Warsaw bridge player.

'Yes, we play every afternoon.'

'Is it sufficiently quiet here for a good game?'

'Of course. We are too close to the German lines for them to bombard us. They might hit their own people.'

'And where are our positions?'

'Here, just on the opposite side of the corridor, in the front room,' our host explained with perfect composure.

We entered the front room, where the floor was covered with sand, and by the window, which was protected by sandbags, stood a motionless sentry of the Home Army, armed with a rifle. Through the opening I had a look at the German side of the street; it was utterly desolate.

'My dear Counsellor,' said K., 'some time ago I made a secret deposit here.'

'That's right. It's there, as you left it.'

'No one has taken anything away?'

'No one has been here since you left it.'

We entered the adjoining room. K. counted the squares in the parquet floor, lifted one with the help of a skewer, and pulled out two bulging silk pouches with their wax seals intact.

'Thank you very much, Counsellor,' said K.

'Don't mention it. But what about a rubber or two some afternoon?'

'With side bets?'

'That goes without saying.'

'Well, I shall try. . . .'

We started on our way back, to the accompaniment of bursting shells, the stench of petrol and the crackle of burning houses. At last we got out of the line of fire and breathed more freely. Covering the pouches with our jackets, we made straight for the Plenipotentiary's office. While crossing a courtyard, we ran into one of its officials, Mr. Y., who had been my adversary in the SWIT affair. I got an idea and said to K.:

'Let's play a joke on him. Don't say anything, but back me up.'

I uncovered the pouch slightly and advanced towards Mr. Y.

We had hardly exchanged a polite 'good morning', when

Mr. Y., eyeing the green pouch, played into my hands by asking:

'What's that, Director, that you're carrying there?'

'This? Oh, it's the mail from London, which was dropped by parachute in the Mokotow Field. Good-bye, Director,' I replied nonchalantly.

Mr. Y. wanted to question me further, but we made off rapidly in the opposite direction. When we delivered the pouches to the Plenipotentiary, he was very pleased, and thanked K. warmly for having saved him a great deal of trouble.

The next day I met the Plenipotentiary as usual. He looked at me enquiringly and asked:

'Mr. Zielinski, what mail did you receive from London yesterday?'

'I didn't receive any, Mr. Plenipotentiary.'

'How can that be. . . ? You told Y. yourself yesterday that you were carrying the mail.'

I could not help smiling.

'No, Mr. Plenipotentiary, what I was carrying were the two pouches we brought you. We thought we would play a joke on Mr. Y.'

Now it was the Plenipotentiary who could not help laughing. There was a twinkle in his tired eyes, marked by so many sleepless nights.

'Ah, Mr. Zielinski, men and women are dying here, houses are collapsing, and you will have your little jokes. . . . Ever since the morning Mr. Y. has been worrying me, complaining that the opening of the London mail is his business not yours. . . .'

'Well, Mr. Plenipotentiary, one has to do something to save oneself from going mad in this hell.'

The Plenipotentiary nodded sadly, and said:

'Perhaps you are right . . . perhaps. . . .'

The Spectre of Capitulation

It had become clear to all that the Soviets wished the Germans to destroy the Capital and its population. They resumed bombing from the air and battered the city with artillery. Warsaw was burning. The spectre of capitulation hovered over the City. I now sent the Government in London a final report on the situation, in three separate telegrams, which deserve to be quoted here:

'Warsaw, September 22, 1944. As Director of the Department for Internal Affairs I am holding regular conferences with local delegates. Here is the report on yesterday's conference. It does not cover Mokotow or Zoliborz, because these sections of the city are completely cut off, and the only means of military liaison are occasional couriers and the radio. In the centre of the city, out of a population of 260,000, more than one half are refugees from other parts of Warsaw. The reserves of food, both military and civilian, amount to about 100 tons of barley and fifty tons of wheat. Fats will give out to-morrow, sugar in four days. We are requisitioning food from traders and from abandoned dwellings, but the results are trifling. We have been without electricity, gas and water for a considerable time. About 92 wells are functioning; some 80 more are being sunk. There is a mild epidemic of dysentery, but nothing worse. Medical service is provided by four doctors to every Commissariat and one to every block of houses. Six hospitals are serving the civilian population and the military, twelve the civilians exclusively, all in vaults.'

'Warsaw, September 23, 1944. Further to my telegram of yesterday: Conditions are slightly better in Zoliborz and Mokotow, which are less crowded and have more vegetables. In the centre of the city trade in water has begun. The wells are soon exhausted and become useless. As from to-day we shall be living on boiled wheat and coffee with sugar. We are under strong howitzer fire.'

'Warsaw, September 26, 1944. On the basis of yesterday's conference with local delegates I am obliged to state that the population is increasingly suffering from hunger. All stocks of wheat have already been distributed, and the remaining 60 tons of barley are being distributed now. There are no reserves left. The population is already killing dogs for food. We are again faced with the spectre of capitulation, or the necessity of sending the civilian population ᵗᵉr to the

German side, because of hunger. Without considerable daily drops we can only last another week, or at the utmost ten days. Twenty cases of scarlet fever have been reported.'

On September 27 the Germans captured Mokotow; on September 29, Bor capitulated to General von dem Bach; and on September 30, after a heroic struggle Zoliborz was captured.

I took part in the sessions of the Council of National Unity concerned with the preparations for capitulation. We were concerned both with the Home Army and with the protection of the civilian population and property from possible German reprisals. The deliberations were carried on at the same time as the negotiations with the Germans, from which it had already transpired that the civilian population would have to leave the City with what they could carry, and that the City itself would be abandoned to the mercy of the Germans. It had been agreed that only the Home Army would go into captivity, and that the political underground and its authorities would be treated as civilians. During this period the Plenipotentiary was greatly concerned with the City, and spent many hours with the former minister, Wachowiak, and myself, discussing the possibility of organising, with the help of the General Welfare Council (GWC), some protection for the abandoned City. After the capitulation, Wachowiak, the deputy mayor of Warsaw, Kulski, and others intervened in vain with the Governor of Warsaw, Fischer, to stop the wanton looting and the systematic destruction of the City by fire.

At the request of the Plenipotentiary, I elaborated a scheme for the underground authorities to re-establish contact with each other after the Rising was over. The scheme was simple; we were to try and meet:

During the first two weeks after the Rising, on odd days, at the first service in the Church in Lesna Podkowa; on even days, in Milanowek; on days divisible by three, in Grodzisk. After two weeks, we should look for each other in Piotrkow; after another two weeks, in Cracow.

The Government Plenipotentiary was already ailing, and whenever I visited him, I found him in bed. I felt pro-

foundly sorry for him. His burden was too heavy for one man
to bear.

The Capitulation

On October 2, 1944, the capitulation agreement was signed
in Ozarow, and the firing ceased. A strange silence fell over
the City. Before the agreement was made known publicly, I
was instructed by the Plenipotentiary to issue a proclamation
ordering the population to abandon the city; but without
informing it that the Home Army was to lay down its arms
and go into captivity. I immediately called a meeting of the
local delegates and the mayor of the City, and issued the necessary instructions to them. The local delegates, in their turn,
called meetings of the block commanders. When our local
delegate, the barrister, Quirini, addressed the assembled
block commanders, numbering about 150, I mingled with
them to observe their reactions. The local delegate calmly
and skilfully informed the meeting of the agreement with the
Germans, as a result of which the population was, as from
the next morning, to leave the City. In spite of the fact that
rumours had already been circulating in Warsaw about negotiations with the Germans, it was obvious that the statement
made a painful impression on those present. There was an
oppressive silence in the room. In accordance with instructions, the local delegate did not mention anything about the
capitulation of the Home Army. When, in conclusion, he
requested that the population should at once be informed,
and urged that the agreement should be executed, a murmur
arose which soon turned into an uproar. A voice shouted:
'May I say something?' And when the delegate, having asked
for silence, invited the man to speak, he promptly asked:
'What is going to happen to the Home Army?' The delegate
was prepared for just such a question, and requested that
military matters, which had to remain secret, should not be
mixed up with civilian affairs, but should be kept separate.
Then a man rushed forward, and turning to the meeting,
shouted:

'Colleagues! I am in command of a block in Marshall Street.

I shall faithfully report to the block the instructions which we have just heard. But I shall also tell them: "Don't leave the City if the Home Army are not to leave with us! If the Home Army remains, let us too remain. If they are to perish, we want to be with them!" '

His words caused another uproar.

'He is right! He is right! Don't let's leave without the Home Army!'

No one would listen to the arguments of the local delegate, and the meeting dispersed, greatly excited over the lack of information about the Home Army.

I went at once to the ailing Government Plenipotentiary to report to him on the meeting. The Plenipotentiary took the only possible course, and ordered the immediate summoning of another meeting, at which the block commanders were informed of the capitulation of the Home Army. The news was received in grim silence, and all dispersed to carry out the order for the evacuation of the population. The following morning, long caravans of emaciated men and women, loaded with bundles, proceeded to the departure points; and slowly the City was deserted. The Germans at the barricades and crossings looked at the sad processions of suffering humanity with eyes that betrayed their uneasy consciences.

At that time I became inseparable from the Government Plenipotentiary, who had another man-to-man talk with me. He showed great solicitude for my safety.

'Mr. Zielinski,' he said, 'I am afraid that despite the terms of the capitulation agreement, the Germans will be looking for you. You were the head of the Directorate of Civil Resistance, and what with the secret courts and death sentences . . . I think it will be best for you to go into captivity as Bor's adjutant. I am sure he will agree if I ask him. And it will be best for you that way.'

I thanked him warmly, but said that only those who could not avoid it should go into captivity, and that all the others should remain in the underground. Moreover, I should try to slip out of Warsaw with the radio station, and attempt to maintain radio liaison with London, which was of paramount importance. This argument made an impression on the Plenipotentiary, and he did not raise the subject again. He only expressed the hope that we should soon meet somewhere near Warsaw.

Bor had already had talks with General von dem Bach, and at a meeting of the Council of National Unity he gave us his impressions. I remember well how he told us that at the outset of the talks Bach was most effusive and outspoken, or pretending to be frank, and said with impressive conviction:

'We must together try to save the magnificent soldiers of the Home Army. It is our common destiny that one day, in the future, no matter under what command, we Germans and you Poles shall fight against the common enemy. . . . When that day comes, these heroic soldiers will be wanted.'

On October 5, I went to Sniadecki Street to say good-bye to Bor and Gregory, who were going into captivity. Walking up to the head of a long column of soldiers, I was frequently hailed by friends; I shook hands with them, and answered 'no' to the many enquiries whether I was going with them. I also met there my sixteen-year-old nephew, Andrew Korbonski.

'How are you, Andrew? Are you going into captivity?'

'Yes, I am going with my unit.'

'Wouldn't you like to stay with me?'

'No, uncle, I prefer to go into captivity, and then I shall try to get away to the West and meet father.'

'God bless you! Good-bye, and good luck!'

We shook hands, little knowing that we were to meet again in London, in 1947.

Bor, Gregory, and their staff were already at the head of the column. Fifty yards away, in the direction of August 6th Street, stood the motionless Germans with rifles at the ready, watching the deep ranks of the Home Army. The day was cold and I felt sad. I again shook hands with many friends, wishing them good luck and receiving similar wishes. At last, all the men in the column bared their heads, and the stirring words of the national anthem, 'Poland shall never perish', rose into the air. All eyes were wet, and voices quivered with emotion. The ranks moved forward, and I started on my way back. I looked compassionately at those young boys and girls, marching with soldierly bearing, their faces set in stony immobility. The muse of history was soaring above that column. But I had to curb my feelings; for I had a hard task before me: how to slip out of Warsaw with my team.

Farewell Warsaw!

I was determined not to let myself be captured but to get out of Warsaw somehow, in order to continue the underground work, and, above all, to maintain radio liaison with London. My decision electrified the whole team, and they all started to make plans to avoid the transit camp in Pruszkow, through which the entire population of Warsaw had to pass. I had my own scheme, but I kept it to myself, as I was not sure whether I should be able to carry it out. However, it came off, and I hurried to our apartment to announce:

'Cheer up, everybody! Everything has been arranged. As from to-day, we are all employees of the General Welfare Council, and we shall be permitted to remain in the City until the evacuation of the population is completed. We have several days in which to make our arrangements for a get-away.'

I handed each person an Identity Card issued by the GWC, and also a stamped armband. We were all full of hope, and our spirits rose. We had still to send out and to receive final messages. We received a telegram from the Prime Minister, thanking us for the work we had done for so many years, and also one from the radio personnel in London, which, in spite of its uplifting tone, was rather grim. It was obvious that they were saying farewell for ever, and regarded the capitulation as putting an end to further contact with us. We were rather annoyed, for at that moment none of us thought either of death or captivity. On the contrary, the worst was behind us, and before us was the prospect of getting out of Warsaw, either as employees of the GWC, or in some other way. The whole team was full of renewed enthusiasm, happy that we had come through the Rising unhurt, which none of us had expected.

In this atmosphere, and amid general applause, I told Jan to send the following telegram to London:

'We shall try to slip out of Warsaw and continue our work.

Listen in after five days, daily at 11 o'clock, on the same wave-length. Till you hear us again!'

We finished our work at a fortunate moment, for no sooner had I gone out into the street, when I ran into the first German patrol, advancing cautiously under the command of an officer. While I was looking at them with some curiosity, there emerged from around the corner a patrol of the Home Army, consisting of three men in helmets, with armlets and automatic weapons slung over their shoulders. The sight of mortal enemies advancing slowly towards each other was rather unusual, and I stopped to watch. I was curious to know what would happen. When the Home Army patrol was only a few yards away from the Germans, the German officer in command raised his hand to his cap, the soldiers slapped the butts of their rifles, and holding themselves stiffly, they stamped the pavement briskly with their boots. The Home Army patrol did a smart 'eyes left'; and in this way the mortal foes, the Poles and the Germans, exchanged honours. I sighed with relief.

Roman assured me that he would be able to find a trans-mitter near Warsaw, or, if it came to the worst, the necessary parts to construct a new one. I had to take into consideration the fact that we could not take a transmitter with us, for if we did and it were found, it would mean the death of all of us; so I decided that we should not keep the 'American beauty', of which Jan was so fond, but together with the other transmitters, we should put it away in a safe hide-out. How-ever, we kept a few quartzes and a few basic valves, and made ready to leave the City at the first opportunity that offered.

Before we left, we went through a short ceremony. Four gentlemen with sorrowful faces lifted on to their shoulders a modest coffin knocked together from rough deal boards, and accompanied by several ladies, who walked behind in a funeral procession, made for one of the nearby cemeteries. There, the coffin was lowered into a prepared grave and care-fully covered with earth, so that in a few minutes the usual mound rose over the grave. In this way we buried our remain-ing transmitters. After Warsaw was 'liberated' by Soviet troops, an 'exhumation' of the transmitters took place, and they came in very handy to us.

We did not know whether we should be able to slip out of Warsaw, but in order to be ready for the eventuality we all moved to one apartment in Mokotow Street, and rested after the hardships of the Rising.

The City presented a sight which would be difficult to imagine. All the inhabitants had already left, and there was a dead silence, broken only by the sound of our footsteps. When I ventured from Mokotow Street into Marshall Street, I returned in a state bordering on panic, horrified by the desolation of the deserted streets and houses, which, only a short time before, had been filled to overflowing. There remained only the innumerable graves in every open space by the streets. On my way back an abandoned and hungry litle dog, a Pekinese, attached himself to me; and when I picked him up, he clung to me and wailed like a little child.

At last there was a great commotion in the GWC. Two German trucks that had brought food supplies for the Home Army hospital, which still remained in the city, were to take all the employees of the General Welfare Council to Pruszkow. When we arrived at the office of the GWC, carrying our heavy rucksacks and bags, the trucks were already full. Everyone was preoccupied with himself, and we were forgotten. This may have been due to the fact that some of the genuine employees of the GWC kept away from our team, knowing that the identity cards and armlets issued to us were a cover for some dangerous work. Fortunately, we were noticed by the well-informed director of the underground Office for the Recovered Provinces, Wladyslaw Czajkowski, whose task it was to prepare plans for the future administration of these provinces; and he invited us to board the crowded truck. With great difficulty and a great deal of squeezing, we were able to get in. We were standing, packed like sardines, when the truck started on its journey through the desolate streets. There was not a living soul to be seen, except for German sentries here and there, regulating the movement of vehicles. Everywhere I noticed broken overhead tramway cables, uprooted lamp-posts, an occasional smashed tram-car, bomb craters galore, barricades and rubble . . . rubble everywhere, and the skeletons of burnt-out houses.

Out of this dead landscape we suddenly emerged into another world, in which the houses were intact, the shops open, people were quietly working in the fields, and normally-attired pedestrians regarded us with curiosity and compassion. We arrived in Pruszkow, and waited anxiously for what was to happen. Would they take us to the camp or not? Should we be searched or should we escape it? Everybody in the truck was worrying about it. At last the trucks turned to the left, and someone who was familiar with Pruszkow cheered us up by saying: 'Thank God! The road leading to the camp was to the right.' The trucks turned sharply into a spacious courtyard, and the two Germans escorting us, whose humanity had been buttressed with a thick wad of banknotes, disappeared behind a nearby door.

'Now we must run for it!' I called in an undertone to my little band. We jumped off the truck, each grabbing his or her baggage; we hustled quickly through the gate, and without being stopped by anyone, ran into the nearby Electric Railway station. The train arrived just as we got there, and with the help of conductors, who guessed where we had come from, we jumped in quickly, and it started right away. We were all perspiring and worn out; but we were dazed by the ease with which everything had happened. We looked at each other with incredulity, rejoicing in our hearts.

All around us was luxury. The coach was clean, the electric light was on, all the passengers well-dressed. At every stop there were stalls with baskets full of bread, cold meat, butter, rolls, and other specialities which we had not seen for two months. Within half an hour we were seated in a bar in Lesna Podkowa; and disregarding our mutual exhortations, we consumed all the delicious foods available. We had to repent it painfully, very soon.

Liaison Re-established

We resumed a relatively normal life. Lesna Podkowa, Milanowek, Grodzisk, all the places along the line of the

Electric Railway were crowded. The whole of Warsaw, including the underground, was there. We were having regular meals, and we lived in houses equipped with windows intact and electric light. Water, too, was plentiful, and we spent hours on end in the bathrooms. What with the clean beds, we felt as if we were in paradise. The Rising was gradually receding in our memories like a terrible but splendid dream. The Germans were everywhere, but they were unable to control the wanderings of the populace of a great City.

Roman and Jan had found a room in a village several kilometres away from Podkowa, and Roman was doing his utmost to construct a transmitter as soon as possible; for unfortunately he had not been able to find one locally. At last he had knocked together something in the nature of a suitable apparatus; he purchased a set of batteries, and as the five days had elapsed, Jan began to call London right away. I visited them both in their new abode, in a substantial brick house. They had a small room there and a hide-out in the cellar. I inspected everything with great care, and to my astonishment found that the aerial came in through the window.

'Are you mad?' I said. 'Why is the aerial outside?'

'Have no fear,' Roman answered. 'The nearest house is so far off that it can't be seen, and Jan has already had a talk with our hosts. They are safe as a rock and won't say a word. The aerial is in the loft and strangers can't see it.'

'Do you think the Germans have a radio interceptor here?'

'Yes, they have. A military one. I saw it at Komorow station, but it's primitive. A German in uniform was walking along the platform with a pack on his back and the earphones on. He was visible for a mile.'

It was eleven o'clock in the morning, so Jan got busy with the transmitter. After a few minutes he turned to me and said:

'They can't hear us at all. . . .'

'What do you think, Roman? What can be the cause of it?'

'The transmitter is very crude, for I couldn't get all the parts. I'll try to remake it, but it would be a good thing to get Jan's transmitter from Warsaw.'

I considered the chances, and by the following day, a boy

I knew for his daring, Antek, was travelling to Warsaw, having joined a squad of workers clearing the barricades under German supervision. I gave him an exact plan and urged him to find the transmitter at all costs and bring it back with him. I was not very optimistic that he would succeed, so I was really amazed when I met him in a bar in the evening and he told me:

'I brought the transmitter back with me and delivered it to your wife. I reached the ruins of the house with the help of the plan you gave me, and there, under the rubble of bricks, I found the transmitter in good order. I wrapped it up in a newspaper, fastened it with a piece of string, and placed it at the bottom of the truck, under the shovels. The Germans searched the truck twice, but so carelessly that they didn't find the transmitter.'

The next day I was again at the station before 11 a.m. It was by now the tenth day since our last telegram had been sent to London. The transmitter, tested by Roman, was functioning perfectly. Both Roman and Jan were excited, though they knew that contact would be established; and I myself could not help feeling excited too.

Punctually at 11 a.m. Jan put on the earphones, listened, and scribbled down for me to read: 'They are calling us. . . .' A moment later he switched over to transmission and replied to London. He switched to reception once more and smiled blissfully. He took his pencil and wrote down: 'OK, OK, we can hear you well!'

Roman and I hugged each other, and we both patted Jan lustily on the back, while he went on taking the message down. Roman got hold of the ciphers and I spelled slowly:

'We send you our heartfelt greetings. Yours is the only station from Warsaw which has managed to save itself.'

CHAPTER XX

The End of German Occupation

'Little London'

By now I had a good idea of the situation along the Suburban Electric Railway. The villas, houses and cottages were overflowing with the exiled people of Warsaw, and even some of the hospitals had found shelter there. On the fences of all the stations were hundreds of notices and the addresses of husbands searching for their wives, parents searching for their children, and people in general announcing where they were. Large crowds stood in front of these 'forwarding offices' from morning till night. At all available corners, women opened provision stalls. People were eating all the time to make good the starvation diet of the Rising. Small restaurants and the ever-popular little café-bars were mushrooming in improvised sheds, some of which were most attractively got up. In short, Warsaw and conspiracy were arising Phoenix-like from the ashes. Men and women rejoiced at having escaped with their lives from the perils of the Rising, and they enjoyed the woods and the fresh air, eating all day long.

The underground was easily re-established. Whenever one went out into the street, one met at every turn somebody one knew, and in this way contacts were re-established. Within a few days we were organising again and had established contact with the Government Plenipotentiary, who, together with the hospital he was in, had been evacuated to Cracow, and with the High Command of the Home Army, which functioned somewhere on the Czestochowa-Cracow line. The bulk of the members of the underground, however, remained in the vicinity of Warsaw, and the Gestapo, who guessed as much, described the localities along the Suburban Electric Railway as 'Little London'. Gestapo agents and gendarmes were swarming everywhere, but their former energy and zeal were gone. Germany's defeat was staring everyone in the eyes.

The looting and burning down of Warsaw was proceeding apace. Columns of thousands of workers marched into the deserted city every day to retrieve everything of any value. Thousands of wagon-loads of furniture, carpets, pictures and clothing were being dispatched into the Reich. All museums, libraries, collections, factory equipment, workshops and laboratories were transported to Germany. The looting assumed gigantic proportions. All efforts to save as much as possible on the part of the Poles who, with the approval of the underground, worked in the German administration of the city under Burgomaster Leist remained ineffective; as were all the attempts at intervention with Governor Fischer, who now resided in Sochaczew.

Wherever the looting had been completed, the Vernichtungskommando got busy, and Warsaw was again enveloped in clouds of smoke. The Germans were systematically setting fire to one house after another, burning down the entire capital; and thousands of Warsavians gazed broken-hearted at the smoke and the blaze consuming their beloved City.

In 1945 I received proofs that the Germans acted in accordance with carefully prepared plans. A member of the former underground supplied me with photographic copies of four plans of the City of Warsaw drawn up by German town-planners, who visited Warsaw for this purpose. One represented the plan of Warsaw in the 16th century; another, in the 18th century; the third, of Warsaw just before the outbreak of the last war; and the fourth, a plan of the future Warsaw under German rule. According to this, it was to be a small town on the banks of the Vistula, reduced to the confined area between Poniatowski and Kierbedz bridges. That was all.

I took steps to ensure that the photographic copies should be put in as evidence at the Nuremberg trial of German war criminals. I had no difficulty, because the two Prosecutors of the Communist Ministry of Justice, Siewierski and Sawicki, took down my depositions and told me openly that I would be a Polish 'star' witness during the trial. However, this did not suit the chairman of the Communist delegation in Nuremberg, a pre-war fellow-travelling lawyer by the name of Warszawski, who in 1945 was already strutting about in the uniform of a colonel under the name of Kurowski. The 'Colonel' would not permit me to be invited to Nuremberg. However, my depositions were not wasted. One day a friend of mine dropped in on me, and producing a copy of the Moscow 'Pravda', asked me to read an article in it. In this way I learned that the Soviet Prosecutor at the Nuremberg trial read the depositions of 'one of the leaders of the Polish people in their struggle against the Germans', one Stefan Korbonski, and requested that the depositions should be entered as evidence.

My friend wanted to know how the 'Pravda' article struck me. I had no illusions, and looking soberly at my position, I said:

'This will postpone my arrest by six to twelve months.'

Departure for Cracow

It became necessary for me to see the Government Plenipotentiary, and having reinforced my forged documents with additional and equally forged endorsements, I climbed through a window into a train in Skierniewice, and travelling in an intolerably crowded compartment, I reached Cracow. On the journey I listened to the conversation going on around me, and I must confess that I was impressed. My travelling companions discussed everything in a most outspoken manner: the defeat of the Germans, the Warsaw Rising (on the whole with adverse criticism), and the approach of the Soviet armies. This last issue dominated the discussion, and everything these simple folk, most of them smugglers, said had in it a great deal of worldly wisdom, realism, common sense, and a quiet but genuine patriotism, bereft of all flamboyance.

Cracow overwhelmed and dazzled me. Having lived for so long amidst the rubble and debris of Warsaw, I was deeply moved by the sight of a beautiful, intact city, which was clean, well-lighted, with running water on tap, and similar luxuries.

With sheer delight I walked along the streets, eyeing everything like a man from another world. I rejoiced that all the
national treasures and shrines of old Cracow were untouched.
But somewhere in the depths of my being I was a little envi-
ous. Where I had come from, heroic, charming and lively
Warsaw was perishing, while here, this sleeping city, en-
grossed in its past, was standing unhurt.

Cracow was brimful of refugees from Warsaw, who were
welcomed hospitably, but rather in the manner in which one
welcomes one's relations whom one has not seen for twenty
years. One knew they were relatives, but there was not much
one could talk to them about.

I found the Plenipotentiary in better health, and he was as
glad to see me as I was to see him. I had a very high opinion
of him, and I knew he liked me. We exchanged information
and discussed current affairs. The Plenipotentiary did not ask
me to move to Cracow, but was himself thinking of transfer-
ring his headquarters to somewhere nearer Warsaw. He was
pleased to know that I had succeeded, with the help of two
inspectors, in establishing contact with all the district plenipotentiaries under German occupation, and was able to tell
him what was happening in the country. We were at that time
preoccupied with the fate of thousands of Warsavians scattered all over the Government General, and, to a lesser extent,
deported to Germany. On his part, he informed me that in
respect of Soviet-Polish relations everything looked unpromis-
ing. With the hindsight of to-day I would say that things were
much worse than the Plenipotentiary realised, and that both
he and the whole underground were not being fully and
honestly informed by the Government in London.

A Rally in Piotrkow

Not long after my return from Cracow, I took a train from
Skierniewice and travelled to Piotrkow. There, having easily
passed the sentry posts of gendarmes and Gestapo agents, who
were as usual snooping around at all railway stations, I
walked into the city. I had firmly impressed in my memory
where to go and how to make contact. After dodging about in

the streets for a little while to see if I was being shadowed, I proceeded straight to the monastery, right in the centre of the city. I could hardly believe my eyes on seeing the assembly. There was the Government Plenipotentiary and the underground Council of Ministers, the new Commander of the Home Army, General Okulicki (pseudonym 'Little Bear', and later, 'Cobra'), the Council of National Unity in full, and almost all the Heads of Departments. If the Gestapo had raided the monastery that day, they would have had a rich haul. The Germans were not yet so absorbed by their defeats that they could not take advantage of such an opportunity, and I found it strange that nothing happened. It must have been either luck or a more profound demoralisation of the Gestapo than I had assumed.

The main business included sessions of the Council of National Unity, attended by all. The deliberations touched upon the international situation, the impending Soviet occupation, our attitude towards the Government in London, where political tension was soon to lead to the resignation of the Mikolajczyk Government, and finally, internal affairs. I have no clear recollection of these deliberations, except that I remember the hopelessness of the atmosphere on the one hand, and the determination to continue the struggle on the other.

In the evening I abandoned myself to the charm of the old monastery. I wandered along quiet, dimly-lit corridors, filled with an air of grave serenity. I lifted the lantern to view some anonymous portraits, I tried to decipher some inscriptions, and rambled aimlessly, meditating on many things.

For the night I was accommodated in a crowded cell, together with a well-known Polish doctor, and a diplomat, Mr. Wielowieyski, who were both members of the Polish Red Cross. I had an upper bunk. I was already stretched out in the twilight, when a monk came along, saying that he was looking for a 'gentleman in top boots who was in contact with the world and knew all that was happening there'. The top boots were standing limply by my bunk; so, reclining on my elbow, I shared with the monk and my companions in the cell, who raised their heads, all that I had heard lately, listening to the

BBC. The monk had not come empty-handed, and as I continued my story, we all drank from one glass the monastery-brewed brandy.

When I had finished, the monk pulled out from under his brown cassock a large, faded photograph showing two rows of monks, and pointing them out to us, he said with pride:

'This one, this one, and this one were in the 1863 Insurrection; and I should also like to tell you that even then emissaries and members of the National Government took refuge in our monastery. We are very proud that to-day our monastery has the honour to provide, within its sheltering walls, hospitality to the underground Government, thereby upholding an old and fine tradition.'

The hospitable monk told us many other things; but when he left, sleep would not come. Thoughts chased through my mind, each more gloomy than the one before. One wave of enemies was receding, another was advancing. Here was the old monastery, here were the underground Government and the Commander-in-Chief, while around them a storm was raging, boding ill for the future. All this had already happened before, the spectacle was familiar, as if the stage of the national theatre had remained unchanged for a hundred years, and the spectators were tired by now. For the first time I felt like one of those tired spectators, and I tossed in my bunk from one side to the other into the early hours of the morning. Sleep would not come.

The Passing of the Front

The headquarters of the Department of Internal Affairs were in Milanowek, while I had a hide-out in Lesna Podkowa. I used to ride to Milanowek on a bicycle, along the Suburban Railway track, or walk there across the fields, dotted with high-tension pylons. This route was forced on me by my forged papers, according to which I was now controller of the electric grid for an area covering three districts; and within these limits I had full freedom of movement. It so happened that I had twice run into a round-up by gendarmes, and thanks to my documents got out of their clutches.

A day came in January 1945, when Soviet guns opened up again, and kept on firing. The Soviet offensive had begun. Zosia and I were in Brwinow when a terrific explosion shook the air. The Germans had blown up a munition dump in the forest of Komorow. While we were on our way home, hurrying along footpaths across the fields to Lesna Podkowa, the retreat to the West of horse-drawn German trains began. I innocently asked one of the elderly German drivers what had happened. His answer was short and to the point: 'Ivan is moving forward'.

The following morning I went on foot to Milanowek, listening to the artillery fire in the East. Milanowek was like a dead town. Not a living soul was to be seen, except along the main street, on the road to Blonie, where a stream of motor vehicles, horse-drawn carts and foot soldiers flowed endlessly by. From Blonie came the sound of aircraft engines and the rattle of machine-guns. Soviet fighters were hitting the retreating Germans.

At the hide-out I found only the frightened liaison-girl, who was astonished to see me.

'There is no one here,' she said. 'The Germans are in retreat. Some German soldiers came here for water, and said that the Russians would be here by the afternoon. . . .'

It was a mistake for me to be there, and I had to go back immediately, so as not to be cut off from the station in Lesna Podkowa, should the front happen to stabilise between Podkowa and Milanowek. I walked along a German column marching in the opposite direction. I was all alone in the street. The Germans were retreating rapidly, but without panic. A German sergeant with a rather intelligent face, stepping off the pavement, asked me for a light. I struck a match and raised it close to his face. While lighting the cigarette he looked me in the eyes, thanked me, and moved on. I saw in his eyes all his tragedy. Fear for his own life, consciousness of defeat, and a vision of a Germany crushed.

The column passed, with two armoured cars and a heavy anti-tank gun bringing up the rear. Except for desultory machine-gun fire from the direction of Blonie, there was a relative lull. I turned into a path running between fences, and there I met a German soldier without arms. He appeared to be lost and wanted to say something as I was passing him, but somehow could not bring himself to do it. He was obviously a deserter, trying to give himself up. In the nearby bushes shells exploded, and on my right a machine-gun opened up. I ducked, and running fast, reached the outskirts of Milanowek, several hundred yards away from the railway track leading to Lesna Podkowa. I examined the neighbourhood carefully. In front of me, far to the left, I could see the shining windows of Brwinow. In the middle of the road leading from there, three grey shapes with rifles at the ready were stalking the enemy. I could feel my heart beating faster. After six years I again beheld Soviet uniforms. I lay down in a trench and waited until they had passed.

When they had disappeared, I leaped across the road, and by familiar paths made my way to Lesna Podkowa. The artillery was by now firing near Grodzisk. A column of tanks advanced across the fields on the distant horizon to the right. I reached the first houses and trees of Lesna Podkowa without further adventure, having crossed the railway track. I sighed with relief. Suddenly I heard the sound of boots, and from the park emerged a platoon of German infantry, with arms at the ready, cautiously reconnoitring the field. They passed me without paying any attention to what I was doing there, and disappeared in the direction of Grodzisk. However, it made me somewhat nervous; for I knew it was not a good thing to be walking about between two fronts. I had already been passed by Germans, then Russians, and again Germans; and I was not at all sure whom I should encounter next. By then, however, I was on the road leading to the main station in Podkowa, among houses and people I knew. From Zarybie came a galloping horse, drawing a little cart with two Soviet soldiers in it. One, without arms, was whipping the horse, the other was manipulating an automatic pistol. They pulled up, shouting:

'Where is the park? The Germans must be there!'

They were completely drunk. I warned them:

'The Germans have just come out of the park and went that way. But be careful, for there are about twenty of them.'

They shouted, 'Thank you!' and drove on like mad in the direction the Germans had taken. I must admit I was impressed. The two of them were taking on ten times their number!

CHAPTER XXI

The Beginnings of Soviet Occupation

First impressions

Our villa housed the staff of a Soviet division, consisting of a General, several officers, and a considerable number of other ranks, in fur jackets and sheepskin caps with earflaps. They were on the whole quiet and embarrassed. The Poles in the house were cool, but correct. The officers showed a complete indiffernce to the welfare of their men. When the owner of the villa offered to put some straw in the hall for the night, so that the soldiers would be more comfortable, the adjutant to the divisional commander, both of whom were accommodated in a warm room, shrugged his shoulders. 'It isn't necessary,' he said. During the night I looked into the hall. The soldiers were asleep on the floor in their fur jackets, and had not even bothered to undo their leather straps. In the ante-room, in front of a transmitter, sat a Soviet soldier fingering the knob of the key. I became interested. When I approached him, he looked up and took one of the earphones off. I greeted him in Russian with words I had learned as a child.

'How are you, stranger?'

'Thanks,' he answered, and went on with his job.

I examined the apparatus with critical eyes. The box was of white metal with slanting walls, and it looked rather crude. But it functioned all right. If I had shown him our 'American beauty', which we kept in reserve, hidden away in the loft, he would have envied us. Even after the Warsaw Rising we had received several new transmitters by parachute drops, and I kept one such apparatus, using only the receiver, to listen to the BBC. To justify my continued presence, I spoke to the soldier again.

'What news do you get from home? When were you last on home leave?'

He lifted his head and regarded me with astonishment.

'Don't you know,' he said, 'that in our army there is no home leave in wartime? I haven't seen my people since 1938, when I was conscripted into the army.'

The conversation stalled, and I went to bed.

Next morning the adjutant asked his host for a glass of vodka for the General. He got two, the second for himself. They drank a large glass each at one go, consumed a large slice of bread with something spread on it and left, following their advancing division.

I took my bicycle and pedalled along the path running by the railway track to Komorow, to see Casimir Baginski. He had been lucky enough to find his wife and little daughter after the Rising, during which they had been cut off by the advancing Germans, and was now living in a peasant cottage. His impressions of the Soviet soldiers were similar to mine.

'They came,' he said, 'and sat down in the snow in front of the cottage, with their rifles between their legs, and dozed. When my host invited them to come inside, they just muttered, "It isn't worth while", and went on dozing.'

Thenceforth every day brought something new. In a large villa in Podkowa, where the Gestapo had had its local headquarters, a new Security Police made its abode. Then placards were posted ordering all members of the underground to register and give up their arms. Soon, other posters introduced a prohibition on listening to Western radio stations. Finally, the first arrests took place; and fear resumed its reign again.

Then one day the news spread that it was possible to go to Warsaw. I took a bicycle and went off right away, though I later regretted it. What I saw was a dreadful graveyard of a City, a stony desert, where before a metropolis had pulsated with life. It was only in Marshall Street and Jerusalem Avenue that I saw little groups of people, the advance guard of the many thousands of Warsavians who soon began to trek back to the rubble and make their homes in it, either in the cellars, or in miraculously preserved rooms perched high up in utterly gutted houses; rooms that could be reached, like pigeon lofts, only by ladders or planks with cross rungs nailed to them. On many houses an inscription could be seen, crudely painted with a tar-brush by the man who first began the re-building of Warsaw. That inscription will remain for me a symbol of the elemental national impulse to rebuild the capital, which continues to this day. It was daubed by the unskilled hand of an unknown soldier of the Zymierski Army, who wanted the people of Warsaw to know that it was he who had opened for them the road back to their abandoned homes and dwellings. The inscription stated concisely: 'Mines removed by Kus, a sapper'.

The underground in territories East of the Vistula had already established contact with us and sent us reports, which were of a depressing uniformity. From all parts of the country we heard the same story. First, units of the Home Army attacked the retreating Germans from the rear, and helped the Soviet Armies to capture a city; then the underground authorities would come out into the open and engage in negotiations with the Soviet command, frequently inaugurated with lavish feasting. Then the NKVD would arrive and demand their subordination to the Communist Union of Polish Patriots, or, a little later, to the Lublin Committee; and, on refusal, all would be jailed and deported to Russia.

The problem of the arrested and deported soldiers of the Home Army was a running sore during the years 1945-1947. When in 1946, as chairman of the Legal Committee of the Polish Peasant Party, I visited the Ministry of Public Security to intervene on behalf of the arrested soldiers of the Home Army and of the Peasant Battalions, requesting their release and permission for them to return to their homes, a Colonel of the Secret Police in a moment of frankness made the position clear to me:

'You are wasting your time,' he said, 'and ours, by raising the matter. Neither you nor we have any say in it. It is exclusively within the competence of the NKVD.'

I also received a reliable report on the talk which the No. 1 Polish Communist, Jacob Berman, had in this matter with the legendary General of the NKVD, 'Malinov', who was none other than the present head of the Soviet Committee of State Security, General Ivan A. Serov. When Ber an tried to convince him that it would help to pacify the country if the soldiers of the Home Army were brought back from Russia, even if they were kept in concentration camps, Serov silenced him with a veiled threat:

'I am astonished, Comrade Berman, that you should take up the cudgels on behalf of men who would certainly contribute nothing to the building up of a people's democracy in Poland, but on the contrary, would obstruct the work. Besides, they live in quite good conditions in the camps, and if you would like to . . . you could find out for yourself on the spot.'

After such an unambiguous allusion, Berman never again dared to raise the question. In time, however, the majority of the Home Army soldiers did come back from Russia.

A typical instance of Soviet treatment of the underground, whenever it came out into the open, was Lublin, where the District Plenipotentiary officially visited the Soviet Command, and where the underground administration took over the city and the county. The officials were installed in public offices, the underground police took over public order; but the final result was the same, for all were arrested and deported to Russia.

Zamosc was another city in which the underground administration passed the test. It so happened that after the German troops had retreated from the city, the Soviet army did not occupy it until a week had elapsed. A few days sufficed for the restoration of order, and general conditions returned to what they had been before the war. All the administrative and municipal offices were taken over by men and women appointed by the underground authorities, and life in the city soon became normal again. The day came when the city was occupied by Soviet troops, and events took the familiar course, leading to a concentration camp in Russia.

Both the Government Plenipotentiary and the Commander of the Home Army were now living near Warsaw. The Plenipotentiary, first in Milanowek, and then in Lesna Podkowa; while 'Little Bear' found a hide-out near Grodzisk. I visited the Plenipotentiary every day, as the Rising had disrupted the monitoring of foreign radio stations, and I had to inform him of all that was happening in the world, on the basis of my own monitoring of BBC broadcasts. Several military and civilian emissaries were dropped into the country by parachute, and the information they brought was far from reassuring. Russia not only dominated the Eastern front, but also world politics; and the spectre of Yalta was already in the air.

The Adventures of 'Little Bear'

One evening we invited 'Little Bear' and Minister Jasiukowicz to dinner, bed and breakfast. I anticipated a pleasant evening, as I had already struck up a friendship with 'Little Bear'; while several days spent in talks with Jasiukowicz after the capitulation of Warsaw, when we stayed together in Mokotow Street, had brought us close to each other. 'Little Bear' came to us rather depressed, and when I asked him what was troubling him, he told me that his radio liaison with London had broken down. I offered to send his telegrams through my station, which pleased him greatly, especially when I told him I could do it as early as the following morning. He at once drafted the telegrams to be enciphered, and this restored his usual cheerfulness.

We sat down to a good dinner and a bottle of tolerable vodka, and listened with fascination to 'Little Bear' recounting his adventures.

'In 1940, when I was in charge of the underground in Soviet-occupied territory, I was living in a hide-out in Lwow. One evening a Soviet Militia car pulled up in front of the house. I didn't suppose that they were looking for me, but to be on the safe side I burnt two little sheets of paper, and waited to see what was coming. I had perfectly forged papers and had no reason to fear anything. However, contrary to my anticipations there was a knock at my door, and to my question, "Who's there?" I received the answer, "This is the Militia. Open the door!"

'When I opened the door, I beheld a strange sight. First to enter were two men with their hands up, and these were followed by a Militia man. The latter, pointing to me, asked them: "Is this the man from whom you bought the sugar?" "That's right", said the two men. I immediately relaxed, for I had never seen the two men before, and I had never sold any sugar to anyone. It was obviously a misunderstanding which, I felt sure, would soon be cleared up. I turned to the Militia man and said: "This must be a mistake. I don't know either of the two men, and I do not trade in sugar". The Militia man said to the two men again: "Have a good look at him, and say whether he did or did not sell you the sugar?" The men, still holding their hands above their heads, said in unison: "Yes, he did". Whereupon the Militia man decided: "In that case, get ready citizen! You will come with us to Militia headquarters, and there they will consider the case". When we left the house, I was somewhat uneasy. I could not understand what it all meant, and what sugar had to do with it. The Militia man opened the door at the back of the van, let in the two men and myself, and locked the door from the outside. Then, when the van started, one of the men said to me: "Colonel Okulicki, let me introduce myself. I am Colonel so-and-so of the NKVD". He was followed by the other man: "I am Major so-and-so of the NKVD. . . ." When I laughed and denied that I was Okulicki, they both said: "Enough of this". I kept hearing those same words for many months, during every cross-examination, whenever I denied that I was Okulicki. Much later, I was told that the comedy in Lwow had been staged to prevent my taking poison, or defending myself against arrest. They organised my arrest in such a way that I shouldn't suspect anything."

As he was telling the story, he became greatly animated, his eyes shone, and I could see that he was re-living his experience. We listened to him with fascination. The Soviets represented to us, veterans of German occupation, a threat which none of us knew from personal experience; and we took in every word, as Okulicki went on with his story, describing the cross-examinations, the tortures, the sleepless nights, the weakening of the body and the breaking down of the spirit. Then came a transformation.

'On the outbreak of the German-Soviet war,' he continued, 'they let me out of prison, half-dead; and from one day to another, I found myself with the Polish Military Mission at a reception in the Kremlin. The luxury there was truly Oriental, with gold plate, jars of caviar, an endless menu of dishes and dozens of toasts. Stalin presided at the table, supported by the highest dignitaries of the regime.

'It was already past midnight when Molotov rose, and continuing the round of countless toasts, raised his glass "in honour of a man present at the table, the leader of the Polish Underground, which has fought the Germans so magnificently: Colonel Okulicki". Though I was not prepared for it, I had to reply. I rose and said: "It is not very far from the Lubianka prison to the Kremlin. But in my case, the road was very long and the journey took many months. If, however, the happiness of Poland required that I had to cover that road, I shall never regret it".

'When I had concluded, to a storm of applause, Stalin rose from his chair, and going all the way round the table, came up to me with a glass of vodka, with which he clicked my glass, and said: "Well spoken! I congratulate you".'

We listened to the story far into the night, and fell into a reverie. What had the future in store for us and for Okulicki? Was it prison, or a banquet in the Kremlin, or both; and which was to precede which? It turned out that it was to be prison; for only a few weeks after that evening, by an accursed fate, Okulicki found himself again in the Lubianki prison, together with Jasiukowicz. While, several months later, I, too, found myself behind bars, in the tender care of the Security Police. But I must not anticipate events.

In the early hours of the morning our guests went to bed, Zosia sat down to encipher the telegrams, and I dozed for an hour. When the telegrams were ready, I took my bicycle and pedalled several miles along country lanes to the station. Roman and Jan were already up and tuning in. I reclined on the bed, and before I had smoked my third cigarette, London confirmed receipt of the telegrams. 'Little Bear' found a note to this effect with his breakfast. He was overjoyed and wanted to show it in some way. 'Put up the names of the men from your station to be decorated. I shall give them each a Cross of Gallantry, for they deserve it.'

Yalta

The London BBC announced the official communiqué on the results of the Yalta conference, while at the same time we received from the Polish Government in London a telegram interpreting its decisions. On learning the truth, even the most hardened optimists were despondent, for a political victory of the Soviets stared us in the eyes. The backbone of a new Polish Government was to be the Lublin Committee, which had already been recognised by the Soviets as the Polish Government; the inclusion of a few Poles from abroad would not change its character in any way.

In a mood of extreme depression, the Council of National Unity met in Lesna Podkowa on February 21 for a two days' session. I arrived early, and thus had an opportunity to listen to the many opinions on what had happened at Yalta. Everyone viewed the situation soberly and critically, nevertheless, each of us was speculating on future chances, principally on the chance of salvaging something of the country's independence, and of introducing into the future Government men from the underground. Casimir Puzak seemed to be more pessimistic than the others, and he was an expert on Russia and the Soviets. But he too thought we should try to salvage as much as possible.

After the discussion had opened, I left the session, for I had other work on my hands. I returned towards the end of the session, to study the resolutions which had been passed. There is a conflict of opinion among Poles abroad about whether the Council of National Unity accepted or rejected the Yalta agreements. The truth is that the Council of National Unity declared its willingness to take the decisions of the Yalta Conference as a basis for talks to regulate Polish-Soviet relations; it declared that the underground should come out into the open, and that a Government of National Unity should be formed as soon as possible. Yalta was regarded as an unavoidable evil, which had grievously wronged Poland, but one to which the country had to adjust itself. In view of this attitude of the Council of National Unity, there can be no question of the Yalta agreements having been either accepted or rejected.

The truth lies half-way between.

The attitude assumed by the Council of National Unity on February 22, 1945, was fully endorsed by the last manifesto of the Council, issued on July 1, 1945, on the occasion of the dissolution of the Council. The manifesto included the following statement:

'In these circumstances, the policy of intransigence towards the Yalta decisions adopted by the Polish Government in London fails to take into account the accomplished facts which Russia has enacted in the country. More especially, the conference in Moscow and the ensuing compromise between the Mikolajczyk group and a number of democratic leaders on the one side, and the Lublin Committee on the other, has produced conditions which Fighting Poland has to reckon with.

'On the formation of a new Government and its recognition by the Western Powers, the possibility of legally carrying on a conspiratorial struggle, based on the generally recognised Government in London, came to an end, and the problem arises of an open struggle on the part of the democratic Parties in Poland for the achievement of national aims and their respective Party programmes.

'In that open struggle, Underground Poland will not impede men of good will who find themselves in the Provisional Government of National Unity. Equally, it will not embarrass individual Parties in their choice of the ways and tactical means they may want, or be obliged, to adopt.

'At the session of July 1, 1945, all the democratic Parties of Underground Poland represented on the Council of National Unity adopted unanimously the resolution dissolving the Council and bringing this fact to the notice of the nation and foreign countries.

'By this act of self-denial, the Council of National Unity desires to give one more proof of its utmost good will, as it gave in its declaration of February 22, and in its acceptance of the Pruszkow talks.'

Such was the 'swan song' of the one and only underground Parliament known in the history of Poland or, perhaps, in the history of the whole world. A future historian, in writing of its activities, will no doubt seize on two manifestoes, those of August 15, 1943, and March 15, 1944. The last one was especially significant; for it bade farewell to the past, pre-war era and attempted to lay the foundations for a better, socially just and democratic Poland. It will be but a slight exaggeration if I say that this was a kind of Constitution of the Third of May, 1791, transferred to the threshold of a new epoch, the epoch that was soon to be born in the deadly vapours of Hiroshima.

A Visit from the Security Police

We no longer felt safe in our latest hide-out. There was nothing definite to fear, but we felt it was time for us to move. For one thing, too many people knew our address. We found a tiny room in a new and clean villa on the periphery of Lesna Podkowa. Our hosts, a lonely, elderly couple, were glad to have someone staying with them in the empty house, and we soon came to terms. Of course they had no idea that we were 'illegal'; but on the contrary, having examined our authentic 'Kennkarten', issued in false names (which meant that they had been issued officially by the Kreishauptmann on the basis of forged birth certificates), the elderly pair regarded us as yet another couple who, expelled from Warsaw because of the Rising, wanted to wait until the new crisis, caused by the Soviet occupation, should pass.

That same evening we packed our scanty belongings and the portable American transmitter on to a toboggan, and taking a roundabout route through the woods, we pulled it over the fresh snow to our new abode.

Our life in that villa was quiet, pleasant and retired; for no one, not even our intimate friends knew our new address. Every morning I left to attend to various matters, while Zosia went out on her affairs. We spent the evenings at home, reading a great deal, and listening to the forbidden London radio. We both felt much better for having settled in a quiet spot.

Several days after we had moved into the villa, in the dead of night, we heard the barking of two dogs kept by our hosts, followed by loud voices in the garden and the ringing of the door-bell. Without turning the light on, I opened the door slightly and listened, while Zosia hurriedly pulled the portable transmitter from under the couch, took it out on to the balcony, and hung it by a leather belt over the rail. The few words I heard from the hall were enough for me to know that it was the Security Police. My heart stopped beating. Had they come for us? I heard the voice ask who else lived in the villa, and the reply, 'A married couple, Mr. and Mrs. Bujnicki, on the first floor'. I gently closed the door, and lay down again on the couch. After a minute I heard a knock. In a sleepy voice I asked, 'Who's there?' and heard the reply, 'Police, open the door'. I switched on the light and said, 'The door is not locked, please come in'.

The man who appeared before us seemed to be the personification of a revolutionary-fighter of the familiar type seen in Soviet propaganda pictures. He was a tall, rather lean man in top boots, a civilian overcoat with a leather belt round it, and a peaked cap; he had an automatic in his hand. He studied us with a sharp, searching look. We were lying motionless on the couch, like two wooden logs, under the light standing on the table; and we looked straight into his eyes. It was the first time we had seen a Security policeman at close quarters, and the sight of the new authority was an exciting experience, not to mention the fright it gave us. He asked us for our documents and examined them carefully. When he handed them back he was a little more polite. He had another look round the room, and as he was preparing to leave, apologised for having disturbed us during the night. This emboldened me to ask:

'For whom are you looking? What has happened?'

'We received a report that a *Volksdeutsche* was hiding here,' he answered.

I laughed with relief, 'In that case it cannot be us!'

'I am sure it's not you. Good night!'

All would have been well, except that a similar visit by another representative of the Security Police took place three days later. This was too much for us. Cursing the 'quiet spot', we moved to a house near Brwinow. Much later, I learned that it was our hosts who were the real cause of the nocturnal visits. That quiet elderly couple were an extraordinary pair. She was of German origin, and had taken advantage of it to protect the life of her much older husband, a Jew. In this way they had lived a life of fear for five years. When the matter was explained, the Security Police left them in peace.

The Arrest of the Fifteen

March 1945 was cold, but the mud dried up and I was able to get around on my bicycle. When I visited the Plenipotentiary, and entered his room on the first floor of the villa in which he had his hide-out, I noticed that he was pre-occupied with some worrying problem. Before I left, I knew what it was; for when I was on the point of going, he handed me a paper saying:

'Read this, and tell me what you think about it.'

As I read the paper I felt increasingly amazed. For it was a letter from a Soviet Army officer, Colonel Pimenov, of the Russian Guards, inviting the Plenipotentiary and the underground authorities to talks with representatives of the Soviet authorities, with the object of finding a solution to the situation created, on the one hand, by the occupation of Poland by the Soviet armies, and, on the other, by the fact that the underground authorities remained in being and continued to function in secret. In conclusion, Colonel Pimenov pledged his word of honour as an officer of the Guards for the safety and liberty of the Polish participants in the proposed talks.

I read the letter, which was written in Russian, twice, and tried to appraise it. To begin with, I suspected that it was a trap. But if it was not a trap, what was to be done? I was of the opinion that if it was not a trap, the proposal should not be ignored; for if we ignored it the Soviets would accuse us before the Allies of having rejected their friendly advance. I thought the talks should be undertaken in agreement with the Polish Government in London, for it was possible that something might come of them. But how to resolve the question of whether the proposal was a straightforward one or a trap? I felt sure that we should never be able to resolve it with absolute certainty, so I recommended that, as a safeguard, the Plenipotentiary and the Commander-in-Chief ought not to take part in the talks personally, but appoint special representatives for the purpose. They themselves should, moreover, increase precautions in communicating with their emissaries, and remain in hiding.

'You are perfectly right,' the Plenipotentiary interposed, 'except that they don't want to talk with representatives, but with me and "Little Bear" in person. They particularly insist that "Little Bear" must be present, as they have already told us through the go-betweens. They said, with brutal frankness, that they are acquainted with the state of our internal affairs, and they know that should the Commander of the Home Army not take part in the talks, he would refuse to recognise their results. I am afraid we shall have to take the risk.'

I was not at all convinced, but realised that matters had already gone too far and were as good as settled. There was no alternative. I was again preparing to leave, when the Plenipotentiary raised another problem.

'You are in charge of our liaison with the world, and to safeguard it, you must break off contact with me, and with those who are to take part in the talks, and remain in hiding. You must watch carefully everything that goes on, and should anything untoward happen, inform the Government in London. Don't call here again unless I summon you, will you?'

'Certainly, Mr. Plenipotentiary.'

'One other thing. Representatives of your Party will be taking part in the talks. Might they want you to participate in the talks as well?'

'I am sure they won't. Ever since I was appointed Director of Civil Resistance my Party has considered that I am responsible to you and not to the Party.'

'I am glad of that, for I wanted to ask you to keep as far away from the talks as possible.'

Next, I had a conversation on the subject with 'Little Bear', who was in hiding near Grodzisk. My bicycle was being repaired, so I set out on foot, taking the lane alongside the Suburban Electric Railway.

I was very fond of bicycling or walking along those narrow,

well-trodden, dry and springy lanes. It was cool and I was covering the distance rapidly, when I ran into 'Little Bear' in the middle of an open field, as he was coming to meet me. There was no shelter at hand, and since we preferred to talk away from other people, we turned into the nearby sand-dunes and settled ourselves in a hollow. It was cloudy and windy, and we had to wrap up well in our overcoats, which we had acquired since the Rising; and there we chatted. In front of us extended a meadow with sparse willow trees, over which crows hovered. It was a typical Mazovian landscape.

Our talk took a course similar to that with the Plenipotentiary, but its conclusion was different. 'Little Bear' was convinced that the letter was a trap, though he agreed that the offer should not be rejected, and that the talks should be conducted by authorised plenipotentiaries. I was relieved when he pressed my hand and said:

'It's agreed, Zielinski. I shall not be going.'

We were both chilled among the sand-dunes, and before parting we dropped in at a wooden shed close to the railway track near Grodzisk, where two young girls welcomed 'Little Bear' as an old friend. We had a glass of 'bimber' and a sausage sandwich, and went out separate ways.

Unexpectedly, after a few days I was again summoned by the Plenipotentiary. He was less worried.

'You may again visit me. The preliminary talks have been concluded. Each Party delegation had separate talks, and all came back without the slightest obstacle. No one shadowed them either before or after the talks. But what is more important, the Russians accepted our pre-condition that our delegation should first be transported to London, and only after that attend the talks.'

I must admit that I felt greatly reassured, and looked upon the whole problem with different eyes. My optimism was not shared by my better half, for Zosia continued to assert with the utmost firmness that it was a trap. This led to much 'domestic strife', in which the male half was repeatedly and heavily trounced for lacking plain common sense. My injunctions 'not to meddle in matters which don't concern you' availed nothing, and even my grumblings that 'here have I been sweating for years and now the others are going on a trip to London', instead of arousing her sympathy, were received with bursts of sarcastic laughter.

The wife of a friend of ours, who was to be a member of the delegation, reacted similarly, warning her husband with exasperating monotony: 'Don't take your wrist-watch with you, Dad, for in "London" the Russians may take it away from you. . . .'

In the meantime, events were moving fast. The Government in London was informed of everything that was going on, and had no objections. It was believed that the delegation might mediate between the London Polish Government and the Soviets, whose representatives did not trouble to conceal their contempt for the Lublin puppets. The Soviet side, described as 'Marshal Zukov's delegates', was supplied with personal data concerning all the people who were to fly to London, so that the necessary travel documents could be issued to them. Our delegates were hurriedly preparing for the journey, and despite the tragic end of the expedition, their eagerness had its comic side. There was keen competition in the Parties for the privilege of being nominated for the delegation, speeches were being prepared in advance, to be delivered in the Kremlin, after the visit to London, and the great receptions were envisioned. There were acute differences of opinion as to the protocol regulations in the Kremlin and the appropriate attire to be worn there.

On March 26, 1945, on the eve of a pre-departure meeting between Soviet representatives and the Government Plenipotentiary, the Commander of the Home Army, and Puzak, I met Okulicki in a little café in Basket Street. As soon as I set eyes on the lady-waitresses and the customers, I knew I was in a place established by the underground. We sipped tea, and leaning over the table, discussed the meeting with the Soviet side that was to take place the next day. Okulicki, who was of a cheerful disposition and had a sound and clear judgement, was now depressed and off his balance.

'I have decided,' he said, 'under pressure from the Plenipotentiary, to take part in the talks; but I feel I was wrong in yielding to that pressure. Should it prove to be a trap, and in the event of my arrest, I have appointed Colonel Rzepecki as my successor. You know him well. After the talks I shall return to Warsaw, and should be glad to meet you, if you are still here.'

We arranged to meet for dinner and to spend the night in my hide-out in Warsaw. The following day I was waiting for 'Little Bear' in front of the door leading to a half-destroyed house. Curfew was approaching and Okulicki had not arrived. I became increasingly worried, but consoled myself with the thought that the talks might have taken longer than antici-pated, or that he might have gone to visit the Plenipoten-tiary, to discuss matters which had arisen from the talks. . . . Zosia and I waited in our hide-out till far into the night, but 'Little Bear' did not come.

On March 28, 1945, the remaining delegates left for Prusz-kow. There was an expectant atmosphere in the underground centres. It is true that we were all rather astonished when observers in Pruszkow reported uniformly that none of the Polish participants in the conference had left the villa which they had all been seen to enter; but it was assumed that the Soviet authorities had prepared hospitality for the night, and that in accordance with their usual practice they were keeping the delegation isolated from the outside world, thus making it easier for them to apply any desired pressure.

During the following days, however, reports arrived stating that in the evening of the day on which the talks began, the buildings adjoining the villa had been occupied by the NKVD, and that several motor-cars had left the villa's court-yard.

All the earlier suspicions were revived, and the monstrous thought intruded that the purpose of the preliminary talks had been simply to weaken our vigilance and bring all the delegates together, especially the distrustful 'Little Bear'; and that when that happened all of them had been arrested on the spot. On the other hand, some people were of the opinion that the talks were continuing; that the Polish representatives had been transported to Marshal Zhukov's headquarters; that they were still being kept isolated, so as to reduce their resistance; but that all the men were tough and would not yield to pressure.

During the whole of this period I cycled every day to a detached village cottage near Otrebusy, where Mrs. Baginska was waiting for her husband. As soon as I got off the bicycle and looked through the window, I would know that Baginski had not come back yet. When I thought of the possibility of his being arrested, I felt terribly sorry for this sterling man, who was closer to me than anyone else in the Party. It was his fate to wander all his life from one prison to another, from a Tsarist jail and the prison of Brest to the prisons of the Security Police in 1946. His uncompromising service to the cause in which he believed, and for which he fought, produced conflicts in which Baginski, as the weaker party, always paid the penalty.

Time marched on, however, and all traces of the delegation vanished. I could not delay any longer, and on Easter Monday I informed London of the position. The conclusion of my telegram shows that I myself had no definite opinion on what had happened:

'We assume that the talks are being continued, or that the delegates have been taken to Moscow, or that they are on the way to London, or that they have been arrested. You must exercise your own judgement.'

When a few days later the BBC broadcast a communiqué from the Polish Government in London, based on the above and subsequent telegrams, which stated that the Polish members of the Pruszkow conference had been arrested (and judging from our radio monitorings this must have made a great impression on world opinion), it still seemed that the statement was too rash. However, all doubts were soon dispelled, not only because of the lack of any Soviet denial, but because of certain news emanating from the Lublin Committee, which definitely stated—with some embarrassment, it is true—that the leaders of the Polish underground had been arrested. The leading Lublin men, however, did not conceal their 'Schadenfreude', and Bierut is reputed to have said to his cronies: 'They wouldn't talk to us, Poles, but only with foreigners; now they have had their talk. . . .'

After the Arrests

The news of the arrest of the underground leaders spread throughout the country with extraordinary speed, and created the most profound consternation. No one had any illusions as to the ultimate aims of Soviet policy, least of all those who had lived through the Warsaw Rising, and had seen with their own eyes and experienced with their own bodies what Soviet 'liberation' meant. But no one would ever have thought it possible that the Soviets would have had recourse to such an infamous and cynical ruse, especially in relation to the four Ministers of the underground Cabinet, who at the request of the Western Allies revealed their names and functions for the benefit of the Soviet side. The shock was all the greater because only the higher leaders of the underground had been informed of the preliminary talks. The nation and the underground masses learnt, from foreign broadcasts, from the underground press, and from whispered news, which circulated with lightning speed, only of the arrests themselves. The outrage produced an explosion of fury and despondency, and there was great tension throughout the country. Plans were made for carrying out a spectacular coup, for reprisals which would satisfy the thirst for revenge and demonstrate that the underground continued to exist, and was able to inflict punishment. Everyone was tensely awaiting the reaction of the Allies. When it came, it was only feeble, and had no prospects of succeeding. Excitement and expectation were replaced by disappointment and boundless discouragement.

Against the background of the kidnapping of the leaders and the hopelessly inadequate intervention of the Allies, people began to realise that at Teheran and Yalta a fourth partition of Poland had been effected; and that, in addition, something worse had happened, which even the boldest and clearest-thinking men and women dared not define. Nevertheless, though shaken, trust in the Allies was maintained; as may be seen from the following incident. On April 12, President Roosevelt died. He was extraordinarily popular in Poland and the country regarded his sudden demise as a great loss. No one at that time realised the immense wrong which

Poland suffered at the hands of this American politician, for no reliable news penetrated into the country. It was natural, therefore, that I should send, on behalf of the Government Plenipotentiary, a message of condolence to the dead leader's successor, President Truman. However, it was a sign of dangerous illusions that I concluded the message by assuring the new President that the trust and hope which the Polish nation had reposed in his predecessor would be transferred to him.

The question arose of how the situation imposed by the Yalta agreement could be resolved if the foremost leaders of the Polish nation in her underground struggle had been kidnapped and deported, instead of being permitted to represent the nation in the solution of that question. Everyone became perturbed by this uncertainty, the uncertainty of what was to come to-morrow, and the fear, which no one would openly admit as yet, that the nation had been sold into Russian slavery again.

The leadership of the Polish underground had been broken up. The entire Council of Ministers, the Praesidium of the Council of National Unity, and the principal Party leaders had been arrested. The Home Army had lost its Commander-in-Chief. The country and the underground were faced, in addition to previous questions, with new problems produced by the Pruszkow crime. How was the Polish question to be solved in face of the dominant role of the Soviets in the settlement in Eastern Europe? What road was the Polish underground to choose? Was it capable of action after the arrest of its leaders? Should the armed partisan detachments still operating in the field carry out an armed demonstration? Was there any sense in keeping these detachments in being? What principles of Civil Resistance should be observed in relation to the new occupying Power? What attitude should be taken towards the problem of the country's reconstruction, and of participation in the Lublin administration? Should the present organisation and methods of action by the underground be maintained, or new methods applied; and if so, what methods? Events moved fast and demanded a clear answer to these questions.

I was now sending one telegram after another, informing

the Government in London of every minute detail of the kidnapping. I also telegraphed the full text of Colonel Pimenov's letter. On the basis of these telegrams, the Government issued statements which the BBC broadcast to the world. The statements were also circulated in Poland by means of radio monitorings and the underground press. The Polish people were profoundly impressed by the declarations of the British Foreign Secretary, Mr. Anthony Eden, at the San Francisco Conference, where the casual explanation offered by Molotov on May 4, 1945, admitting the arrest of the underground leaders, removed all doubts and uncertainties as to their fate.

CHAPTER XXII

The Final Months of the Polish Underground State

A Session in Warsaw

I now entered on the most difficult period of my life, and spent many hours rambling through the woods and thickets of Lesna Podkowa, meditating on the situation and trying to find a way out. It was springtime, and nature was awakening to new life, but I felt sad at heart. As head of Civil Resistance and director of the Department of Internal Affairs I was the senior member of the Government Delegation. The deputies of the Plenipotentiary, who were members of the underground Cabinet, were themselves under arrest, and they had no deputies. In these circumstances, I had to take the initiative myself. Apparently others were of the same opinion, though for somewhat different reasons; and the director of the Government Plenipotentiary's office, Miklaszewski, approached me with a proposal, which though superficially attractive seemed to me but a new version of the competition for 'first place under the gallows'.

'After the arrest of the Plenipotentiary,' said Miklaszewski to me, 'authority over the underground should be assumed by a triumvirate, consisting of yourself, as chairman, the director of the Department of Press and Information, and myself. We should take everything into our hands and carry on.'

I decided to reject this proposal outright, but before doing so, I wanted to find out what was really in Miklaszewski's mind.

'What would be the legal source of our authority,' I asked.

'The offices we already occupy,' he answered.

I refused to be a party to it, and told Miklaszewski what I intended to do.

'In view of the fact that the Council of National Unity has been disrupted by the arrests, I have decided, as the senior member of the Delegation, to convene a meeting of plenipotentiary members of the Parties which form the Council, to determine our future course.'

The meeting took place in Warsaw in about the middle of April 1945. I went to Warsaw on my bicycle from Lesna Podkowa. It was my second visit to the capital since the 'liberation', and its inhabitants were returning to it from all parts of Poland. The capital had such a strange power of attraction that people frequently left towns and villages unaffected by the war, in which they had already settled, to live in the rubble and ruins of their beloved City.

I could not find the hide-out in which the meeting was to take place. Everywhere, as far as the eye could reach, there were great mounds of rubble and bricks, over which footpaths had already been well trodden. I found the path I had to follow and reached the gutted house in which we were to meet. The delegates were arriving one after another. It was the first time since the arrests in Pruszkow that we were meeting in such large numbers. We were ten in all, most of those present being members of the Council of National Unity; and all were visibly affected by what they had gone through. The Pruszkow crime was in everyone's mind, and we sat there in a solemn mood, full of grim determination.

The chair was taken by one of the senior members of the Council, who called upon me to present the agenda and to explain the purpose of the meeting. The Parties were more or less aware of what was intended; for I had requested that representatives with full powers should be appointed, who could make decisions binding on the Parties; but I had to explain the situation in detail. I placed before the meeting the complete dossier concerning the Pruszkow talks, I read all the telegrams sent and received, I analysed the situation, and in conclusion, I declared for the continuation of underground activities, for the reconstruction of the Council of National

Unity with a reduced membership, and for the maintenance of the most important departments of the underground Government. The ensuing discussion showed that there were no conflicts of opinion. All those present had a clear view of the situation and of the new problems, and were not afraid to accept responsibility. No one as much as mentioned the liquidation of the underground; for everyone realised that the existence of the Polish Underground State was the foundation of the Polish Government in London and all its activities; and that the liquidation of the underground would clear the way for the Allies to recognise the Lublin Government, and would in any case give a monopoly in politics to the Communists. In order to counteract the consequences of the arrests, the purpose of which was the disintegration and disorganisation of the underground, it was necessary to close ranks and endure, so as to demonstrate before the world the existence of an independent Poland. As far as organisation was concerned, the opinion prevailed that the Council of National Unity still existed, though with reduced membership. With regard to the appointment of a successor to the Government Plenipotentiary, it was unanimously agreed, on the motion of the representative of the National Democratic Party, to propose to the Government in London that I should take over the office until the position of the arrested leaders had been clarified. The discussion showed complete unanimity on the necessity of retaining the kidnapped leaders in their previous offices, and that all their successors should be appointed as only acting on their behalf. We were of the opinion that this would become an embarrassment to the Soviet authorities; while their release from the offices they occupied would weaken their position and narrow down the ground of Allied intervention; as to which, we deluded ourselves that it would lead to the release of the arrested leaders. No one anticipated at the time that the Allies would be guilty of such weakness and helplessness in their dealings with the Soviets, and that the Moscow show trial would take place.

On the other hand, the meeting decided not to reconstruct the underground Council of Ministers, for in the existing circumstances it would have been superfluous, as the Cabinet was practically a replica of the Praesidium of the Council of National Unity, and acted only in an advisory capacity.

This solution of our current problems, speedily approved by the Polish Government in London, was very timely, and prevented the carrying out of all sorts of 'coups d'état' by various groups which had assumed that all the Government centres had been smashed, and wanted to seize control of the underground movement and carry on under their own particular flags. The nation was informed of the actual position by Government declarations, broadcast by the BBC, to the effect that authority in the country under occupation continued to rest with the new Government Plenipotentiary and the Council of National Unity. These declarations, repeated several times by radio and circulated by the underground press, enabled us to keep the situation under control.

In possession of a clear authorisation, I proceeded speedily with the reorganisation of the office of Government Plenipotentiary, which had been planned even earlier, by Plenipotentiary Jankowski. During the following few weeks most of the departments were liquidated. The entire conspiratorial administration was concentrated in the Department of Internal Affairs, the Department of Information, and the Department of Social Welfare, which was taken over by Francis Bialas, who succeeded Judge Mateja, killed during the Rising. The underground journal, 'The Republic', continued to appear. The Department of Social Welfare carried on its work in the centres to which the population of Warsaw had been evacuated after the Rising. Contacts with District Plenipotentiaries were maintained. They carried on their activities on the same reduced scale as the central office, but even so they had to take into account the fact that the Security Police were on their trail, and arrests were multiplying. The first Communist concentration camp in Central Poland, established in Rembertow, was soon filled.

Liaison with the Government in London continued without interruption, and was limited only by the capacity of the transmitters. Unfortunately, from the time of the arrest of the leaders of the underground until the dissolution of the office of Government Plenipotentiary and the Council of National

Unity on July 1, 1945, not one official emissary from the Government in London to the Plenipotentiary arrived in Poland.

A New Commander of the Home Army

Colonel Rzepecki, a squat, balding man of about forty-seven, who went into German captivity after the Rising, but was able to make his way back into Poland, took over Okulicki's functions as Commander-in-Chief of the Home Army. He came straight to my hide-out, and remained with me in seclusion for two days, talking day and night. In these talks we touched upon everything, the past, present and future. We delved deep into history, searching for precedents and guidance. The road before us was hard and long, but we had to enter upon it. We were both coffee addicts, so we stimulated our minds by countless cups of this refreshing beverage. I knew Rzepecki well; we addressed each other by our Christian names, and our talks were most amicable throughout. Though he sympathised with 'Little Bear', he blamed him for acting contrary to the orders of the Supreme Commander in London, General Sosnkowski, not to take part in talks with the Russians; and he also blamed the Plenipotentiary for having exerted such strong pressure on Okulicki. The fact that Rzepecki was politically-minded facilitated our mutual understanding, and we were unanimous in almost all the matters we discussed.

Our talks began with an exaggeratedly solemn declaration by Rzepecki that he recognised my political authority, to which he was subordinate; and after a full exchange of information, we attempted to appraise the actual situation. The result was exactly the same as that of the meeting of the Parties, and the conclusions were identical, especially as to the necessity of continuing underground activities.

To begin with, we discussed the question of 'No', the organisation called into being by the Home Army, on the justified assumption that underground anti-Soviet activities would have to break off contact with the maternal organisation. In my opinion, 'No' had been uncovered by NKVD agents, as both numerous arrests and confidential information indicated; and, moreover, the methods of action adopted by the Home Army against the Germans were in the present phase politically obsolete. I was of the opinion that the underground had to find new forms in which to manifest the desire for independence of the Polish Nation; forms which would be appropriate to NKVD methods, and which offered chances of survival. I emphasised to Rzepecki the fact that 'No' had been founded without the knowledge of the Government Plenipotentiary, and that I had been requested by competent persons to inform him of its existence at a meeting of the Cabinet and the Council of National Unity in Piotrkow during the winter of 1944, which, however, failed to take place.

Rzepecki was of the same opinion, and we both agreed to approach the authorities in London with the proposal that 'No' should be dissolved. I do not know whether it was on account of this initiative, or because of a decision that had been reached by London in the meantime, that the 'No' organisation was dissolved; but we were informed of it by the Government in a telegram received during May 1945. All this took place several weeks before the Moscow trial of Polish leaders, which confirmed our worst fears.

At the same time, and because of certain suggestions I had already received, I told Rzepecki that any attempts against leading Lublin or Soviet personalities, by way of reprisals for the kidnapping of our leaders, would be inadvisable, and that I should not agree to them. They could only endanger the lives of the arrested leaders and lead to greater reprisals. The NKVD and Security Police would no doubt welcome them as a justification for further arrests of men and women whom they regarded as hostile. The beneficial results which reprisals might produce, such as the demonstration of the strength of the underground, the intimidation of Lublin or Soviet agents, and the impression they might make at home and abroad, would not offset the obvious disadvantages.

Rzepecki agreed with my opinion and undertook to issue instructions accordingly; though his liaison with district organisations was precarious, and discipline was breaking down. However, we decided that exceptionally cruel or overzealous officials of the Security Police would be severely punished by the underground.

Finally, the most important matter, which we agreed upon, was the problem of the partisan units of the Home Army, which still operated in the forests, fighting the aggressive troops of the NKVD and the Security Police, and carrying out special tasks, such as the liberation of prisoners, the liquidation of agents of the Security Police, etc. We had to reach a grim decision; for we both clearly saw the hopelessness of further armed struggle, in which the gallant fighters would inevitably be exterminated. After Teheran and Yalta, in the face of 'appeasement', which was discernible even in our country, cut off as it was from the world, and in face of the dominant rôle of the Soviets in Eastern Europe, recognised by the free world, we came to the conclusion that the struggle for independence by means of armed demonstrations undertaken by partisan units was useless, because militarily it had no chance, while politically it would have been senseless. We agreed, therefore, to issue instructions to the partisan units to disband; and in order to endow the instructions with greater authority, we decided to issue a joint manifesto on the matter.

In conclusion, Rzepecki informed me that he had appointed as his successor Colonel Bokszczanin, whose soldierly virtues he extolled in glowing terms. For my part, I considered that Rzepecki's rank did not endow him with sufficient authority, so I suggested in a telegram to London that he should be promoted to the rank of general. My telegram was disregarded, and Rzepecki was given the militarily unimpressive title of 'Delegate for the Armed Forces of Poland'.

He arranged two meetings for me with the commanders in the field, Colonel Radoslaw, whom I already knew, and Colonel Mscislaw (Colonel Wladyslaw Liniarski), commander of the Bialystok district, whom I had not met before. Rzepecki and I met the latter in a bombed building, in a little room that was perched up in the gutted house like a cage on a tree, except that it was not visible from the street.

I eyed Mscislaw with great interest, for he had the reputation of being a brilliant commander, and his exploits in the Bialystok district had become almost legendary. For some time now he had been engaged in fighting the troops of the NKVD and the Secret Police, which were attempting to encircle his forces and exterminate them; but so far without success. The partisans of Bialystok had an especially redoubtable reputation, and as chairman of the Peasant Party in that district, I was proud of the tough attitude of our people, on whose ardent patriotism we could always rely.

I asked Mscislaw what tactics he was employing to avoid encirclement by Soviet troops. His explanation was simple and reminded me of what the partisan leader, Andrew, had told me some years before.

'We have adopted a new system,' said Mscislaw. 'We maintain only small cadres in the forests, which can easily hide and slip out; while the bulk of the detachments consists of local inhabitants who lead a normal life. They are mobilised from time to time, whenever an action is being prepared, and afterwards they return to their homes.'

Mscislaw did not escape the fate which overtook so many others; he was captured by Soviet troops. As far as I remember, he was sentenced to only (!) ten years in prison; for the Communist military court took into consideration the mitigating fact that Mscislaw had been mentioned several times in the dispatches of the Soviet commander for his sector of the front, for the excellent co-operation of his partisan units in the fighting against the Germans.

Sessions of the Council of National Unity

During May and the early part of June several sessions of the Council were held near Warsaw with reduced attendance. It was late spring and the countryside was in full bloom. Through lanes, fields and woods we arrived singly at a secret hide-out in a little house surrounded by trees. There we deliberated for many hours. The analysis of the international situation which was made at each session was not encouraging. The Council continued to be guided by the February resolutions, while still recognising the Polish Government in London. The Council had no further means of action, except to wait for developments in the situation produced by the agreements of Teheran and Yalta. However, its hostility to the Lublin Committee was uncompromising.

In the course of our deliberations, the Peasant Party ('The Triangle') revealed its strong opposition to the Arciszewski Cabinet in London. The Peasant Party refused to support this Government, and energetically demanded its resignation, threatening to leave the Council should its demands be disregarded. During several debates on this subject, all Parties insisted on the necessity for the return of the Peasant Party to the Government, which would lose its representative character without it. At one of the meetings, however, Stanislaw Wojcik reasserted the Party's opposition to the Government of Arciszewski, and declared that he was withdrawing from the Council of National Unity. This greatly depressed all the remaining members of the Council, who appealed in vain to the Peasant Party to change, or at least to postpone, its decision.

At each session I reported to the Council on the international situation and the position at home. I submitted also reports received from the district centres and the texts of outgoing and incoming telegrams; and in addition I reported on my conversations and agreement with the Delegate for the Armed Forces concerning 'No'. Finally, after considering the state of our organisation, the Council entrusted me with wide powers as a Government Plenipotentiary and Deputy Prime Minister. Taking into account the possibility of my being arrested, the Council appointed against this eventuality two temporary successors, the first of whom was Francis Bialas. Should I be arrested, he was to take over my functions until the Government appointed a new Plenipotentiary.

The last session of the Council was adjourned without a date being fixed for another meeting. The Government in London was informed by radio of the business transacted at each session.

The Manifestos

The atmosphere of waiting on events and the uncertainty continued. The Yalta Agreement, the negative attitude which the Government in London had assumed towards it, the February resolutions of the Council of National Unity, recognising the necessity of taking the fact of the agreement into consideration, the kidnapping of the underground leaders, who had been animated by the utmost goodwill as far as co-operation with the Soviets was concerned, all combined to make a completely hopeless picture. Nevertheless, there were certain problems in the country which required a solution. The nation was implacably hostile to the new occupying power and hated the new regime, desiring to remain loyal to the underground authorities, whose instructions and guidance during the German occupation it had been accustomed to follow. Innumerable requests were made for the underground authorities to express an opinion on such questions as accepting office under the Lublin administration, and as to co-operation in the fields of education, national economy, and reconstruction. It also became necessary to define clearly the relationship of the Parties towards the Lublin authorities and the Communist Party (PPR).

To meet the emergency, I issued, on May 17, 1945, a manifesto signed by me as Acting Government Plenipotentiary and the Council of National Unity. I drafted the manifesto while walking in the fine garden of a villa in Lesna Podkowa, amid pine trees, shrubs and flowers, looking their best in the spring. All around were other gardens and detached villas, contributing to the serene atmosphere of an idyllic countryside; except that the Security Police were snooping around after the new Plenipotentiary and members of the Council of National Unity.

My life was that of a voluntary prisoner. I never ventured on to the roads or streets, I never used the Suburban Electric Railway, or visited the stations and the little café-bars. Like a shadow I flitted on my bicycle along little-frequented lanes, making my way to Warsaw, or to the secret hide-outs in which I met the men and women of the underground. The efficient Intelligence Service of the Government Plenipotentiary's Office had excellent contacts, and it warned me that the Security Police knew the identity of the new Plenipotentiary, and that he was hiding in the vicinity of the Suburban Electric Railway. They were out to capture me at all costs. I imposed the strictest discipline on myself and those nearest to me, and broke off all superfluous contacts. I even gave up visiting the radio station, which functioned perfectly and, in comparison with conditions under the German occupation, with relative safety. Personally, I missed the company of Roman and Jan very much. Within the narrow confines of the fenced-off garden, I pondered the heavy problems which had so fatefully devolved on to my shoulders. When the draft of the manifesto was ready, I secured the approval of the Council of National Unity, and it was issued on May 17, 1945. Here it is:

'To the Polish Nation.

'The war in Europe has come to an end. The wild beast of Nazism lies crushed at the feet of the victorious Allies. The war in the Far East will only indirectly affect the course of events in Europe. World opinion has turned its attention to the problem of a just peace and liberty, while the Governments are about to find ways to give it expression.

'The war has ended, but the struggle continues. The struggle for the realisation of the ideals embodied in the Atlantic Charter, the struggle for genuine liberty, democracy and a just peace.

'Poland has become the principal problem in this struggle and the crucial test for the victors. On the decision determining our fate will depend whether the coming world will be better, and whether peace will reign in it, or whether it will be plunged into the turmoil of an even more terrible war.

'What do we expect? What do we believe?

'We believe that the honest opinion of the whole world has been convinced that by the resolution of the Council of National Unity of February 22, 1945, declaring our readiness to accept, as a basis for further talks, which are to regulate Polish-Soviet relations, the decisions of the Crimea Conference, we went so far towards meeting Russia, by giving up values which every Pole holds dear, that any further concession would mean national suicide. However, to-day it has become clear to all, especially to the Western Allies, that Russia is delaying the carrying out of the decisions of the Crimea Conference concerning Poland, and that the matter remains open and unregulated.

'We believe that the entire world has been convinced of our sincere desire to enter into friendly relations with Russia, whose great power and position we recognise, and with whom we shall for ever remain neighbours, and with whom we do not desire ever to fight in the future. This our sincere assurance has greater weight than the vociferous and servile declarations of the imposters of Lublin.

'We expect that, in spite of everything, a Provisional Government of National Unity will be formed, based on the representatives of our genuine democracy, in the sense in which we understand the word, and not on the Lublin puppets; not on the despots from the Lublin Committee, who, with the word "liberty" on their lips, have shackled the hands of the Polish Nation and now gag its mouth and blindfold its eyes; not on the imposters of Lublin, who were responsible for the rejection of our hand, outstretched in friendship, and who now kill or banish into exile the best sons of our Motherland, the soldiers of the Home Army, admired by the whole world. We have lived to see the infamy of the Lublin security authorities outrivalling the Gestapo, with the name "Rembertow" acquiring the same reputation for horror as "Auschwitz".

'The crowning deed in the infamous activities of the Committee "governing" our country was the treacherous luring to Pruszkow on March 27 and 28 of the fifteen leading representatives of Underground Poland, their arrest and their deportation to an unknown destination. It was treacherous because they had been invited to a conference with a plenipotentiary of Marshal Stalin, Colonel-General Ivanow, which was to enable them to take an open part in the political life of the country. Among them were the deputy Prime Minister of the Polish Government in London, Jan Jankowski, a former minister and member of Parliament; the chairman of the Council of National Unity, Casimir Puzak, condemned to death by a Tsarist Court, his sentence being commuted to imprisonment for eight years in the fortress of Schlisselburg; and General Leopold Okulicki, the last Commander-in-Chief of the Home Army, a former Chief of Staff of the Army of General Anders. It was in this way that the Lublin Committee rid itself of its rivals.

'We expect that the fifteen arrested representatives of Underground Poland will take part in the formation of the Provisional Government of National Unity; that with its formation will be restored freedom of speech, freedom of the press, assembly and association; that the Nazi prohibition of listening to foreign radio stations will be rescinded; that there will follow the return of our heroic Army from the West, the return of prisoners-of-war, prisoners, workers, and emigrés from all countries of the world; that the elections to the Seym, which are to produce the first normal Polish Government, will be held in conditions of full freedom and complete peace, after the Soviet Army has left Polish territories, the Army which, with our modest support, liberated our country from the Nazi invasion, for which our gratitude will not be inhibited by fear and memories of violence; that the just achievement of agrarian reform, the nationalisation of the means of production, the democratisation of the Army, and the other plans enumerated in the manifesto of the Council of National Unity of March 15, 1944, will be carried out in order to reconstruct our system, and not for purposes of political agitation; that besides friendly relations with Russia, we shall preserve our most intimate relations with our Western Allies.

'We expect that the great Allies will bring their work to such a conclusion. The recent events in the international sphere, especially the fourfold rejection of the candidature of the Lublin Committee at the San Francisco Conference and the speech made on May 13 by Prime Minister Churchill, justify these our hopes.

'We believe, finally, that in the future, as a result of peaceful and friendly relations, it will be possible, with the approval of Soviet Russia, in an atmosphere of mutual trust, to resume the attempts to repair, be it only in part, the wrongs which the Yalta agreement inflicted on the Polish Nation.

'Such are our hopes for the immediate future. If these hopes were to be disappointed, which we do not anticipate, there will remain to us only further struggle for the recovery of genuine independence, which we shall never renounce.

'Fellow countrymen!

'No matter what the future has in store for us, the present requires from you that you should persevere in the attitude of resistance assumed by all social classes of our nation. Misfortunes have united us as we were never united before. We are united to-day in our thoughts and actions. We are united in distinguishing between chaff and grain, between truth and the falseness of the impostors of Lublin, in whatever fine words it is expressed. The flood of Lublin lies has yielded no results. We have closed our ranks, and we shall oppose all attempts to deprive us of our liberty and independence.

'Our unitedly negative attitude towards the present policy of the impostor "government" of Lublin must not retard the work of reconstruction in the country. We see chaos and anarchy rampant in all fields, which is harmful to our national interests. The dishonest Lublin Committee, striving for other, concealed, political aims, cannot master the situation. We therefore appeal to you to take the social initiative in the work of reconstruction. Report spontaneously for constructive work in all fields of reconstruction, in industry, commerce, agriculture, communications, education, etc.; in short, wherever you can work without abandoning your convictions, and without collaborating with the debasing policy of the Lublin Committee. This principle requires you to boycott all work in the political administration, propaganda and Security services, whose organisation and loathsome methods are alien to the truly free system of government which we desire to establish.

'Civil servants of the Lublin administration!

'Remember that your only legal and constitutional authority is the Government of the Polish Republic in London, recognised as such by the whole world, except Russia and her vassals, and that Government's deputed authority within the country. We request you to act in conformity with the national interest. While serving impostors, some of whom are not even citizens of Poland, be careful to preserve our spiritual and material values; do not take part in the political machinations of foreign agents in the Lublin Committee, threatening our independence, but oppose them.

'Countrymen!

'Do not let yourselves be provoked into an armed struggle. It could not now bring any advantage to the aims for which we are striving, but would expose ardent, and often most valuable individuals to doom. We appeal to the young people who sought shelter from mass persecutions and arrests in the forests to try to go back to normal life and productive work wherever it is possible to do so. Your remaining in the forests has already become the cause of a bloody pacification campaign. You are doomed to perish there, whereas your destiny is to live and to work for the Motherland, not to die without any advantage to it. Should you be compelled to serve in the army, you must preserve the attitude of good Poles, though without letting yourselves be used in actions directed against your countrymen or in a struggle for an alien cause, and avoiding deportation to the East, beyond the frontiers of Poland.

'May 17, 1945.   The Council of National Unity.
Acting Plenipotentiary for
Poland of the Government of the
Polish Republic in London.'

In connection with this manifesto I should like to point out that it announced in advance a demand for a revision of the Yalta agreement, expressing this demand in a form that took into account the situation in the country, in whose name the demand was put forward, which was entirely occupied by the Soviet power. This advance announcement, while leaving open the possibility of talks concerning the problem under dispute, indicates clearly that the stipulations of the Yalta agreement were not accepted. This paragraph of the manifesto should be studied carefully by those who desire to re-define, as far as it is possible, the attitude of the underground authorities towards Yalta.

The manifesto also defined the terms put forward by the underground movement concerning the formation of a Provisional Government of National Unity, the first condition of which was to be its foundation on truly democratic elements, and not on the usurping Lublin Committee, and the demand for the inclusion in it of the fifteen arrested representatives of Underground Poland, which has been brutally and tragically denied.

The manifesto advanced the demand that before the elections were held, Soviet troops should leave the country. I did not anticipate at the time that a few years later a similar demand to Russia would be made by the Western Powers in connection with a divided Germany and the occupied countries of Eastern Europe. The manifesto also put an end to any armed struggle, and appealed to young people to go back to normal life and productive work, wherever it was possible to do so, which meant without 'reporting' to the Communist authorities. This helped to produce a considerable efflux of young people from the forests and from the underground, and moulded an attitude to the conspiracy which even to-day dominates Polish public opinion.

Finally, the manifesto dealt exhaustively with the work of reconstruction in the country, appealing to all for 'social initiative in the work of reconstruction' without regard, or even in opposition, to the Lublin Committee. However, the manifesto contained a categorical prohibition on any work in the political administration, propaganda and security service. This part of the manifesto has undoubtedly greatly influenced the shaping of conditions in the new state of affairs imposed on Poland. It caused a mass of professionals and technicians, who up till then had been passively observing what was happening and waiting for guidance from the underground authorities, to rush to take part in the work of reconstruction; and it is to this that the Communists owe the great success achieved in this field. The entire immense group of engineers, administrators and technicians prepared by our Office for the Recovered Territories, was soon busy in the Ministry for the Recovered Territories, and played an important part in the rehabilitation of these areas.

It was through this attitude of the underground authorities that the Polish people were able to achieve so much in the realm of reconstruction, into which they put a superhuman effort. In undertaking this effort, the Polish people had no trust in Communist rule. The effort was prompted by the profound conviction that whatever was repaired or constructed in the country would remain and would serve the nation in better times, which every Pole at that time believed were coming.

At about the same time I collaborated with Rzepecki in drafting an appeal to the soldiers of Polish detachments in the fields and forests; this was signed by Rzepecki and me and issued on May 27, 1945, being widely circulated in the press and by leaflets.

'Soldiers of Polish Forest detachments!

'The whole world is already aware of your five-year-long devoted struggle against the German invaders, the intensity of which grew to such a high pitch when the German-Soviet front rolled into Polish lands, into Volhynia and Vilna. It is no longer a secret to the world that our Soviet Ally eagerly took advantage of the battle-readiness of the Home Army, only to disarm its soldiers brutally and cynically; and, using the meanest ruses, it imprisoned them, or forced them into the ranks of its own army, or executed them.

'Under these morally revolting conditions you nevertheless fought; because the interest of Poland demanded it; because you were ordered to do so by the legal Polish Government; because you understood that the military effort had to serve the political aims of the nation, and that these aims justified the heaviest soldierly sacrifice. By your conduct you have demonstrated the supreme values which can be expected from soldiers. We know to-day that your sacrifices have not been wasted.

'In the part of Poland liberated from the German pest, our Russian "ally", and the traitors from the Lublin Committee serving him, produced such vile conditions that it proved impossible to bring about what we had dreamed, that your detachments, which had covered themselves with glory, should be formed into divisions and corps and take part in the liberation of the Western part of the Motherland, and revenge the wrongs done by Poland's hereditary enemy.

'In these circumstances, the supreme authorities of the State demanded from you new and grave sacrifices, by self-immolating yourselves as soldiers. A decree of the President of the Republic ordered the dissolution of the Home Army and released you from your oath, while the Commander-in-Chief ordered you to return to constructive work in the re-habilitation of the country.

'This open, soldierly road, too, has been blocked to many of you by the perverse policy of the Soviets and their servile agents, by producing conditions equally as painful as the previous occupation. We know that many of you are still in hiding in the forests, and that your ranks are even being increased by those seeking shelter from the terror of the NKVD and the "Polish" security service. Unfortunately, such are conditions in Poland to-day, which the usurpers in their mockery call "democratic", that the best citizens, those who desire to serve their Motherland, must seek protection from the hostility of the alleged "allies" and traitors by hiding.

'In your tragic situation, however, you must realise that this is not a time for armed struggle; that the Government of the Republic expressly ordered the dissolution of the Home Army; that it has not declared armed opposition to the pre-sent occupying power, considering it to be harmful; and that it has appointed a Plenipotentiary for the Armed Forces in the country for the regulation of other military matters. Do not, therefore, trust either German *agents provocateurs* or those of the NKVD, who are trying to infiltrate into your ranks, even if they should show you printed orders of the Government or the Commander-in-Chief. Neither should you trust those reckless Poles, who, though prompted by patriotic motives, tempt you to continue partisan warfare, by referring to alleged orders of Polish authorities. Remember that even the finest soldierly exploits are useless if they are not carried out at the right time, and if they do not serve a purpose indi-cated by competent authorities. And, to-day, the competent authority in Poland is the Government Plenipotentiary and the Plenipotentiary of the Commander-in-Chief.

'Therefore, as behoves good and disciplined soldiers, carry out the difficult order of the President of the Republic and the Commander-in-Chief: go back to the work of reconstructing the country; though observe the necessary caution, so as to avoid treacherous persecution.

'May 27, 1945.　　Acting Government Plenipotentiary, Plenipotentiary for the Armed Forces.'

After the manifesto had been circulated through the service channels of the Home Army and all other underground channels, the efflux of partisans from the forests increased. Nevertheless, during the trial which the Security Police subsequently staged against Rzepecki, after the latter had been arrested, he was accused of not including in the manifesto an appeal for the soldiers to report to the Security Police and give up their arms. It is true that the manifesto did not include such an appeal, for that would have been too much. On the contrary, the manifesto of May 27 ordered that proper precautions should be taken against the possibility of treacherous persecution, which plainly indicated that the partisans were not to report to the Security Police.

Here I should like to mention that the problem of the partisan forest detachments involved me as late as 1947.

I was elected a member of Parliament by the City of Warsaw, and delivered in the Seym a single speech, devoted to the question of amnesty for members of the underground movement. After I had delivered this speech, I received several visits in my office at the headquarters of the Peasant Party in Jerusalem Avenue from young men, each of whom, talking to me confidentially, and pretending to be an emissary of the forest detachments, asked me whether my speech in the Seym was meant seriously, or whether it was only made as a matter of political expediency, and whether partisans should really take advantage of the amnesty. Fortunately, in the very first young man, I immediately recognised a security policeman, and knew that I was dealing with a clumsy act of provocation. With the utmost gravity, therefore, I answered my questioners by saying that my speech had been meant in all seriousness; and it was with great satisfaction that I noticed how disappointed the young men were with my replies.

Apart from this, I had several visits from genuine emissaries of the underground, who sought information and guidance.

An Emissary from Hungary

I was informed of the arrival of an emissary from the Government post in Hungary, who wanted to see me. By then, we had few safe hide-outs left, and the Security Police were exceptionally active along the Suburban Electric Railway. I decided to meet the emissary in the forest, at a spot familiar to me, to which my visitor would be brought by a trusted contact-girl. I reached the spot in good time, and sat on a boulder waiting for the emissary. The sky became overcast and it started to rain hard, when two rain-drenched shapes emerged from among the trees. Our conversation opened to the accompaniment of a heavy downpour.

The young emissary gave me an account of the Polish emigrés in Hungary. They had been hospitably received by the Hungarians; arrests by the Germans had followed, and then a desperate situation had arisen after the occupation of Hungary by the Soviets. The Government post's liaison with London had been disrupted, and the emigrés wanted to know whether they should return to their country, or wait for further developments; and the emissary had been sent to Poland to find out what the underground authorities had to say.

During his long discourse the rain lashed his tired face. I could sense from his expression how depressed he was by the fact that we had to meet in a wood, with no roof over our heads to protect us from the rain. Through the sparse trees I noticed a motor-car driving slowly along a nearby track, so we withdrew deeper into the forest, under a still heavier downpour. Reading his mind, I asked him:

'Over there, in Hungary, you did not guess how hard-pressed we were here?'

'We assumed that things must be difficult here, but we didn't think it would be as bad as it is,' he answered with warm sympathy.

I gave the emissary a full explanation of how matters stood; I surveyed all the pros and cons of a return of the emigrés to

Poland, and concluded in a way which was unlikely to satisfy those who had dispatched him.

'There is no sense in remaining in a foreign country which is, and will continue to be, occupied. If one is to suffer, it is better to be with one's own people. But you must decide yourselves, whether to return to Poland now, or wait a little longer; or try to move to the West. Whatever decision is made, it will affect the individual's whole life, so each must decide for himself. We have no instructions from the Government concerning this matter; but we shall enquire, and request that their opinion be communicated to you direct.'

I assured him that I would telegraph to London all the information he had imparted to me, and we agreed on the means of communication, via London, between the post in Hungary and the posts in Rumania.

Before parting, I wished the young man a safe journey back, shook his hand, and by a roundabout way made for my hide-out, trying to dispel the dark thoughts which beset me after the talk with the emissary. Here was a new problem, new worries, and further delays; while the thousands of homeless wanderers were waiting like the Hebrews in the desert for the flaming bush which would show them the way to go.

And as if to mock me, the rain stopped and the sun came out. I entered my favourite thicket of young pines, and each tree was scintillating with millions of raindrops as if with diamonds. A wonderful rainbow in the sky linked the two horizons; but all its splendour failed to convince me that it was a good omen.

A Mean Attempt foiled

In June 1945 I received an unexpected invitation to meet Josef Niecko of 'The Triangle'. I was somewhat surprised by the proposal; for Niecko was a hopeless coward. During the Warsaw Rising, he spent 23 days in a vault before revealing his presence in Warsaw. I knew he was in some safe place, and if he now proposed to leave his hide-out, the matter must indeed be of some importance.

During our talk Niecko was very amiable and accommodating. He showered me with compliments, extolled my services, and, in short, sugared me up for something he had concocted in his head. As in my former dealings with him, I said nothing, waiting for what was concealed behind his hedging. Niecko seemed to be embarrassed by my reserve, and finally blurted out what was in his mind.

'As you know, our Party is in opposition to the Arciszewski Government. As this has not brought about any changes in London, we decided at a Party meeting to strengthen our opposition. In considering ways and means of doing this, we came to the conclusion that it would be necessary to withdraw all members of our Party from the Government Plenipotentiary's Office. In this connection I wanted to ask you to resign. I find it very difficult to make this request, in view of the fact that. . . .' and Niecko repeated all the compliments he had already showered on me, and finally appealed to me to resign for the sake of the movement to which I had belonged for so many years, and to which I had rendered such signal service during the war. . . .

Contrary to Niecko's expectations, I was not at all taken by surprise. I had already had many indications from my friends in 'The Triangle' that opposition to the London Government was growing; and, moreover, I was myself of the opinion that since my Party had left the Government in London and the Underground Council of National Unity, a rather strained situation had arisen, with a member of a Party in opposition occupying the office of Government Plenipotentiary. I considered, therefore, that from this point of view Niecko's request was justified. So much for the political side of the problem. As far as other aspects of it were concerned, I was of the opinion that the decision to withdraw members of the Party from the underground Government was neither timely nor loyal to our partners in the underground. It might have looked like rats scuttling from a sinking ship. I assured Niecko that I should unconditionally and immediately obey the decisions of the Party authorities and resign, but at the same time I also let him have my views on the ethics of the matter.

Here I had a surprise. Niecko thought for a while, pacing the room; then he stopped in front of me and said:

'I am not thinking of leaving a sinking ship. On the contrary, I am considering how to save the ship, and I can see a way out. When your resignation is accepted, do not cede your functions, either as Government Plenipotentiary or as head of radio liaison, to the new Plenipotentiary whom the Government will appoint, but hand them over to a new centre, which, together with you and other members of our Party, I shall organise. The Arciszewski Government is following a mistaken policy, and we must make an end of it here.'

I was indignant at this cynical proposal. To-day, writing of it after a lapse of years, I have come to the conclusion that Niecko could have been prompted by two considerations. One, which he mentioned himself, was the formation in the country of a centre independent of the Government in London. The other, much more likely, was that he intended to hand over everything to the Communists, and thus buy for himself a place in the new Government set-up in Poland. The office of Government Plenipotentiary was to be a kind of dowry, which Niecko wanted to bring with him into the union. I looked at Niecko with a certain curiosity and a great deal of loathing. I thought that the peasant movement, which produced the largest underground organisation under the German occupation, including about one hundred and fifty thousand soldiers in the Peasant Battalions, the pillars of Civil Resistance in the villages, and delegated five members who occupied leading positions in the underground Government, deserved better leaders than Niecko.

I tore his proposals to shreds and declared once more that I should resign immediately, which I did the following day by a telegram to London; but, at the same time, I told Niecko categorically that when my resignation was accepted I should hand over everything to my successor, appointed by the Government, and to no one else.

Our parting was far from friendly, and my loathing for him remained undiminished to the end of my stay in Poland.

The Trial and the Conference in Moscow

On June 17, 1945, the talks in Moscow opened, with the participation of Mikolajczyk, Grabski, and Stanczyk, from London; and Professor Stanislaw Kutrzeba, Zygmunt Zulawski, Professor Adam Kryzanowski, Dr. Henryk Kolodziejski, and Wladyslaw Kiernik, who deputised for President Witos— who pretended to be ill and refused to attend—from Poland. Witos, an old hand in politics, knew that the conference would not yield anything beneficial to Poland, and preferred not to take part in it. The Lublin Committee were represented by Bierut, Osobka, Kowalski, and Gomolka.

When the Communist press in Poland announced the names of the delegates, our hearts sank. Except for Zulawski, there were no men of sufficiently strong moral fibre among them. Krzyzanowski and Kutrzeba had no political experience; Kolodziejski, though a man of high intelligence, was too scared to be of any use; while Kiernik, devoured by a morbid ambition, would be primarily concerned with securing a high office for himself. As Witos said of him, 'If a bishopric fell vacant, Kiernik would probably offer himself as a candidate.' Of all the men who went to Moscow from Poland, Mikolajczyk would be able to rely on Zulawski alone.

These pessimistic forecasts were soon confirmed by a man from the underground, who, for conspiratorial reasons, maintained contact with the Communist Ministry of Foreign Affairs. 'There is great merriment and satisfaction in the Ministry,' he said. 'A telegram has arrived from Moscow to the effect that the Lublin delegates promised Stanczyk a seat in the Cabinet, and he agreed to support them without reservation.'

We were thus confronted with treason within the London delegation, on the part of a member of the Polish Socialist Party. I tried to imagine the painful impression which Stanczyk's treachery would make on Tomasz Arciszewski, one of the finest and most idealistic personalities in Polish public life.

But all this was nothing compared to the shock produced in the country by the simultaneous opening in Moscow of the trial of sixteen Polish underground leaders. (To the fifteen kidnapped in Poland, a sixteenth had been added, arrested earlier.) It was unbelievable that, on the one hand, the Soviets were sponsoring negotiations with Bierut, which actually meant negotiations with the Soviets, for the formation of a Government of National Unity, while on the other, the self-same Soviets were simultaneously trying members of the existing constitutional Government, who were pre-eminently suited to take part in the new Government. Reality had surpassed the wildest dreams of the most fertile imagination; and before the eyes of an incredulous country, a drama was unfolded, on the characters and action of which only history can pronounce the final verdict. No one can do it yet; for the drama continues; the curtain has not yet descended.

The underground was seething against Mikolajczyk; the general opinion was that he should not have taken his seat at the conference table until the arrested men had been released. There were a few contrary voices, of those who considered that in a struggle casualties were inevitable. No one can say how posterity will judge this painful case. If at the price of sacrificing the sixteen, Mikolajczyk should have succeeded in saving at least something of Polish independence, history may yet give a verdict in his favour. But events have moved in the opposite direction, and one is entitled to have grave doubts about his conduct. In any case, the 'casualties' were put away behind bars with savage sentences, while the new Government landed on the Okecie airfield in Warsaw on June 27, 1945.

Farewell to the Underground

On the same day, June 27, 1945, a meeting of the Council of National Unity was convened in Cracow. I intended to resign my office despite the fact that no telegram from the Government in London had arrived yet accepting my resignation and appointing my successor. I decided to do so in order to frustrate Josef Niecko's attempts to liquidate the office of Government Plenipotentiary. He might have succeeded in doing so, if I continued to occupy the office after Mikolajczyk's arrival in Poland, when 'The Triangle' would have to come out into the open. We were too closely knit together for such a state of affairs to continue. It was obvious that my com-

ing out into the open, while still occupying the office of Plenipotentiary, would have automatically brought about the
liquidation of the office. To prevent such an eventuality, I
decided to hand over my functions beforehand, and to cut
myself off from the underground.

I left Warsaw in the early morning, in a motor-car at the
disposal of the underground, accompanied by Zosia. I wanted
to give her an opportunity to relax in a different atmosphere,
and to visit Cracow, a city she had not seen for so many years.
The day was exceptionally fine and sunny, and it was a real
pleasure to travel by car. We were happy to see the open
fields and extensive forests after our long confinement in
Lesna Podkowa, within the four walls of the fence surrounding our villa. We stopped for lunch in Kielce, reached Cracow
by nightfall of June 26, 1945, and were accommodated in a
private apartment belonging to a charming elderly lady.

The next day I attended the meeting, while Zosia went out
sightseeing. In the hide-out I met my old friends, in an atmosphere of expectation and faint hopes. We anticipated a
struggle against the Communists, but in a more moderate
form. Some hoped that the compromise reached in Moscow
would facilitate a compromise in the country as well, and
that the Mikolajczyk group in the Government would have
'the powerful support of the Western Powers', who would see
to it that the elections were free. All this held out promise of
an improvement.

With regard to the underground, the prevailing view was
that it should be liquidated, and that we should resume open
and legal political activities. I shared this opinion; for
though I viewed the future less rosily and reckoned with the
need for a new conspiracy, I thought that its present forms
were obsolete, both with regard to organisation and methods
of action, and, moreover, that it had by now been infiltrated
by the Communists and the NKVD and Security Police.

Once again, as so many times before, I reported to the
Council on the international and internal situation, and on
the state of our organisation; and I read the incoming and
outgoing telegrams, etc. All those present listened with great
attention, mingled with sadness, and perhaps also a little

envy, that one of them should be leaving the assembly to resume a different life, while they were to remain in the old one, until existing difficulties had been solved. My report was accepted, and the moment arrived for me to lay down the functions of Government Plenipotentiary, and to bid farewell to the Council of National Unity. Since the then chairman of the Council, George Braun, observed that my two successors had been appointed only against the possibility of my being arrested, which had not occurred, I handed over my functions as Plenipotentiary to him, as chairman of the Council. In a short speech, Braun thanked me for my collaboration, and, profoundly moved, we embraced each other warmly. My eyes were misty as I pressed the hands of my comrades, and with a lump in my throat I hurriedly left the meeting.

During the following days the Council óf National Unity continued its sessions and resolved to abolish the office of Government Plenipotentiary and the Council itself; and on July 1, 1945, it issued its last manifesto 'To the Polish Nation', which I have already quoted. A special committee was appointed to liquidate all the current affairs of the Government Plenipotentiary's office, which within a short time brought its labours to a close, thus putting an end to the conspiracy of the years 1939-1945.

Out of the remains of the war-time underground, out of the terror and persecution of the new rulers, and out of the ever-living, unconquerable Polish spirit, there began to come into being a new underground, which continues to this day, and I am sure will continue until, in the words of a Polish partisan whom I met on the forest road near Pultusk in 1946, 'the last Soviet soldier has left the soil of Poland'.

CHAPTER XXIII

In the Clutches of the Security Police

The Arrest

I left the meeting in a depressed mood. One more chapter of my life was closed, and the prospects for the new chapter were not very promising. I had no illusions on that score. My mind was still occupied with the experiences of the last few hours. The sorrowful look on the faces of my comrades in the struggles and labours of the past years, the farewells, the handshakes—all this caused me to return to the hide-out, where Zosia was waiting, a nervous wreck.

The following day we were to return to Warsaw, so we decided to go for a stroll in Cracow, to rejoice in the charms of the city before going back to the ruins of the capital. We returned to our hide-out rather late that night, the night of June 28-29, 1945.

We had already turned in and were on the point of falling asleep, when we heard a knock at the front door. Both Zosia and I were wide awake at once, and we became all ears. My heart sank with an evil foreboding. I looked at Zosia. She had the same feeling. After a while I could hear the voice of the landlady talking to someone, the creaking of opening doors, and the footsteps of some men entering the house. Then came a knock at our door; the landlady poked her head in and told us that it was nothing more serious than a check on personal documents. Her head disappeared, and three men in mufti entered the room, led by a tall, young, good-looking, fair-haired man in a light and somewhat dirty raincoat. His companions had their automatics ready.

The leader came up to our beds, asked our names, and demanded to see our papers. The latter were in perfect order, and I handed them to him with considerable self-assurance; though I did not assume for one moment that an inspection of our identity cards was all they had come for.

I awaited further developments. The fair-haired young man sat down on the edge of my bed, and with sufficient civility asked why we had come to Cracow. Still in bed, I proceeded to give him the answers I had carefully prepared for such an occasion. The man listened, examined our identity cards, shook his head, and finally said apologetically that the matter needed further investigation; in view of which we must dress and accompany him to the police station. He ordered his two companions to leave the room, while he himself turned his back to us.

We dressed without hurry, exchanging furtive glances which acknowledged simply that 'this was the end'. The shock was too sudden and too potent for clear thinking. We were under arrest, but not yet fully aware of the fact. Unexpectedly, I felt a surge of anger mounting in me, and I said rather cuttingly that the present time did not differ at all from the time of the Nazi occupation, when the Gestapo used to knock at doors in the dead of night and drag people away from their homes. The young man did not seem to pay any attention to this insulting comparison. After we had dressed, he summoned his two henchmen, and they carried out a minute search. After another half-hour we left the apartment, and escorted by a squad armed with automatics, we were led through the empty streets of the city. Our escort was swelled by several men who had been waiting in front of the house, which was obviously surrounded by armed police. We did not have far to walk; for it turned out that the house in which we had been staying was only some two hundred yards away from the local headquarters of the Secret Police.

As soon as we entered a brightly lit building, teeming with armed men, and before I realised what was happening, I was separated from Zosia, without being able to say good-bye. I was then conducted into an office in which two young men were seated behind a desk, one a civilian, the other in the uniform of a lieutenant. My escort vanished.

There followed an examination lasting several hours, during which I discovered that the young man in mufti was a big-mouthed semi-literate, while the lieutenant was a stupid martinet. They did not know how to put their questions, and though I was still under the impact of the shock, I had full control of the situation. They demanded that I should reveal my real name, because, they said, the identity-card issued in the name of Bujnicki was forged. They let fall that they knew who I was, and that it was senseless to conceal anything.

During the examination I underwent something in the nature of a 'split' in my personality. One 'I' answered the questions, while my other ego controlled him, whispering counsel, praising or censuring him, and even attempting to anticipate the next question. This collaboration between my two egos went on throughout the entire period of my imprisonment.

After several hours of cross-examination, during which I kept repeating the same statements, i.e., that my name was Bujnicki; that together with my wife I resided in Lesna Podkowa; that I was registered there (here is the registration card); that I had come to Cracow with a view to settling in the city; that I knew no one there, etc., they gave up. I had been able to explain satisfactorily even the most ticklish question—how I had been able to get a room in a private apartment—by mentioning the fictitious name by which my landlady knew the man from the underground who had booked the room for me. They could search for a man of that name till doomsday.

I was left in the room, guarded by a silent sentry armed with a revolver. It was time to take stock of the position, and to regain some sort of balance. So I spread my overcoat on the floor, and pretending that I wanted to get some sleep, I lay down.

My two egos immediately opened a debate. The first asked, 'Do they know who I am?' and the other replied, 'The fact that the house was surrounded indicates that they knew you were there, and that they came to fetch none other but you. The allusions made by the two youngsters of the Security Police leave no room for doubt.' 'That's true,' said the first ego, 'but if so, why did they not address me by my right name at once?' 'That's one of their tricks, which you can't know about,' answered the second ego. 'That's true. But the question is shall I tell them my name and my function in the underground if they press me, or shall I go on denying everything?' 'I am not infallible, and I cannot exclude the possibility that they do not know who you are. My advice, therefore, is to admit nothing until they have said it first. But if they do, it would be senseless to deny it. It would even be undignified. It wouldn't be seemly.' 'Supposing they know, is there any chance of getting out of it?' 'None whatever. Remember the Trial of the Sixteen. You will be deported to Russia, and that will be the end of it. Zosia, too, will get several years. Have no illusions. Your future is settled, and all you can do now is to conduct yourself in a manner worthy of the position in which fate has placed you. Most important of all, you must not give anyone away. Remember that you must not mention yesterday's meeting of the Council and your own resignation from office.' The first ego agreed, and the 'discussion' came to an end. I fell into a restless sleep.

The NKVD Colonel Vorontsov

In the morning I was given a cup of coffee and a slice of larded bread. I was looking greedily out of the window, saying farewell to the view of trees and lawns, when the Security Police lieutenant whom I already knew appeared and escorted me along the corridors. We descended some stairs and then mounted some more. I gathered that we had entered a wing of the Security Police Headquarters. Then a door opened, and I beheld the young man who had arrested us the day before in the uniform of a Captain of the NKVD. He stood behind a desk, by the side of a man of about fifty in the uniform of a Colonel of the NKVD. The Colonel waved me to a chair and said in Russian:

'Good morning Mr. Plenipotentiary Zielinski. Please be seated.'

I replied courteously:

'Good morning Colonel.'

'Allow me to introduce myself. My name is Colonel Vorontsov. What is your name?'

I reciprocated without a moment's hesitation.

'My name is Stefan Korbonski.'

The SP man was shaken, as if an electric current had passed
through him. It was obvious that he had not known who I
was. The Colonel on the other hand was visibly pleased.

'Ah, that's right, that's how it should be, Mr. Prime
Minister. It will greatly facilitate matters.'

'I am not a Prime Minister, but only Acting Plenipotentiary of the Government you have jailed,' I corrected.

'Don't be so modest; we know very well what the function
of the Government Plenipotentiary is. We also know quite a
lot about you, and we have been searching for you for some
months. Now we have made your acquaintance here.'

The Security Police man, who had been containing himself
restlessly, butted in:

'Why didn't you tell me this yesterday?' he asked.

I let myself go:

'You are too young to listen to such confessions.'

The SP man wanted to say something, but the Colonel
stopped him with a look of disapprobation, and continued to
question me.

'Do you speak Russian?'

'Not very well, though I understand it sufficiently.'

The Colonel was again pleased.

'That is exactly my case. I do not speak Polish well, but I
understand it sufficiently. May I suggest that I speak in Russian and you in Polish?'

And that was how the cross-examination, which lasted several hours, proceeded. The Colonel, who had a full grasp of
the case, questioned me about the past, about the activities of
Civil Resistance, about the Rising, about the manifestos I
had signed as Government Plenipotentiary, and casually enquired how Colonel Rzepecki was getting on.

In the course of the examination I requested that Zosia
should be brought in. The Colonel motioned to the Captain,
and a minute later Zosia entered the room, escorted by another
Colonel of the NKVD. She was pale, but self-possessed. It was

evident that she was being cross-examined in an adjacent office. Zosia fixed her enquiring eyes on me. I could sense her whole being in that look. I informed her in a few words:

'These gentlemen know who I am. It would make no sense to deny it.'

And looking at her I added meaningly.

'They know I acted as Government Plenipotentiary.' I wanted Zosia to understand that they did not know I had been directly responsible for radio communications, which Vorontsov had not even mentioned. Zosia received my statements quietly and was led out of the room.

I learned afterwards that she had obstinately refused to admit who she was, and her examiners had been on the point of losing their patience. She understood my look and my explanatory words perfectly.

After my release I found that the tactics I chose were right. Contrary to my initial assumption, the news of my arrest spread immediately all over Cracow, and reached Zygmunt Zulawski at about the time I was being cross-examined by Vorontsov. Zulawski at once informed Mikolajczyk, who had just arrived in Cracow to visit Vincent Witos, and Mikolajczyk immediately undertook steps to ensure my release, rightly mentioning my authentic name and my true function in the underground. As the examination proceeded, it transpired that the NKVD had been informed that I should be visiting Cracow. Agents of the Security Police had shadowed me while I was on my way there by car, but lost the trail when we arrived in the city. It also transpired that all houses within a certain radius of the Security Police Headquarters were watched by informers, and one of them had reported that a couple whose description tallied with us had been staying for two days in that particular house without registering. That was how they had picked up the lost trail. My own subsequent investigation showed that the thread which led to my arrest passed through the Boleslav Piasecki group, Fascist before the war and fellow-travelling now. The same group was responsible for the arrest of Colonel Radoslav, which occurred much later. It is only fair that this should be mentioned in my reminiscences.

There followed a question for which I had been waiting:

'Why did you come to Cracow?'

I replied glibly:

'I came to meet Mikolajczyk. I was sure that before doing anything else, he would want to meet the Leader of the Party, Witos, and that he would fly straight from Moscow to Cracow. I decided to wait for him here, so as to meet him without delay.'

The Colonel must have been confounded, for my explanation sounded plausible. But it did not dispel his suspicions.

'We have different reports about the purpose of your visit. You came here to meet other members of the underground.'

I had to preserve my calm and determination now, because one wrong step might have incriminated me.

'That is not true. Why should I want to meet members of the underground if Mikolajczyk's arrival meant that our party was henceforth to act openly and legally? I have met no one here. I went sightseeing with my wife; we visited restaurants, we went to a cinema, and that was all.'

Colonel Vorontsov shook his head in disbelief, but he must have reached some decision, for he concluded the examination by saying:

'That's all for to-day.'

I was escorted back to another room or cell, in which there was a bed, a table and two chairs. A sentry stood in the corridor by the door. I paced the room trying to analyse the course of the preliminary investigation, and I thought the outcome not too bad, although in the long run the situation appeared hopeless to me. A strange reaction set in, confirming the adage that uncertainty is sometimes worse than knowledge of even the most unpleasant fate. I regained my composure. Worrying was no remedy. The prospect was obvious, though it was as gloomy as night itself. I was obsessed with the thought of what was going to happen to Zosia, though it seemed that there was a chance for her.

In the evening, a woman brought my supper. Eyeing the closed door, she whispered:

'I am a prisoner myself. I took supper to your wife too, and she told me to give you her regards, should I happen to see you.'

I had an idea.

'Will you be taking supper to her to-morrow evening?'

'I think so.'

'Would you give her a note from me?'

'Certainly.'

'I shall have it ready to-morrow at noon.'

I immediately sat down to pen the gist of my depositions. If the woman was a stooge of the Security Police, all that would happen was that Zosia would not get my note. And no harm would be done if the police got hold of a report of what I had actually said.

While I was writing, I overheard a voice outside the door. Someone was speaking to the sentry in Russian. Straining my ears, I heard:

'If he tries to escape, don't kill him. You understand? You must not kill him. Shoot at his legs.'

With such a 'good-night' I lay down in bed and fell asleep.

A Nocturnal Visitor

By noon the following day my notes for Zosia, written in microscopic letters, were ready. When the woman brought me my lunch, as I took the bread and soup from the tray, I put the folded notes on to it, and gave her a wink. She glanced at the door and secreted them in her blouse. After a few hours, along with my supper, she brought a message from Zosia. I gave a sigh of relief. She had got the notes. Communication with Zosia was established.

Resigned to my fate, I lay down and tried to get some sleep. In the course of the whole day I had not been summoned for examination, which gave me much food for thought. I came to the conclusion that they were consulting Warsaw, or perhaps Moscow. In the dead of night the door creaked and a face appeared through the opening. Wide awake, I looked silently at a strange pair of eyes. The intruder noticed that I was not asleep, and a second later entered the room. The man, whom I shall call Conrad, seated himself on the edge of my bed and whispered excitedly:

'What a calamity that they've got you. Oh God, what a

disaster! Jankowski has been sentenced to eight years, and now they've got you.'

I did not quite trust him.

'Who are you, and why have you come?'

There ensued one of the strangest talks I have ever had in my life. Here I was, in a dark room, illumined only by the dim light penetrating from the corridor through the glass door, lying in bed and receiving the confessions of an unknown individual. Conrad was a Security Policeman, an ex-partisan who had chanced to enter the People's Army; like so many others who joined the first armed detachment they came across, in order to fight against the Germans. He had already been with the partisans a little while before he realised who they were. He kept his eyes open, and noticed that men who criticised the treatment Russia meted out to Poland, or failed to attend lectures on Communism, used to vanish without trace. He dug in his heels and held his tongue. He was taken for a Communist, became a member of the party, and, as a trusted comrade, was attached to the Security Police. But he could not stick it any longer, and would rather shoot himself. The Russians were in command everywhere, and no Pole had any say in anything. Even Security Policemen, convinced Communists, were disgruntled, but could do nothing, with the threat of death hanging over them.

My first ego talked to him for several hours, while the other considered whether it was advisable to trust the man, and came to the conclusion that it was. There was burning sincerity in his every word, and what he was saying was so downright and convincing, his oppressive suffering was so genuine, that my intuition resolved my doubts in his favour. I decided to play for the highest stake and asked him:

'Can you deliver a note to someone in the city?'

'I can, without any difficulty.'

I slid out of bed, and by the light coming from the corridor I scribbled on a scrap of paper:

'Dear X. Together with my wife I am under arrest. I have mentioned no names and revealed no addresses, and I know I shall not do so. Be easy.'

Conrad seized the scrap of paper, whispered good-night, and disappeared the way he had come.

The Third Day

I saw him again during the night. He glided in like a shadow, seated himself on the edge of my bed, and whispered:

'I delivered the note. Someone opened the door and took fright at the sight of my uniform. I placed the note on a table and left.'

I thanked him warmly, and asked him if he knew anything about my case. He leant over and whispered, with his lips close to my ear:

'The day after to-morrow you will be transported in a lorry to the Ministry of Security in Warsaw. Perhaps it will be better for you that way. If I and my friend should be in the escort, we shall shoot the others and escape to the woods.'

I gazed at him in amazement. There was cold determination in his eyes and he proceeded to instruct me:

'When we get under way, watch me carefully. I shall shoot at the man nearest to you. You must at once get hold of his revolver and shoot at the others.'

When he left, I was beset by doubts.

'Was he a patriot or an *agent provocateur?* How does he manage to get by the sentry posted in the corridor? Was it not an old ruse, to get myself killed while attempting to escape?'

Without being able to decide one way or the other, I fell asleep. However, I resolved to be on guard, and not to yield to hopes of escape. When the day broke, I could hardly believe in the reality of Conrad's existence.

On the Way to Warsaw

The following day I was again escorted into Colonel Vorontsov's room. The conversation was brief; the Colonel was formal and unbending. He told me in a few words of the important decision concerning me.

'We are not interested in your case. We shall hand you over

to your Polish Minister, Radkiewicz.' He pronounced the word 'Polish' with a sardonic smile.

He asked me if I had any complaints, or something to that effect, and when I said I had none, he ironically wished me a happy journey and motioned the escort to take me away.

On the way back I gave myself up to speculation. On the whole, the case looked slightly better. In surveying the situation I came to the conclusion that they were not going to deport us to Russia, which in itself represented a considerable improvement in our position. I inclined to the belief that the Trial of the Sixteen had yielded the Soviets all they desired, and that it would make no sense for them to repeat the trial on such a miniature scale. Besides, the information I had received from my nocturnal visitor seemed to be coming true. Would that his other schemes succeeded! Here, the second ego protested and advised me to reflect rather on what might occur at the Ministry of Security than think of rescue. Escape and freedom seemed too good to be true!

On the morning of the fifth day after my arrest, I was conducted to the front of the Security Police building and put into an enclosed lorry, in which Zosia was already crouching on some straw. There was also an unknown young man, who was able to whisper to us during the journey that his name was Korwin-Piotrowski. I learned afterwards that he was executed. Our escort in the lorry consisted of a sergeant and three soldiers armed with automatics. My heart sank. Conrad was not in the escort. I was glad I had refused to succumb to idle dreams. The convoy was commanded by a Captain of the Security Police, who strictly forbade us to talk to each other, and instructed the sergeant to enforce the prohibition. He took his place by the side of the driver, and we moved off.

I managed to get as close to Zosia as possible, happy to be with her again. We moved swiftly through the streets of Cracow, and were soon on a main highway. I tried to discover which road we were taking, but through the back of the lorry I could see only the tops of houses, and later only the sky. We did not talk to each other, but I succeeded in squeezing into Zosia's hand detailed notes, which I had prepared in advance, with further advice on what line to follow. She read them later on, in Warsaw. During the journey, we stopped for half an hour in Czestochowa, which I knew well from my school-days, and then resumed our drive. In the evening we reached the suburbs of Warsaw, and in another half-hour we pulled up in front of the Ministry of Security Headquarters at 6, Brukowa Street.

Cross-examination in Warsaw

Under a new guard we were taken to the third floor, where we were kept waiting for some time in a corridor full of policemen, who eyed us with curiosity. We seemed to be the sensation of the day. Some time later a door opened, and a man from the underground, whom I knew well, was led out, under guard. When he saw me, he stopped dead. He recognised me, and realising that I was under arrest, was horrified. But the policeman gave him a shove from behind, and they moved on. From another door a woman emerged, also under guard. When she reached the staircase a piercing cry of horror rent the air, there was a commotion, and a second later the woman was carried back in a state of collapse. I was reminded of my visit to the Gestapo after the arrest of Rataj, and I realised where I was. The slight satisfaction I had felt at being in Warsaw again soon vanished.

A tall officer in the uniform of a captain, with a square, peaked cap pulled down over his brow, appeared in the corridor. He was rather dark-skinned and had deep-set, fierce, unpleasant eyes. He quickly separated us, and taking me by the arm led me into a small, brightly-lit room, filled with officers of the Security Police. The room looked like an orderly room, or a waiting room; as it turned out, I had to spend several weeks in it. The young policemen eyed me with curiosity, and exchanged whispered comments.

After half an hour the captain appeared again, took me into his room, and opened the cross-examination. During the several hours it lasted I had ample opportunity to observe him closely. He had a lean, ascetic face, a sharp nose, and most prominent of all, a pair of cold eyes. I was fated to look into those eyes for many a day and night, and I well remember every one of their expressions. Captain of the Security Police Rozanski, as he was then, though by the time I made my escape from Poland, in 1947, he had already become a Colonel, was in charge of the Investigations Department of the Ministry of Security; and the fact that he had been entrusted with my case was a distinction which bode me no good. He was a brother of the well-known and influential Communist George Borejsza. Their real name was Goldberg.

The cross-examination opened with the same questions as those that had been put to me in Cracow. When I remarked that I had already answered them all during previous examinations, and that my depositions had been taken down, Rozanski said briskly:

'You'd better forget everything that happened in Cracow. You could tell them all sorts of fairy tales, but not me. Please answer the question why you went to Cracow and whom you met there.'

I proceeded to repeat for hours the answers I had given in Cracow, while Rozanski openly jeered at them. I could see that I was dealing with an intellectual, one who was thoroughly familiar with the affairs of the underground and in possession of ample information about it, with which he often surprised me. Nevertheless, I stuck to my original story and did not change the slightest detail in my previous depositions.

Rozanski closed this part of the cross-examination with the ironic observation:

'I quite understand that you are determined not to give away anyone in Cracow, and for the time being we shall not proceed with it, as there is a more important matter I want to take up with you. When and where did you last meet Colonel Rzepecki?'

I answered that it had been a month previously, in Independence Avenue. Rozanski looked at me with approval.

'What number?'

'In Mokotov Fields. The contact met me under the Sapper monument and then led me to Mokotov Fields, where Colonel Rzepecki was waiting for me.'

Rozanski was furious.

'Don't talk such nonsense! You used to meet him at. . . .'

Here he consulted a slip of paper and rolled off a number of addresses which had served as Rzepecki's hide-outs. I was startled. I had never imagined they had got as close to Rzepecki as that. Things looked pretty grim.

Dawn was already breaking when Rozanski left, together with the shorthand writer, who took down the depositions, and he was replaced by a Lieutenant of the Security Police. A young, thick-set, fair-haired man, he had a piece of paper with a list of questions on it, which had been left by Rozanski, and he started the examination with the old question: why had I gone to Cracow and whom had I met there. He was a perfect ass, hardly literate, and he had difficulty in taking down the minutes. I resolved to have a breather while he was with me; for I realised that my cross-examination was going to be carried on uninterruptedly for some time. I answered every question exactly as before, and I was careful not to wear myself out. I felt sleepy, but I was far from being completely exhausted physically. I frequently refreshed myself with a glass of water, which he did not deny me, and in order to stretch my legs I repeatedly went to the lavatory in the company of the Lieutenant, whether I needed it or not. He did not press me very hard; he was obviously scared and sleepy himself. I am inclined to think that his main and only task was not to let me fall asleep.

At about noon Rozanski, fully rested and refreshed, came back and took up the same old questions. Now, however, his tone was more threatening.

'I would advise you to tell the whole truth, and not force me to apply measures which have induced tougher men than you to speak.'

I consistently repeated my previous answers, determined not to mention any names or addresses. Rozanski was furious, but did not go so far as to put his threats into effect; and at eight o'clock in the evening, after a cross-examination lasting twenty-four hours, he suspended the hearing.

By now I was utterly worn out, and after I had had a mug of some sort of soup and a slice of bread, I asked the sentry in the guard-room where I was supposed to sleep. He pointed to the desk; so I rolled up my overcoat, put it under my head, and immediately fell asleep, undisturbed by the powerful electric light bulb which hung over my eyes. The policeman made himself comfortable on a chair by the side of the desk, with an automatic across his lap. I had hardly closed my eyes when someone pulled me by the arm. Rozanski was standing by the desk.

'Get up. Let's have another little talk.'

I rose without a word, gritting my teeth, and the next moment I was again seated in front of Rozanski in his room. From the clock on the wall I could see that he had allowed me to sleep for two hours. I decided to change parts with Rozanski and spoke first:

'If you go on without any sleep, you won't last long,' I said.

I must have touched a sensitive spot, for Rozanski wiped his face with a handkerchief and went on to tell me how overworked and exhausted he was. His former rudeness disappeared, and he became quite chatty. He told me that he had known me before the war, when he had been working for a lawyer in Warsaw; that I had the reputation of being a good democrat; and that it was strange that I should have remained in the Underground after democracy had come into power, and more of such nonsense. He spoke with forced politeness, he did not revert to earlier questions, he made no threats, and behaved as if he were not the same man as the one who had examined me before. In the end I realised what he was getting at. After a prolonged discourse on the subject of the new Poland and her prospects, Rozanski proceeded to enumerate all the blunders the Underground had made in relation to the Communist Government and the Soviets, and ended up with a startling proposal:

'You ought to admit that you made a mistake in remaining in the Underground after the liberation, and sign a declaration to that effect. If you do this you will immediately be released, and what is more, you will be appointed to such a high office that in future I shall have to stand to attention in your presence. I know all the plans concerning you.'

It would not be easy to describe all the details of the discussion which ensued; but as the subject is altogether too familiar generally to need rehashing, it is hardly necessary. The condemnation of one's mistakes is a primary tenet of the Soviet method of breaking a man's character, and this was being applied to me. My answers boiled down to the statement that though I was an ordinary person, with no hankering to be a martyr, I did not want to save my skin at the price of condemning something which represented the most valuable part of my life. I would have preferred to remain in jail rather than walk in freedom without daring to look people straight in the eye.

Rozanski shook his head disapprovingly, and by way of example mentioned some Soviet Marshals, Rokossowski for one, who had been in prison, had admitted their guilt, and yet to-day were worshipped by the entire Russian nation. Finally, carried away by his own impatience, he came out with an astounding remark, which solved for me the riddle of why I was being treated with so much consideration.

'If you had been arrested a few months ago, I wouldn't be treating you so gently, or persuading you to sign a declaration. A bullet would have settled you, or you would be left to rot in jail. You are lucky to have been arrested just after the formation of the Provisional Government of National Unity. To-day, we are having an idyllic interlude and trying to collaborate, and that is why I am talking to you as I am. If it hadn't been for that, you would be hearing a different tune.'

Here, Rozanski pierced me with his notorious eyes, as sharp as daggers, and rose from behind the desk. Outside, it was already broad daylight.

The temptation continues

Rozanski continued to harass me day after day, and night after night. The only remaining issue was the persistent demand that I should condemn the activities of the Underground under the Soviet occupation. Rozanski used ever new means of exerting pressure, but refrained from physical torture. Once, for instance, he woke me up in the dead of night, took me to his room, and ordered me to sign the receipt of a formal decision concerning my arrest, together with the order for my removal to Mokotov prison, where, as he said, I should not be as comfortable as in the Ministry. On another occasion he used a more serious threat. I was fast asleep on the hard desk, when he woke me up and read me a summary of the numbers of officers and men of the Soviet Army, Security Policemen, and Militiamen 'murdered by the reactionary Underground during the time the office of the so-called Plenipotentiary of the Polish Government in London was occupied by Stefan Korbonski, who used the pseudonym Nowak or Zielinski', and he asked me if I accepted responsibility for the death of some 1,500 people enumerated in the summary. The largest number of the alleged murders were supposed to have occurred in the County of Bialystok. Shrugging my shoulders, I replied that I could not accept direct responsibility for all this, because, far from having ordered the executions, in a manifesto issued on May 27, 1945, and addressed to partisans in the field, I ordered a cessation of hostilities.

If, however, any killings had occurred during the period in which I was carrying out the functions of Plenipotentiary, there could only be a question of political responsibility, which represented a much more complicated problem. Rozanski would not agree to such a distinction; but in the end he recorded my words in the statement exactly as I dictated them, and declared solemnly that my admission would suffice as a basis for a sentence of death; in view of which he was suspending the examination for the time being, and would remit the documents of the case to a higher authority for its decision. Seeing that I remained unimpressed, he resumed the cross-examination the following day; and on this occasion he tried to intimidate me by saying that through my obstinacy I was sealing the fate of Zosia, who might have been saved.

During the intervals between investigations, I either slept on the desk, or sat on a bench by the sink, reading Zakrzewski's Universal History, which I chanced to find in the guard-room. Day and night an armed officer of the Security Police sat by my side. Sometimes in the evening, when there was no examination and the hubbub in the building had subsided somewhat, I chatted with the sentry, to while away the time. Some of the sentries were quite talkative, and one of them was openly sympathetic. On one occasion I told the latter that the Soviets must have lost interest in my case, because since my arrival at the Ministry of Security in Warsaw I had seen no Russians. His answer was altogether unexpected:

'Every statement in your cross-examination is being sent to the Soviet adviser, whose office is on the same floor. He and not Rozanski is issuing all the instructions, and is in charge of everything.'

I also asked him what was wrong with Rozanski's hand, that he had it bandaged. He replied venomously:

'Because he is not allowed to do so with you, he is taking it out of the others. During a cross-examination he hit a prisoner so hard with his fist that he hurt himself.'

The same policeman, while guarding me during the night, told me stories similar to that of Conrad. What he said would explain much to those of my compatriots who, living abroad, cannot comprehend how a Pole can serve in the Security Police. Apart from the 'élite' of the Rozanski type, and a few convinced Communists or cynical careerists, the lower ranks consisted of young men in their twenties, who could be divided into two groups. Some of them lost their parents in Russia, were deported to concentration camps, or sent to prisons, and were offered their freedom in return for entering the police service, for which they underwent thorough training. Subsequently, promoted to the rank of officers in the Security Police, they were transferred to Poland; and they were already sufficiently Russianised to have to grope for the right Polish words. The other group consisted of boys who drifted by accident into the People's Army, and from there were detailed to the Security Police, quite ignorant of what was happening to them. When they realised it, it was too late. At about that time I heard a saying which was popular among the Security Policemen: 'The only exit from service in the Secret Police is the grave'. All boys in the latter group received their training in the NKVD school in Kaluga, Russia. It was one of them who, on one occasion, turning towards the window so as to conceal his face from me, asked me what I thought of the decision of the Allies concerning the occupation of Germany for a period of fifty years? Did I interpret it literally, that Germany would be occupied for fifty years? I said that this was the only possible interpretation. His reaction was altogether unexpected.

'In that case we shall be encircled by the Ruskis for fifty years. That's bad, that's very bad. . . .'

Some readers, who have read a great deal about the horrors of the Security Police, may find my account somewhat innocuous. I must point out, therefore, that all this happened in July, 1945, and that at that time the Security Police was just being organised and in process of being manned. Moreover, this was a period when the Communists still hoped to come to an understanding with Witos and Mikolajczyk. These very same policemen who chatted with me more or less frankly would not have hesitated for a moment to murder me, if they had been ordered to do so; and one of them admitted to me that he had shot an escaping officer of the Home Army. During one of my cross-examinations, or rather during a nocturnal discussion with Rozanski, when I accused the Security Police of having recruited murderers and bandits, he finished the sentence for me by adding:

'And reactionaries. I have just come from the execution of eight of these bandits who had infiltrated our ranks.'

I learned in 1946 that the Cracow Security Police had been completely recast. The men were either transferred to other units or arrested and executed.

The Ministry of Security hummed with feverish activity. The offices and the entire building were illuminated throughout the night. The traffic in the corridors continued day and night, and most of the cross-examinations took place at night. At every turn there were armed sentries; and they were especially numerous on the staircases and at the entrance to the building, where motor-cars arrived and departed continuously day and night.

The young officers of the Security Police were on duty twenty-four hours a day. Some of them were occasionally told they could go home to rest, but not before eight o'clock in the evening. They were being trained continuously and had to attend daily lectures. They were terrorised to such an extent that none of them ever dared speak to me in the presence of another. Only when alone and when the traffic in the corridors had subsided, which was usually late in the evening, did they risk talking to me, sometimes quite frankly.

Zosia's experience was similar. At some time or other she casually mentioned to the sentry that she could read the cards. He brought her a pack, and thenceforth they all came in one after the other and asked her to tell them their fortunes. When she was supposed to be telling them about their past lives, and said . . . 'I can see you performing some hard labour, but that was some time ago', the policeman admitted, 'Yes, I was in a forced labour camp then, in the North. . . .' One of them, while describing his hard life in Russia, told her something which, though it was known to everyone in the Ministry, came as a great surprise to her:

'Did you know, Captain Rozanski himself was in a forced labour camp, and worked in the mines?'

If Rozanski should ever write a book he might give it the telling title, 'From Forced Labourer to Colonel'.

My Meeting with Mikolajczyk

One evening a Captain arrived and took me to the barber, who trimmed my hair and shaved off the accumulated growth from my chin. While in the barber's chair I entertained all sorts of ideas; was I, for instance, being treated in accordance with the peace-time custom by which the condemned man is given food and drink, in addition to having his hair cut and his beard shaved before being led to execution? But that evening I had an ordinary meal with no extras. When I asked the Captain bluntly what all this careful grooming meant, he would tell me nothing; and after the barber had finished with me, he led me, not up the stairs into the guard-room, but to the entrance hall on the ground floor. I wondered what was coming to me. In front of the building stood a fine, new, black, high-powered American car, guarded by two armed Security Policemen. The Captain opened the door and motioned me to get in. I took my seat, followed by the Captain and the two policemen, and the car moved off. In front I could see the red tail-lights of the car that was preceding us, while at the back the beams from the headlights of another car shone through the window. I was being driven under a strong escort. My guards remained silent; but although I was somewhat perturbed, everything indicated that I was not being driven to a place of execution. The drive took only about ten minutes or so, and we pulled up in front of a brightly-lit building in the suburb of Praga. I got out, and surrounded by a crowd of armed policemen, entered the building. It was only now that the Captain told me where I was going.

'You are going to meet Prime Minister Mikolajczyk.'

I was flabbergasted. First a drive in a fine car, then a new and intact, brightly-lit building with clean corridors, and now a meeting with a man who had come from the dreamed-of free world. Did all this mean that I was to be set free? To make sure, I asked the Captain:

'What is going to happen after the meeting?'

The instructions he had received must have been precise, for he said:

'After the meeting you will be taken back to the Ministry.'

A door opened and I found myself in a large well-appointed room with a fine carpet in the middle, while Mikolajczyk's secretary, Paul Siudak, took me in his arms. The policemen remained in the corridor, by the open door, and I could see their inquisitive glances and the butts of their revolvers.

From a side door Mikolajczyk emerged, seized me by the hand, and noticing the armed guard, pulled me into his office. Our talk lasted the best part of two hours. The sudden change was confusing. There was the prison, here the office of the deputy Prime Minister. I was utterly unprepared for such a sudden transformation. I made no attempt to question Mikolajczyk about his plans. I knew that I was going back to prison, where Rozanski would be waiting for me. Besides, Mikolajczyk's answer to the first question I asked him was a heavy blow to me, which absorbed all my being. I learned that my brother Stanislav had been killed by a V1 bomb in London. No one had ever mentioned it before, and the sad news overwhelmed me. Only after my release did I find out that the Government in London had informed Plenipotentiary Jankowski, who had issued a strict order that I was not to be told. 'Zielinski has enough worries and troubles already, why add to them. . . .'

It was not much comfort to me when Mikolajczyk told me that as a result of his efforts, the Council of Ministers had passed a resolution that I should be released from prison, and that in a few days I ought to be free. I returned to the Ministry profoundly depressed. I lay down on the desk as usual, to collect my wits and to think. I had hardly closed my eyes when Rozanski appeared.

'Get up! We are going to have a little talk.'

Another cross-examination followed, with the same old questions. Perhaps Rozanski thought that the meeting with Mikolajczyk might have gone to my head, and wanted to bring me back to a sense of reality. This time, however, I was in an exceptionally bad mood for being cross-examined, and I told Rozanski the sad news of my brother's death, hoping that he would leave me alone. He condoled with me, asked me a few polite questions concerning my brother, and then fired the question which must have been bothering him all along:

'What did you talk about with Mikolajczyk?'

I was not mistaken in my surmise. The beast wanted to know at once what Mikolajczyk had told me, and not even the affliction that had befallen me would dissuade him from harassing me with his questions. My blood was up, and without considering the consequences I resolved to frighten Rozanski. Outwardly calm and collected, I improvised with the utmost self-assurance:

'In a few days I shall be free, and then we shall see. . . . I have been told that as a result of Allied pressure there will be a switch-over to the Peasant Party, and that we shall take over the Government. Then we shall have a little talk. . . .'

I continued with such empty boasts and threats for some time. Rozanski was impressed. Profoundly surprised by the strange transformation in me and the self-assurance with which I spoke, he gazed at me without uttering a word. When I was through, he suspended the examination saying:

'Ah, do you remember what I told you? The time will come when I shall have to stand to attention in your presence.'

I returned to my uncomfortable resting place on the desk,

and for the first time since my arrest I could not sleep that night.

General of the NKVD Malinov

Notwithstanding the resolution of the Council of Ministers, I remained in jail and the cross-examinations continued. I was confronted with a new demand, namely that as Government Plenipotentiary I should issue a manifesto to the Underground calling upon its members to report to the 'state authorities', which in practice meant to the Security Police. I refused categorically, asserting in the first place that a manifesto issued from prison would be worthless, and in the second place, that my Party had already come out into the open, and that I could not therefore undertake any action without first consulting the leader of the Party, Vincent Witos. Rozanski was furious; he threatened, coaxed, and persuaded in turn, but I would not yield. What he demanded of me would be directed against the Underground, and that I could not do. Colonel Radoslaw and Colonel Rzepecki, who were subsequently arrested, acted differently. Each of them issued from prison a manifesto summoning the Underground to come out into the open. Apart from the sorry fact that they yielded under duress, in my opinion they acted rightly. The war-time Underground was by then so thoroughly cornered by Communist intelligence that it was impossible for its members to return to normal life without coming out into the open. Taking no account of whatever the future may have in store for them, the men who came out into the open have enjoyed for a number of years the 'freedom' that it is possible to enjoy in present-day Poland. And in any case, even that freedom was better than the prisons and the concentration camps.

Some days later the SP Captain turned up in the morning, and again took me to the barber, who did his best to make me look like a bridegroom. From the barber we went along the corridors of the Ministry of Security, led by Rozanski, and I was soon facing a young man in his thirties, with a dry, lean and unpleasant face, seated behind a large desk. Also behind the desk, by the side of the fair young man, was a SP Major.

I looked around. The office was equipped with easy chairs and carpets, which were not to be seen in Rozanski's room; and judging from this, I gave the young man in front of me the rank of Colonel. I was not mistaken; for I stood before SP Colonel Romkowski, who by the time I escaped from Poland in 1947 had already become a General. Next to him was Major Czaplicki, dubbed by the men of the Underground 'Akover', not only because he was of Jewish descent and his name an assumed one, but also because he was in charge of the Department for the Liquidation of the Home Army (in Polish A.K.) in the Ministry of Security.

The fair young man motioned me into the easy chair, ordered Rozanski to take down my depositions, and opened the examination with the same old sterile questions. I repeated all my answers, which by then I knew by heart, and Rozanski took them down, utterly bored. Czaplicki listened; but Romkowski was much more aggressive than Rozanski and pressed me hard, as if he were quite ignorant of the resolution of the Council of Ministers. He peremptorily demanded that I issue the manifesto. As before, I gave him my stereotyped reasons why I could not do it, determined not to pay such a price for my freedom.

During this wordy duel the side-door opened noiselessly, and into the room came a man of about fifty, in a dark civilian suit with some Soviet decoration on the lapel of his jacket. All the men present, except myself, jumped up and stood to attention. The newcomer, with a casual wave of his hand, made them resume their seats and take up the cross-examination. Without saying a word, he seated himself on the arm-rest of an unoccupied easy chair and listened to my depositions for about an hour. I could observe him out of the corner of my eye, as he sat to one side of me. He had dark hair, his face, with a healthy tan, had no 'special characteristics', but the look of his eyes expressed authority, and there was an impressive self-assurance in his every movement. It was evident that his presence was embarrassing to everyone, and the examination went on rather lamely. After an hour he rose from his chair, everybody stood to attention, and he left the room without having uttered a single word.

I was escorted back by one of the more gregarious of the SP men. I was interested to know who the impressive stranger had been, and asked my guard. There was no one near us in the corridor, so moving closer to me he whispered:

'He's the top dog in the Ministry, a General of the NKVD, who gives orders to the Minister himself!'

As I found out later, I had happened to come into contact with the lord-lieutenant of Poland, the Soviet *eminence grise*, the NKVD General who was known to the initiated by the name of Malinov. God only knows if that was his real name.[1] He always went about in mufti, he drove about in an old jeep, and attended no celebrations or receptions; but at the secret meetings which took place every Thursday in the apartment of Gomolka in Szucha Avenue, he told Bierut, Berman, and the other rulers of Poland what they were to do.

I met Romkowski again in 1947, by which time he was a General. On January 19, 1947, in spite of indescribable election frauds, I was elected Member of Parliament for the City of Warsaw as a member of the anti-Communist Peasant Party. The people of the Capital, as of the whole country, went to the polls *en masse* to cast their votes, in the knowledge that the elections represented the last chance, which was not to be missed. As a deputy I was appointed a member of a Committee which was to prepare a new Amnesty Bill for the anti-Soviet underground. The Bill was broadly conceived and made only one exception, concerning those soldiers of Zymierski's Army who deserted to join the partisans. Overcoming my loathing, I took Romkowski aside and persuaded him that if any group of partisans should be excluded from the amnesty a nucleus for a new partisan movement would remain. After some argument he agreed, and an appropriate amendment was passed without difficulty. All the members of the Committee, who up till then had attacked my amendment sharply and venomously, immediately changed their attitude when Romkowski declared that the amendment was reasonable, and voted for it.

When the Bill was introduced, I delivered my only speech

---

[1] It was disclosed in 1954, that his true name is Ivan A. Serov, an NKVD General, at present head of the Soviet State Security Committee.

on the floor of the House; in it I demanded the immediate release of all the arrested members of the underground. When I mounted the rostrum, the hubbub in the House suddenly subsided, and the air became tense in anticipation of some sensational development. I looked round the House. On the Government side, to the right, I noticed on the front bench the bald head of the 'Prime Minister', Cyrankiewicz. I raised my eyes. In a box in the gallery I could see the broad face of the Soviet Ambassador Lebedev. That Soviet reincarnation of the Tsarist Ambassador Repnin[1] had his eyes on me. The galleries were crowded with SP men, while in front of me I had the cold and hostile faces of Berman, Mazur, Chelchowski, Zambrowski, and others. Only below the Government benches, further down, could I see the familiar and friendly faces of the deputies of the Peasant Party.

I proceeded to attack the Government in violent terms. I accused them of liquidating one Underground only to produce another. The latter was being joined by all who had passed through the prisons, persecution and terror of the Security Police; by those hundreds of thousands of patriotic Poles whose names had been struck off the electoral register under the insulting pretext that they had collaborated with the Germans; by all those who were being tortured and persecuted. . . .

The House was howling with rage. About a score of Peasant Party deputies were applauding. I could see only their clapping hands, for their voices were drowned in the clamour. With my lips almost touching the microphone, and thus mastering the storm, I was able to shout my speech through to the end.

I was followed on the rostrum by the leading Communist orator, Zambrowski, who counter-attacked. Someone had to break the spell which my speech had cast, and most of it was expunged from the Official Report. A few days later I learned from Communist circles that with that speech I had sealed my doom.

---

[1] The Ambassador to Poland of Catherine the Great, who played then a role similar to that of Lebedev in 1947.

The release of Zosia.

One day at noon, I was escorted to Rozanski's room. Scarcely had the SP man opened the door when I noticed a woman sitting with her back to me, and recognised Zosia. From behind the desk Rozanski waved me to the other chair. I sat down and looked closely at Zosia. She was much paler and thinner. Her face spoke of nocturnal cross-examinations, of anxieties and worries. She too was looking at me intently. We exchanged glances and smiles, happy to see each other again. The silence was broken by Rozanski, who said in his most polite manner:

'Your wife is being released, and I wanted to give you an opportunity to see her and say good-bye to her.' He paused and added, 'After all, we are not the beasts you think we are. You can say good-bye now, and then you will go back to where you have come from.'

At that very moment the telephone bell rang. Rozanski was annoyed, but took up the receiver, after warning us threateningly:

'I forbid you to talk.'

I had a sudden inspiration: Zosia could carry out an important errand, which I had had very much at heart during my whole confinement. I leaned towards her, and as I kissed her on the cheek, I whispered the message in her ear. She nodded slightly, confirming that she had understood what I wanted. When I looked at Rozanski I beheld the embodiment of fury. He raised his fist, and his eyes were alight with anger; but he continued to report in Russian, with the deference of a subordinate talking to his superior, that 'the person in question cannot be examined for the time being, because the wound is rather serious and it will be necessary to wait for some weeks. . . .'

When he replaced the receiver, he was livid with rage.

'What did you say to your wife? Speak! Or I shall send you to the cellars and cancel your wife's release!'

I withstood the storm and explained calmly that I had only said a few loving words to Zosia by way of good-bye, and that there was no reason for all the shouting. Rozanski's polite manner disappeared altogether, and I hardly had time to embrace Zosia before the guard hurried me off to 'where I had come from'.

My Talk with the Minister of State Security, Radkiewicz

This time everything looked more imposing than on the previous occasions. They not only trimmed my hair and had me shaved, but supplied me with a cloth and boot-brushes so that I might improve my general appearance. I asked the policemen ironically whether they were going to take me to a ball at the Ministry; but they held their tongues. In their company I visited in turn all my old acquaintances, beginning with Rozanski, who joined us and conducted us to Romkowski. The latter, too, joined our group and led the way; so that in the end the procession consisted of five men marching along the corridors of the Ministry to a destination unknown to me.

The procession entered a well-appointed, carpeted room, which, judging from the presence of several young SP men with slightly more humane faces, must have been an orderly room, as indeed it was. Here, the two SP men remained behind, while I was ushered into a large office; there, behind a huge desk, sat a man of about forty with a handsome, olive-skinned face and dark hair. The man fixed his cold, expressionless eyes on me for a while, and finally motioned me to a chair placed in front of his desk. All Security Policemen on such occasions used the same energetic, authoritative gesture, a quick wave of the hand.

I sat down without uttering a word, waiting to see what was to come. Romkowski and Rozanski took less conspicuous seats by the wall. At last, the man broke the silence, which had begun to be rather oppressive.

'You are being released. Have you any complaints?'

His voice was clear and high-pitched, and he spoke with an accent which sounded like a mixture of borderland Polish and Russian. Though my heart quickened, I replied with restraint and without emotion:

'I have no complaint.'

The man shifted his position in his chair and continued:

'Before you leave, I should like to have a little talk with you on some subjects of topical interest.'

Though I could guess who the man was, I wanted to make sure and interposed:

'Am I speaking to Minister Radkiewicz?'

'Yes, you are,' he confirmed; and proceeded to discourse at length on our former anti-German underground activities, criticising our refusal to co-operate with the Communist underground, the 'treacherous' policy of the Polish Government in London, the 'reactionary' character of the Supreme Command of the Underground Army, and the murder of Communists alleged to have been committed by our Underground; he finally wound up with our 'felonious' persistence in remaining underground after the 'liberation' of Poland by the 'allied' Soviet Army.

I listened attentively, wondering what Radkiewicz was driving at. All he said was familiar to me. Reading the Communist press sufficed to make one realise what accusations and charges had been concocted. What was interesting, however, was the manner in which Radkiewicz spoke. He uttered his words slowly, in the quiet voice of a man accustomed to weighing each one. His Polish was correct, but his distinct accent left no room for doubt that he must have spent a considerable time in Russia. He spoke calmly but with great force and conviction, which indicated that he was either a fanatical Communist or a perfectly schooled agent.

He charged the anti-Soviet underground with short-sightedness, because it disregarded the fact that the Soviets were Poland's neighbour, and, moreover, that they had liberated Poland from a nightmarish occupation by the Germans. Reliance on the West and hostility to Russia were grievous errors. The existence of an Underground directed against Russia, its hostilities against the 'liberating' Soviet Army, had frustrated all the efforts of the Lublin Government, and was now frustrating the efforts of the Government of National Unity. The pre-war system had collapsed, never to be restored again.

In the new Poland, genuinely democratic elements had emerged, which, with the support of a friendly Russia, would at last assure the country peace, economic progress, and democracy.

His tirade went on for nearly half an hour, and when he stopped at last, I sensed that he expected an answer from me. I took up the challenge and delivered myself of a kind of political defence of the anti-German and anti-Soviet Underground. When I mentioned the Warsaw Rising and the halting of the Soviet offensive just before Warsaw, Radkiewicz, for the first and only time during the whole of our conversation, lost his temper, cut me short, and with the utmost passion presented the familiar Communist thesis that although the Rising had been directed against the Germans militarily, politically it had been aimed against the Soviets. Rozanski and Romkowski eagerly, though silently, approved, nodding their heads. I could feel that for the Communists, the matter was a rather delicate one and that I had touched on a sore point. This gave me momentarily a feeling of ascendancy in the discussion. When I in turn proceeded to attack the disarmament of the Home Army units and the subsequent mass-arrests and killings, in face of which the continued conspiracy of the Underground could be regarded simply as an act of self-defence, Radkiewicz replied energetically; but nevertheless, he admitted one 'mistake', by stating that the murder in the municipal park in Cracow of Narcyz-Zawojna, the Commander of the Peasant Battalions of the Cracow region, was 'a crime', and he assured me that the guilty SP men had suffered exemplary punishment. He tried to explain that such 'trespasses' were due to lack of training among the SP personnel, which had had to be schooled from scratch, 'because we did not want any of the Blue police scum in our ranks'.

I still could not make out what Radkiewicz was driving at. During my discussion with him, I again applied my earlier system of splitting my personality. One 'I' argued, replied, and explained; the other tried to guess the purpose of the conversation and watch for pitfalls. It was well after the discussion had entered its second hour that I began to realise what Radkiewicz was angling for.

'We recognised that the manifestos of May 17 and 27 were the first signs of awakening commonsense,' he said, 'because,

although you heaped abuse on the SP and the PPR, you
nevertheless summoned the nation to work for the reconstruction of the country and called upon the partisans to cease
fighting.'

Romkowski, unable to contain himself, burst out:

'But the manifesto of May 17 incited men to desert from our
army. The underground rag of the National Armed Forces
quoted it even in its most recent issue. . . .'

Radkiewicz must have found this apposite remark rather
embarrassing, for he brushed it aside.

'Anyone can pick a sentence from the manifesto and twist
it to his liking,' he said; and resuming his argument with me,
continued:

'I think these two manifestos you issued should be comple-
mented by yet another one, in which, as Plenipotentiary of
the London Government, you should call upon the Underground to report to the Security authorities, to lay down their
arms, and to submit to the Government.'

Here was the rub! Here was the demand made towards the
end of my cross-examination by Rozanski and repeated by
Romkowski being put forward once again by Radkiewicz;
and it seemed certain that my compliance would be a condition of my release from prison, and that only now was this to
be made clear.

For a moment I reflected deeply. I tried to gauge all the
elements in a lightning review of the position. On the one
hand I saw the prospect of freedom at the price of capitulation, on the other, the iron bars of a jail, with no hope of
ever emerging from it. I had already considered the matter
fully during the long series of examinations. I was determined
to persevere in my resistance, and to refuse to issue the manifesto. I told myself once again what I had resolved God knows
how many times before, that if I was to walk as a free man
again, it would have to come about in such a way that I
should be able to look people straight in the eye. Otherwise
it would have been better to remain in prison. Freedom purchased at the price demanded by Radkiewicz had no attrac-
tions for me. It was only much later that I reached the conclusion that the unmasking of the Underground was inevi-

table. In the existing circumstances, and in the position I was in, I regarded compliance with the demands of the Security Police as a betrayal of the cause I served. As dispassionately as I could, I told Radkiewicz exactly what I had told Rozanski and Romkowski during earlier examinations. In particular, I emphasised that my arrest must have been generally known, and that no one would respond to the manifesto, because everyone would regard it as having been issued under duress and contrary to my real convictions. Besides, it would be regarded as a rather clumsy trap set by the Security Police to catch the Underground. Moreover, I said, I was sure that the problem of the Underground would form the subject of consultations which the Leader of the Party, Witos, intended having with myself and others, and that we would undoubtedly deal with it.

Radkiewicz would not give up, and went on repeating his demand, advancing ever new arguments; while I continued to refuse, and also advanced new arguments why my answer had to be no. Listening to this duel, Rozanski and Romkowski cast threatening glances at me, and displayed palpable impatience, and silent dissatisfaction with the correct manner of the Minister.

However, for some reason or other, my unconditional re-lease must have been decided upon at a high level; for in the end Radkiewicz got up from his chair and concluded with a sigh:

'I am sorry you won't accept good advice. But that's that. Nevertheless, I hope we shall not regret having set you free in future, and that your activities will be useful to the country.'

He got up, we shook hands, and accompanied by my escort I left the ministerial offices.

Now, things began to move fast. In Rozanski's room I was given back some personal trifles, and a document stating that during the period specified I had been 'at the disposition of the Ministry of Security'; then Rozanski, somewhat disheartened, ordered a guard to conduct me past the various sentry posts into the street. I descended the staircase rapidly, and in no time found myself free and on my own in Brukowa Street.

I stopped behind the wooden barrier separating the street

from the carriage-way leading to the Ministry, and looked around. After several weeks in prison, it was a strange experience to be in an open space without bars. What a surprise! Down the street came Zosia, running towards me. Arm in arm we hurried towards the bridge over the Vistula, to get as far away as possible from the accursed Security Police. There was an enormous amount of traffic over the bridge, but it did not interfere with our feverish conversation. Zosia related her experiences and described the various tricks that had been played on her in Cracow, in order to intimidate her and force her to 'confess'. During her examination, for instance, two SP men would enter in their shirt-sleeves, sit down on either side of her, and without uttering a word, roll up their sleeves, preparatory to a beating. Zosia would not be intimidated, and she either modestly disclaimed any knowledge of her husband's affairs, or answered in accordance with the hurriedly scribbled notes I had been able to pass her. On another occasion, while Zosia was being cross-examined, a screaming woman rushed into the room and ran towards the window, as if to jump out. The two SP men dashed after her and seized her 'just in time', when she was already on the window sill. That trick, too, remained unavailing, and Zosia did not squeal or mention anyone by name. She also told me that she had found a message at home from the Polish Government in London, informing me that my resignation had been accepted, and thanking me for discharging the duties of Plenipotentiary of the Government during a most difficult period.

I drew up a balance-sheet of my dealings with the Security Police, and had no reason to be dissatisfied with it. I had not divulged a single name or address, and I had refused to condemn my activities in the underground or issue a manifesto. So far so good. But what was going to happen in the days to come? That question was already worrying me and intruding on the joy of freedom regained.

I was wondering why they had set me free. Zosia, who had already had an opportunity to see Mikolajczyk and Kiernik, gave me an explanation of a sort. I had been set free for various reasons, but primarily in order that I might join the fraudulent National Council, which happily I escaped. From the political point of view this information confirmed Rozanski's indiscretion, and meant that the Communists really were trying to gain the support of the Peasant Party.

In the meantime we had reached the Cracow Suburb and it was a joy to behold familiar sights. By that time the roadway had been cleared of rubble, but it was flanked on either side by spectres, the burnt-out ruins of buildings that had during the long years of the occupation given us shelter, and to which we owed so much. Drab and emaciated men and women moved about with unsmiling faces. Something about their appearance struck me as being distinctly similar to something I had noticed at an earlier period; it occurred to me that people in Warsaw had looked exactly like this during the first few months of the German occupation. They had been similarly dressed and had assumed the same closed facial expression. This look more than anything else was eloquent testimony that we had passed from one occupation to another.

In the welter of questions and answers one question kept intruding: what could we expect? What did the future hold for us? The chapter in our lives entitled 'Conspiracy' was closed. A new chapter was opening.

I listened with great attention to all the information Zosia had been able to gather, trying to gauge and appraise the situation. In the end I ventured on a prophecy:

'The present period may drag on for about two years or so, but after that our choice will be between jail or an escape to the West.'

It turned out that I was about three months out in my calculations; for I was forced to escape with Zosia, in somewhat dramatic circumstances, on November 5, 1947, when we made our way to Sweden. But that is a part of another story.